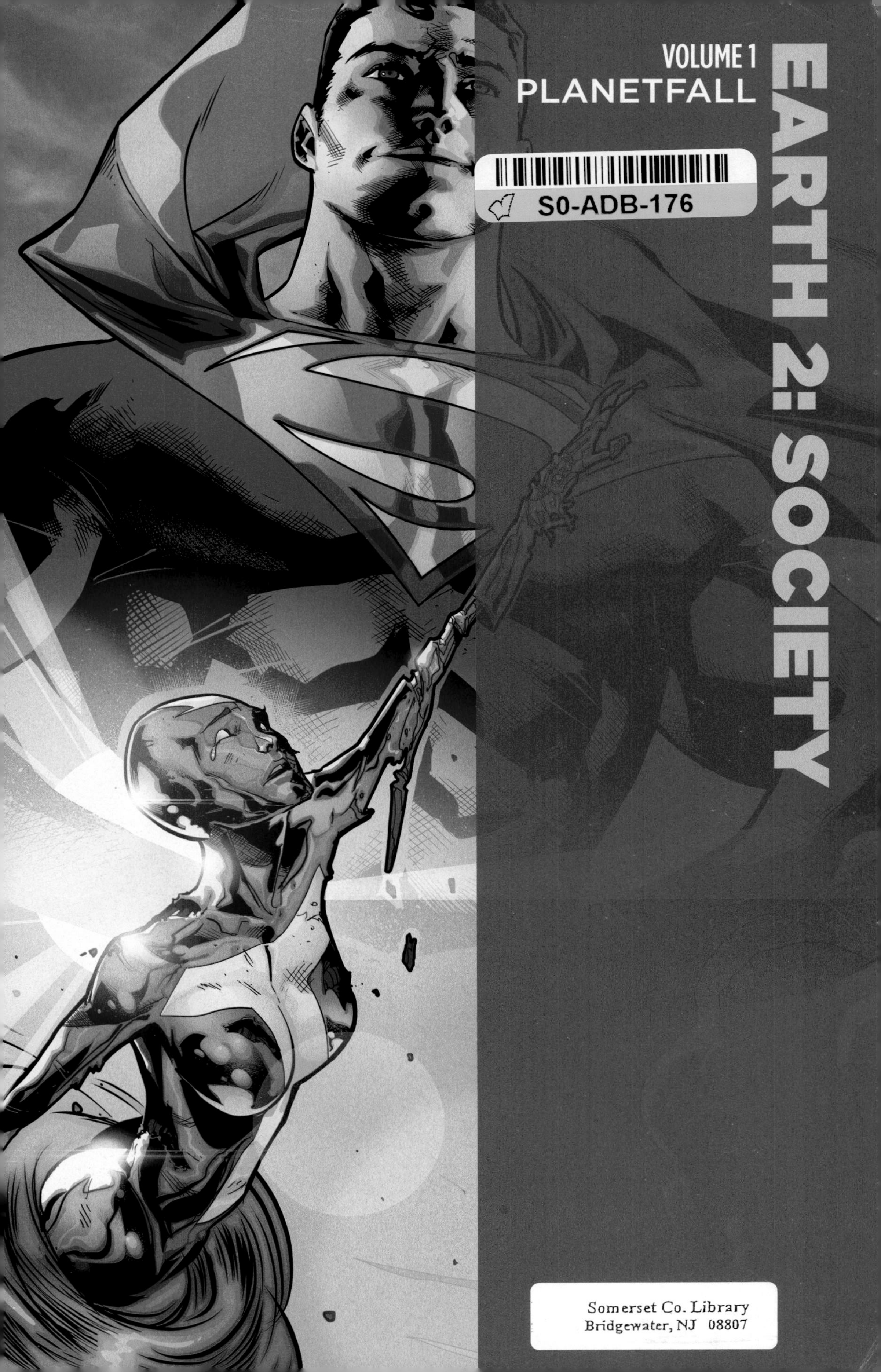

EARTH 2: SOCIETY

VOLUME 1
PLANETFALL

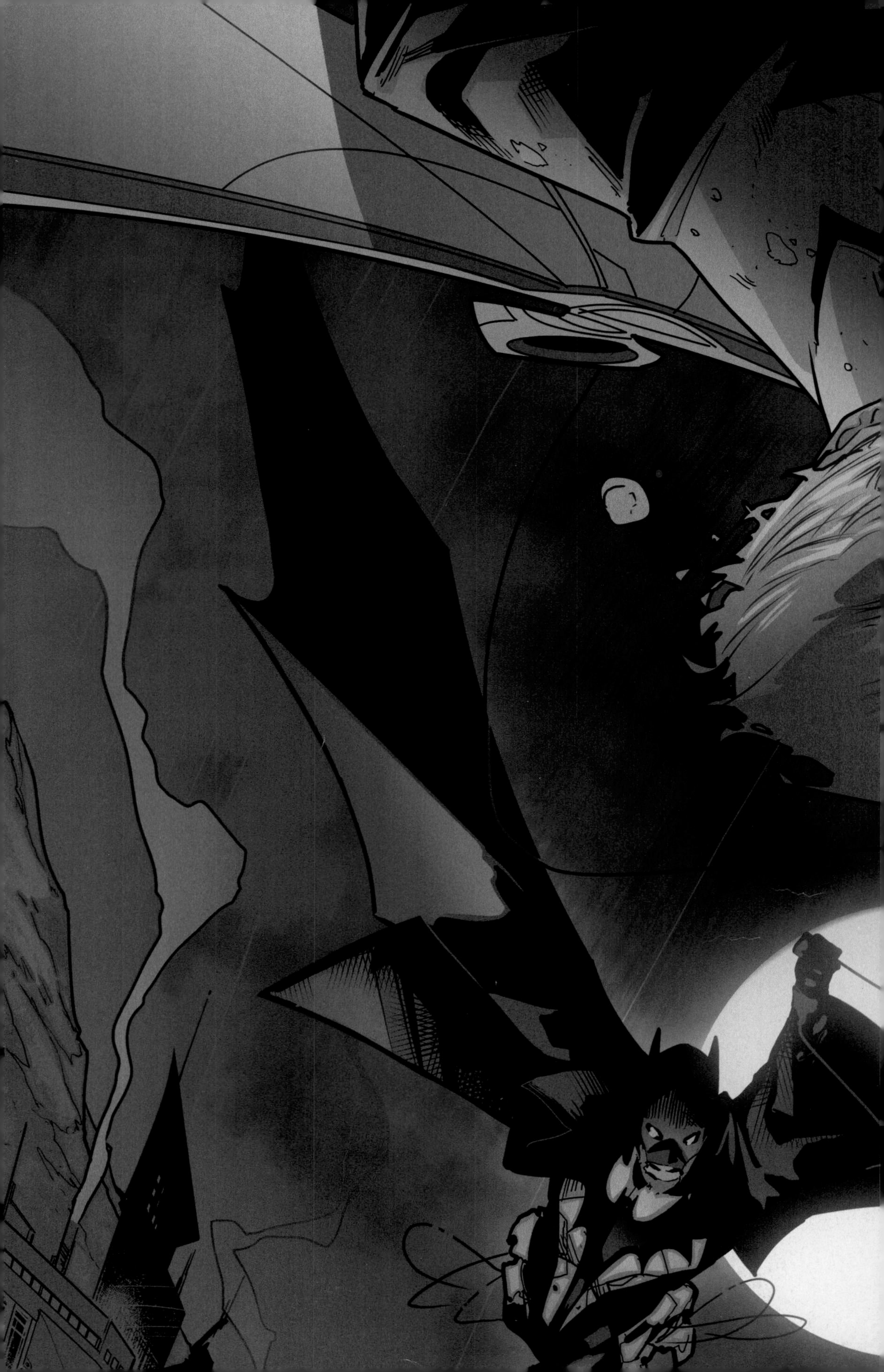

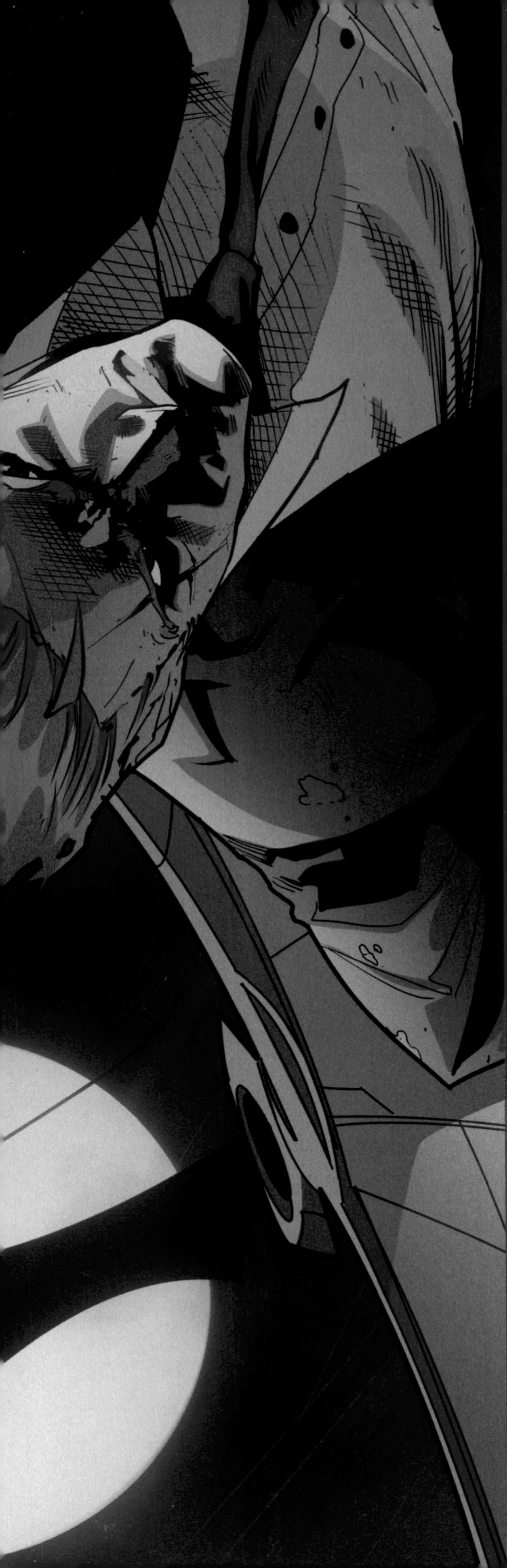

EARTH 2: SOCIETY

VOLUME 1
PLANETFALL

WRITTEN BY
DANIEL H. WILSON

ART BY
JORGE JIMENEZ
ALISSON BORGES

COLOR BY
ALEJANDRO SANCHEZ
JOHN RAUCH
ANDREW DALHOUSE
BLOND

LETTERS BY
TRAVIS LANHAM
PATRICK BROSSEAU

COLLECTION COVER ART BY
JORGE JIMENEZ
& JOHN RAUCH

SUPERMAN CREATED BY
JERRY SIEGEL &
JOE SHUSTER
BY SPECIAL ARRANGEMENT
WITH THE JERRY SIEGEL FAMILY

THE FLASH/JAY GARRICK CREATED BY
GARDNER FOX

EARTH 2: SOCIETY VOLUME 1: PLANETFALL

Published by DC Comics. Compilation and all new material Copyright © 2016 DC Comics. All Rights Reserved.

Originally published in single magazine form in EARTH 2: SOCIETY 1-7 and online as DC SNEAK PEEK: EARTH 2: SOCIETY 1 Copyright © 2015 DC Comics. All Rights Reserved. All characters, their distinctive likenesses and related elements featured in this publication are trademarks of DC Comics. The stories, characters and incidents featured in this publication are entirely fictional. DC Comics does not read or accept unsolicited ideas, stories or artwork.

DC Comics, 2900 West Alameda Ave., Burbank, CA 91505
Printed by RR Donnelley, Salem, VA, USA. 2/5/16. First Printing.
ISBN: 978-1-4012-6123-8

Library of Congress Cataloging-in-Publication Data is available.

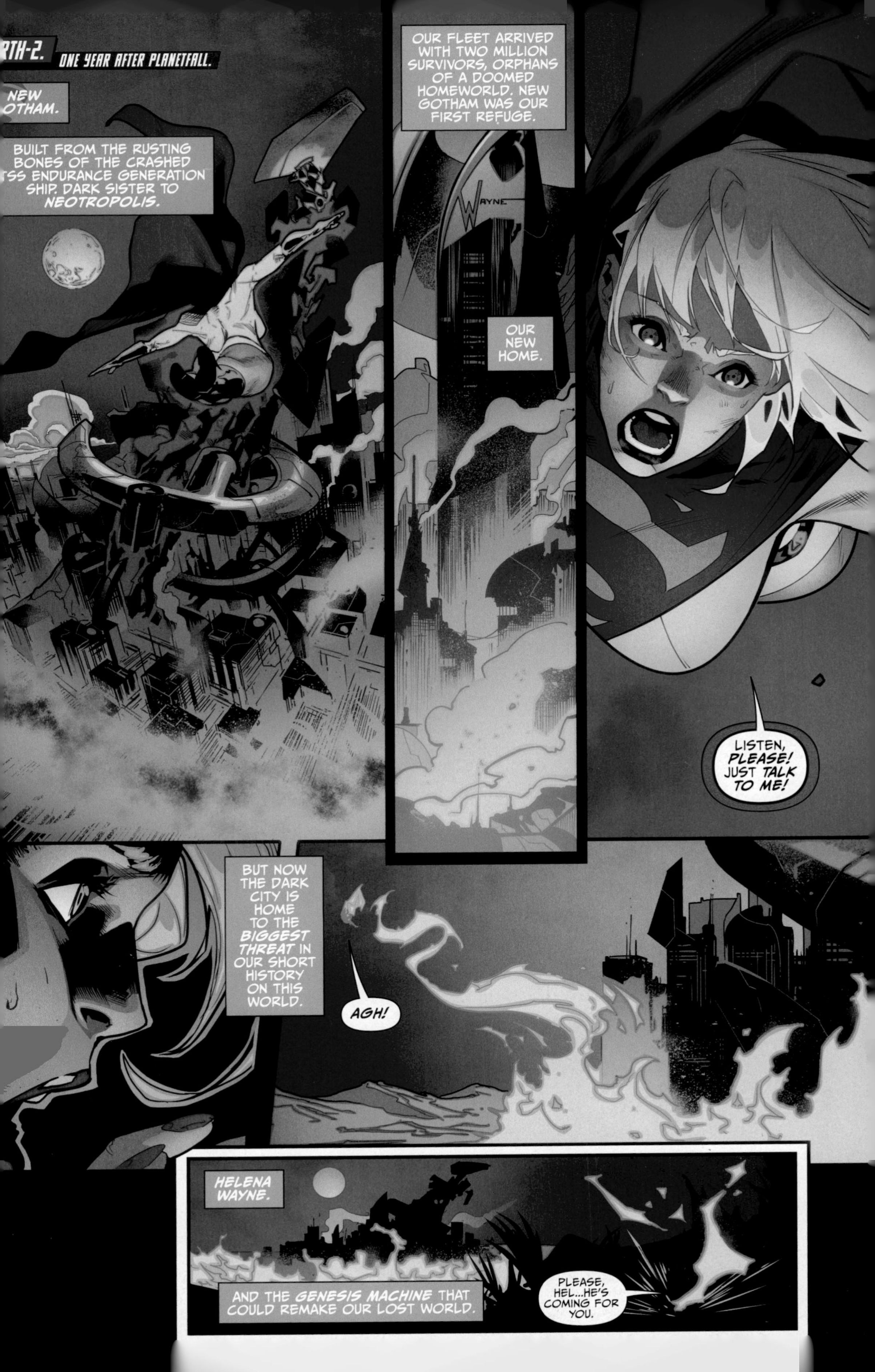
RTH-2. ONE YEAR AFTER PLANETFALL.
NEW OTHAM.
BUILT FROM THE RUSTING BONES OF THE CRASHED TSS ENDURANCE GENERATION SHIP. DARK SISTER TO NEOTROPOLIS.
OUR FLEET ARRIVED WITH TWO MILLION SURVIVORS, ORPHANS OF A DOOMED HOMEWORLD. NEW GOTHAM WAS OUR FIRST REFUGE.
WAYNE
OUR NEW HOME.
LISTEN, PLEASE! JUST TALK TO ME!
BUT NOW THE DARK CITY IS HOME TO THE BIGGEST THREAT IN OUR SHORT HISTORY ON THIS WORLD.
AGH!
HELENA WAYNE.
AND THE GENESIS MACHINE THAT COULD REMAKE OUR LOST WORLD.
PLEASE, HEL...HE'S COMING FOR YOU.

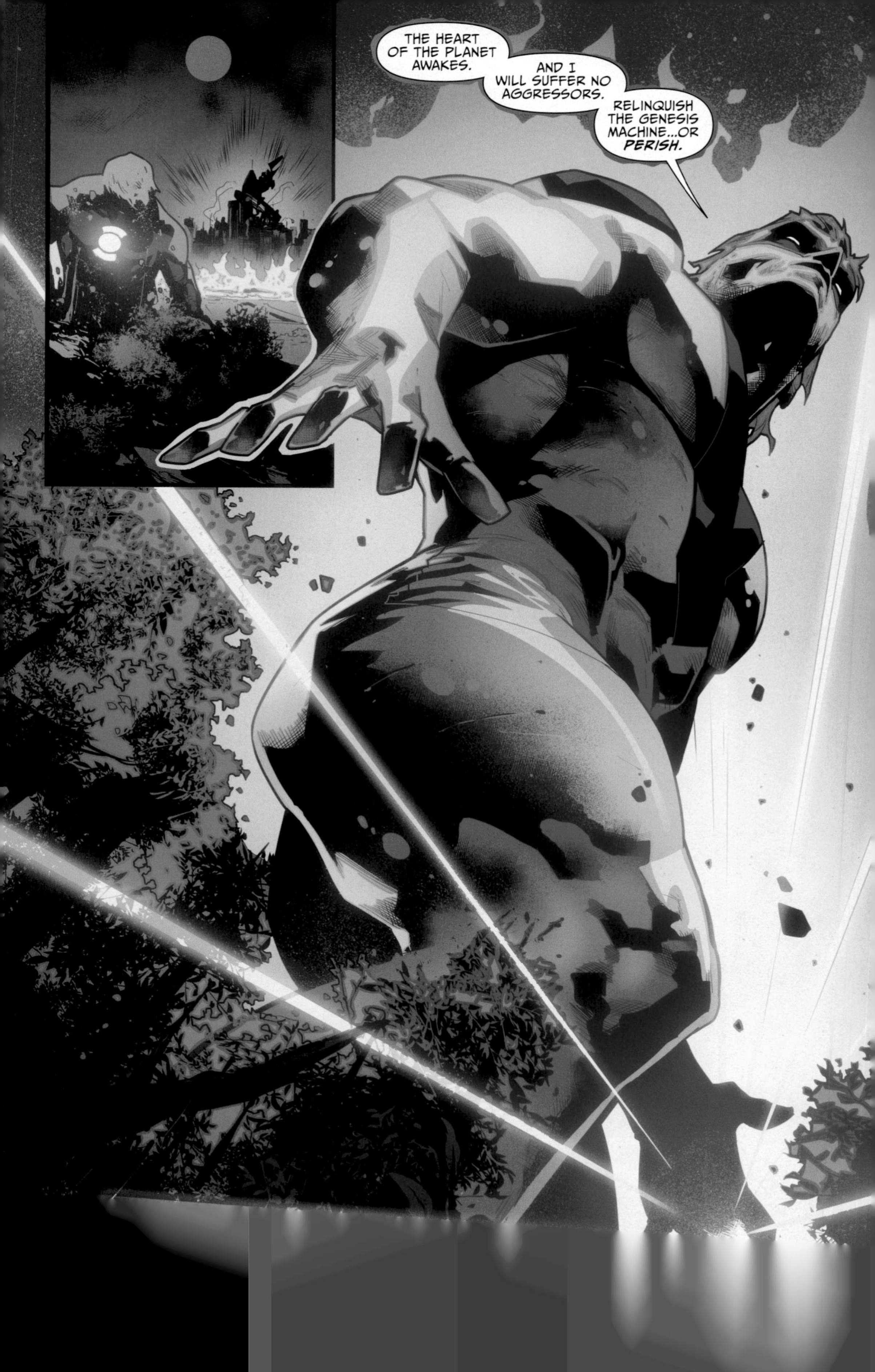
THE HEART OF THE PLANET AWAKES.
AND I WILL SUFFER NO AGGRESSORS.
RELINQUISH THE GENESIS MACHINE...OR *PERISH.*

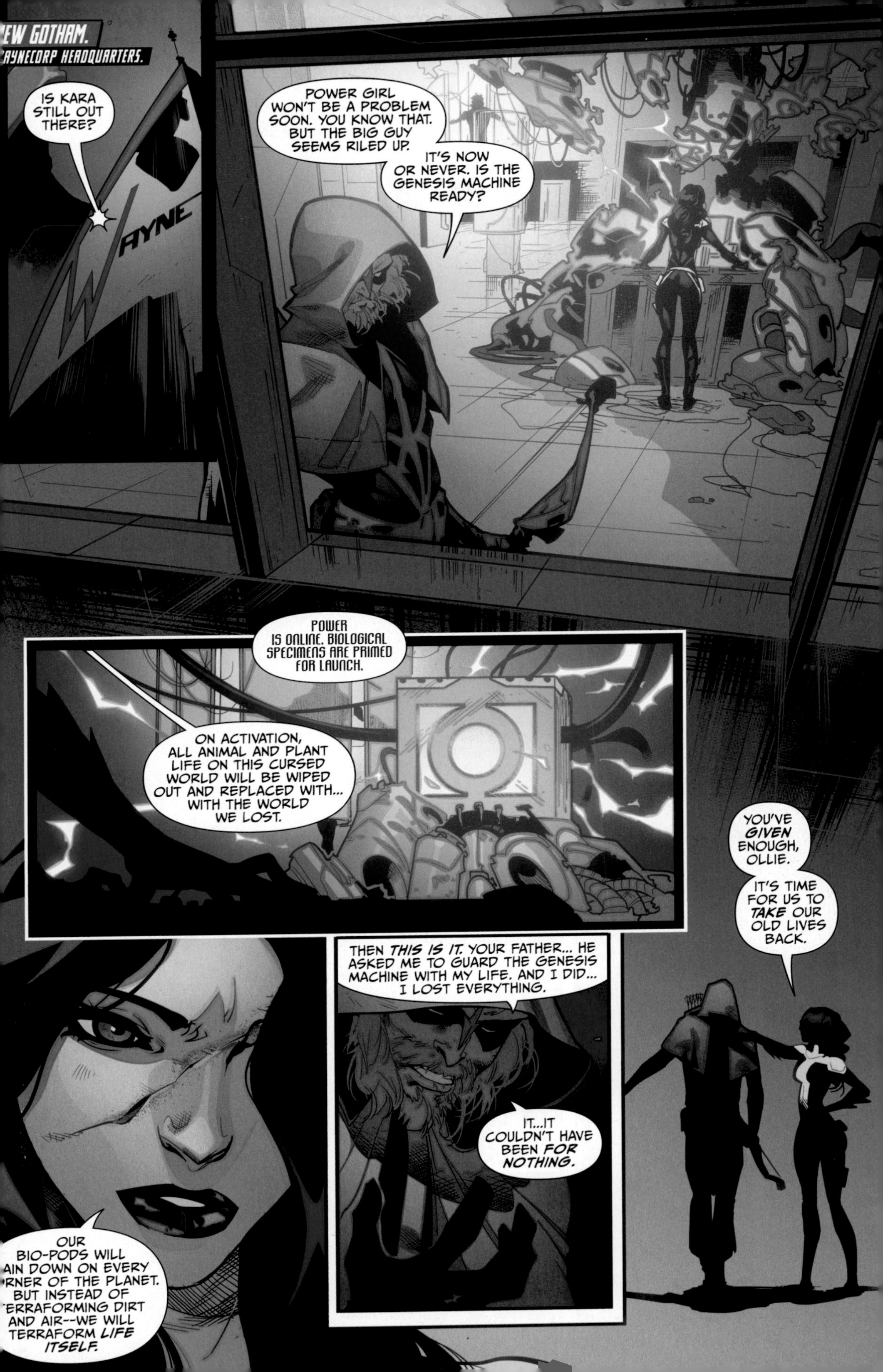

EW GOTHAM.
AYNECORP HEADQUARTERS.
IS KARA STILL OUT THERE?
WAYNE
POWER GIRL WON'T BE A PROBLEM SOON. YOU KNOW THAT. BUT THE BIG GUY SEEMS RILED UP.
IT'S NOW OR NEVER. IS THE GENESIS MACHINE READY?
POWER IS ONLINE. BIOLOGICAL SPECIMENS ARE PRIMED FOR LAUNCH.
ON ACTIVATION, ALL ANIMAL AND PLANT LIFE ON THIS CURSED WORLD WILL BE WIPED OUT AND REPLACED WITH... WITH THE WORLD WE LOST.
OUR BIO-PODS WILL AIN DOWN ON EVERY RNER OF THE PLANET. BUT INSTEAD OF ERRAFORMING DIRT AND AIR--WE WILL TERRAFORM LIFE ITSELF.
THEN THIS IS IT. YOUR FATHER... HE ASKED ME TO GUARD THE GENESIS MACHINE WITH MY LIFE. AND I DID... I LOST EVERYTHING.
IT...IT COULDN'T HAVE BEEN FOR NOTHING.
YOU'VE GIVEN ENOUGH, OLLIE.
IT'S TIME FOR US TO TAKE OUR OLD LIVES BACK.

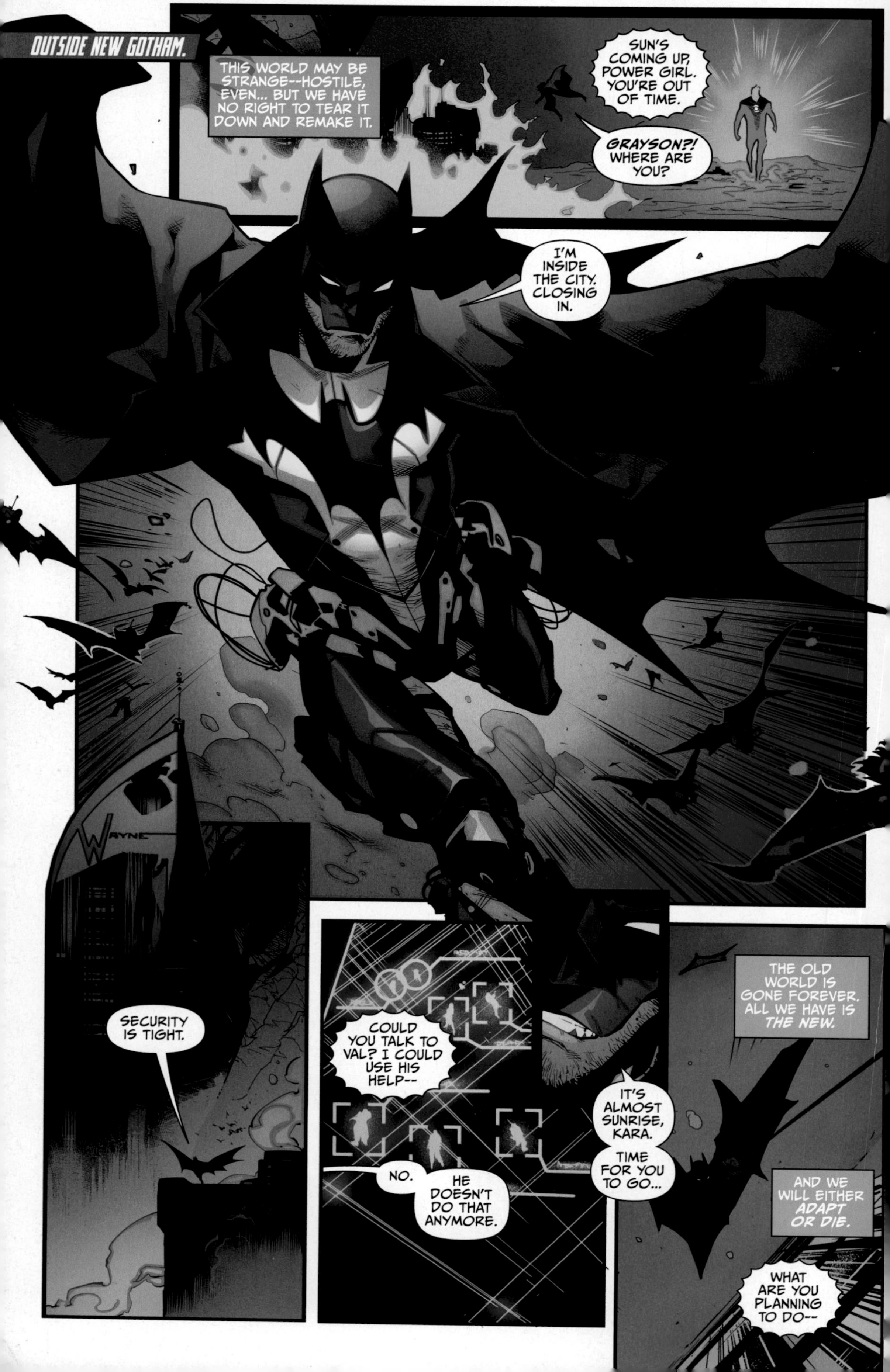
OUTSIDE NEW GOTHAM.
THIS WORLD MAY BE STRANGE--HOSTILE, EVEN... BUT WE HAVE NO RIGHT TO TEAR IT DOWN AND REMAKE IT.
SUN'S COMING UP, POWER GIRL. YOU'RE OUT OF TIME.
GRAYSON?! WHERE ARE YOU?
I'M INSIDE THE CITY. CLOSING IN.
SECURITY IS TIGHT.
COULD YOU TALK TO VAL? I COULD USE HIS HELP--
NO.
HE DOESN'T DO THAT ANYMORE.
IT'S ALMOST SUNRISE, KARA.
TIME FOR YOU TO GO...
THE OLD WORLD IS GONE FOREVER. ALL WE HAVE IS THE NEW.
AND WE WILL EITHER ADAPT OR DIE.
WHAT ARE YOU PLANNING TO DO--

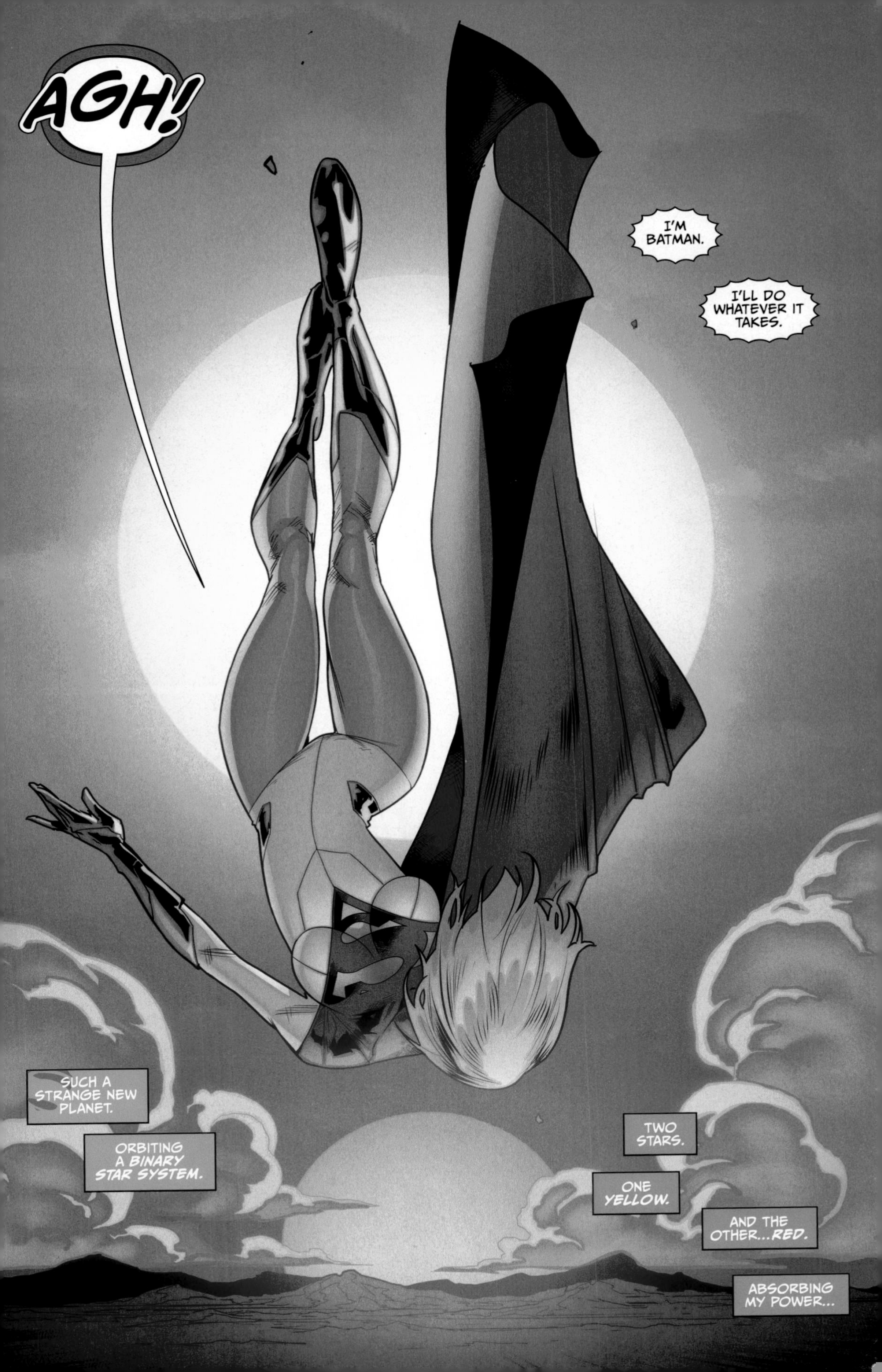
AGH!
I'M BATMAN.
I'LL DO WHATEVER IT TAKES.
SUCH A STRANGE NEW PLANET.
ORBITING A BINARY STAR SYSTEM.
TWO STARS.
ONE YELLOW.
AND THE OTHER...RED.
ABSORBING MY POWER...

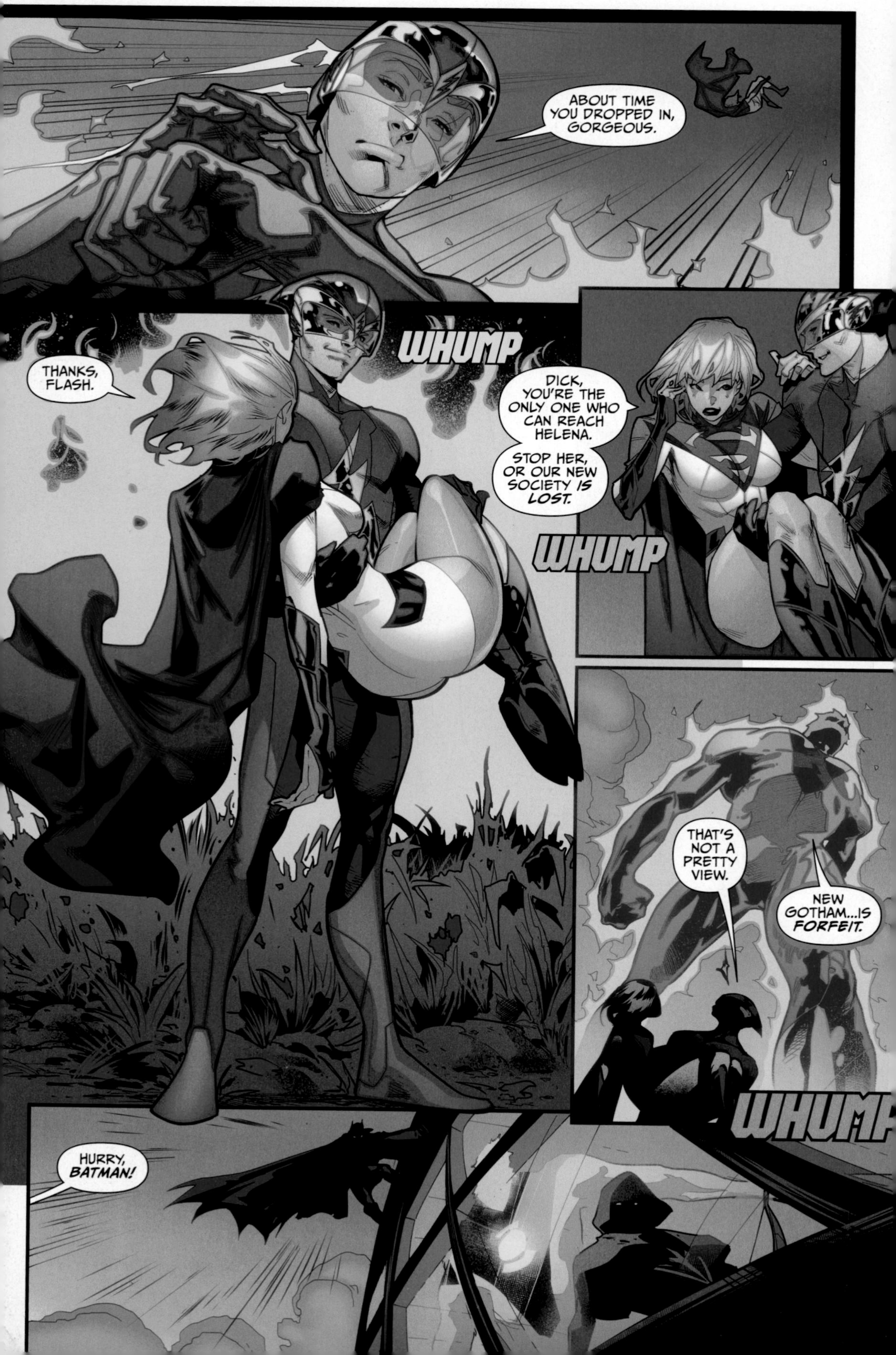

ABOUT TIME YOU DROPPED IN, GORGEOUS.
THANKS, FLASH.
WHUMP
DICK, YOU'RE THE ONLY ONE WHO CAN REACH HELENA.
STOP HER, OR OUR NEW SOCIETY *IS* *LOST.*
WHUMP
THAT'S NOT A PRETTY VIEW.
NEW GOTHAM...IS *FORFEIT.*
WHUMP
HURRY, *BATMAN!*

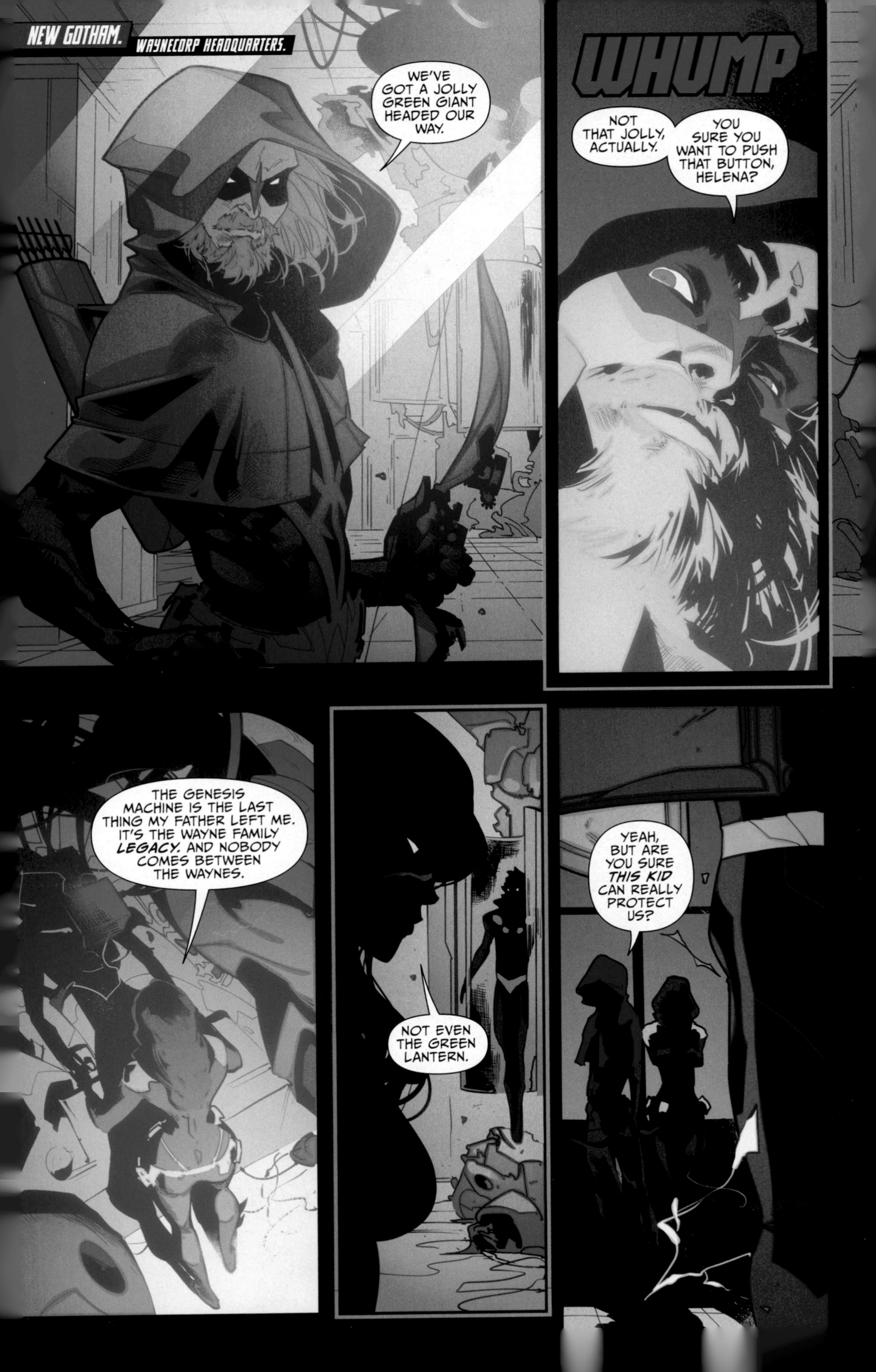
NEW GOTHAM.
WAYNECORP HEADQUARTERS.
WE'VE GOT A JOLLY GREEN GIANT HEADED OUR WAY.
WHUMP
NOT THAT JOLLY, ACTUALLY.
YOU SURE YOU WANT TO PUSH THAT BUTTON, HELENA?
THE GENESIS MACHINE IS THE LAST THING MY FATHER LEFT ME. IT'S THE WAYNE FAMILY LEGACY. AND NOBODY COMES BETWEEN THE WAYNES.
NOT EVEN THE GREEN LANTERN.
YEAH, BUT ARE YOU SURE THIS KID CAN REALLY PROTECT US?

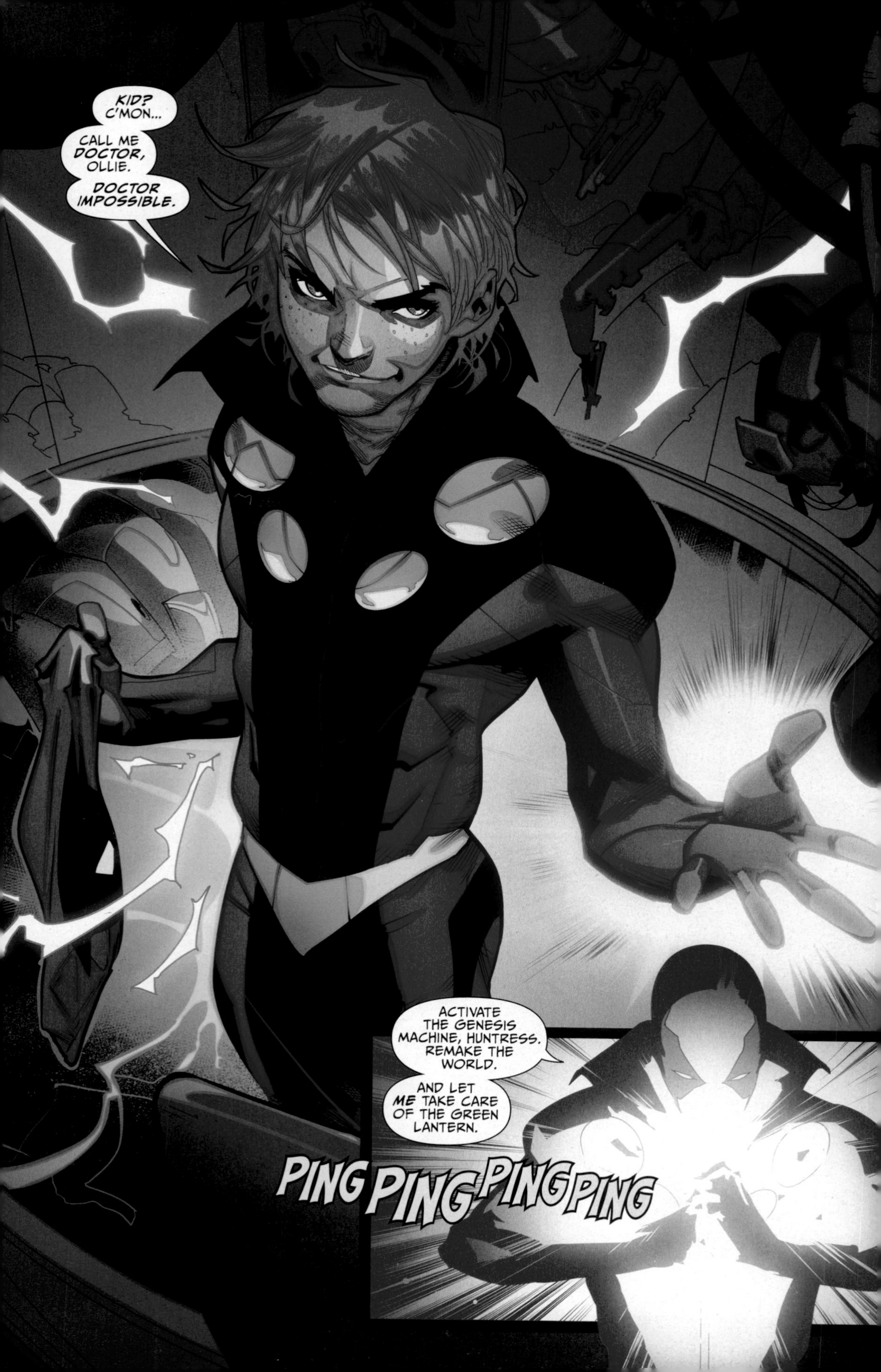
KID? C'MON...
CALL ME DOCTOR, OLLIE.
DOCTOR IMPOSSIBLE.
ACTIVATE THE GENESIS MACHINE, HUNTRESS. REMAKE THE WORLD.
AND LET ME TAKE CARE OF THE GREEN LANTERN.
PING PING PING PING

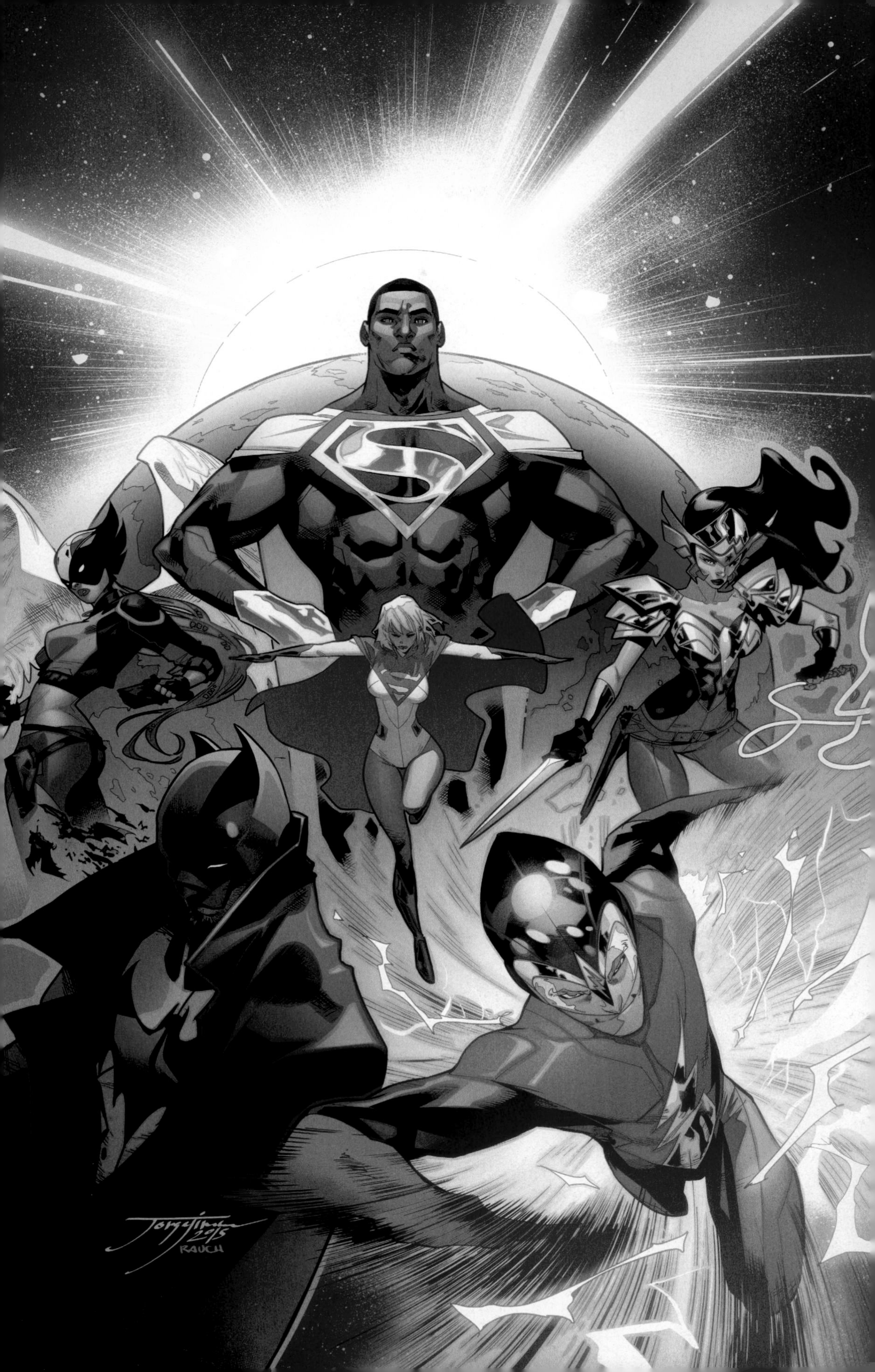
RAUCH

PLANETFALL

DANIEL H. WILSON writer JORGE JIMENEZ artist JOHN RAUCH colorist TRAVIS LANHAM letterer cover by JIMENEZ & RAUCH

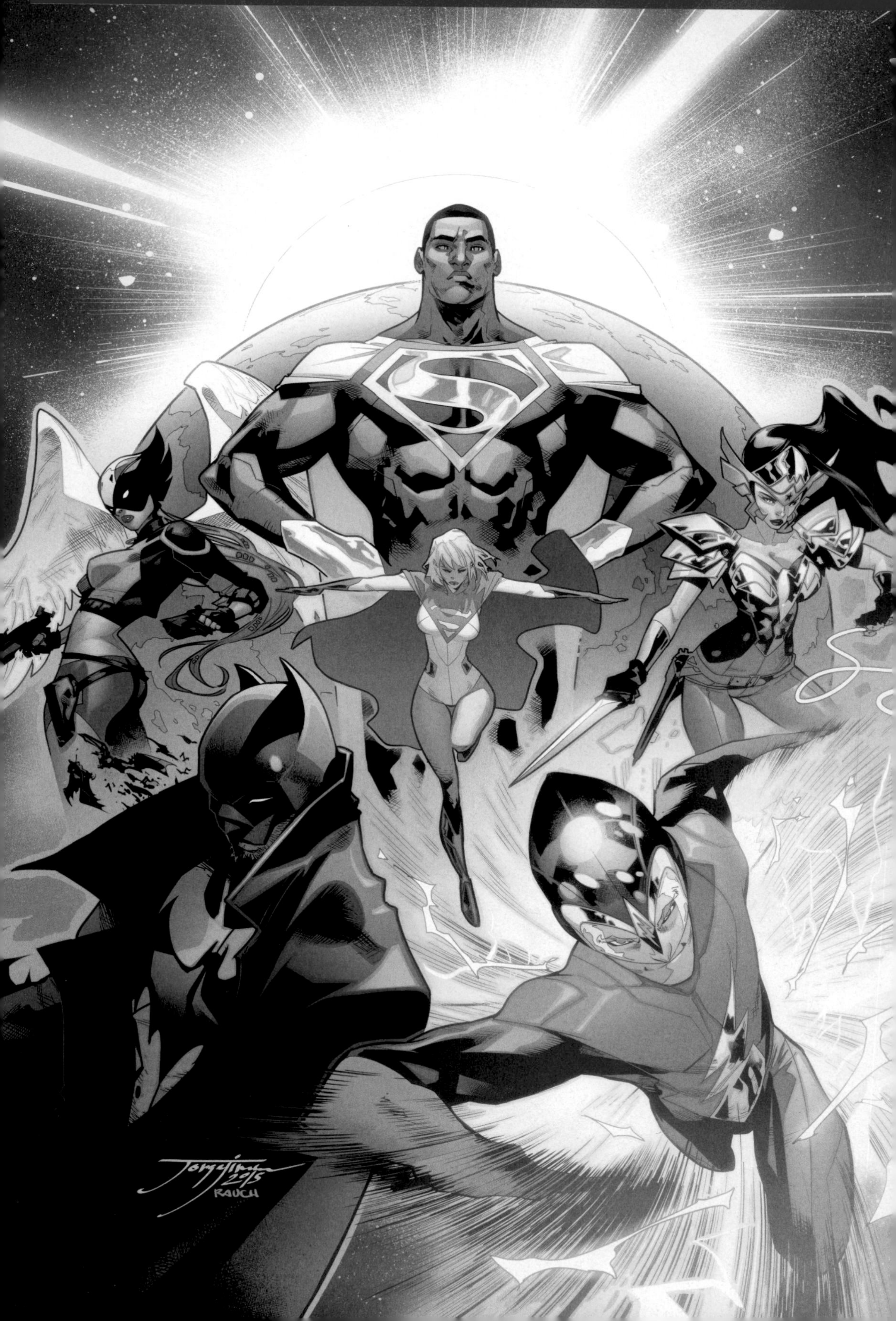

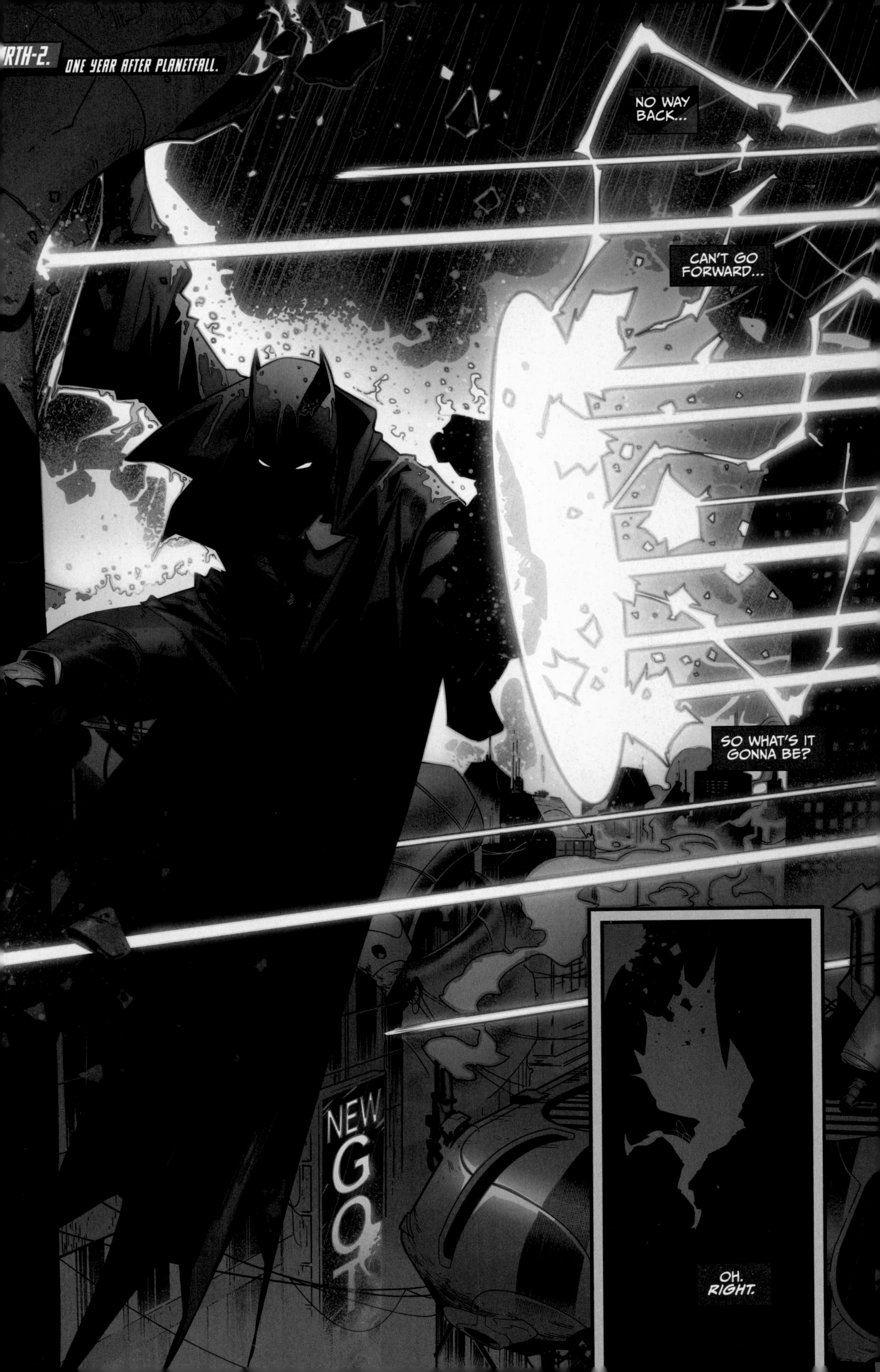
RTH-2. ONE YEAR AFTER PLANETFALL.
NO WAY BACK...
CAN'T GO FORWARD...
SO WHAT'S IT GONNA BE?
OH. RIGHT.
NEW GOT

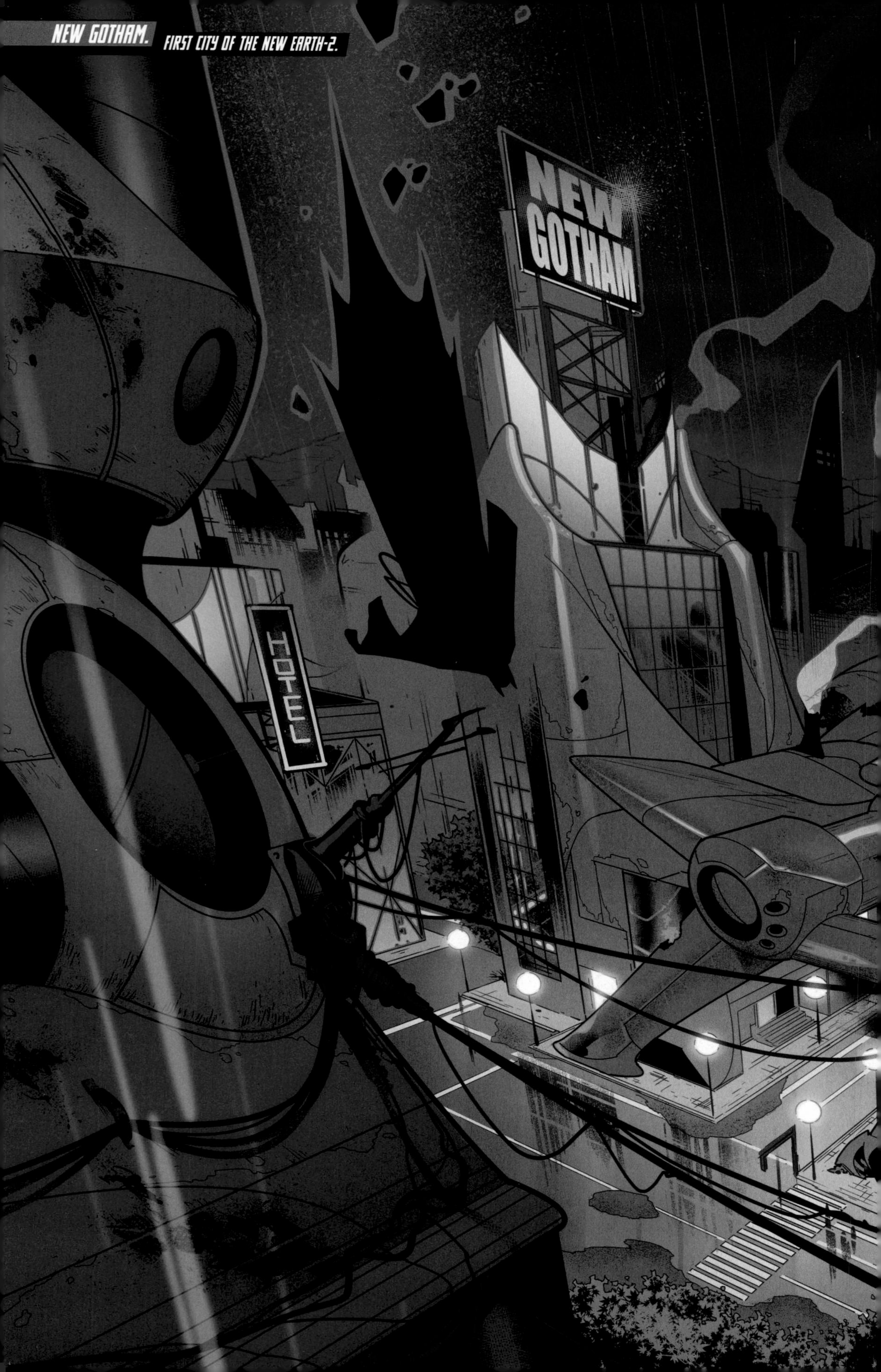
NEW GOTHAM.
FIRST CITY OF THE NEW EARTH-2.
NEW GOTHAM
HOTEL

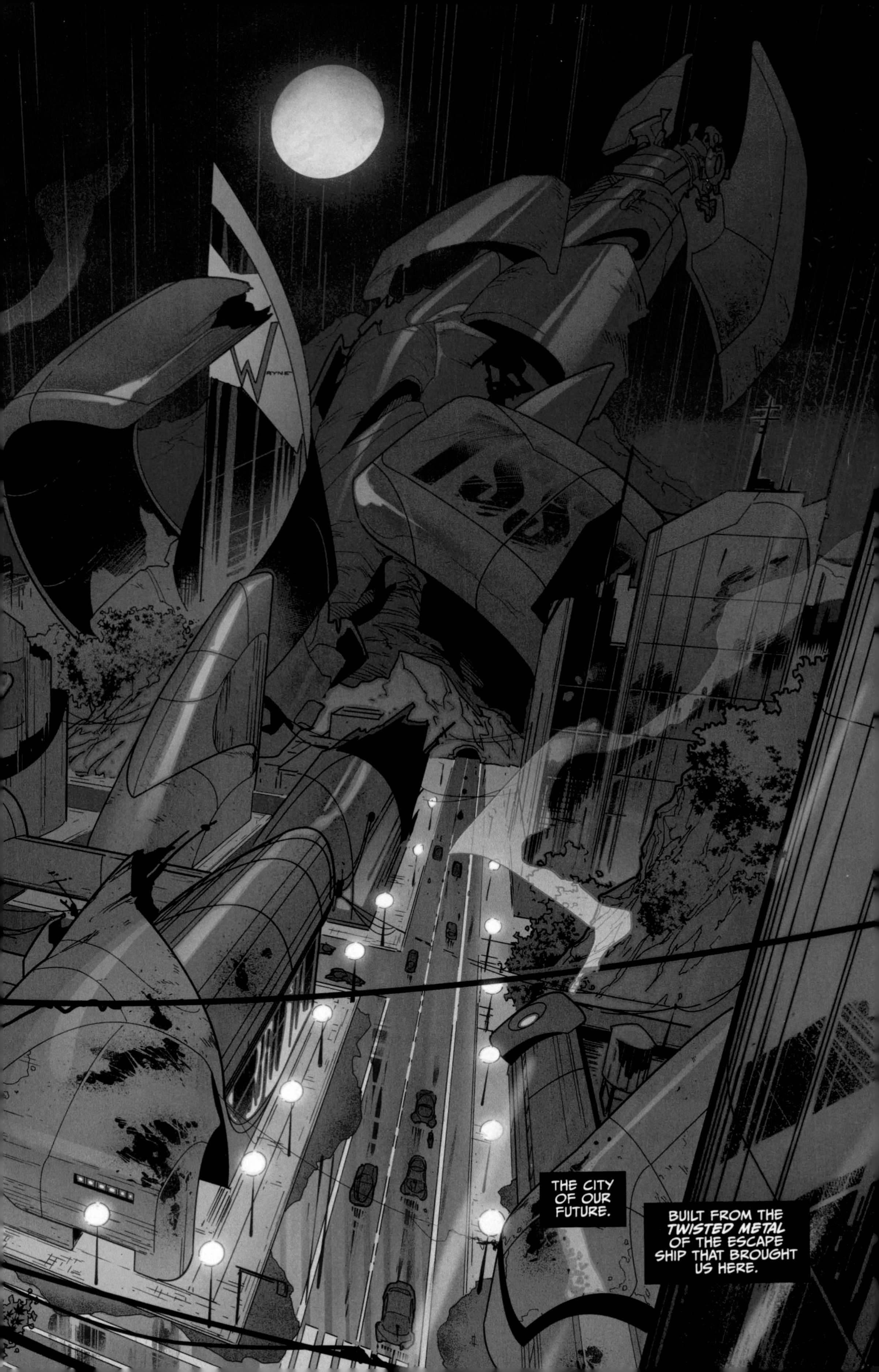
THE CITY OF OUR FUTURE.
BUILT FROM THE *TWISTED METAL* OF THE ESCAPE SHIP THAT BROUGHT US HERE.

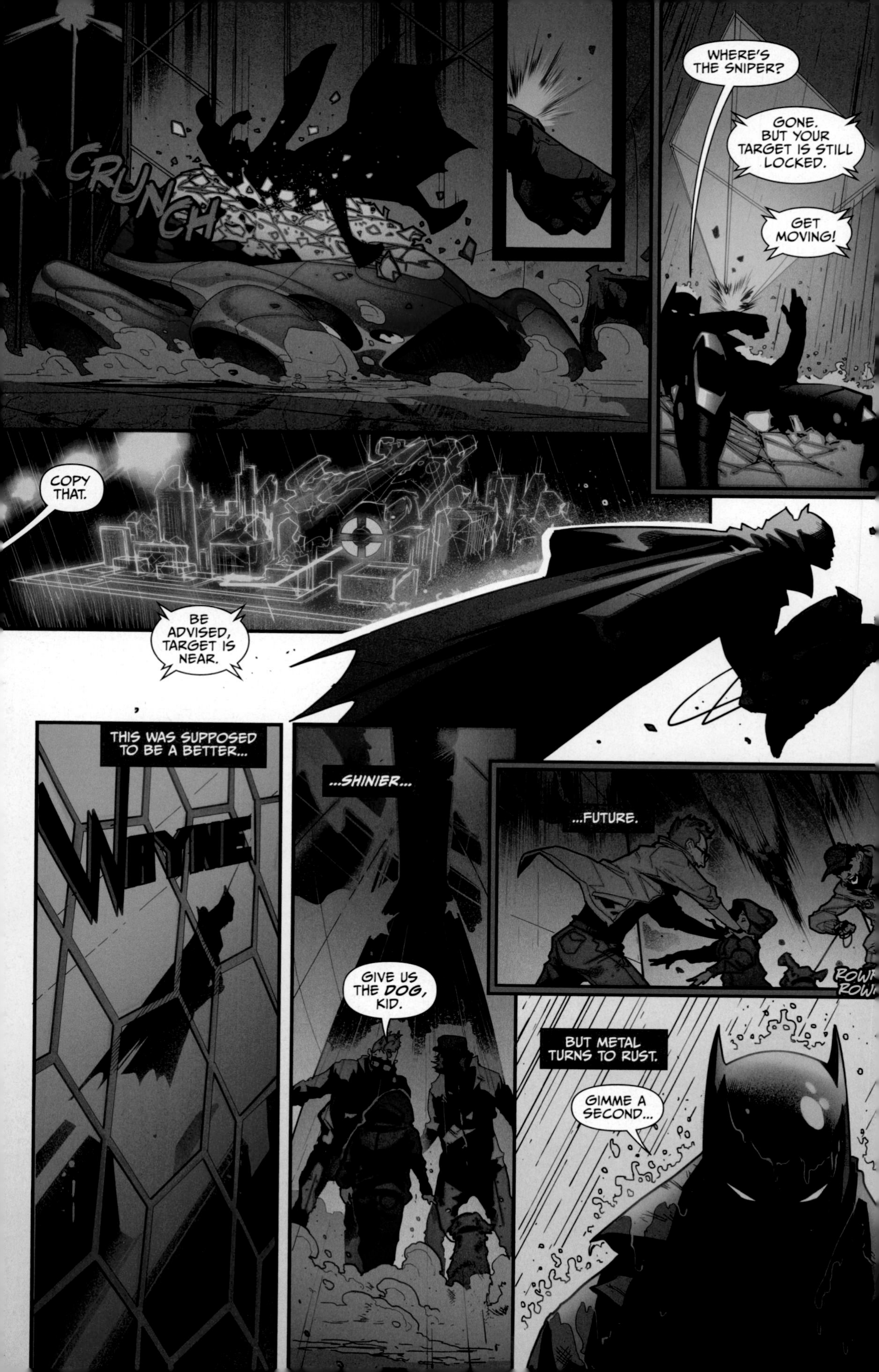
CRUNCH
WHERE'S THE SNIPER?
GONE. BUT YOUR TARGET IS STILL LOCKED.
GET MOVING!
COPY THAT.
BE ADVISED, TARGET IS NEAR.
THIS WAS SUPPOSED TO BE A BETTER...
WAYNE
...SHINIER...
...FUTURE.
GIVE US THE DOG, KID.
BUT METAL TURNS TO RUST.
GIMME A SECOND...

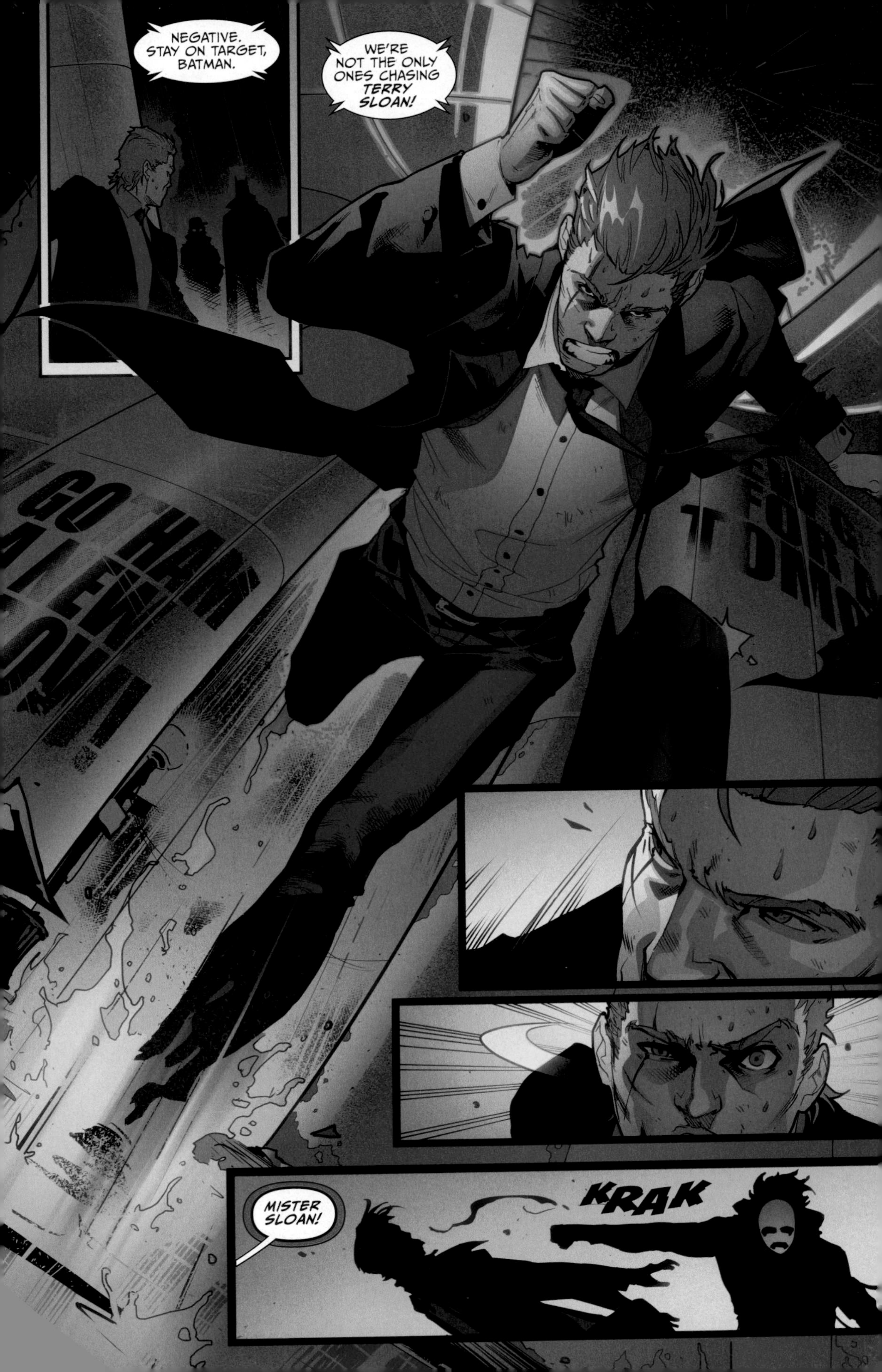
NEGATIVE. STAY ON TARGET, BATMAN.
WE'RE NOT THE ONLY ONES CHASING TERRY SLOAN!
MISTER SLOAN!
KRAK

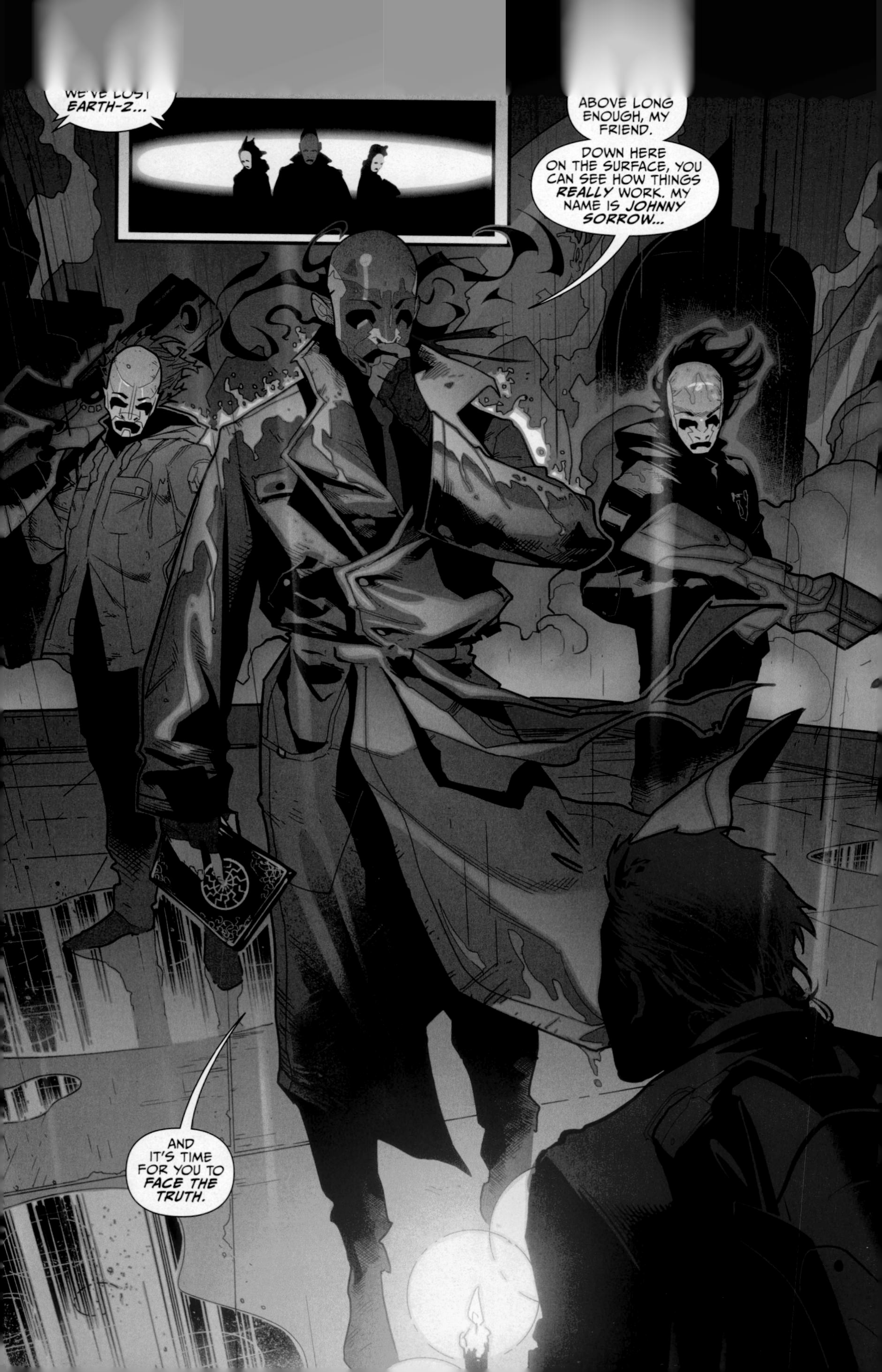
WE'VE LOST EARTH-2...
ABOVE LONG ENOUGH, MY FRIEND.
DOWN HERE ON THE SURFACE, YOU CAN SEE HOW THINGS REALLY WORK. MY NAME IS JOHNNY SORROW...
AND IT'S TIME FOR YOU TO FACE THE TRUTH.

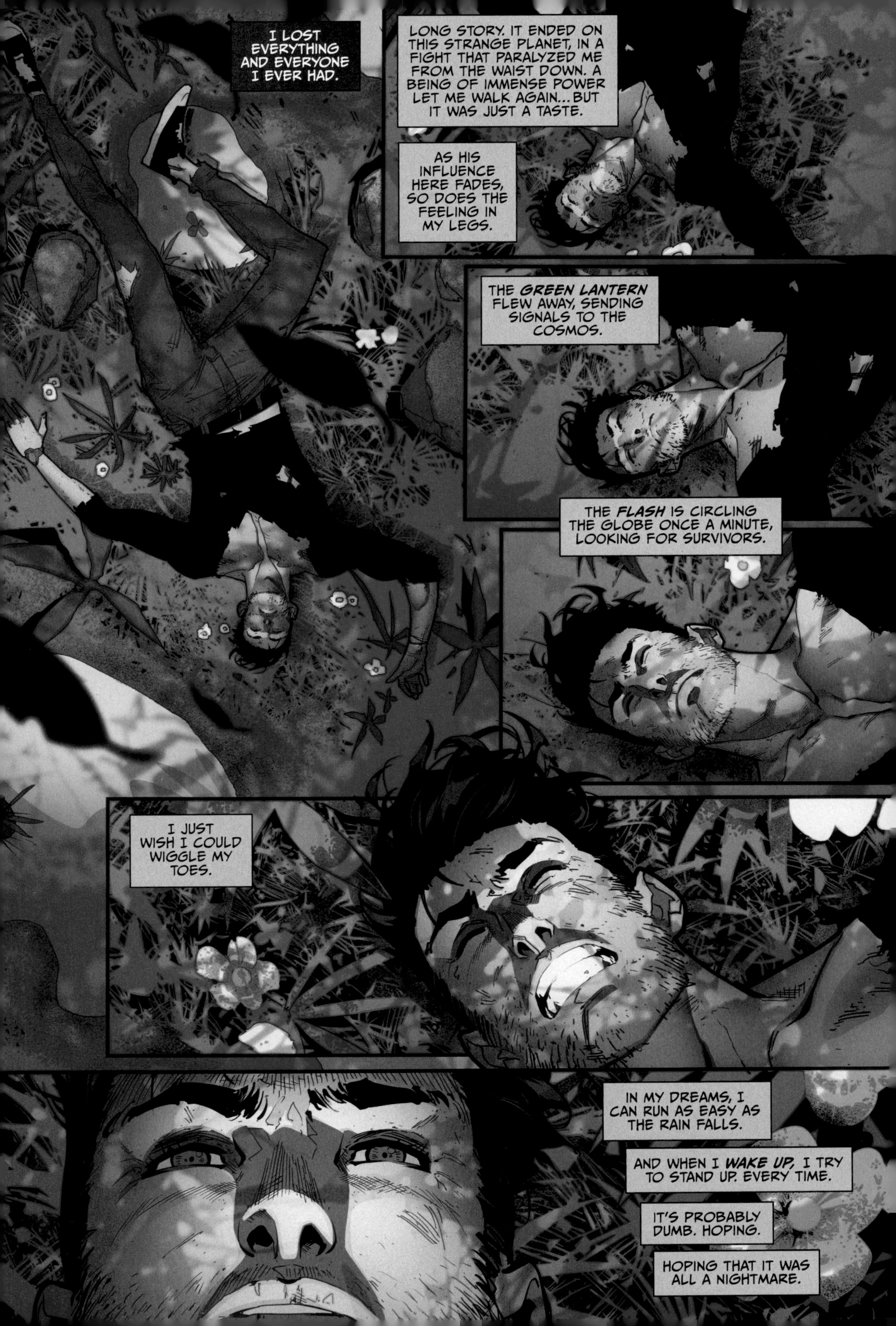
I LOST EVERYTHING AND EVERYONE I EVER HAD.
LONG STORY. IT ENDED ON THIS STRANGE PLANET, IN A FIGHT THAT PARALYZED ME FROM THE WAIST DOWN. A BEING OF IMMENSE POWER LET ME WALK AGAIN... BUT IT WAS JUST A TASTE.
AS HIS INFLUENCE HERE FADES, SO DOES THE FEELING IN MY LEGS.
THE GREEN LANTERN FLEW AWAY, SENDING SIGNALS TO THE COSMOS.
THE FLASH IS CIRCLING THE GLOBE ONCE A MINUTE, LOOKING FOR SURVIVORS.
I JUST WISH I COULD WIGGLE MY TOES.
IN MY DREAMS, I CAN RUN AS EASY AS THE RAIN FALLS.
AND WHEN I WAKE UP, I TRY TO STAND UP. EVERY TIME.
IT'S PROBABLY DUMB. HOPING.
HOPING THAT IT WAS ALL A NIGHTMARE.

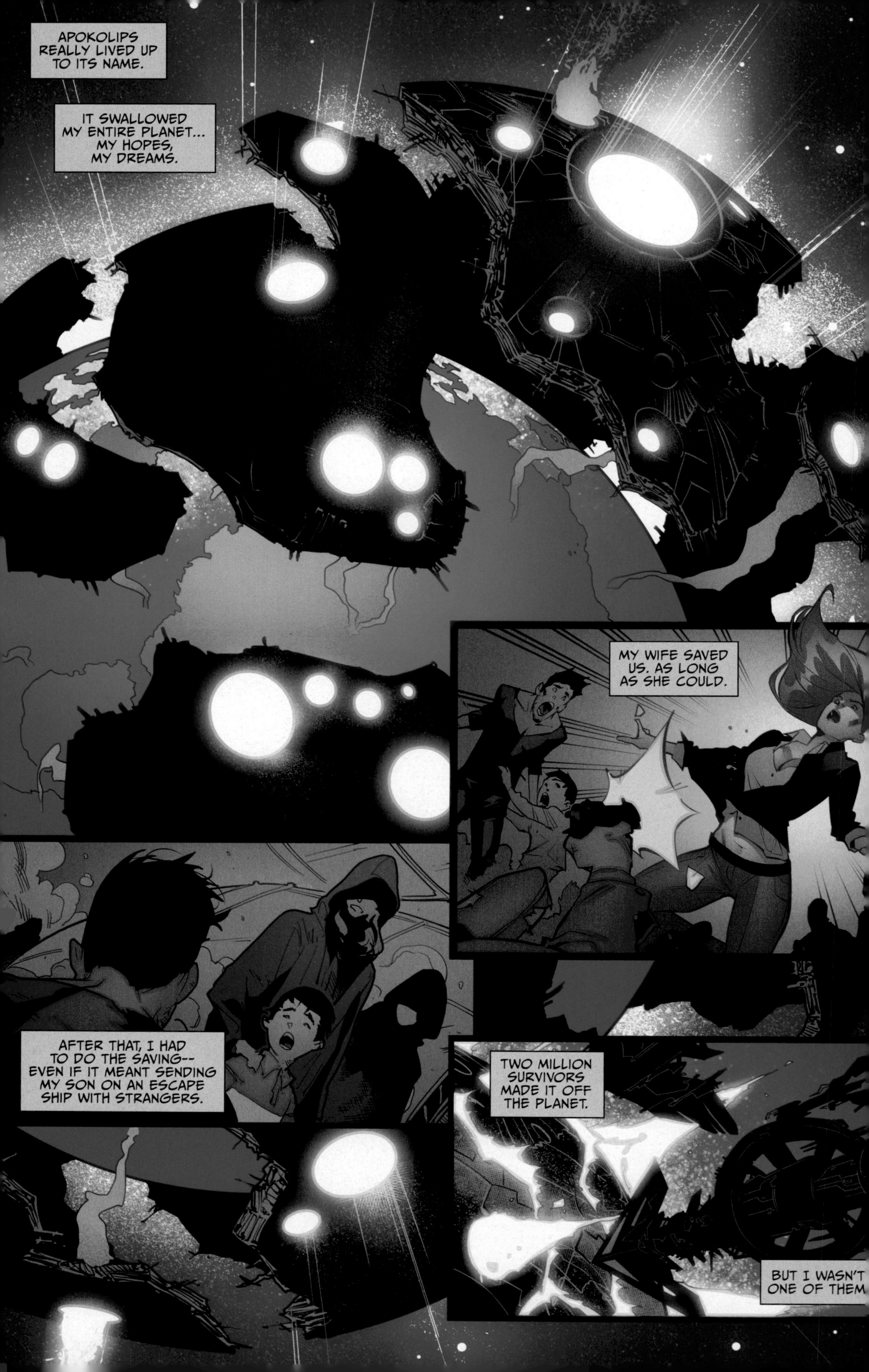
APOKOLIPS REALLY LIVED UP TO ITS NAME.
IT SWALLOWED MY ENTIRE PLANET... MY HOPES, MY DREAMS.
MY WIFE SAVED US. AS LONG AS SHE COULD.
AFTER THAT, I HAD TO DO THE SAVING-- EVEN IF IT MEANT SENDING MY SON ON AN ESCAPE SHIP WITH STRANGERS.
TWO MILLION SURVIVORS MADE IT OFF THE PLANET.
BUT I WASN'T ONE OF THEM

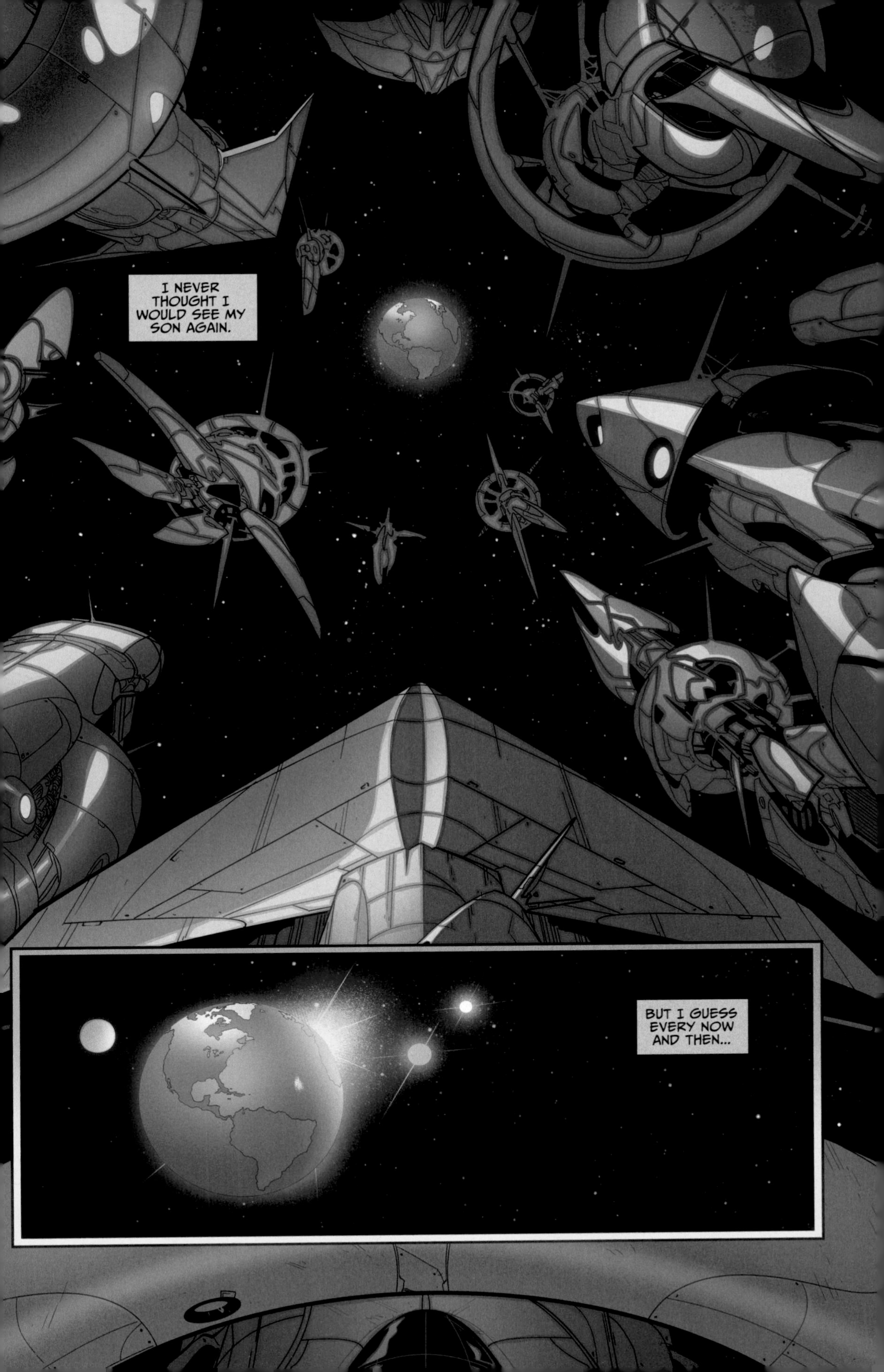
I NEVER THOUGHT I WOULD SEE MY SON AGAIN.
BUT I GUESS EVERY NOW AND THEN...

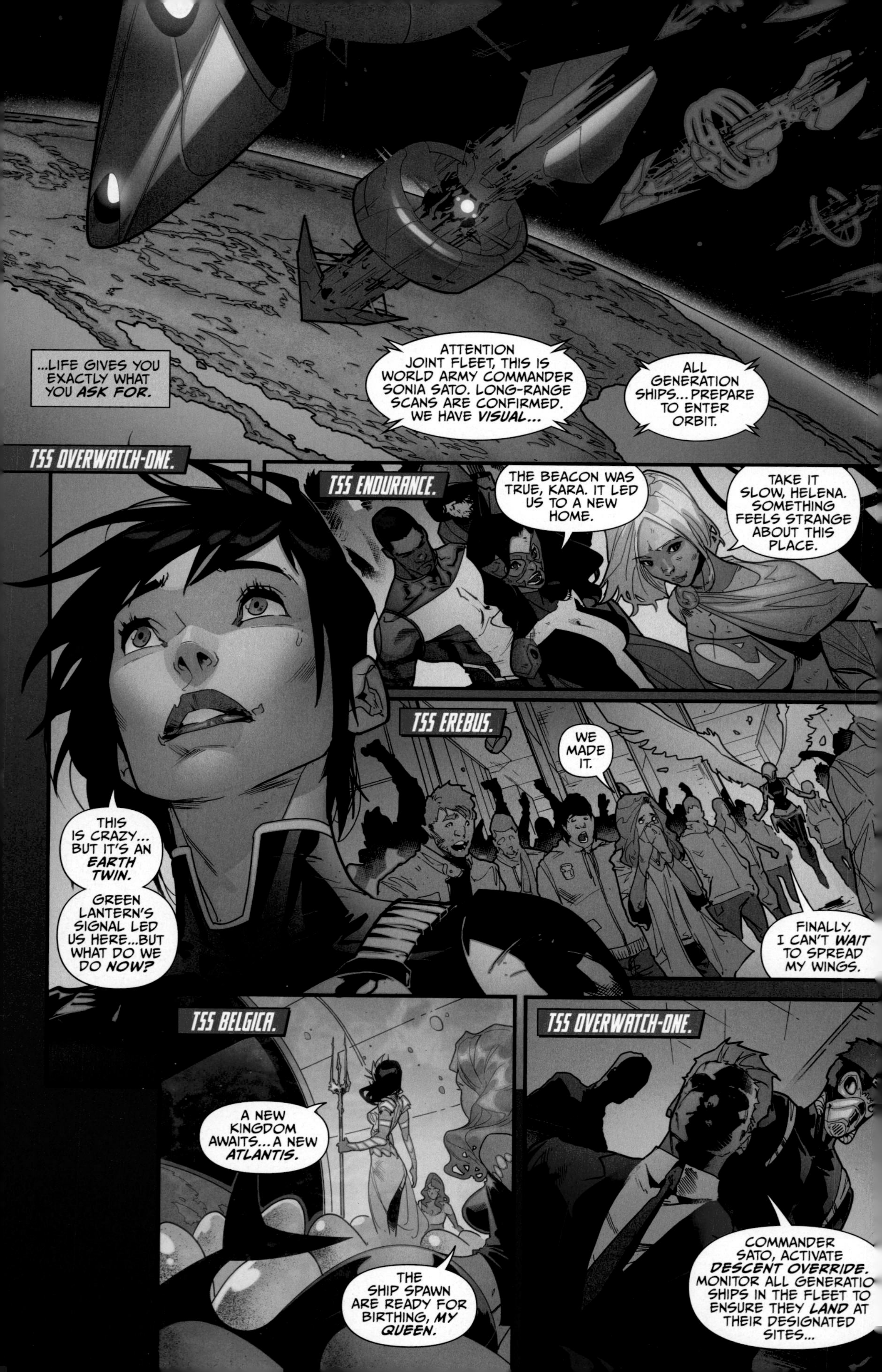
...LIFE GIVES YOU EXACTLY WHAT YOU ASK FOR.
ATTENTION JOINT FLEET, THIS IS WORLD ARMY COMMANDER SONIA SATO. LONG-RANGE SCANS ARE CONFIRMED. WE HAVE VISUAL...
ALL GENERATION SHIPS...PREPARE TO ENTER ORBIT.
TSS OVERWATCH-ONE.
THIS IS CRAZY... BUT IT'S AN EARTH TWIN.
GREEN LANTERN'S SIGNAL LED US HERE...BUT WHAT DO WE DO NOW?
TSS ENDURANCE.
THE BEACON WAS TRUE, KARA. IT LED US TO A NEW HOME.
TAKE IT SLOW, HELENA. SOMETHING FEELS STRANGE ABOUT THIS PLACE.
TSS EREBUS.
WE MADE IT.
FINALLY. I CAN'T WAIT TO SPREAD MY WINGS.
TSS BELGICA.
A NEW KINGDOM AWAITS...A NEW ATLANTIS.
THE SHIP SPAWN ARE READY FOR BIRTHING, MY QUEEN.
TSS OVERWATCH-ONE.
COMMANDER SATO, ACTIVATE DESCENT OVERRIDE. MONITOR ALL GENERATIO SHIPS IN THE FLEET TO ENSURE THEY LAND AT THEIR DESIGNATED SITES...

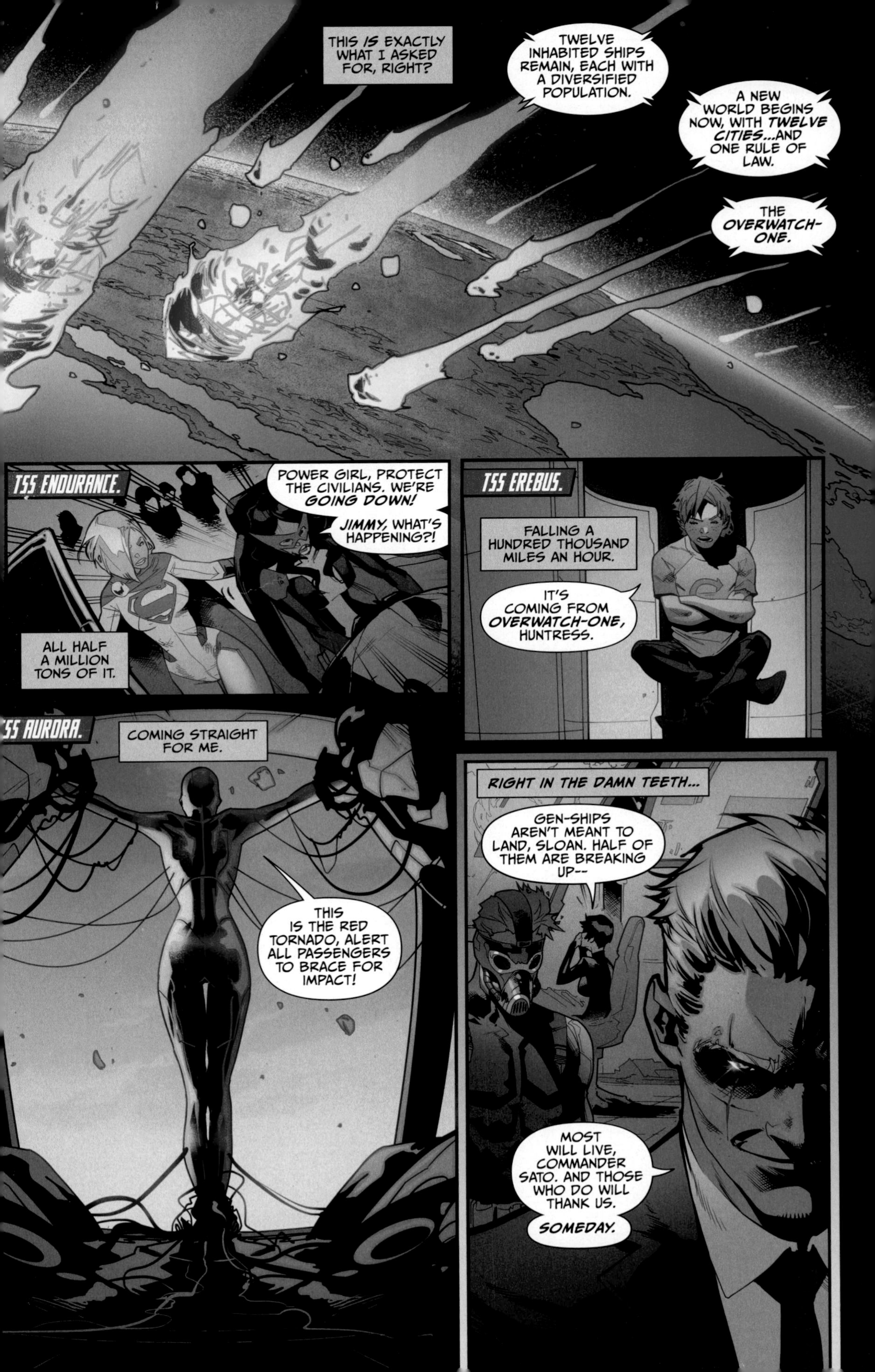
THIS IS EXACTLY WHAT I ASKED FOR, RIGHT?
TWELVE INHABITED SHIPS REMAIN, EACH WITH A DIVERSIFIED POPULATION.
A NEW WORLD BEGINS NOW, WITH TWELVE CITIES...AND ONE RULE OF LAW.
THE OVERWATCH-ONE.
TSS ENDURANCE.
POWER GIRL, PROTECT THE CIVILIANS. WE'RE GOING DOWN!
JIMMY, WHAT'S HAPPENING?!
ALL HALF A MILLION TONS OF IT.
TSS EREBUS.
FALLING A HUNDRED THOUSAND MILES AN HOUR.
IT'S COMING FROM OVERWATCH-ONE, HUNTRESS.
TSS AURORA.
COMING STRAIGHT FOR ME.
THIS IS THE RED TORNADO, ALERT ALL PASSENGERS TO BRACE FOR IMPACT!
RIGHT IN THE DAMN TEETH...
GEN-SHIPS AREN'T MEANT TO LAND, SLOAN. HALF OF THEM ARE BREAKING UP--
MOST WILL LIVE, COMMANDER SATO. AND THOSE WHO DO WILL THANK US.
SOMEDAY.

TSS ENDURANCE. *CRASH LANDING.*

...SO SMILE.

PLEASE. WHOEVER IS UP THERE. WHOEVER IS LISTENING.

I DON'T LIKE YOU. AND YOU *DEFINITELY* DON'T LIKE ME.

BUT *PLEASE.*

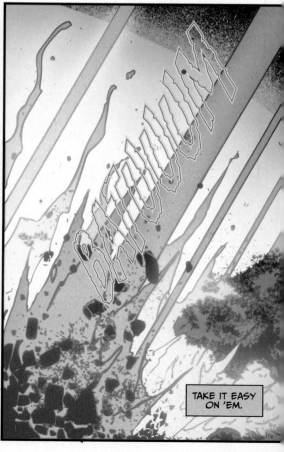

TAKE IT EASY ON 'EM.

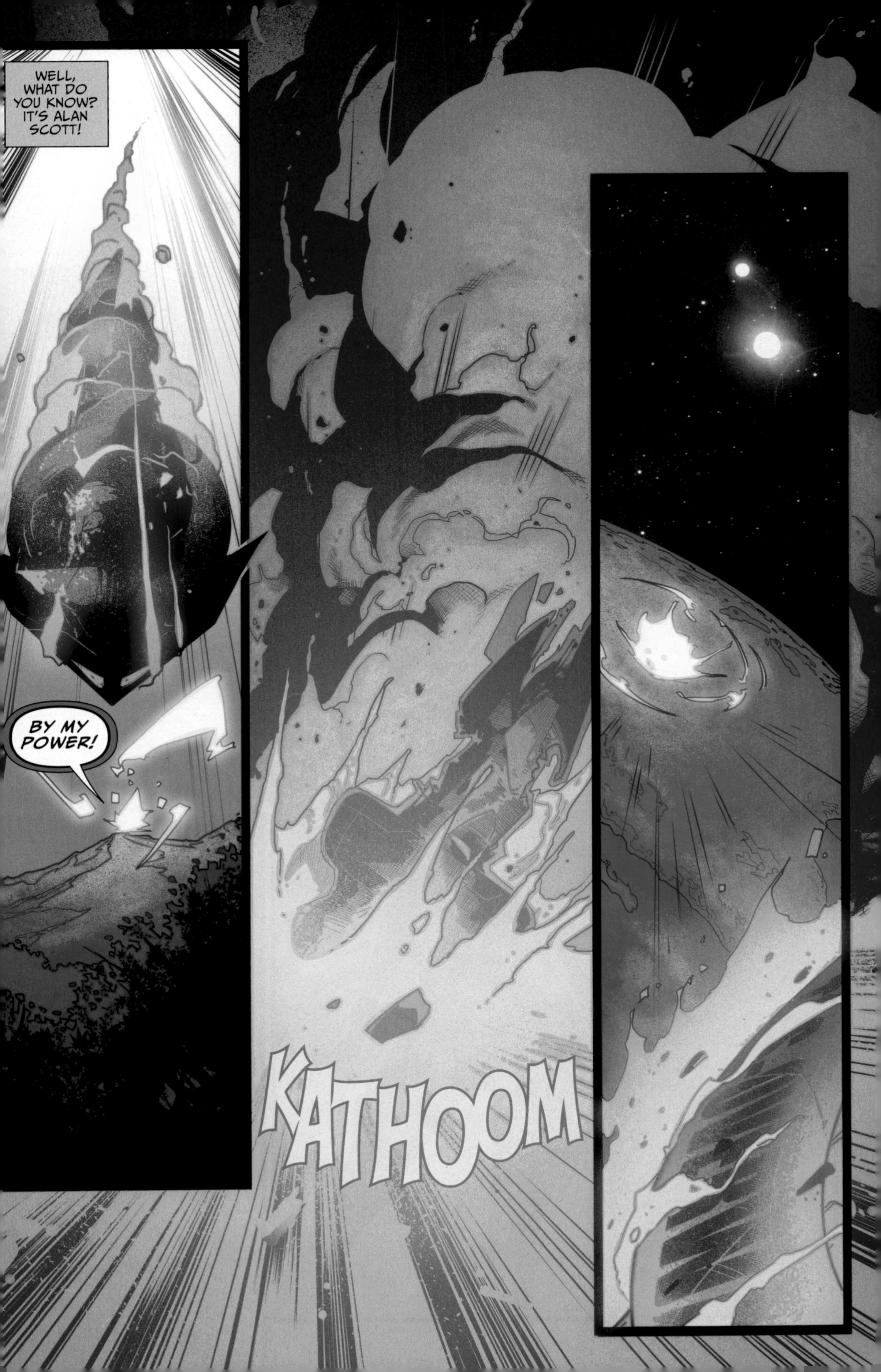
WELL, WHAT DO YOU KNOW? IT'S ALAN SCOTT!
BY MY POWER!
KATHOOM

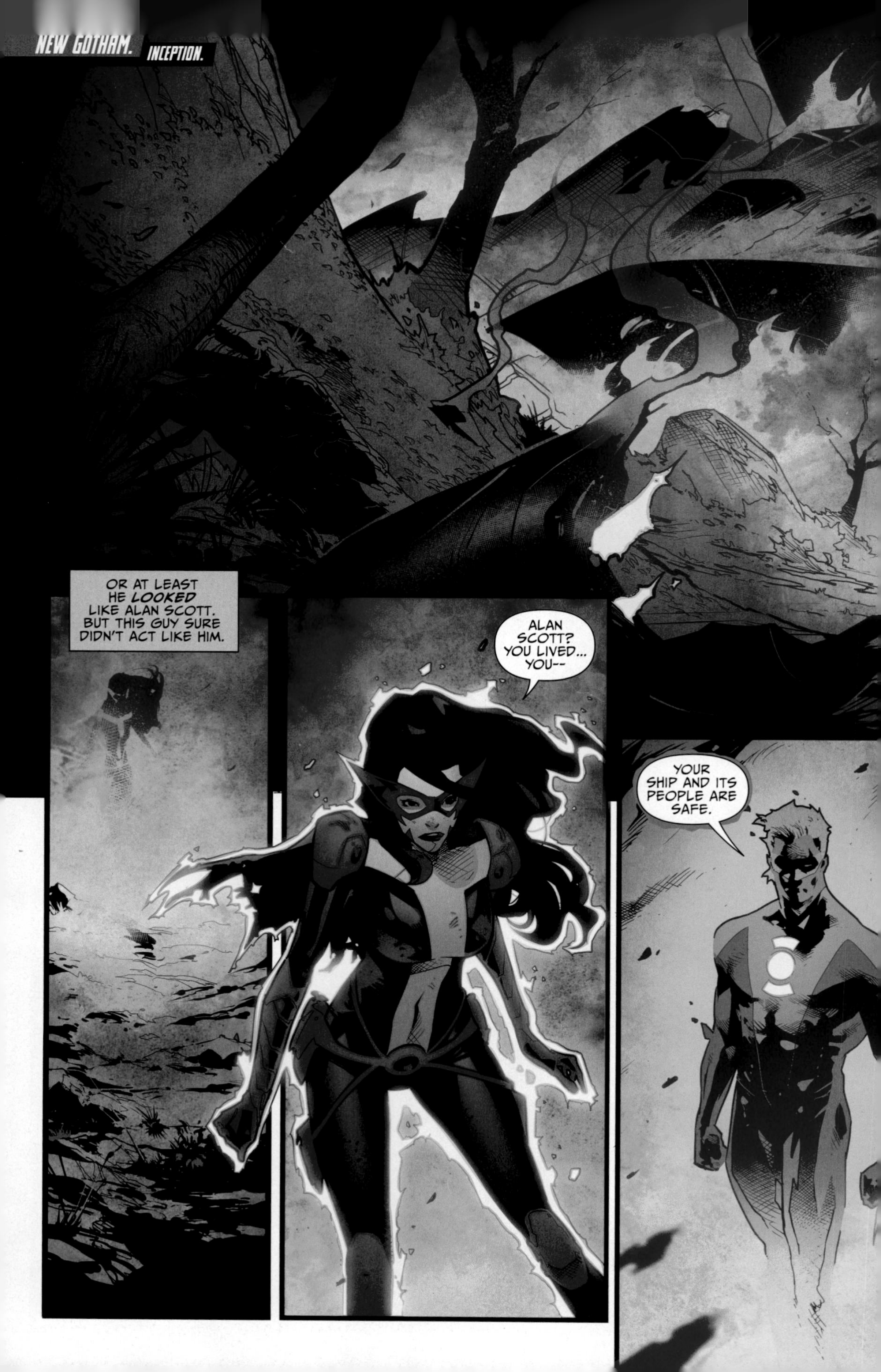
NEW GOTHAM.
INCEPTION.
OR AT LEAST HE LOOKED LIKE ALAN SCOTT. BUT THIS GUY SURE DIDN'T ACT LIKE HIM.
ALAN SCOTT? YOU LIVED... YOU--
YOUR SHIP AND ITS PEOPLE ARE SAFE.

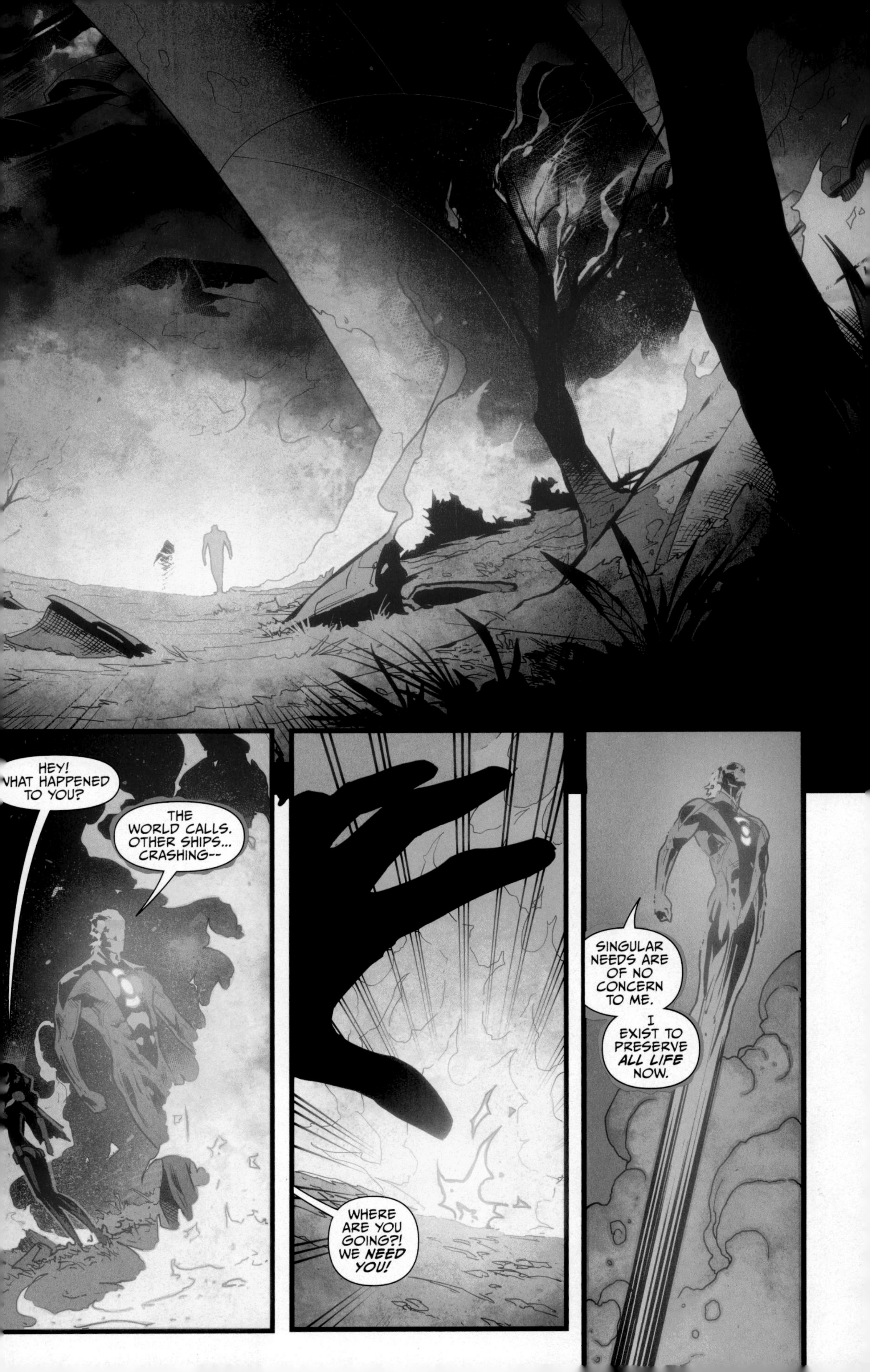
HEY! WHAT HAPPENED TO YOU?
THE WORLD CALLS. OTHER SHIPS... CRASHING--
WHERE ARE YOU GOING?! WE NEED YOU!
SINGULAR NEEDS ARE OF NO CONCERN TO ME.
I EXIST TO PRESERVE ALL LIFE NOW.

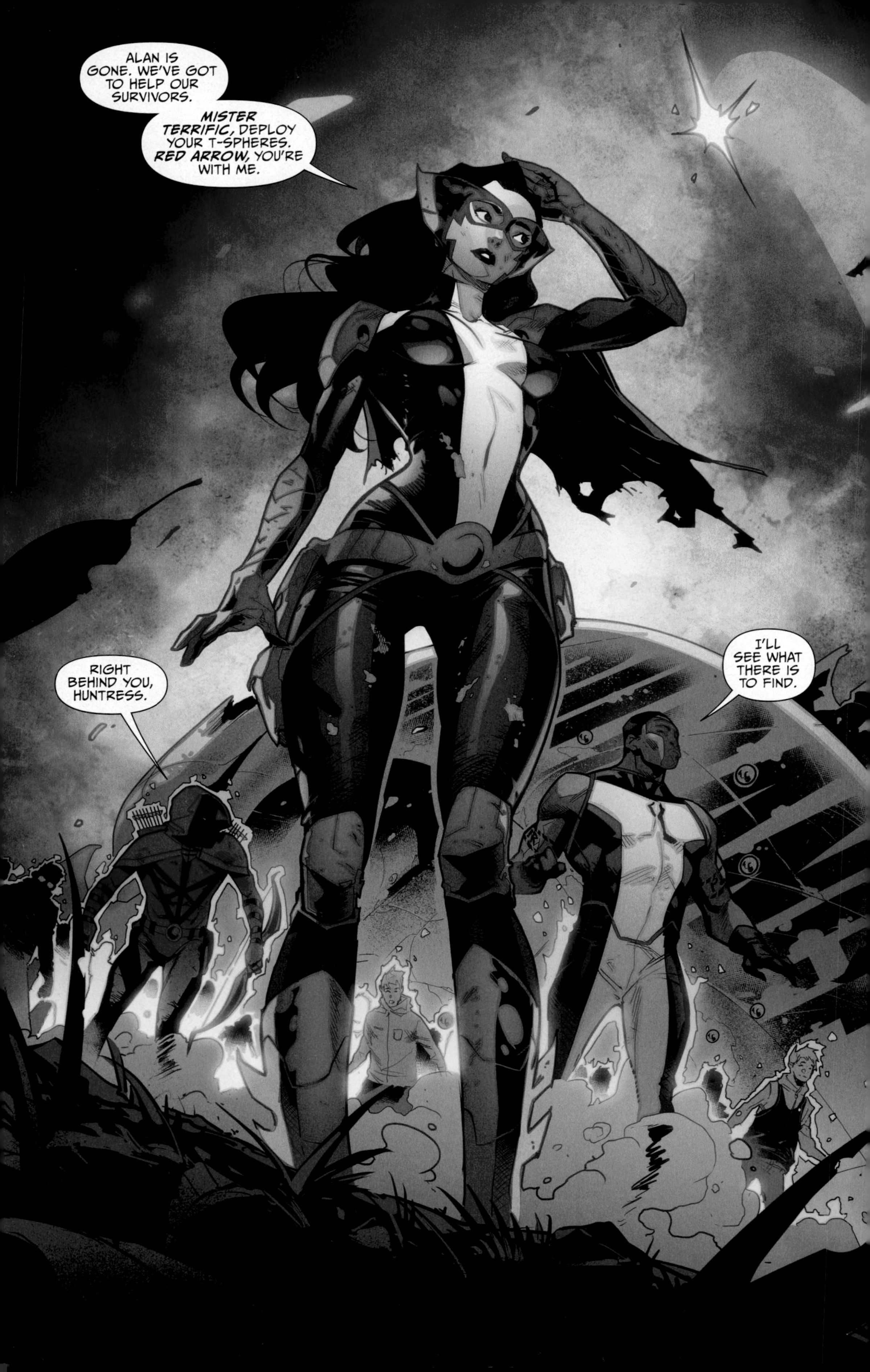
ALAN IS GONE. WE'VE GOT TO HELP OUR SURVIVORS.
MISTER TERRIFIC, DEPLOY YOUR T-SPHERES. RED ARROW, YOU'RE WITH ME.
RIGHT BEHIND YOU, HUNTRESS.
I'LL SEE WHAT THERE IS TO FIND.

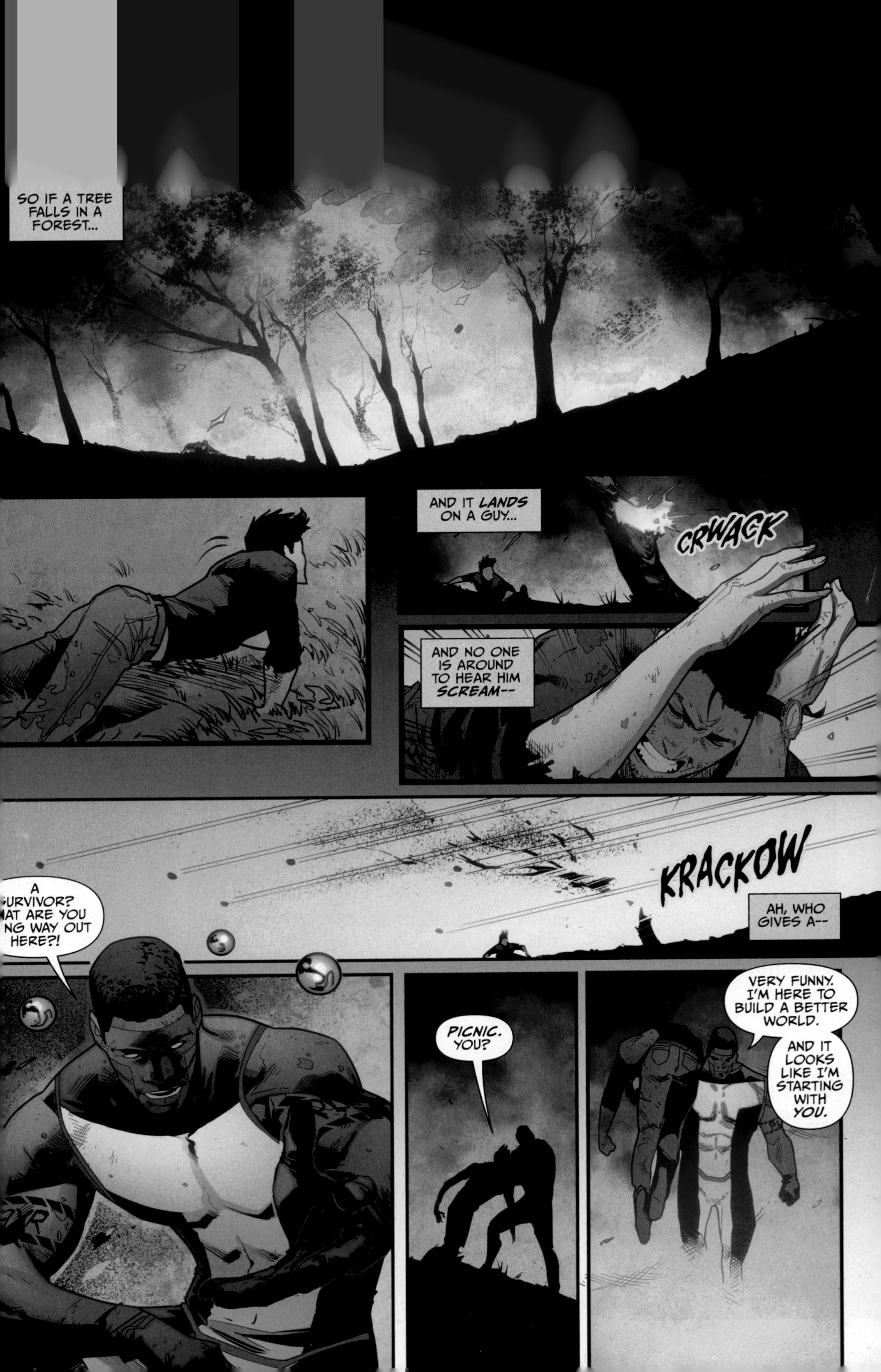
SO IF A TREE FALLS IN A FOREST...
AND IT LANDS ON A GUY...
CRWACK
AND NO ONE IS AROUND TO HEAR HIM SCREAM--
KRACKOW
AH, WHO GIVES A--
A SURVIVOR? HAT ARE YOU NG WAY OUT HERE?!
PICNIC. YOU?
VERY FUNNY. I'M HERE TO BUILD A BETTER WORLD.
AND IT LOOKS LIKE I'M STARTING WITH YOU.

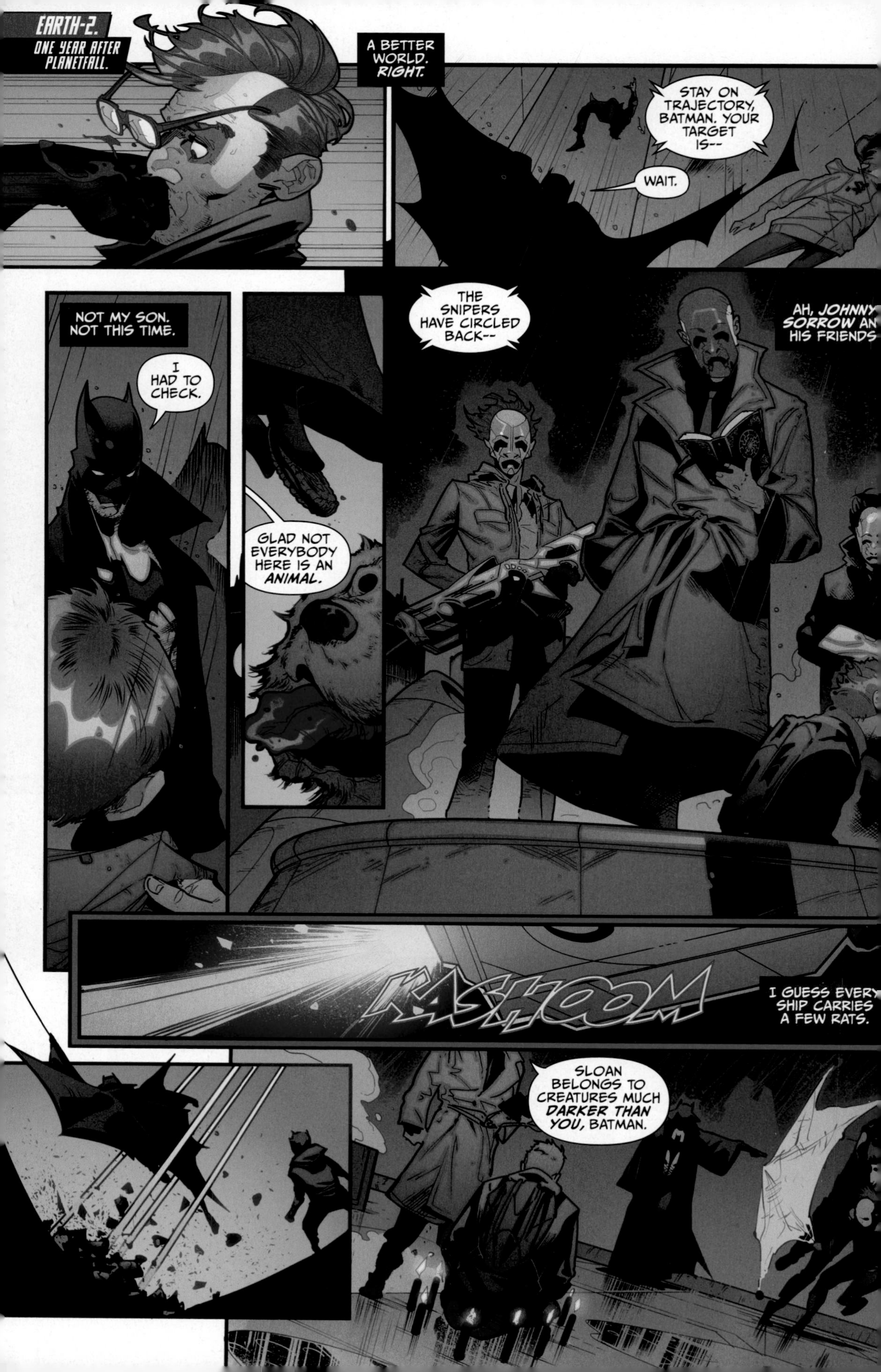
EARTH-2.
ONE YEAR AFTER PLANETFALL.
A BETTER WORLD. RIGHT.
STAY ON TRAJECTORY, BATMAN. YOUR TARGET IS--
WAIT.
NOT MY SON. NOT THIS TIME.
I HAD TO CHECK.
GLAD NOT EVERYBODY HERE IS AN ANIMAL.
THE SNIPERS HAVE CIRCLED BACK--
AH, JOHNNY SORROW AN
HIS FRIENDS
KASHOOM
I GUESS EVERY
SHIP CARRIES
A FEW RATS.
SLOAN BELONGS TO CREATURES MUCH DARKER THAN YOU, BATMAN.

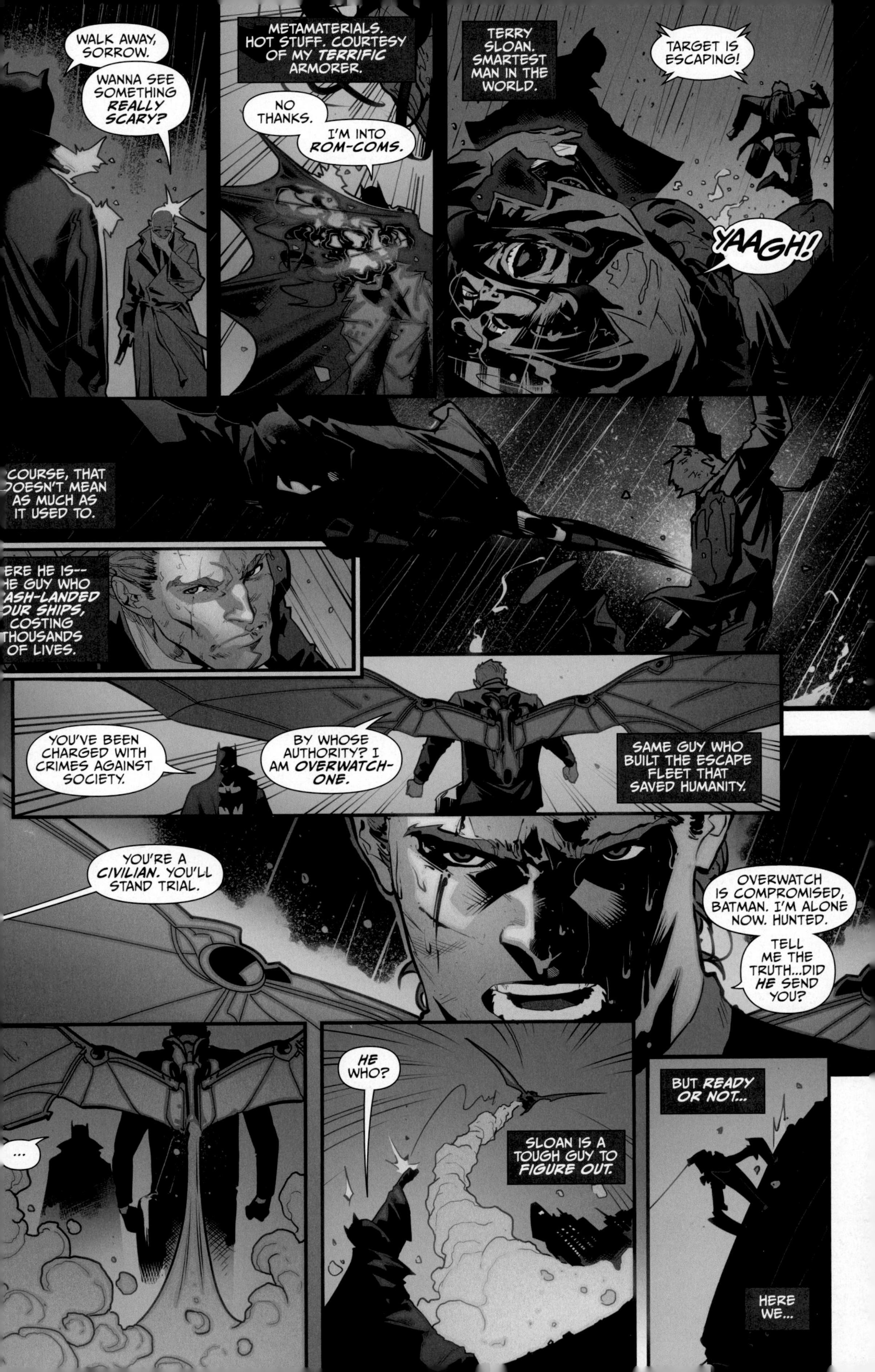

WALK AWAY, SORROW.
WANNA SEE SOMETHING REALLY SCARY?
METAMATERIALS. HOT STUFF. COURTESY OF MY TERRIFIC ARMORER.
NO THANKS.
I'M INTO ROM-COMS.
TERRY SLOAN. SMARTEST MAN IN THE WORLD.
TARGET IS ESCAPING!
YAAGH!
COURSE, THAT DOESN'T MEAN AS MUCH AS IT USED TO.
ERE HE IS-- HE GUY WHO ASH-LANDED OUR SHIPS, COSTING THOUSANDS OF LIVES.
YOU'VE BEEN CHARGED WITH CRIMES AGAINST SOCIETY.
BY WHOSE AUTHORITY? I AM OVERWATCH-ONE.
SAME GUY WHO BUILT THE ESCAPE FLEET THAT SAVED HUMANITY.
YOU'RE A CIVILIAN. YOU'LL STAND TRIAL.
OVERWATCH IS COMPROMISED, BATMAN. I'M ALONE NOW. HUNTED.
TELL ME THE TRUTH...DID HE SEND YOU?
...
HE WHO?
SLOAN IS A TOUGH GUY TO FIGURE OUT.
BUT READY OR NOT...
HERE WE...

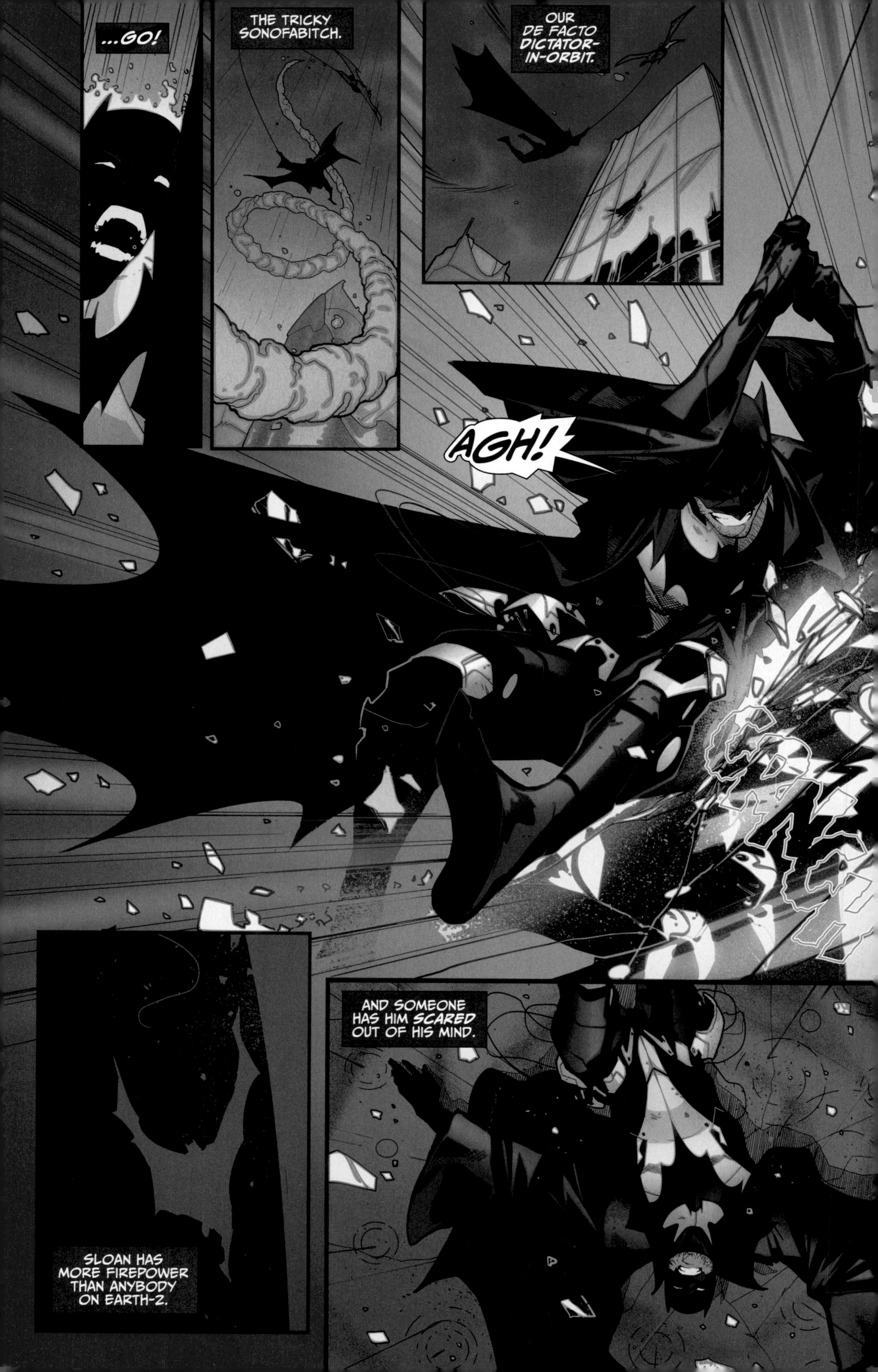
...GO!
THE TRICKY SONOFABITCH.
OUR DE FACTO DICTATOR-IN-ORBIT.
AGH!
SLOAN HAS MORE FIREPOWER THAN ANYBODY ON EARTH-2.
AND SOMEONE HAS HIM SCARED OUT OF HIS MIND.

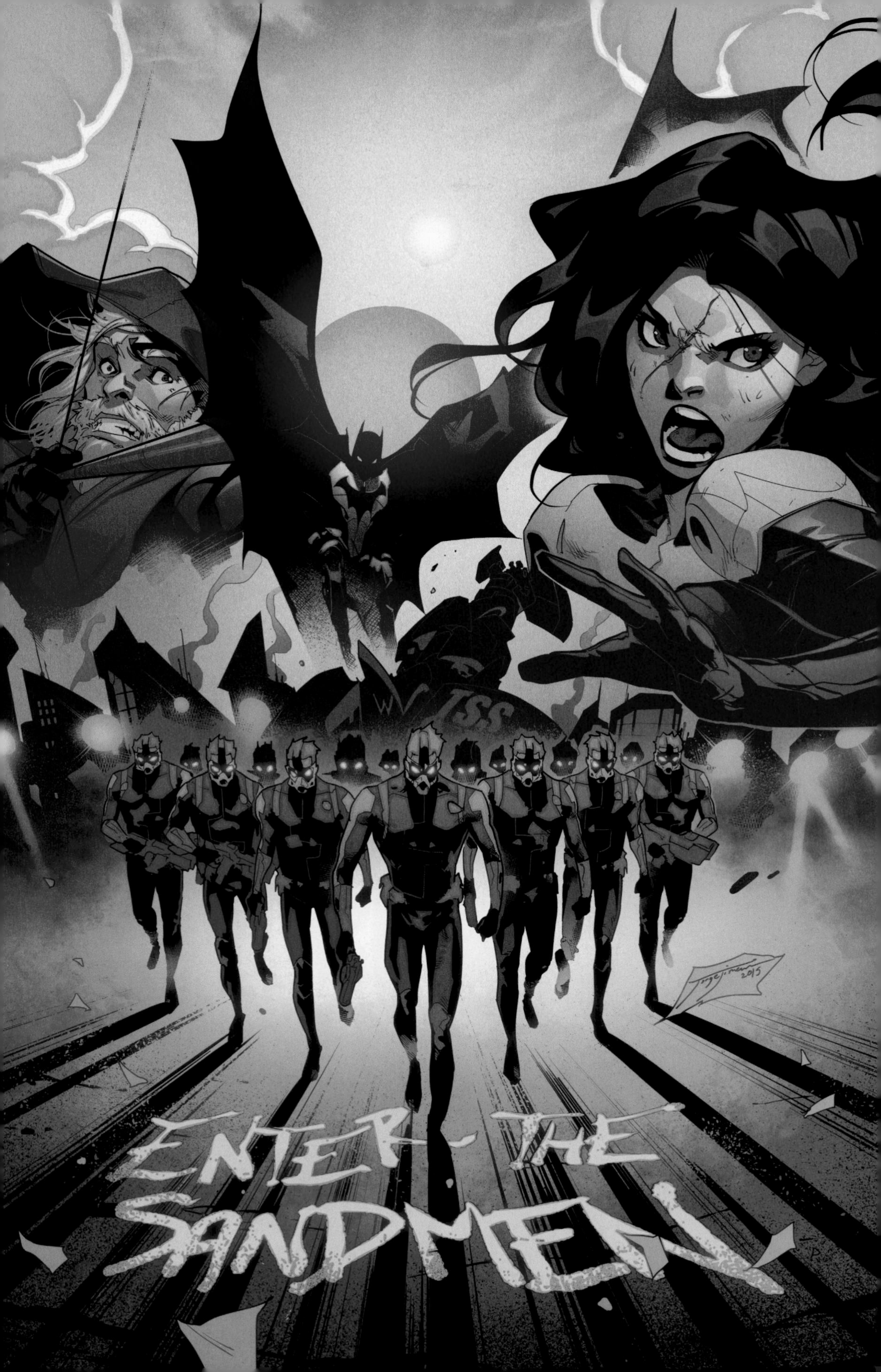
ENTER THE
SANDMEN

GUARDIAN ANGEL

DANIEL H. WILSON writer JORGE JIMENEZ artist JOHN RAUCH ANDREW DALHOUSE colorists TRAVIS LANHAM letterer cover by JIMENEZ & RAUCH

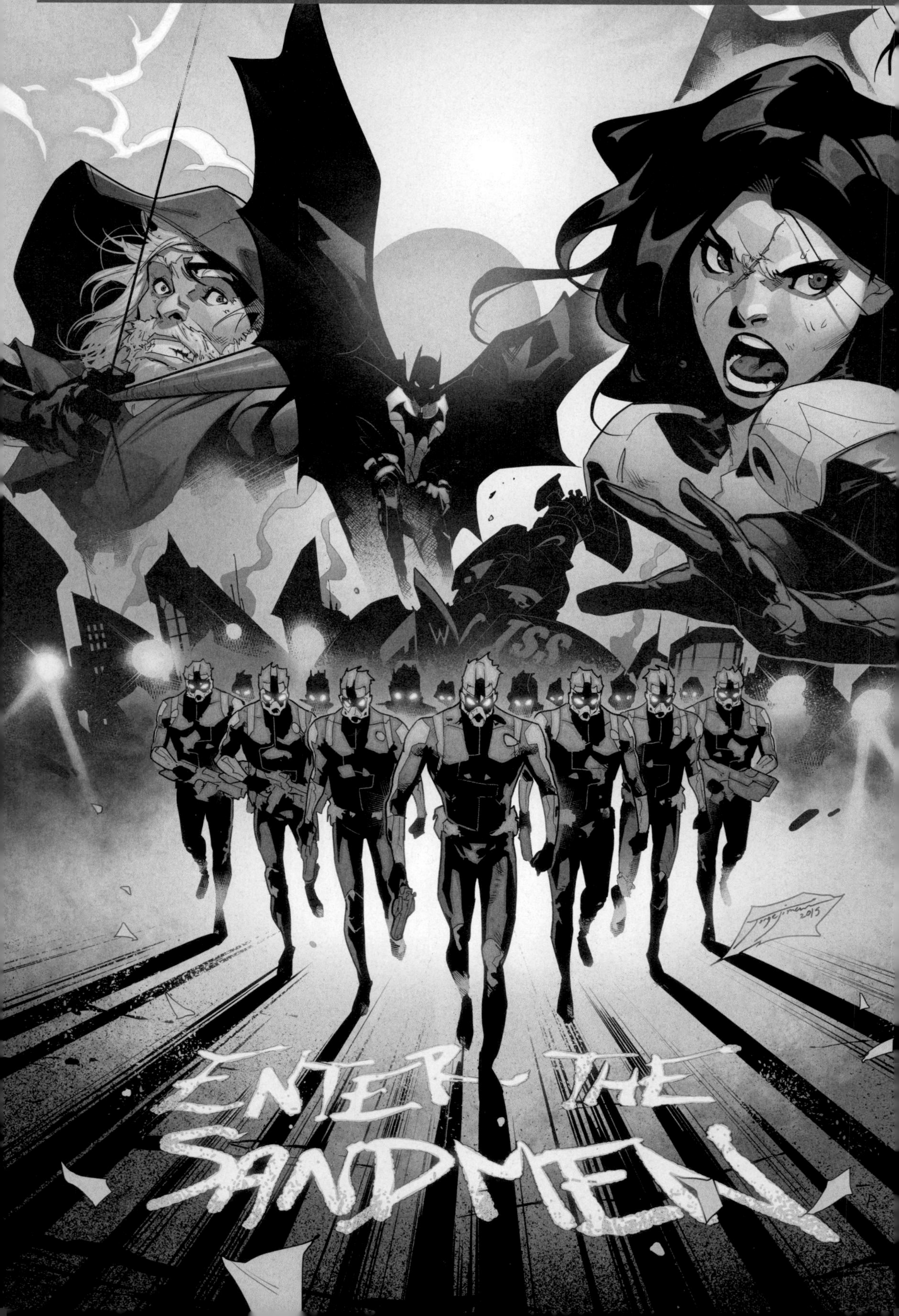
ENTER THE SANDMEN

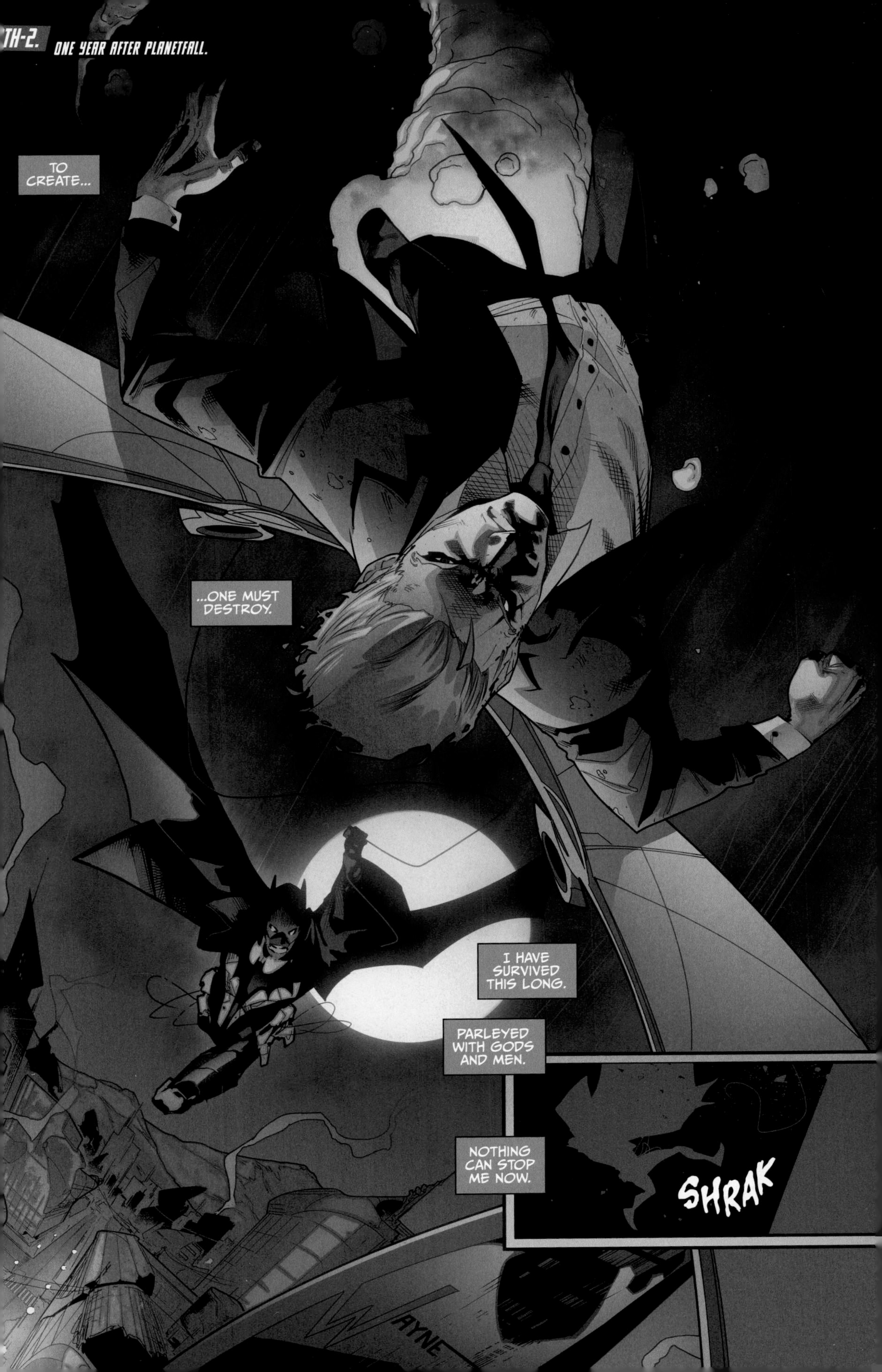
TH-2.
ONE YEAR AFTER PLANETFALL.
TO CREATE...
...ONE MUST DESTROY.
I HAVE SURVIVED THIS LONG.
PARLEYED WITH GODS AND MEN.
NOTHING CAN STOP ME NOW.
SHRAK

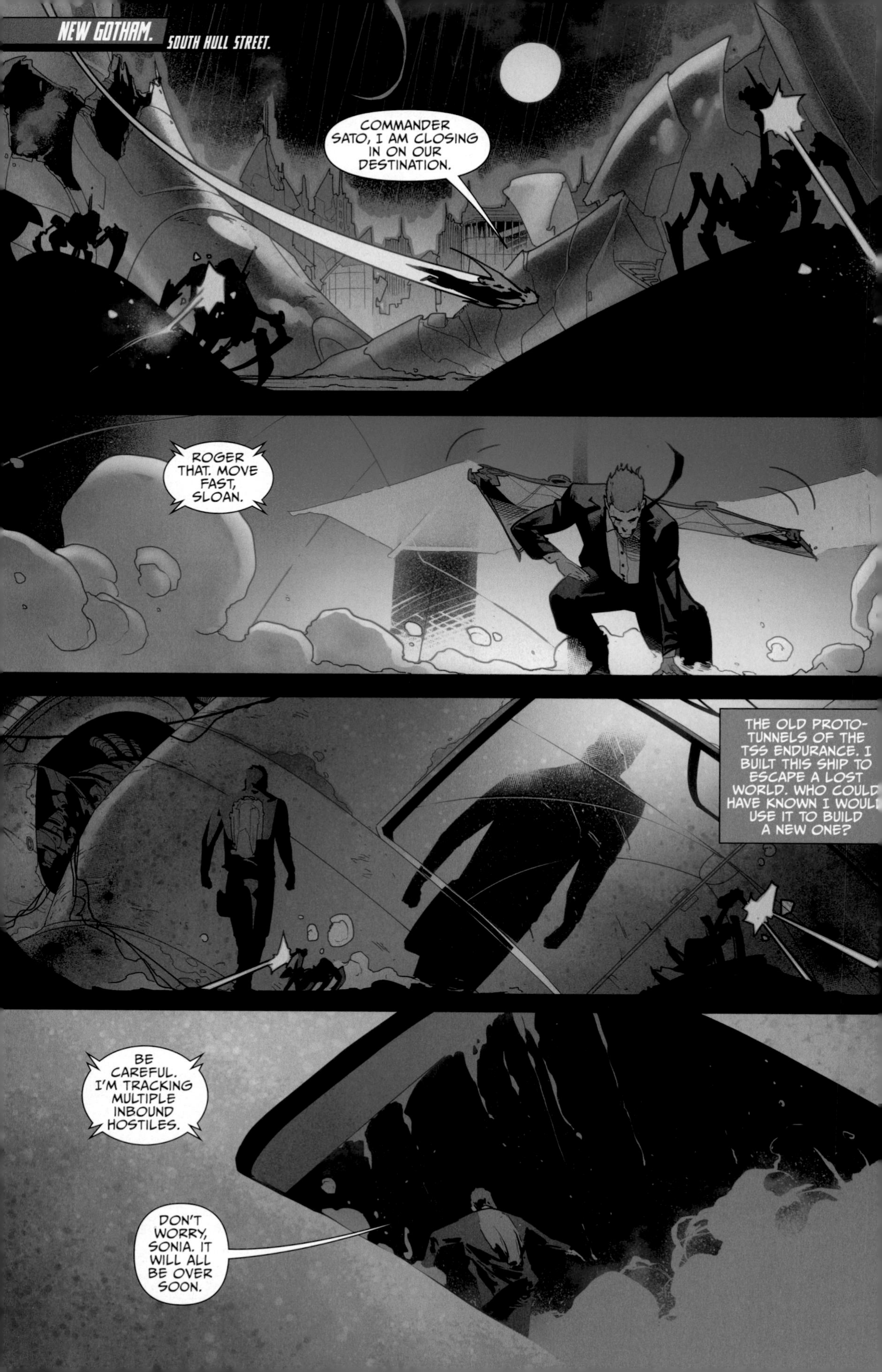
NEW GOTHAM.
SOUTH HULL STREET.
COMMANDER SATO, I AM CLOSING IN ON OUR DESTINATION.
ROGER THAT. MOVE FAST, SLOAN.
THE OLD PROTO-TUNNELS OF THE TSS ENDURANCE. I BUILT THIS SHIP TO ESCAPE A LOST WORLD. WHO COULD HAVE KNOWN I WOULD USE IT TO BUILD A NEW ONE?
BE CAREFUL. I'M TRACKING MULTIPLE INBOUND HOSTILES.
DON'T WORRY, SONIA. IT WILL ALL BE OVER SOON.

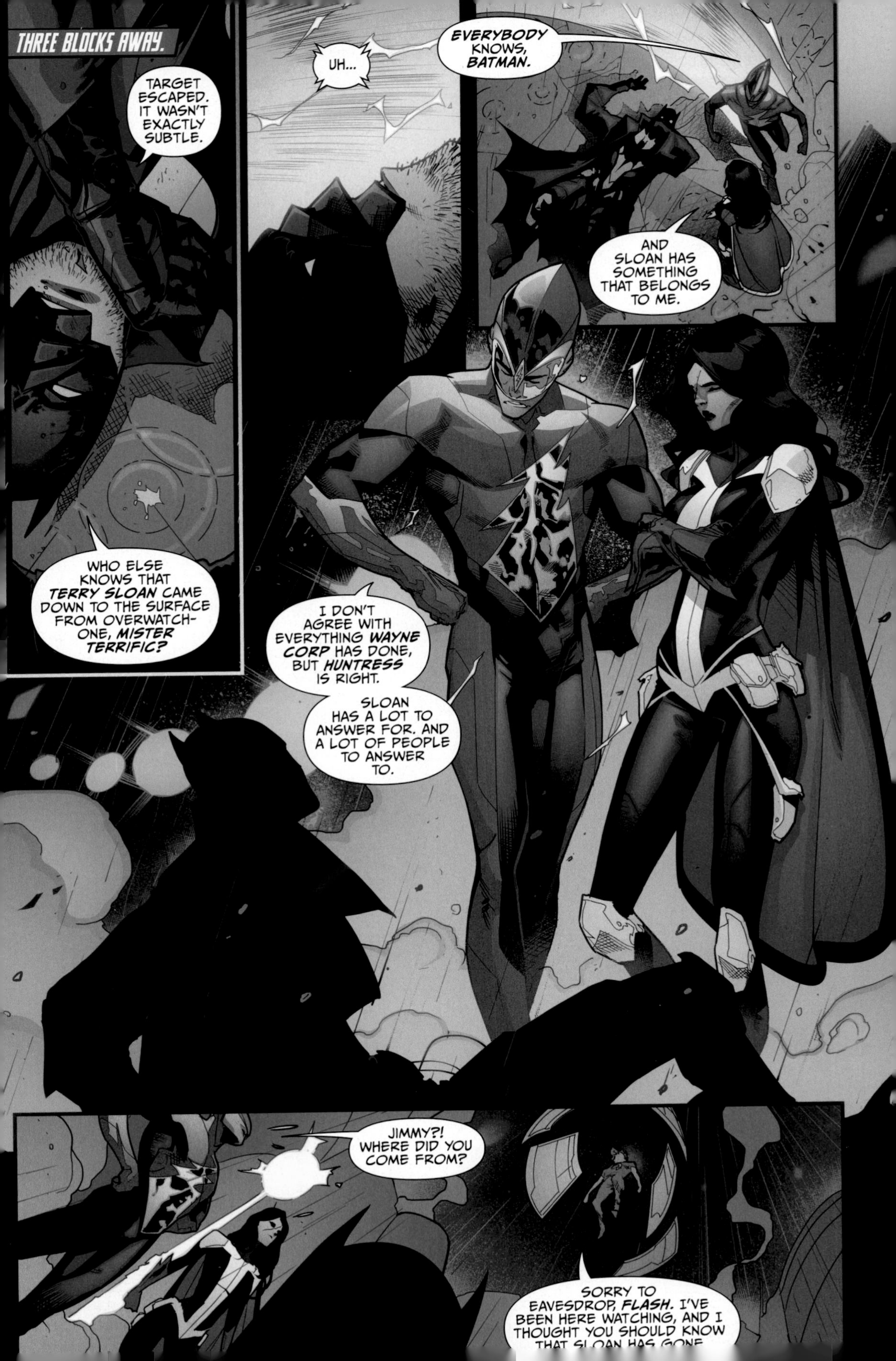
THREE BLOCKS AWAY.
TARGET ESCAPED. IT WASN'T EXACTLY SUBTLE.
UH...
EVERYBODY KNOWS, BATMAN.
AND SLOAN HAS SOMETHING THAT BELONGS TO ME.
WHO ELSE KNOWS THAT TERRY SLOAN CAME DOWN TO THE SURFACE FROM OVERWATCH-ONE, MISTER TERRIFIC?
I DON'T AGREE WITH EVERYTHING WAYNE CORP HAS DONE, BUT HUNTRESS IS RIGHT.
SLOAN HAS A LOT TO ANSWER FOR. AND A LOT OF PEOPLE TO ANSWER TO.
JIMMY?! WHERE DID YOU COME FROM?
SORRY TO EAVESDROP, FLASH. I'VE BEEN HERE WATCHING, AND I THOUGHT YOU SHOULD KNOW

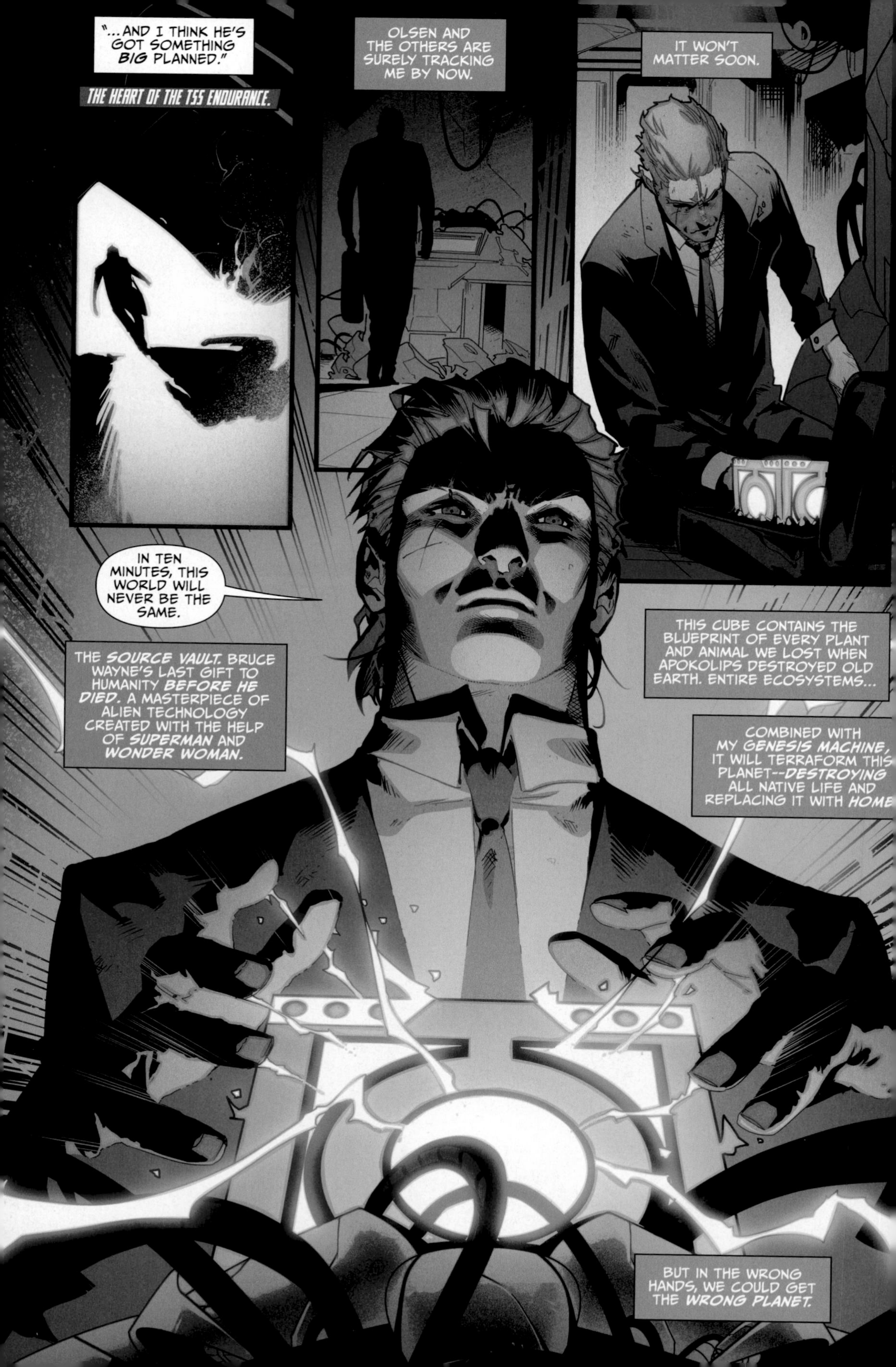
"...AND I THINK HE'S GOT SOMETHING BIG PLANNED."
THE HEART OF THE TSS ENDURANCE.
OLSEN AND THE OTHERS ARE SURELY TRACKING ME BY NOW.
IT WON'T MATTER SOON.
IN TEN MINUTES, THIS WORLD WILL NEVER BE THE SAME.
THE SOURCE VAULT. BRUCE WAYNE'S LAST GIFT TO HUMANITY BEFORE HE DIED. A MASTERPIECE OF ALIEN TECHNOLOGY CREATED WITH THE HELP OF SUPERMAN AND WONDER WOMAN.
THIS CUBE CONTAINS THE BLUEPRINT OF EVERY PLANT AND ANIMAL WE LOST WHEN APOKOLIPS DESTROYED OLD EARTH. ENTIRE ECOSYSTEMS...
COMBINED WITH MY GENESIS MACHINE, IT WILL TERRAFORM THIS PLANET--DESTROYING ALL NATIVE LIFE AND REPLACING IT WITH HOME.
BUT IN THE WRONG HANDS, WE COULD GET THE WRONG PLANET.

MONTHS AGO.
OVERWATCH-ONE. ARRIVAL.

ATTENTION, JOINT FLEET, THIS IS WORLD ARMY COMMANDER SONIA SATO. LONG-RANGE SCANS ARE CONFIRMED. WE HAVE *VISUAL*...

THIS IS CRAZY BUT...IT'S AN *EARTH TWIN*.

THIS IS INCREDIBLE, SLOAN...

THIS PLANET HAS BEEN TRANSFORMED INTO A *ROUGH COPY* OF EARTH. IT'S HABITABLE, AND IT LOOKS LIKE HOME...BUT THE SCANS OF THE PLANTS AND ANIMALS ARE UNDENIABLY *ALIEN*.

WHOEVER DID THIS COULD BE DANGEROUS. LET'S JUST *OBSERVE* FOR A WHILE--

BWEEEP BWEEEP

WHAT'S WRONG?

SOMEONE OR SOMETHING... IS BREACHING OUR *CONTROL SYSTEMS*.

OH MY GOD--

BWEEEP BWEEEP

WE'RE UNDER ATTACK!

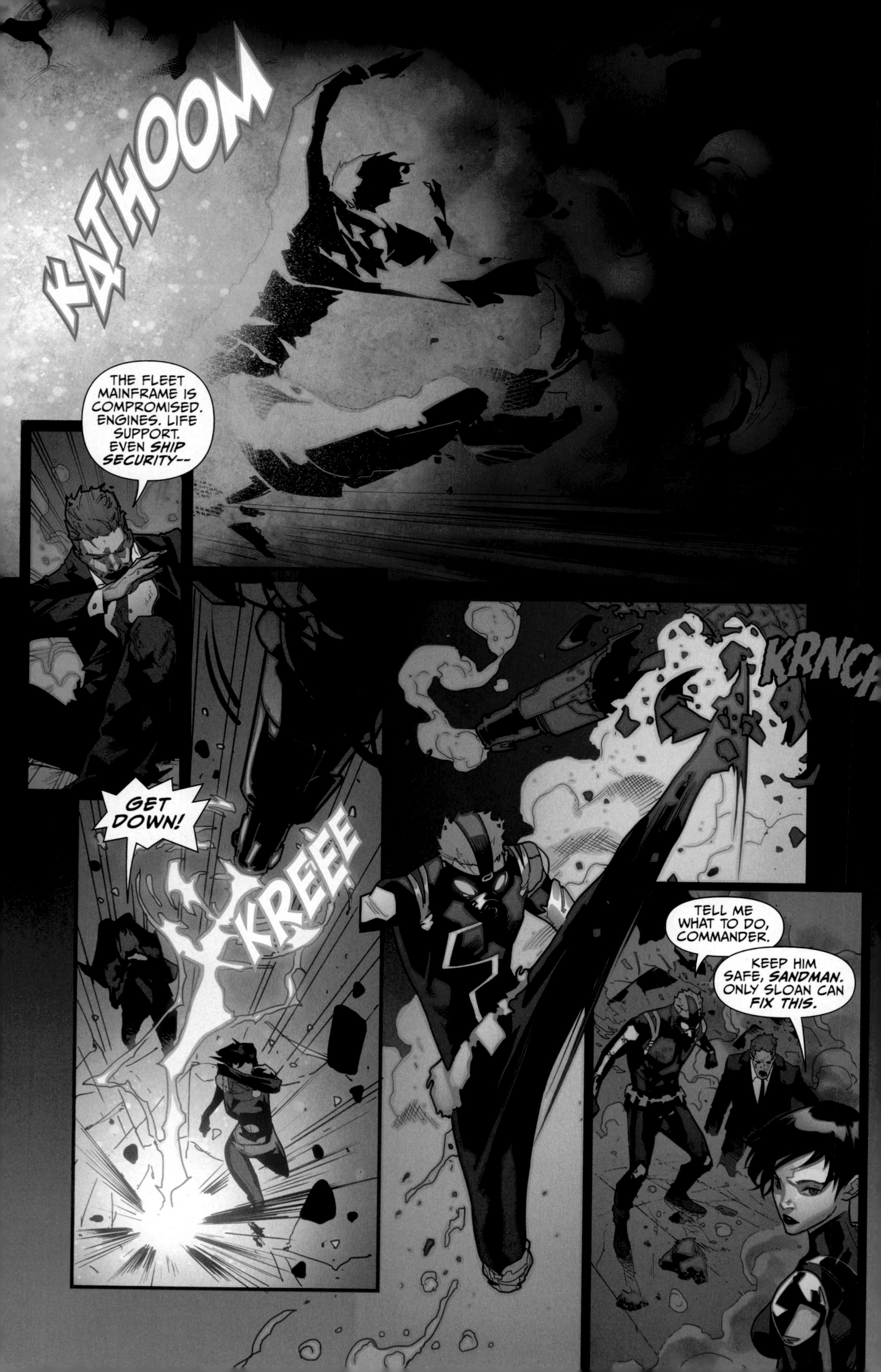
KATHOOM
THE FLEET MAINFRAME IS COMPROMISED. ENGINES. LIFE SUPPORT. EVEN SHIP SECURITY--
KRNCH
GET DOWN!
KREEE
TELL ME WHAT TO DO, COMMANDER.
KEEP HIM SAFE, SANDMAN. ONLY SLOAN CAN FIX THIS.

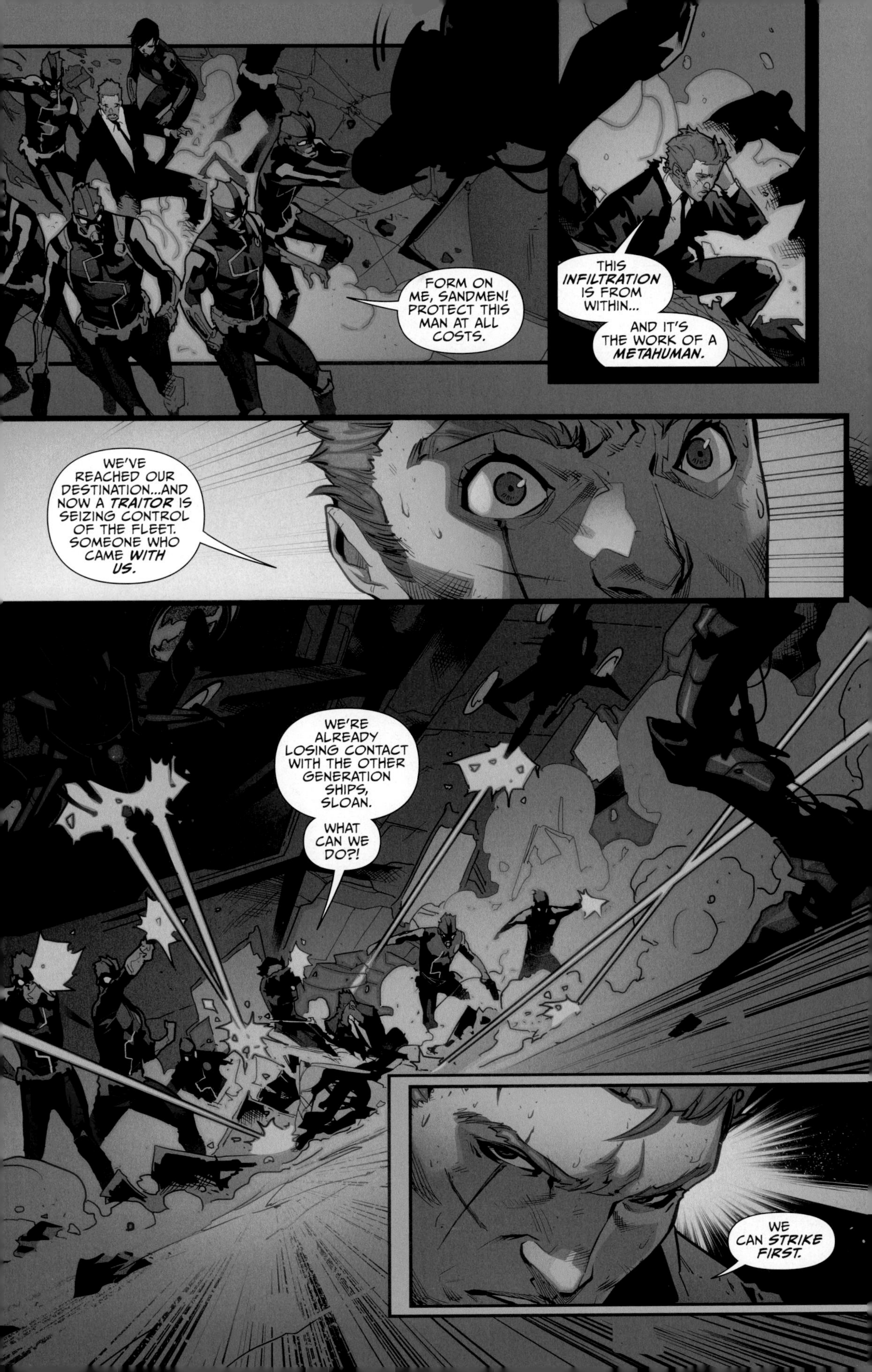
FORM ON ME, SANDMEN! PROTECT THIS MAN AT ALL COSTS.
THIS INFILTRATION IS FROM WITHIN...
AND IT'S THE WORK OF A METAHUMAN.
WE'VE REACHED OUR DESTINATION...AND NOW A TRAITOR IS SEIZING CONTROL OF THE FLEET. SOMEONE WHO CAME WITH US.
WE'RE ALREADY LOSING CONTACT WITH THE OTHER GENERATION SHIPS, SLOAN.
WHAT CAN WE DO?!
WE CAN STRIKE FIRST.

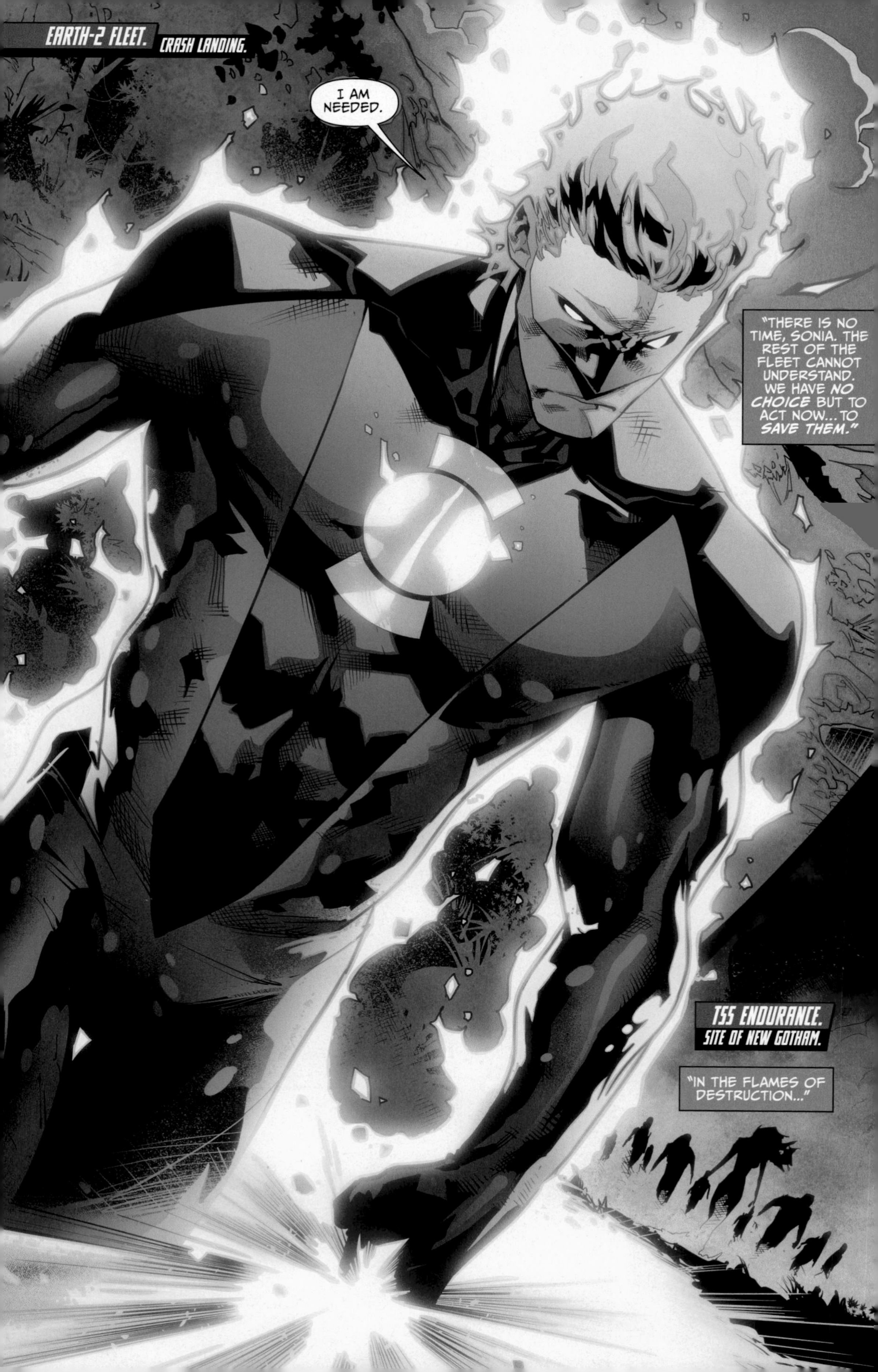
EARTH-2 FLEET.
CRASH LANDING.
I AM NEEDED.
"THERE IS NO TIME, SONIA. THE REST OF THE FLEET CANNOT UNDERSTAND. WE HAVE NO CHOICE BUT TO ACT NOW...TO SAVE THEM."
TSS ENDURANCE.
SITE OF NEW GOTHAM.
"IN THE FLAMES OF DESTRUCTION..."

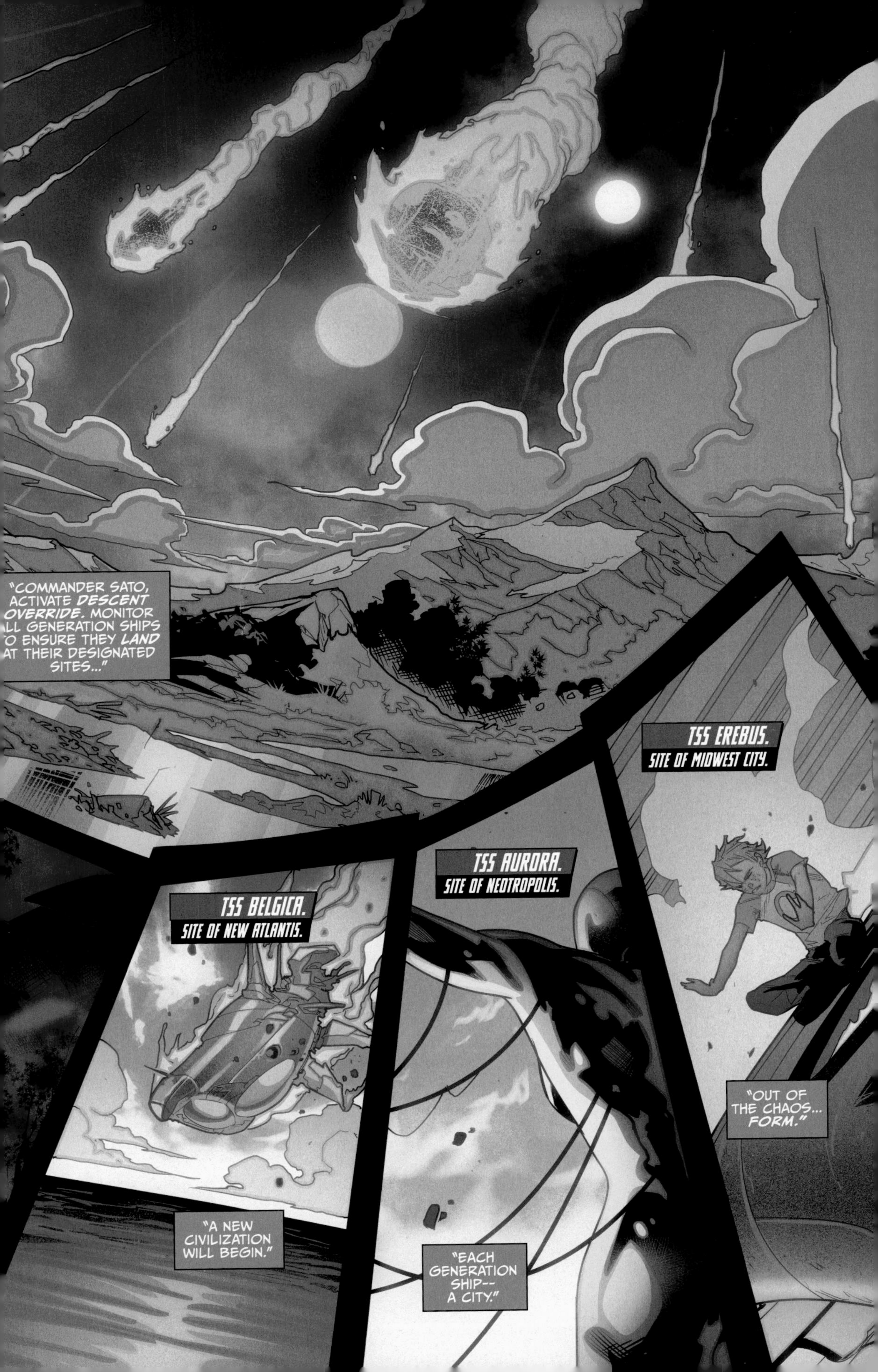
"COMMANDER SATO, ACTIVATE DESCENT OVERRIDE. MONITOR ALL GENERATION SHIPS TO ENSURE THEY LAND AT THEIR DESIGNATED SITES..."
TSS EREBUS.
SITE OF MIDWEST CITY.
TSS BELGICA.
SITE OF NEW ATLANTIS.
TSS AURORA.
SITE OF NEOTROPOLIS.
"OUT OF THE CHAOS... FORM."
"A NEW CIVILIZATION WILL BEGIN."
"EACH GENERATION SHIP-- A CITY."

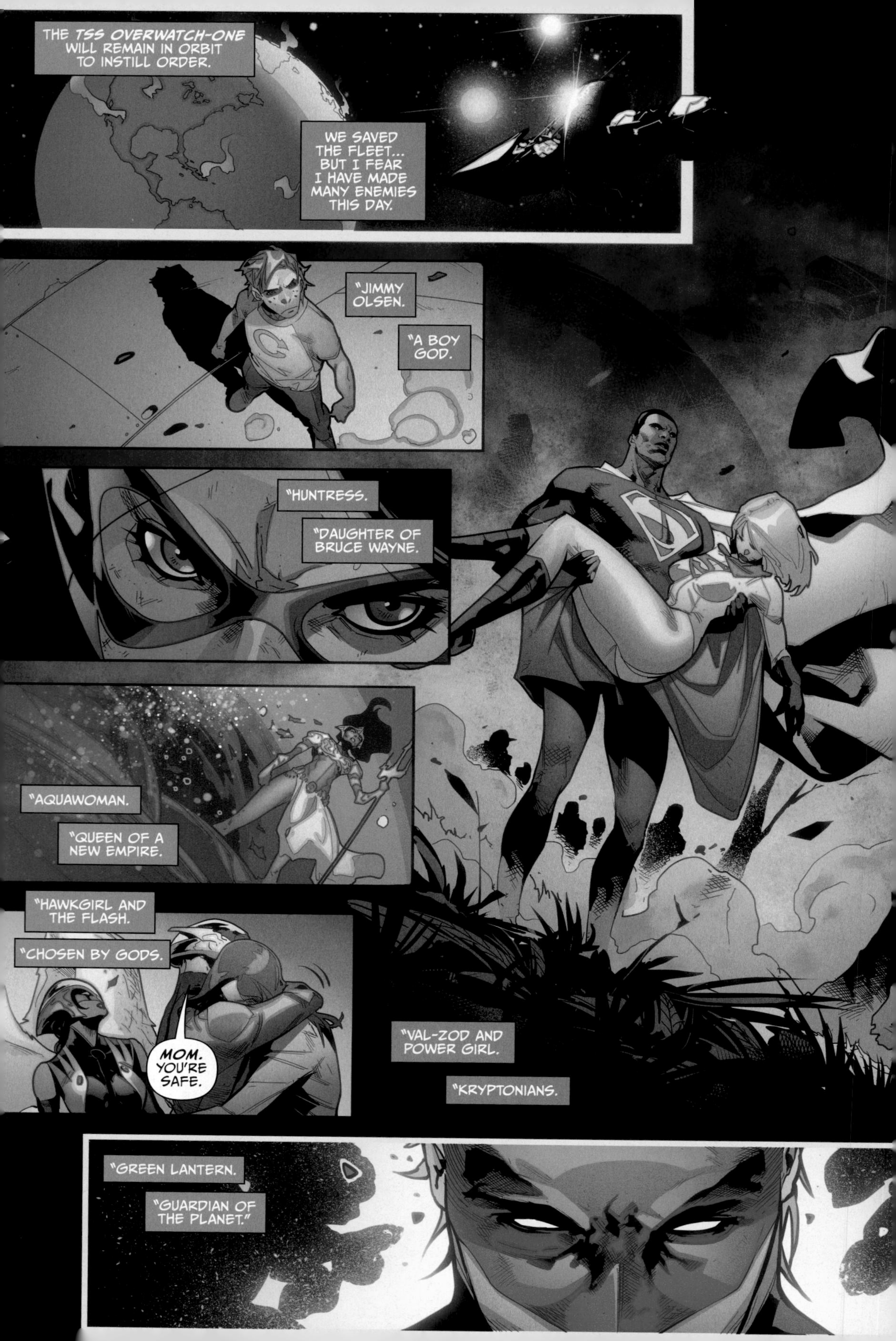
THE TSS OVERWATCH-ONE WILL REMAIN IN ORBIT TO INSTILL ORDER.
WE SAVED THE FLEET... BUT I FEAR I HAVE MADE MANY ENEMIES THIS DAY.
"JIMMY OLSEN.
"A BOY GOD.
"HUNTRESS.
"DAUGHTER OF BRUCE WAYNE.
"AQUAWOMAN.
"QUEEN OF A NEW EMPIRE.
"HAWKGIRL AND THE FLASH.
"CHOSEN BY GODS.
MOM. YOU'RE SAFE.
"VAL-ZOD AND POWER GIRL.
"KRYPTONIANS.
"GREEN LANTERN.
"GUARDIAN OF THE PLANET."

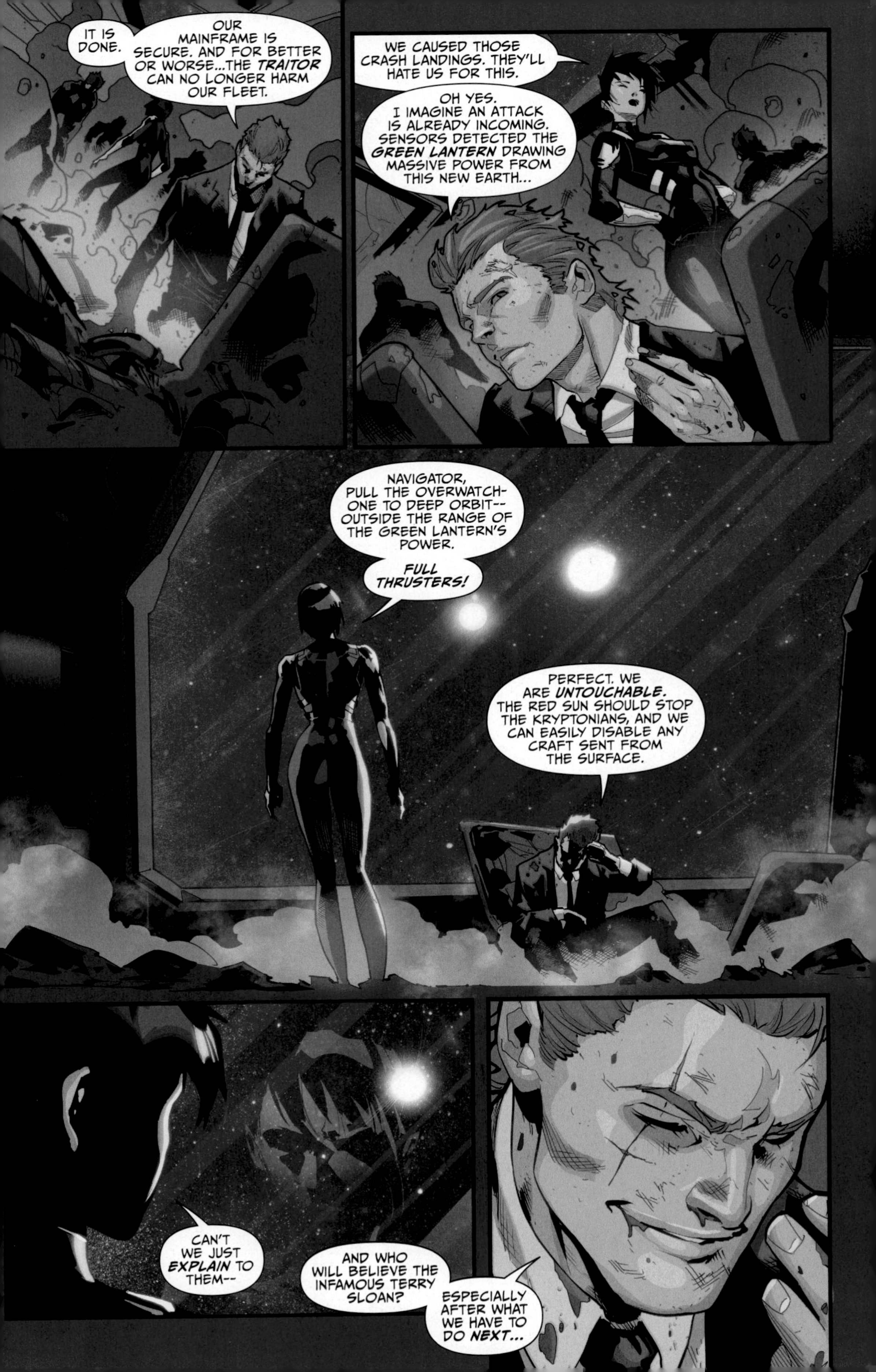
IT IS DONE.
OUR MAINFRAME IS SECURE. AND FOR BETTER OR WORSE...THE *TRAITOR* CAN NO LONGER HARM OUR FLEET.
WE CAUSED THOSE CRASH LANDINGS. THEY'LL HATE US FOR THIS.
OH YES. I IMAGINE AN ATTACK IS ALREADY INCOMING. SENSORS DETECTED THE *GREEN LANTERN* DRAWING MASSIVE POWER FROM THIS NEW EARTH...
NAVIGATOR, PULL THE OVERWATCH-ONE TO DEEP ORBIT--OUTSIDE THE RANGE OF THE GREEN LANTERN'S POWER.
FULL THRUSTERS!
PERFECT. WE ARE *UNTOUCHABLE.* THE RED SUN SHOULD STOP THE KRYPTONIANS, AND WE CAN EASILY DISABLE ANY CRAFT SENT FROM THE SURFACE.
CAN'T WE JUST *EXPLAIN* TO THEM--
AND WHO WILL BELIEVE THE INFAMOUS TERRY SLOAN?
ESPECIALLY AFTER WHAT WE HAVE TO DO *NEXT...*

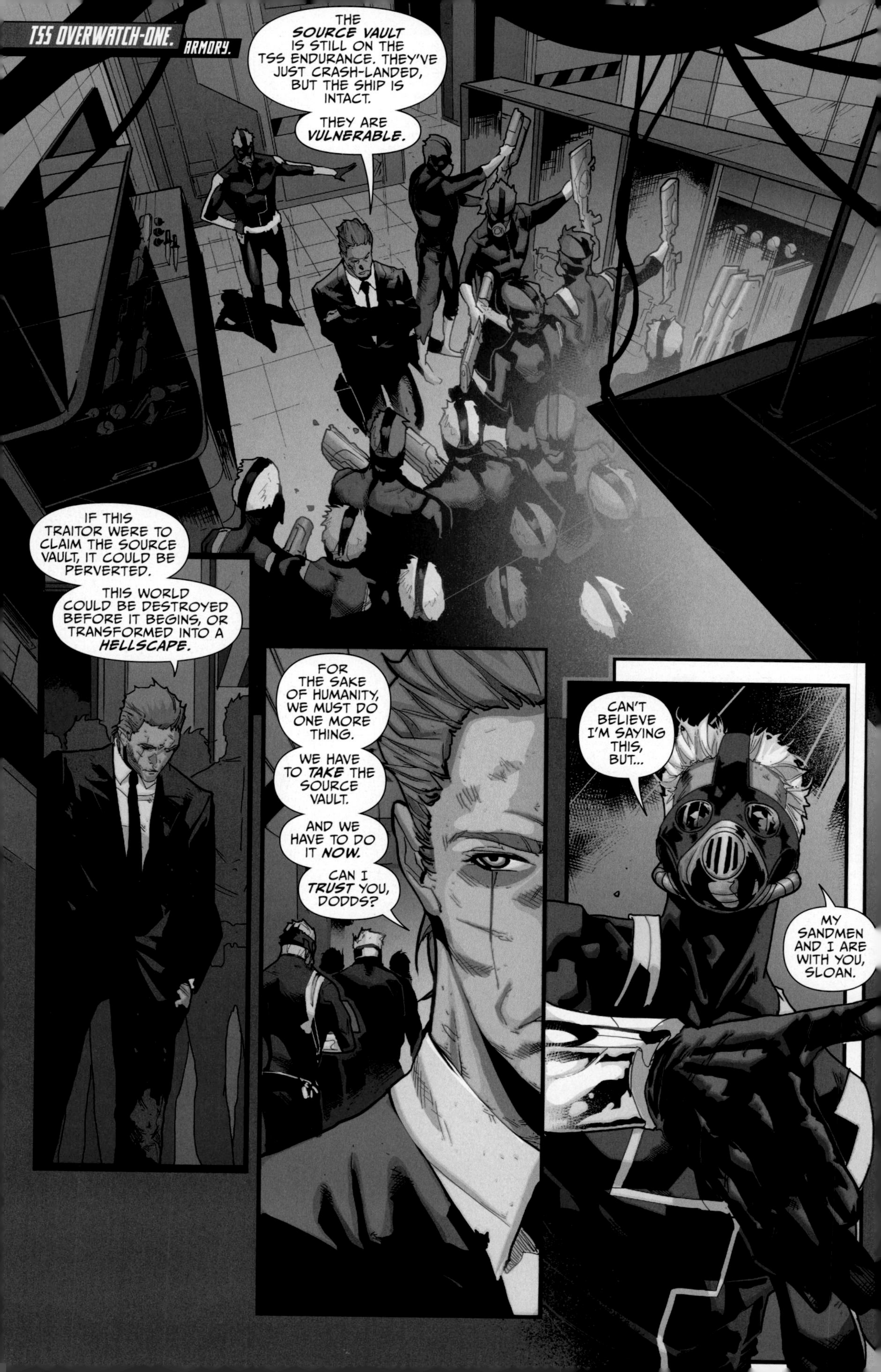
TSS OVERWATCH-ONE.
ARMORY.
THE SOURCE VAULT IS STILL ON THE TSS ENDURANCE. THEY'VE JUST CRASH-LANDED, BUT THE SHIP IS INTACT.
THEY ARE VULNERABLE.
IF THIS TRAITOR WERE TO CLAIM THE SOURCE VAULT, IT COULD BE PERVERTED.
THIS WORLD COULD BE DESTROYED BEFORE IT BEGINS, OR TRANSFORMED INTO A HELLSCAPE.
FOR THE SAKE OF HUMANITY, WE MUST DO ONE MORE THING.
WE HAVE TO TAKE THE SOURCE VAULT.
AND WE HAVE TO DO IT NOW.
CAN I TRUST YOU, DODDS?
CAN'T BELIEVE I'M SAYING THIS, BUT...
MY SANDMEN AND I ARE WITH YOU, SLOAN.

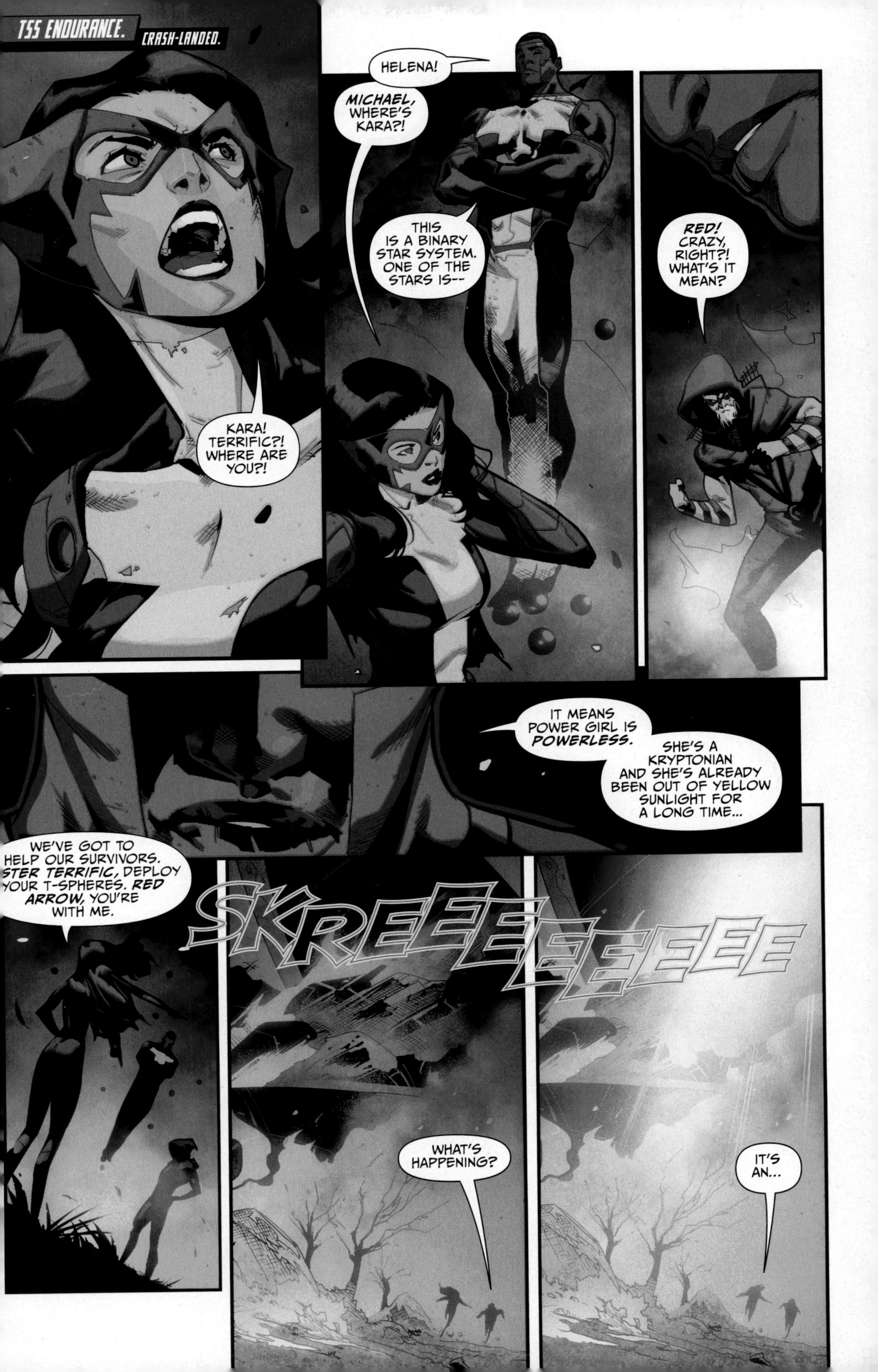
TSS ENDURANCE.
CRASH-LANDED.
KARA! TERRIFIC?! WHERE ARE YOU?!
HELENA!
MICHAEL, WHERE'S KARA?!
THIS IS A BINARY STAR SYSTEM. ONE OF THE STARS IS--
RED! CRAZY, RIGHT?! WHAT'S IT MEAN?
IT MEANS POWER GIRL IS POWERLESS.
SHE'S A KRYPTONIAN AND SHE'S ALREADY BEEN OUT OF YELLOW SUNLIGHT FOR A LONG TIME...
WE'VE GOT TO HELP OUR SURVIVORS. STER TERRIFIC, DEPLOY YOUR T-SPHERES. RED ARROW, YOU'RE WITH ME.
SKREEEEEEEEE
WHAT'S HAPPENING?
IT'S AN...

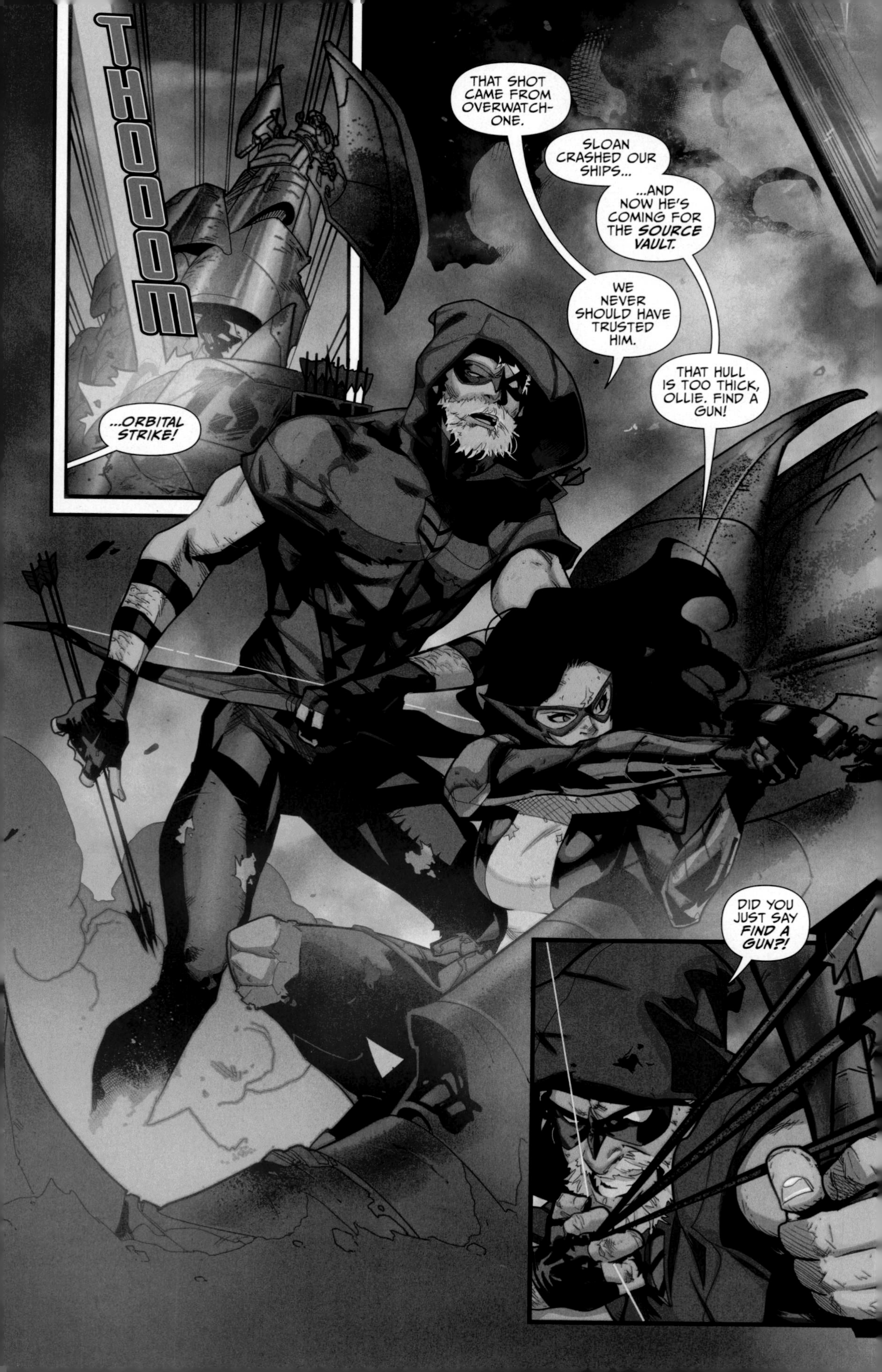
THOOOM
...ORBITAL STRIKE!
THAT SHOT CAME FROM OVERWATCH-ONE.
SLOAN CRASHED OUR SHIPS...
...AND NOW HE'S COMING FOR THE SOURCE VAULT.
WE NEVER SHOULD HAVE TRUSTED HIM.
THAT HULL IS TOO THICK, OLLIE. FIND A GUN!
DID YOU JUST SAY FIND A GUN?!

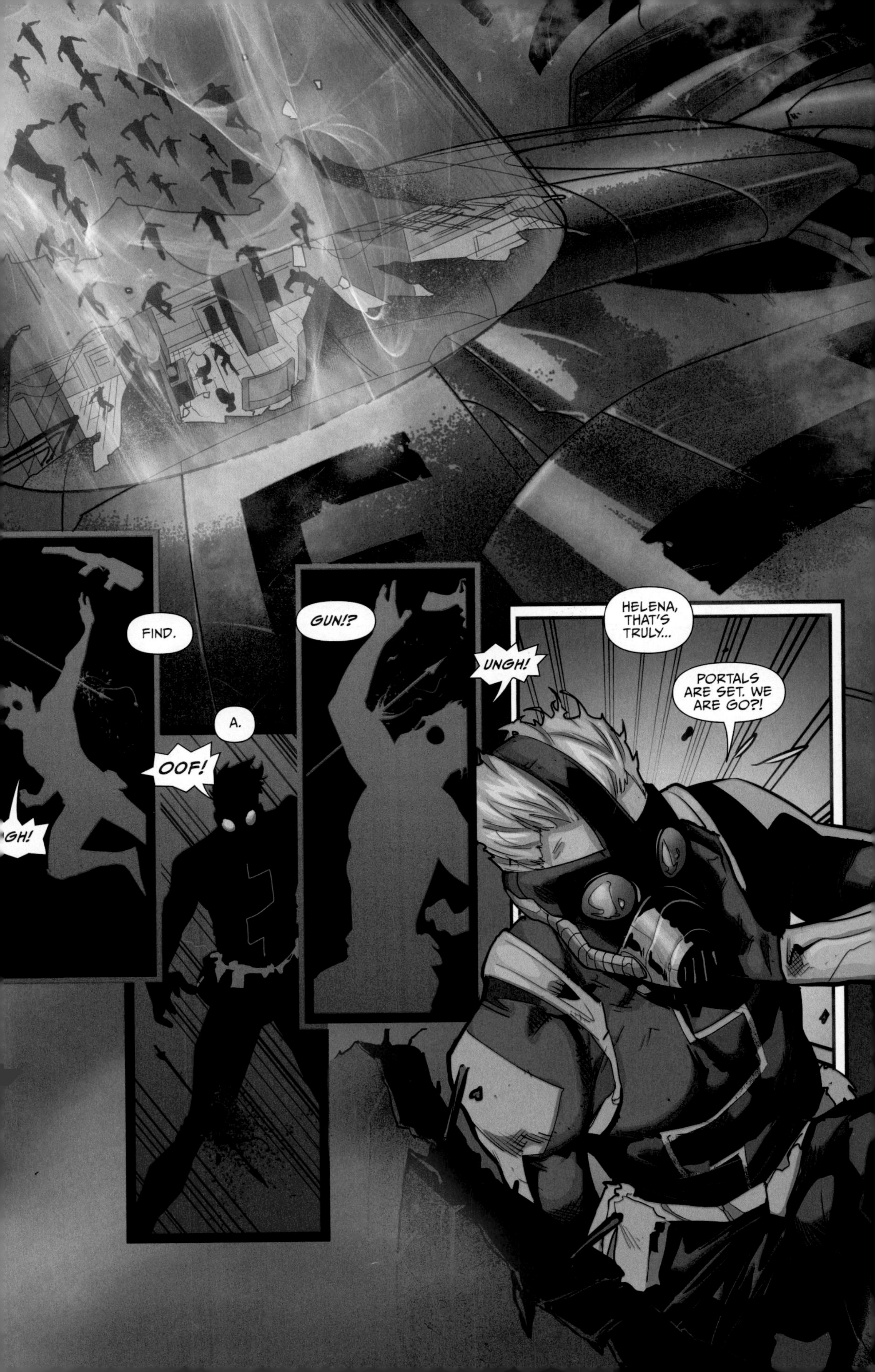
GH!
FIND.
A.
OOF!
GUN!?
UNGH!
HELENA, THAT'S TRULY...
PORTALS ARE SET. WE ARE GO?!

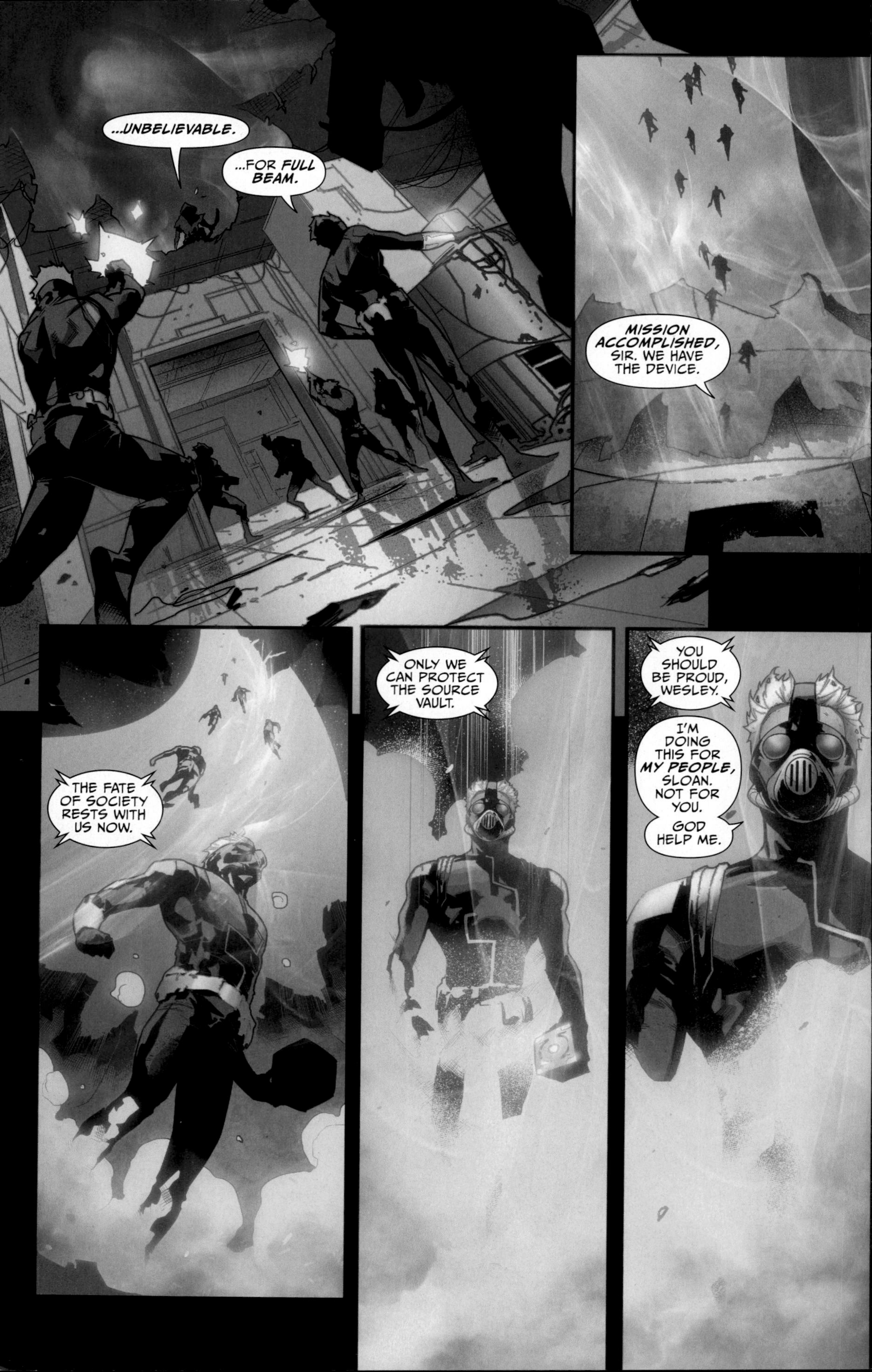
...UNBELIEVABLE.
...FOR FULL BEAM.
MISSION ACCOMPLISHED, SIR. WE HAVE THE DEVICE.
THE FATE OF SOCIETY RESTS WITH US NOW.
ONLY WE CAN PROTECT THE SOURCE VAULT.
YOU SHOULD BE PROUD, WESLEY.
I'M DOING THIS FOR MY PEOPLE, SLOAN. NOT FOR YOU.
GOD HELP ME.

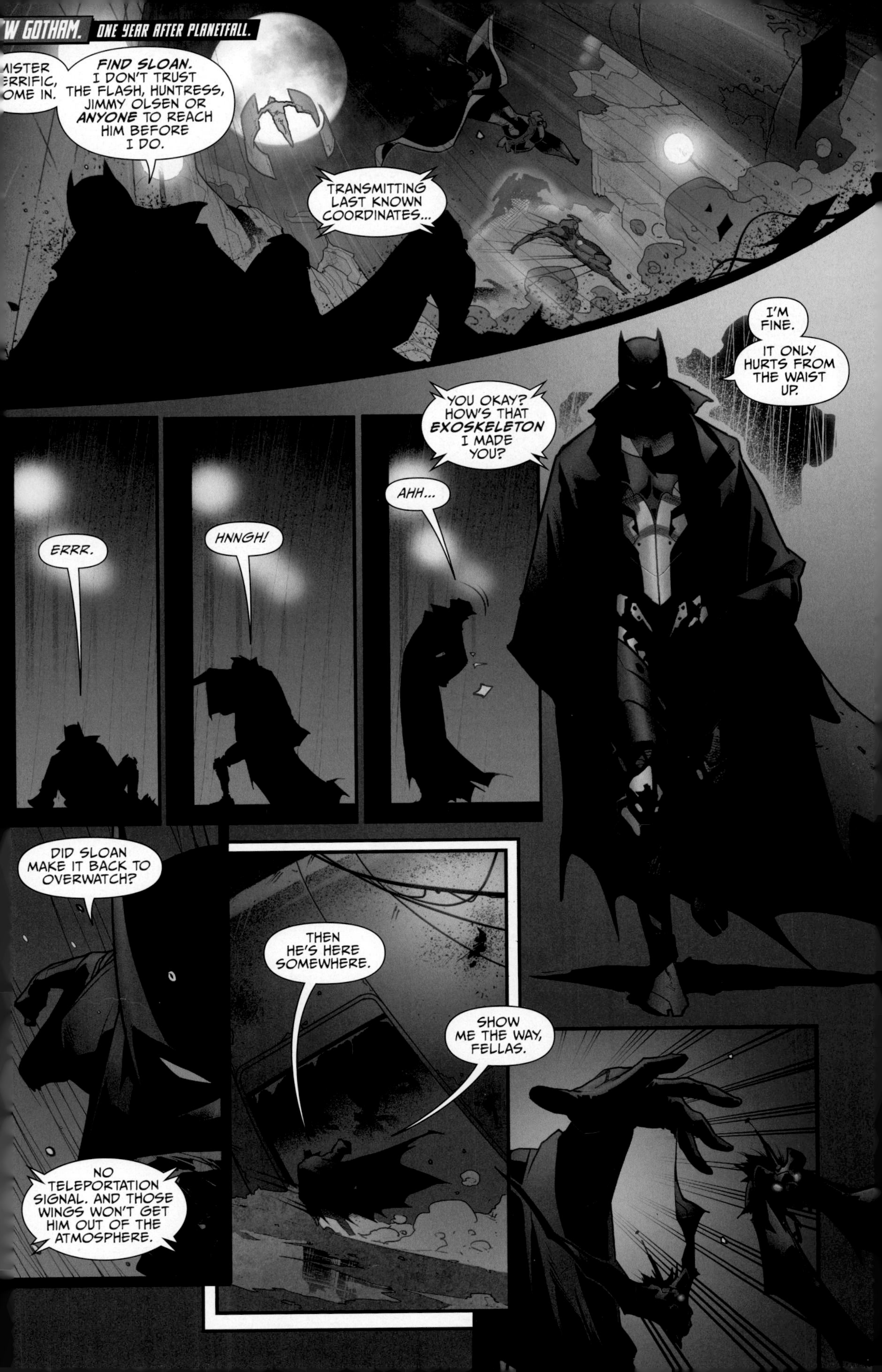

W GOTHAM.
ONE YEAR AFTER PLANETFALL.
MISTER ERRIFIC, OME IN.
FIND SLOAN. I DON'T TRUST THE FLASH, HUNTRESS, JIMMY OLSEN OR ANYONE TO REACH HIM BEFORE I DO.
TRANSMITTING LAST KNOWN COORDINATES...
ERRR.
HNNGH!
AHH...
YOU OKAY? HOW'S THAT EXOSKELETON I MADE YOU?
I'M FINE.
IT ONLY HURTS FROM THE WAIST UP.
DID SLOAN MAKE IT BACK TO OVERWATCH?
NO TELEPORTATION SIGNAL. AND THOSE WINGS WON'T GET HIM OUT OF THE ATMOSPHERE.
THEN HE'S HERE SOMEWHERE.
SHOW ME THE WAY, FELLAS.

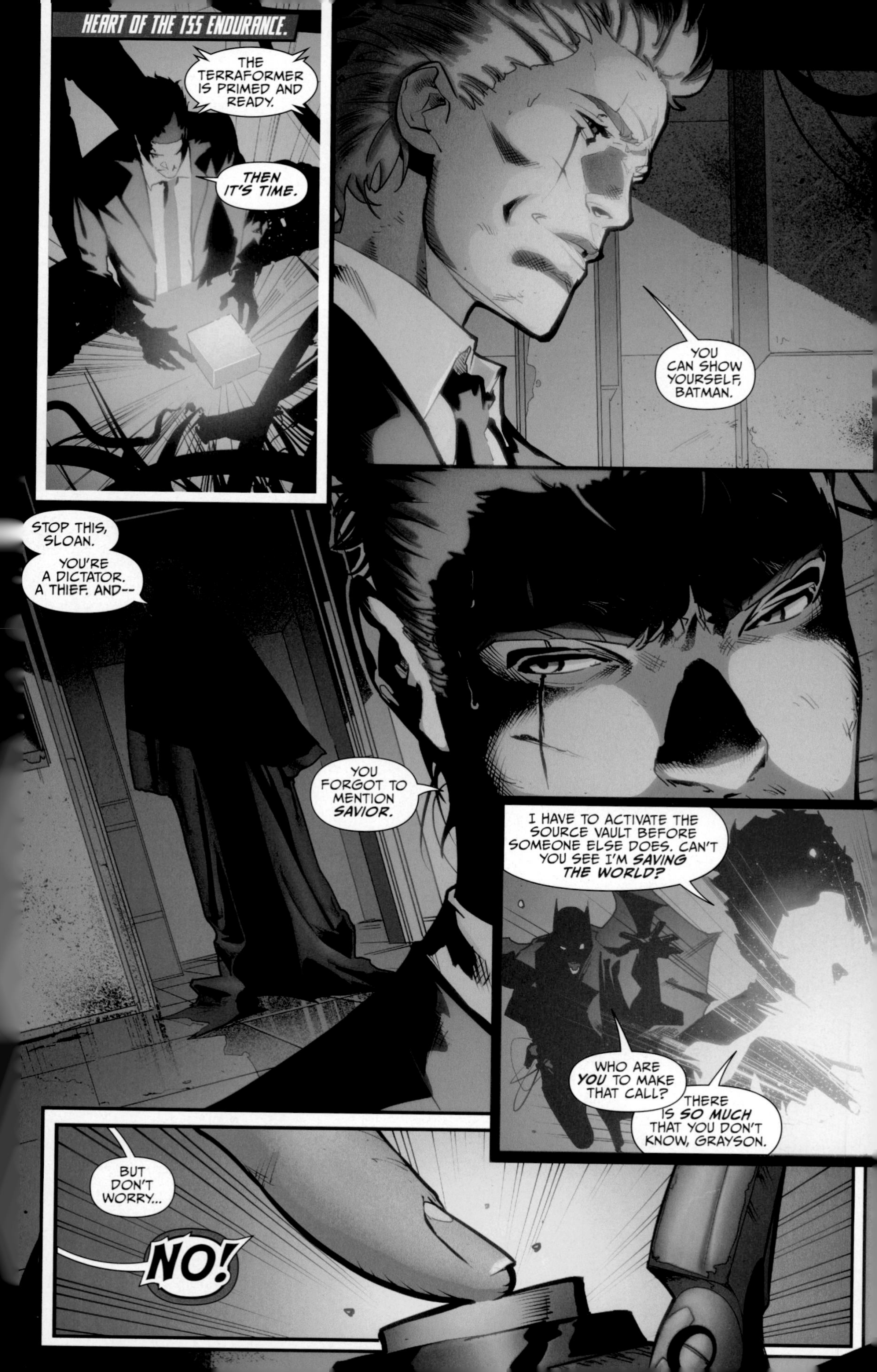
HEART OF THE TSS ENDURANCE.
THE TERRAFORMER IS PRIMED AND READY.
THEN IT'S TIME.
YOU CAN SHOW YOURSELF, BATMAN.
STOP THIS, SLOAN.
YOU'RE A DICTATOR. A THIEF. AND--
YOU FORGOT TO MENTION SAVIOR.
I HAVE TO ACTIVATE THE SOURCE VAULT BEFORE SOMEONE ELSE DOES. CAN'T YOU SEE I'M SAVING THE WORLD?
WHO ARE YOU TO MAKE THAT CALL?
THERE IS SO MUCH THAT YOU DON'T KNOW, GRAYSON.
BUT DON'T WORRY...
NO!

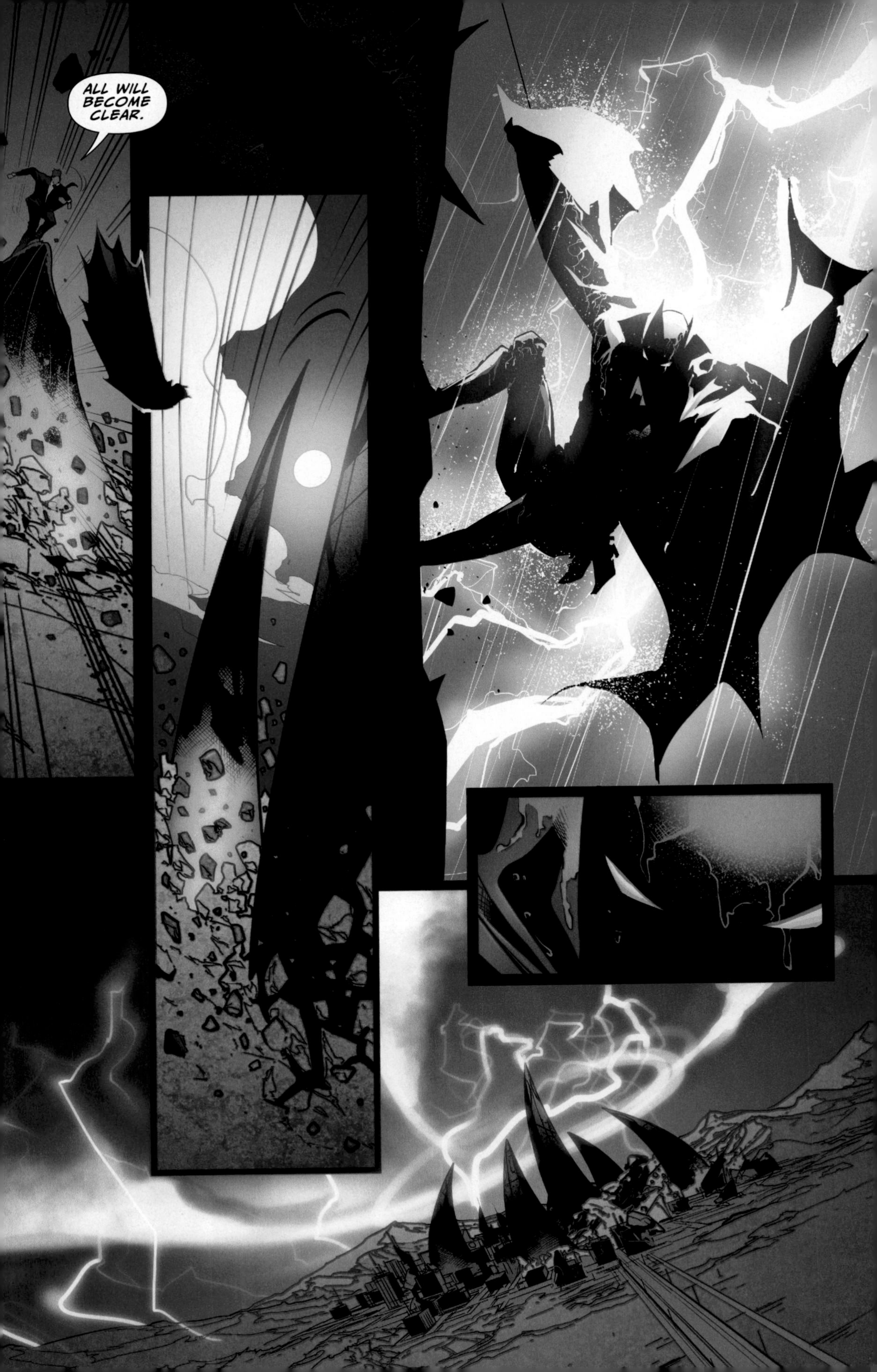
ALL WILL BECOME CLEAR.

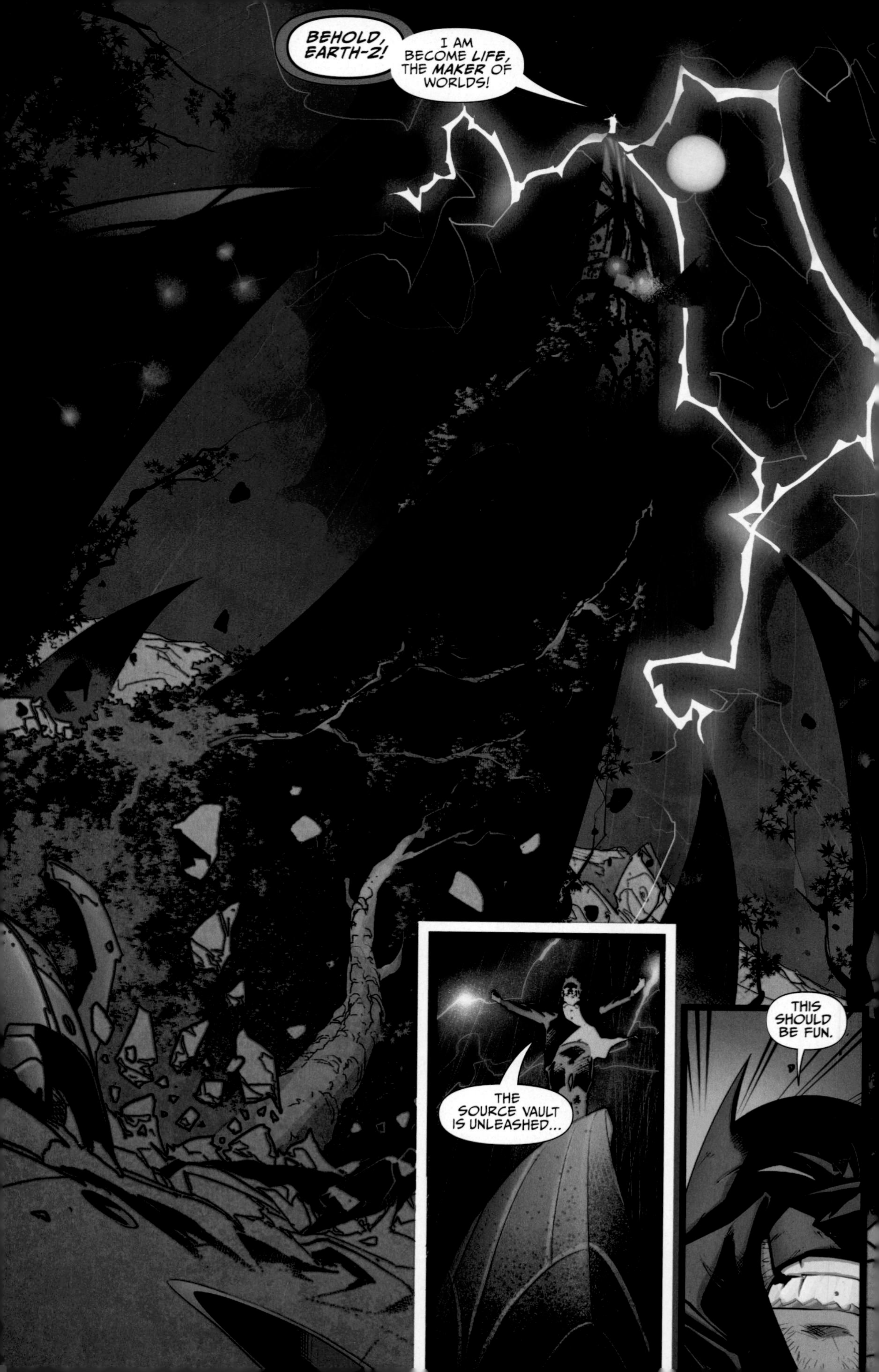
BEHOLD, EARTH-2!
I AM BECOME LIFE, THE MAKER OF WORLDS!
THE SOURCE VAULT IS UNLEASHED...
THIS SHOULD BE FUN.

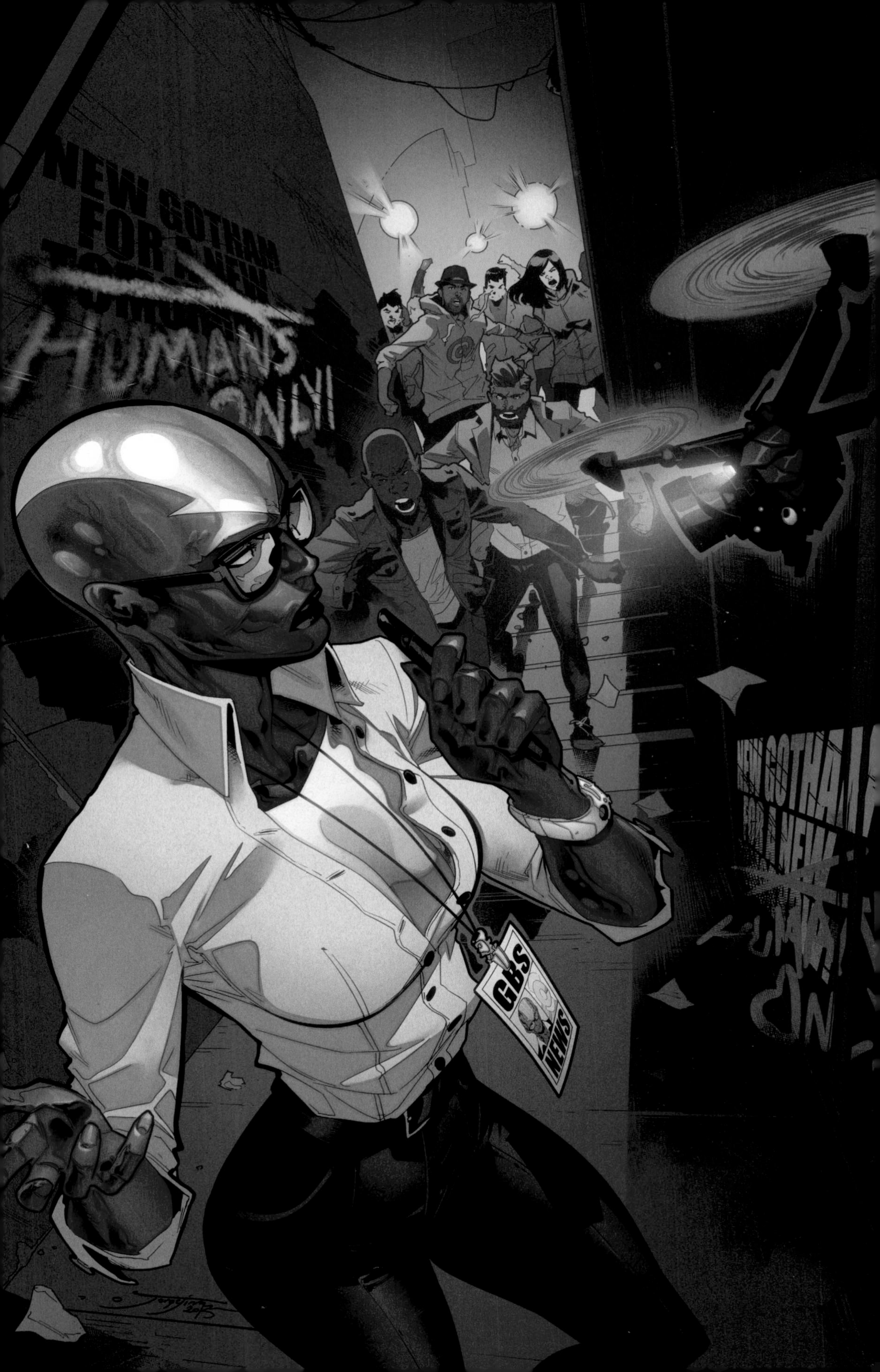
NEW GOTHAM
FOR A NEW
HUMANS
ONLY!
GBS
NEWS
NEW GOTHAM
FOR A NEW

SOLACE

DANIEL H. WILSON writer JORGE JIMENEZ artist ALEJANDRO SANCHEZ colorist TRAVIS LANHAM letterer cover by JIMENEZ & RAUCH

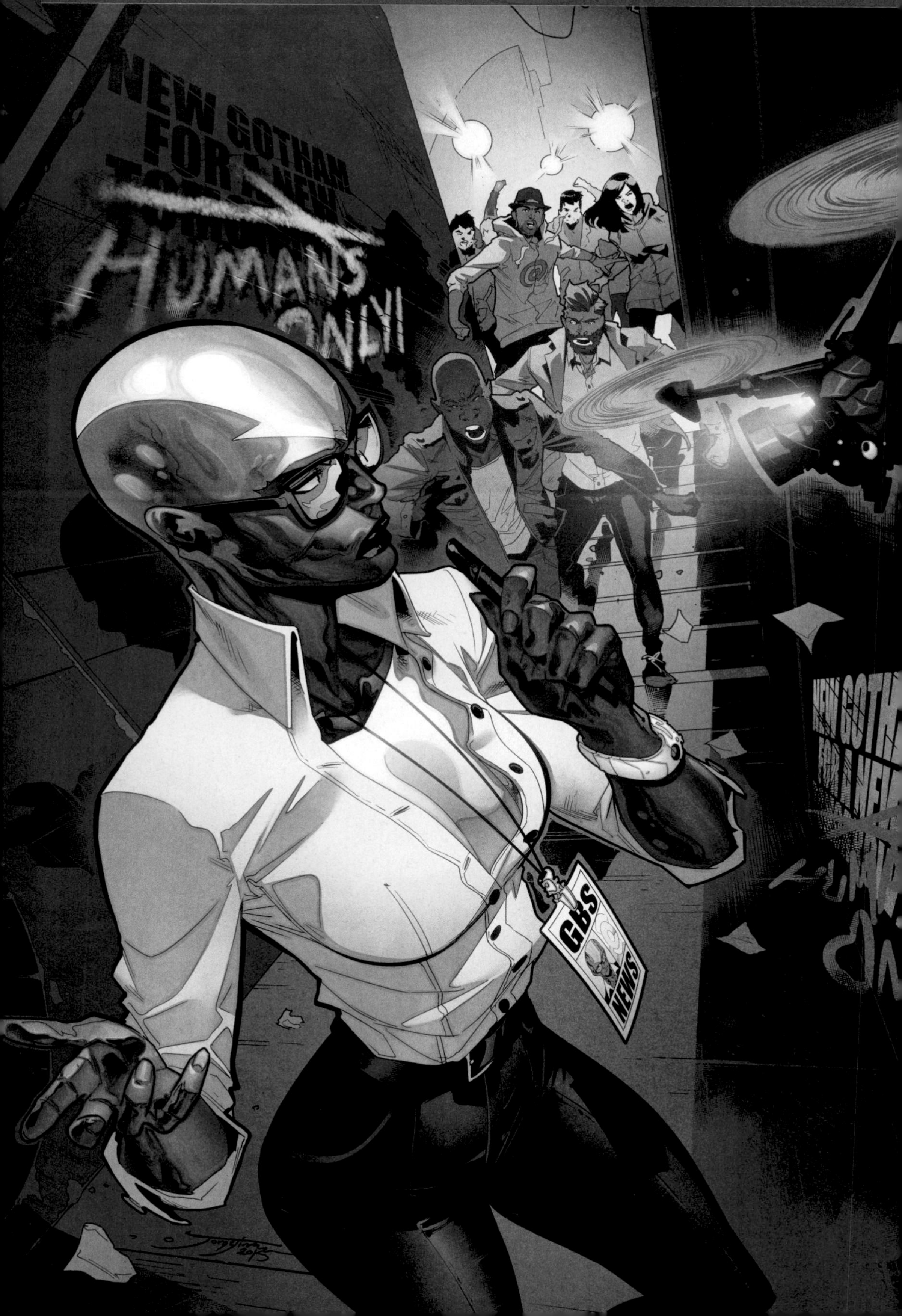
NEW GOTHAM FOR A NEW
HUMANS ONLY!
GBS NEWS

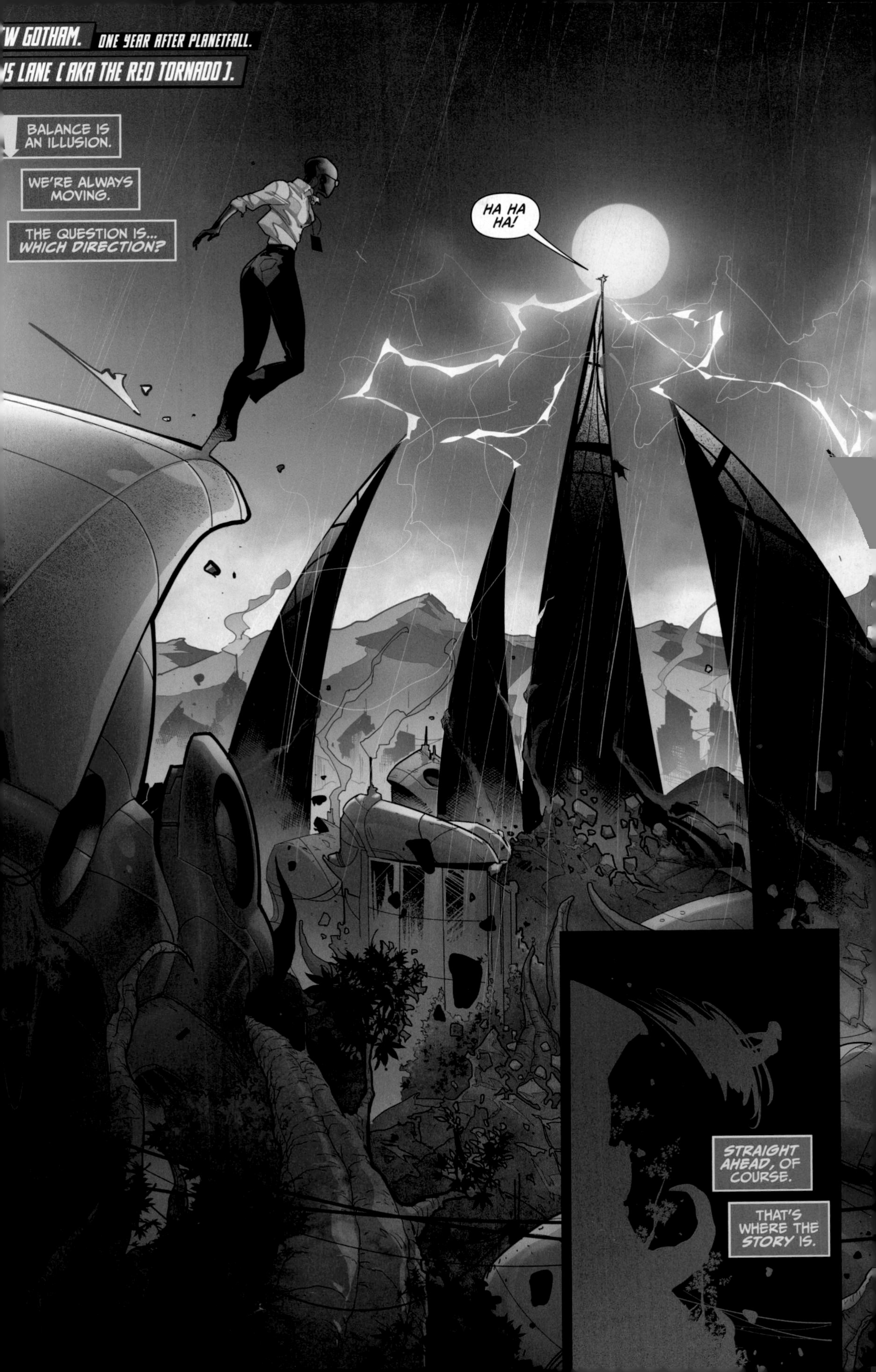

W GOTHAM.
ONE YEAR AFTER PLANETFALL.
S LANE [AKA THE RED TORNADO].
BALANCE IS AN ILLUSION.
WE'RE ALWAYS MOVING.
THE QUESTION IS... WHICH DIRECTION?
HA HA HA!
STRAIGHT AHEAD, OF COURSE.
THAT'S WHERE THE STORY IS.

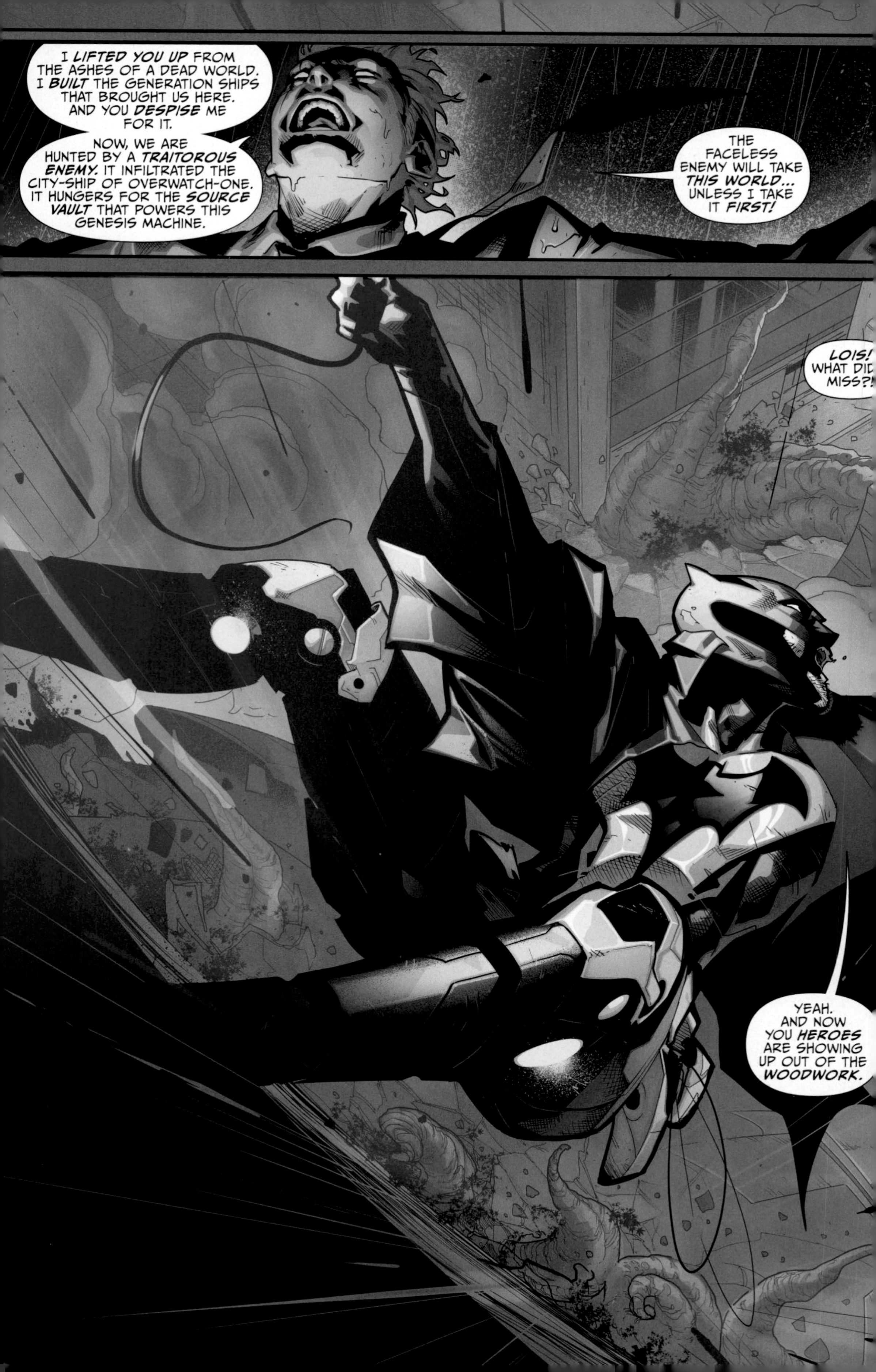
I LIFTED YOU UP FROM THE ASHES OF A DEAD WORLD. I BUILT THE GENERATION SHIPS THAT BROUGHT US HERE. AND YOU DESPISE ME FOR IT.
NOW, WE ARE HUNTED BY A TRAITOROUS ENEMY. IT INFILTRATED THE CITY-SHIP OF OVERWATCH-ONE. IT HUNGERS FOR THE SOURCE VAULT THAT POWERS THIS GENESIS MACHINE.
THE FACELESS ENEMY WILL TAKE THIS WORLD... UNLESS I TAKE IT FIRST!
LOIS! WHAT DID
MISS?!
YEAH. AND NOW YOU HEROES ARE SHOWING UP OUT OF THE WOODWORK.

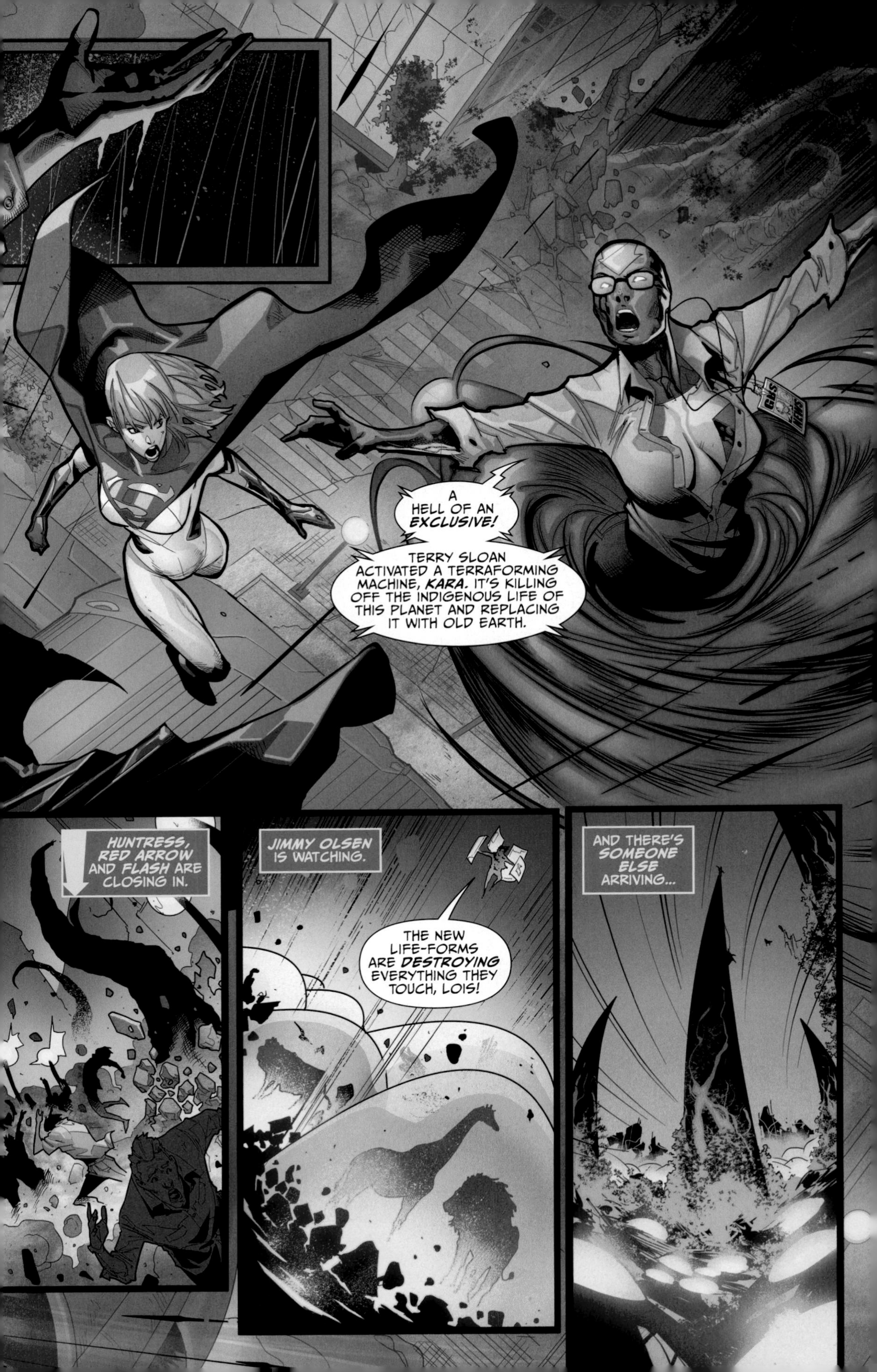
A HELL OF AN EXCLUSIVE!
TERRY SLOAN ACTIVATED A TERRAFORMING MACHINE, KARA. IT'S KILLING OFF THE INDIGENOUS LIFE OF THIS PLANET AND REPLACING IT WITH OLD EARTH.
HUNTRESS, RED ARROW AND FLASH ARE CLOSING IN.
JIMMY OLSEN IS WATCHING.
THE NEW LIFE-FORMS ARE DESTROYING EVERYTHING THEY TOUCH, LOIS!
AND THERE'S SOMEONE ELSE ARRIVING...

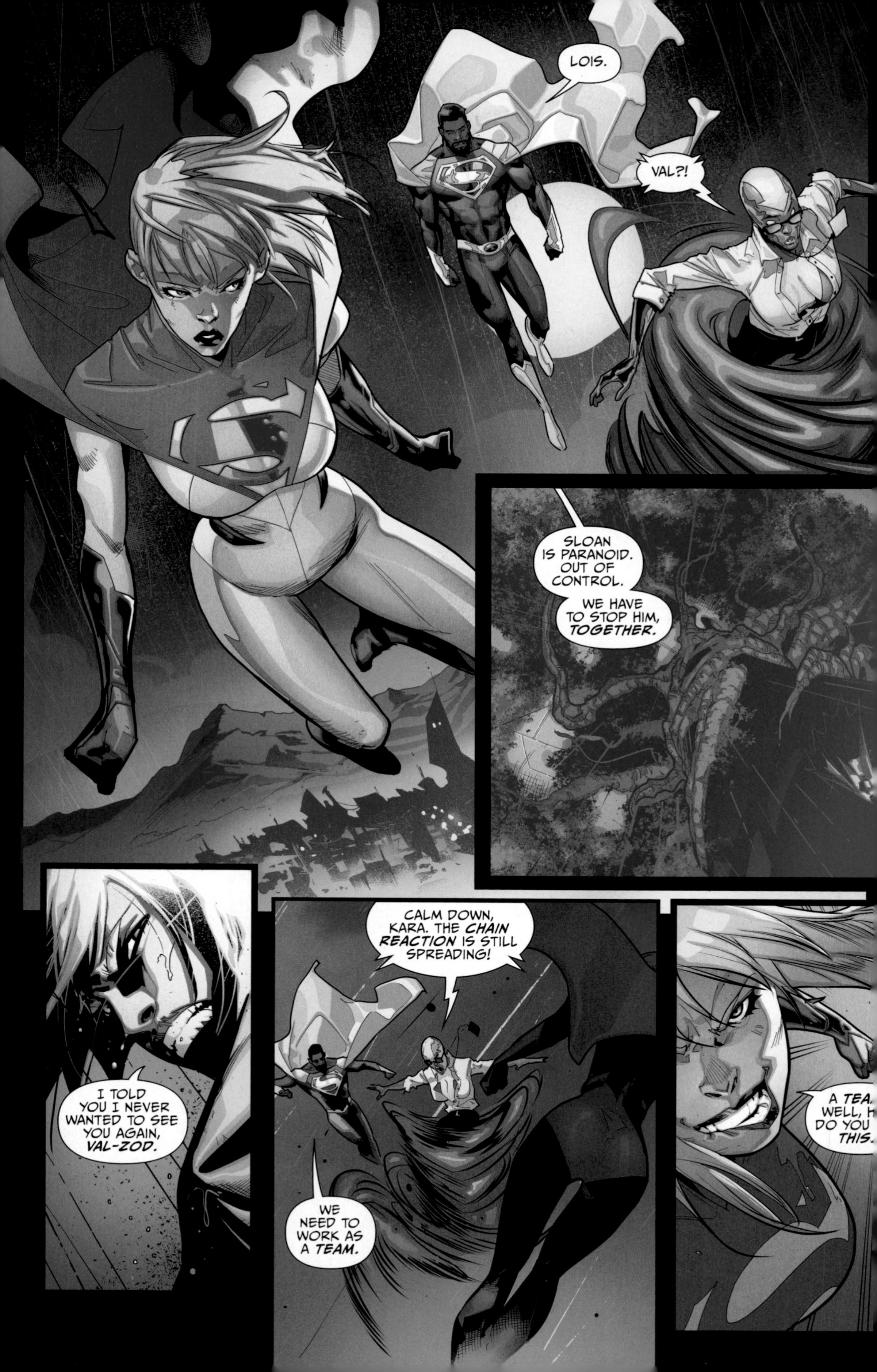
LOIS.
VAL?!
SLOAN IS PARANOID. OUT OF CONTROL.
WE HAVE TO STOP HIM, *TOGETHER*.
I TOLD YOU I NEVER WANTED TO SEE YOU AGAIN, *VAL-ZOD*.
CALM DOWN, KARA. THE *CHAIN REACTION* IS STILL SPREADING!
WE NEED TO WORK AS A *TEAM*.

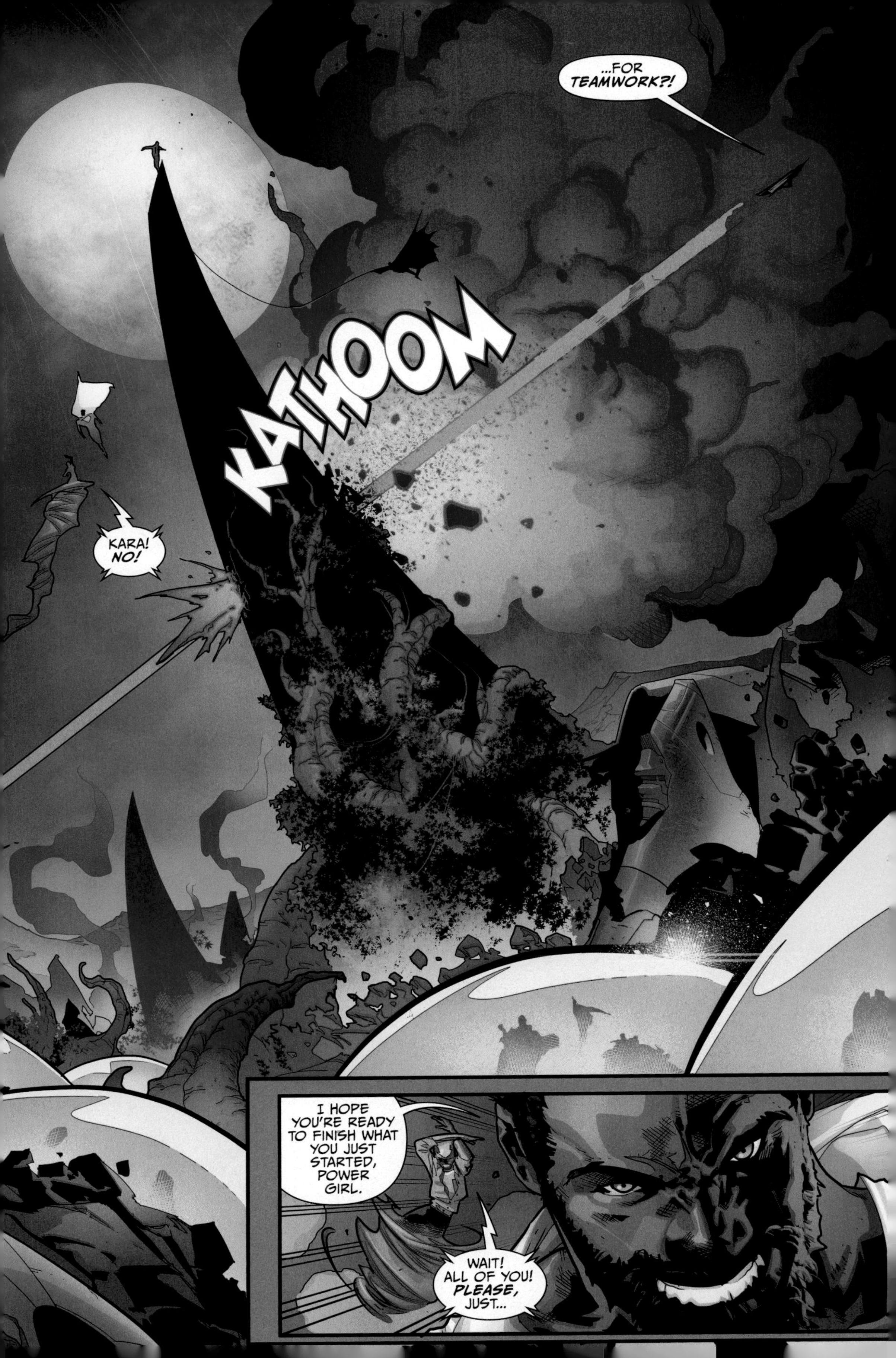
...FOR TEAMWORK?!
KATHOOM
KARA! NO!
I HOPE YOU'RE READY TO FINISH WHAT YOU JUST STARTED, POWER GIRL.
WAIT! ALL OF YOU! PLEASE, JUST...

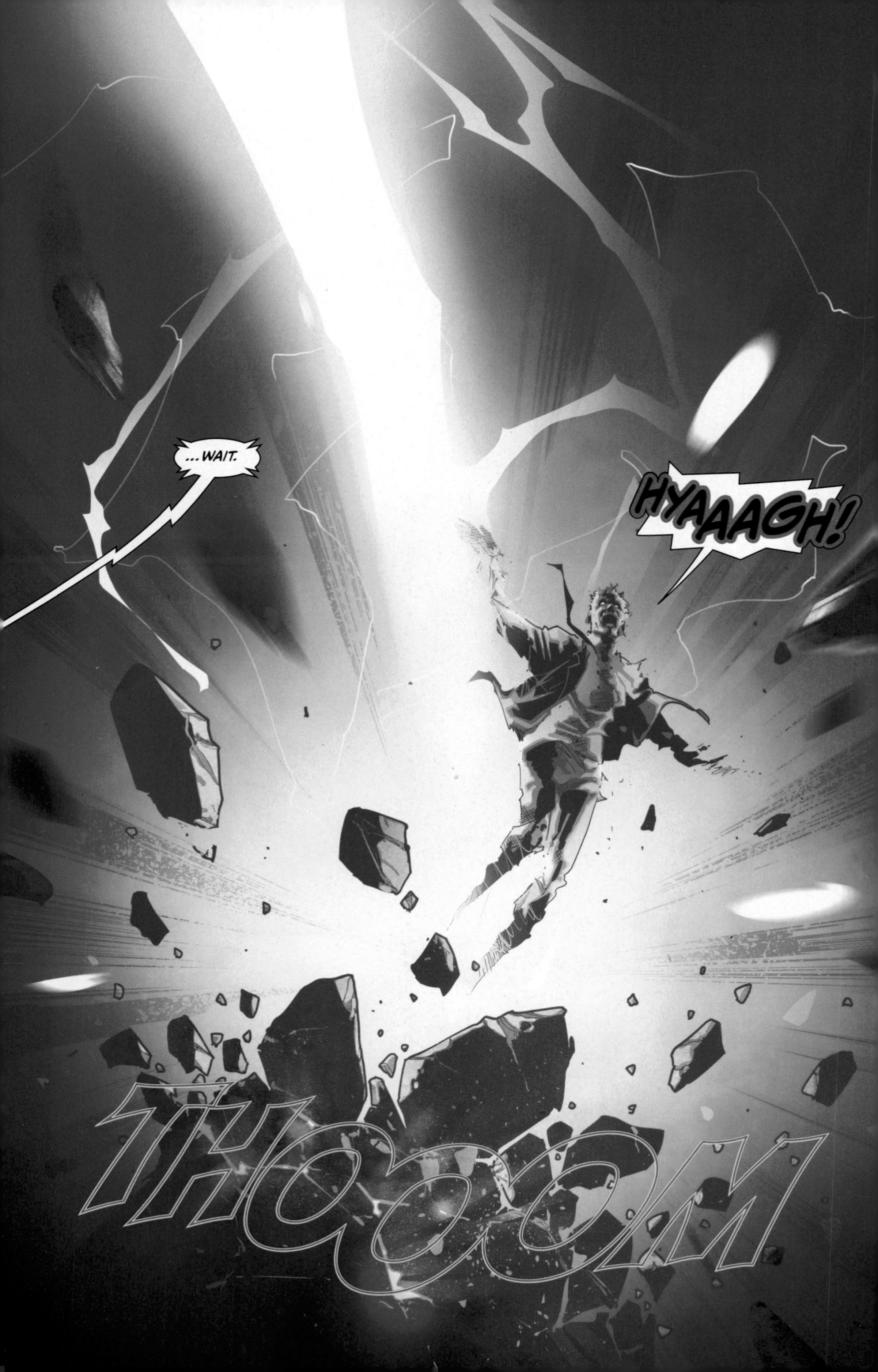
...WAIT.
HYAAAGH!
THOOOM

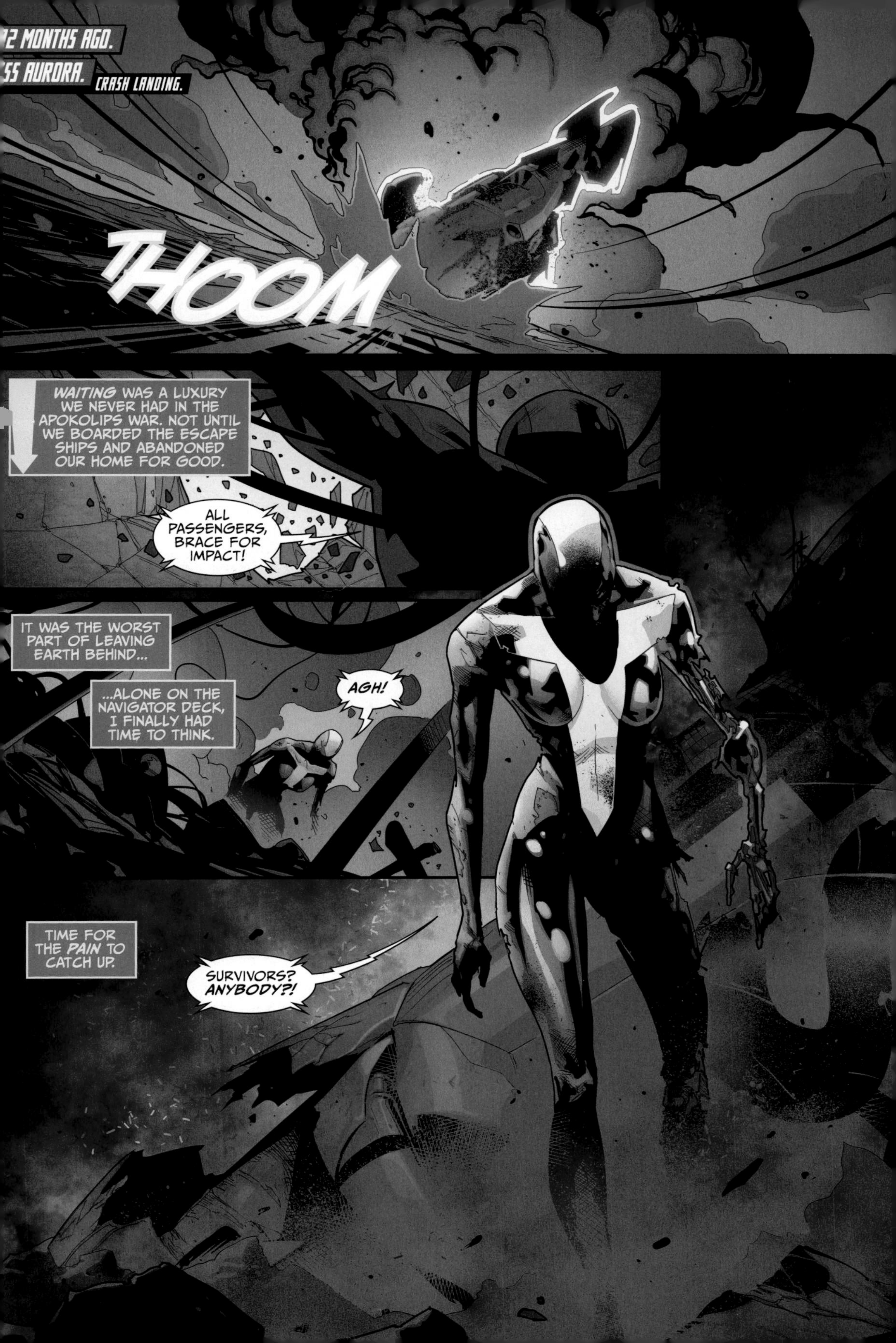
2 MONTHS AGO.
SS AURORA.
CRASH LANDING.
THOOM
WAITING WAS A LUXURY WE NEVER HAD IN THE APOKOLIPS WAR. NOT UNTIL WE BOARDED THE ESCAPE SHIPS AND ABANDONED OUR HOME FOR GOOD.
ALL PASSENGERS, BRACE FOR IMPACT!
IT WAS THE WORST PART OF LEAVING EARTH BEHIND...
...ALONE ON THE NAVIGATOR DECK, I FINALLY HAD TIME TO THINK.
AGH!
TIME FOR THE PAIN TO CATCH UP.
SURVIVORS? ANYBODY?!

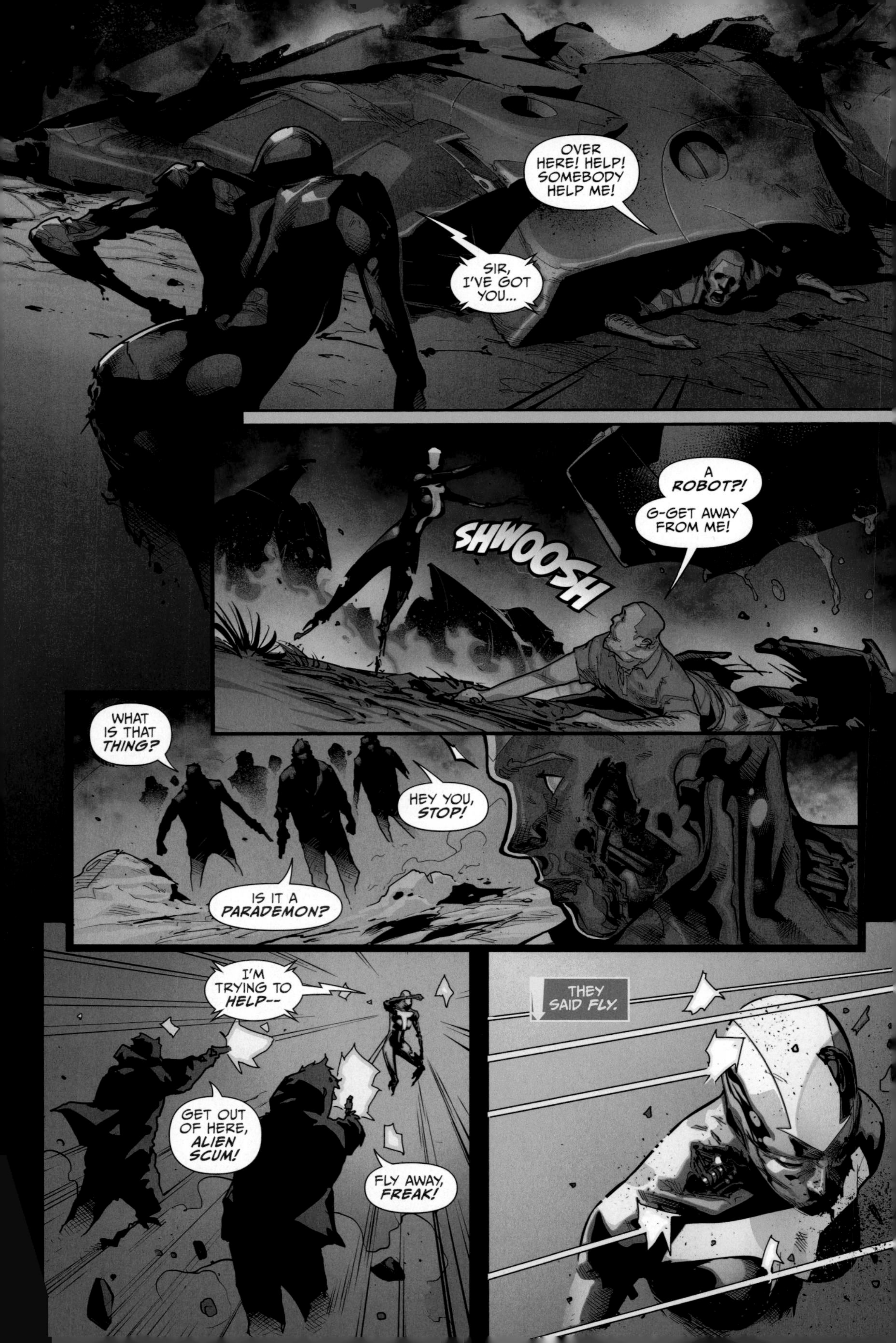
OVER HERE! HELP! SOMEBODY HELP ME!
SIR, I'VE GOT YOU...
A ROBOT?!
G-GET AWAY FROM ME!
SHWOOSH
WHAT IS THAT THING?
HEY YOU, STOP!
IS IT A PARADEMON?
I'M TRYING TO HELP--
GET OUT OF HERE, ALIEN SCUM!
FLY AWAY, FREAK!
THEY SAID FLY.

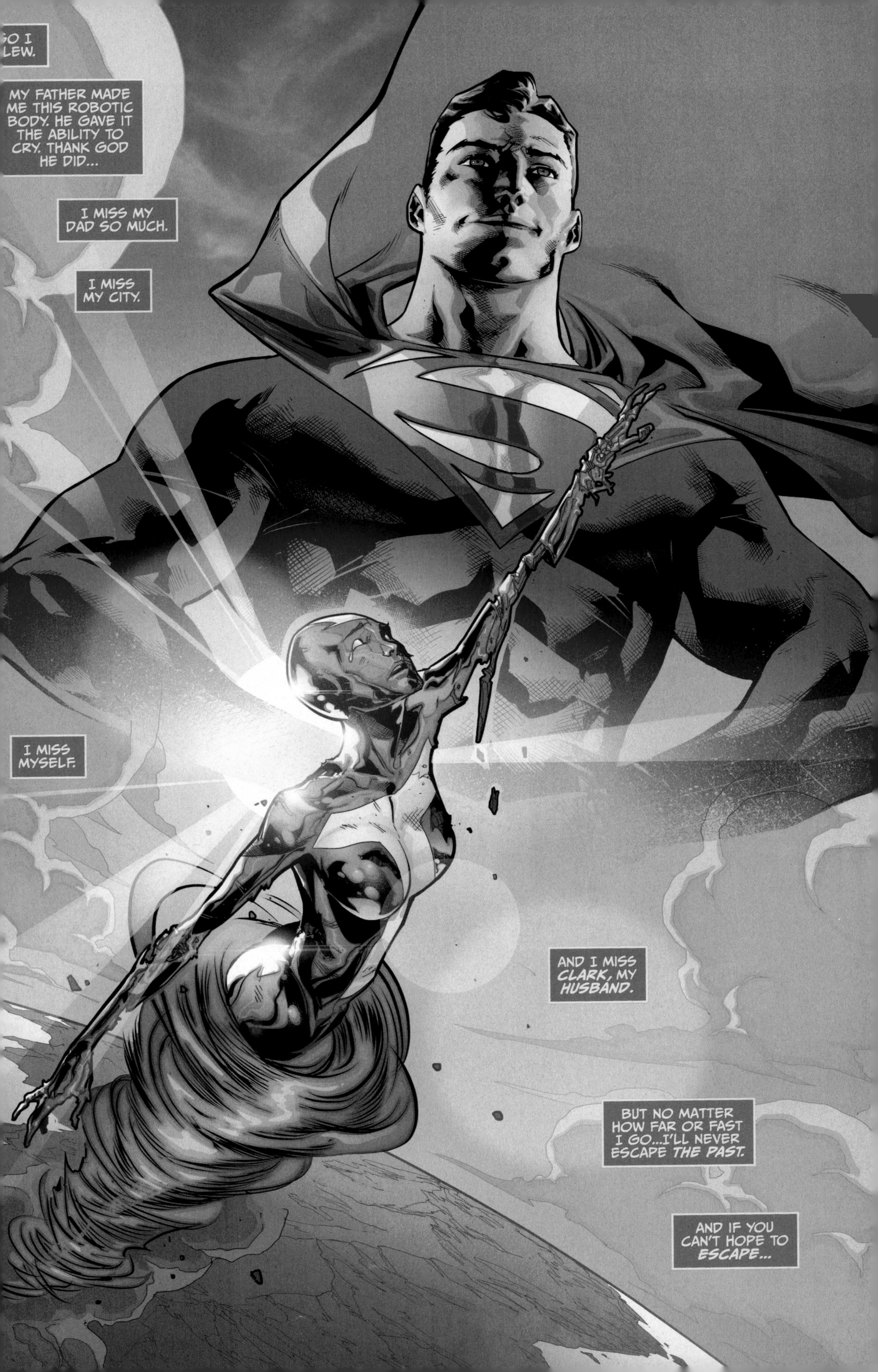

SO I
FLEW.
MY FATHER MADE ME THIS ROBOTIC BODY. HE GAVE IT THE ABILITY TO CRY. THANK GOD HE DID...
I MISS MY DAD SO MUCH.
I MISS MY CITY.
I MISS MYSELF.
AND I MISS *CLARK*, MY *HUSBAND*.
BUT NO MATTER HOW FAR OR FAST I GO...I'LL NEVER ESCAPE *THE PAST*.
AND IF YOU CAN'T HOPE TO *ESCAPE*...

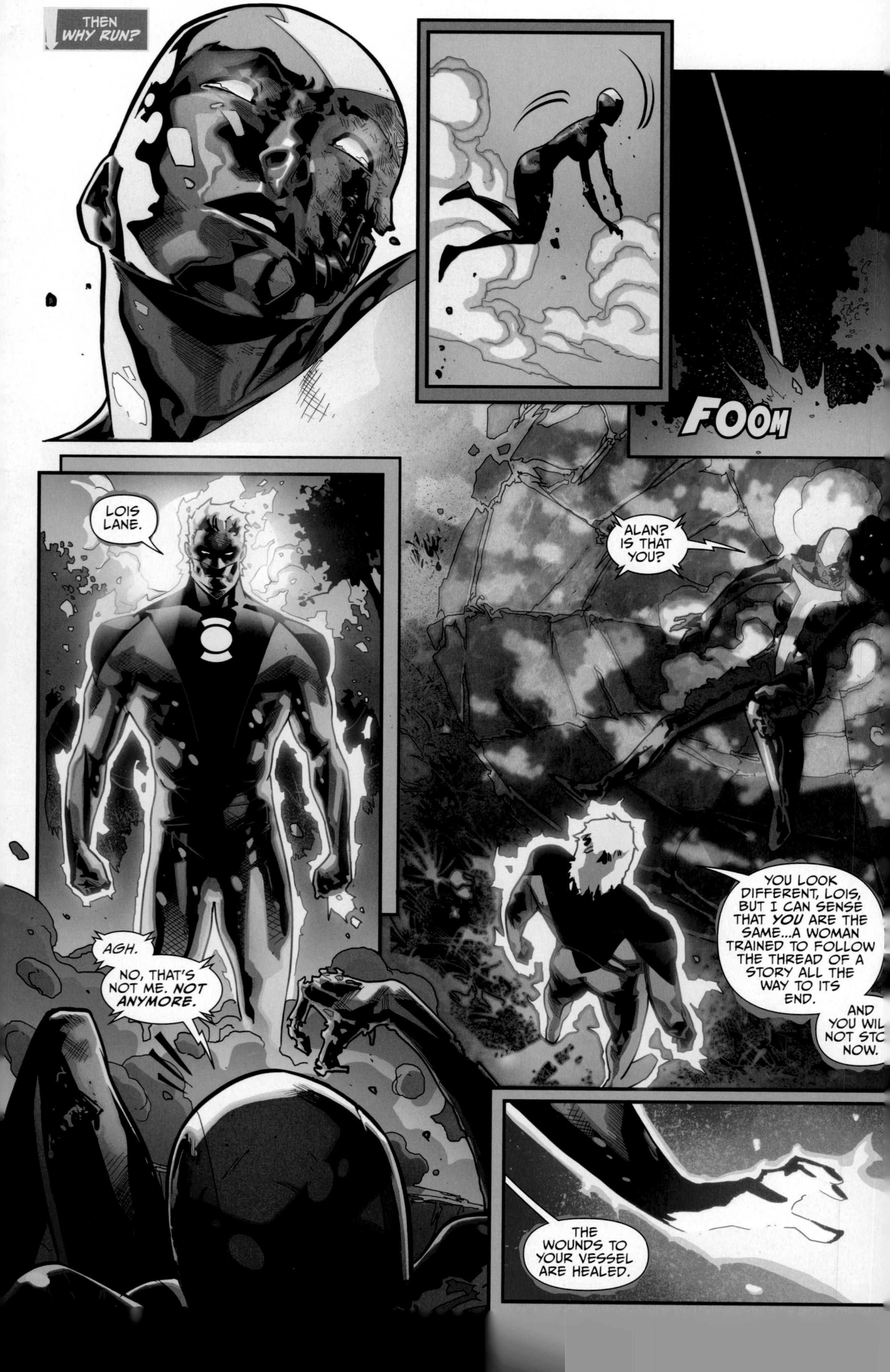
THEN WHY RUN?
FOOM
LOIS LANE.
ALAN? IS THAT YOU?
AGH.
NO, THAT'S NOT ME. NOT ANYMORE.
YOU LOOK DIFFERENT, LOIS, BUT I CAN SENSE THAT YOU ARE THE SAME...A WOMAN TRAINED TO FOLLOW THE THREAD OF A STORY ALL THE WAY TO ITS END.
THE WOUNDS TO YOUR VESSEL ARE HEALED.

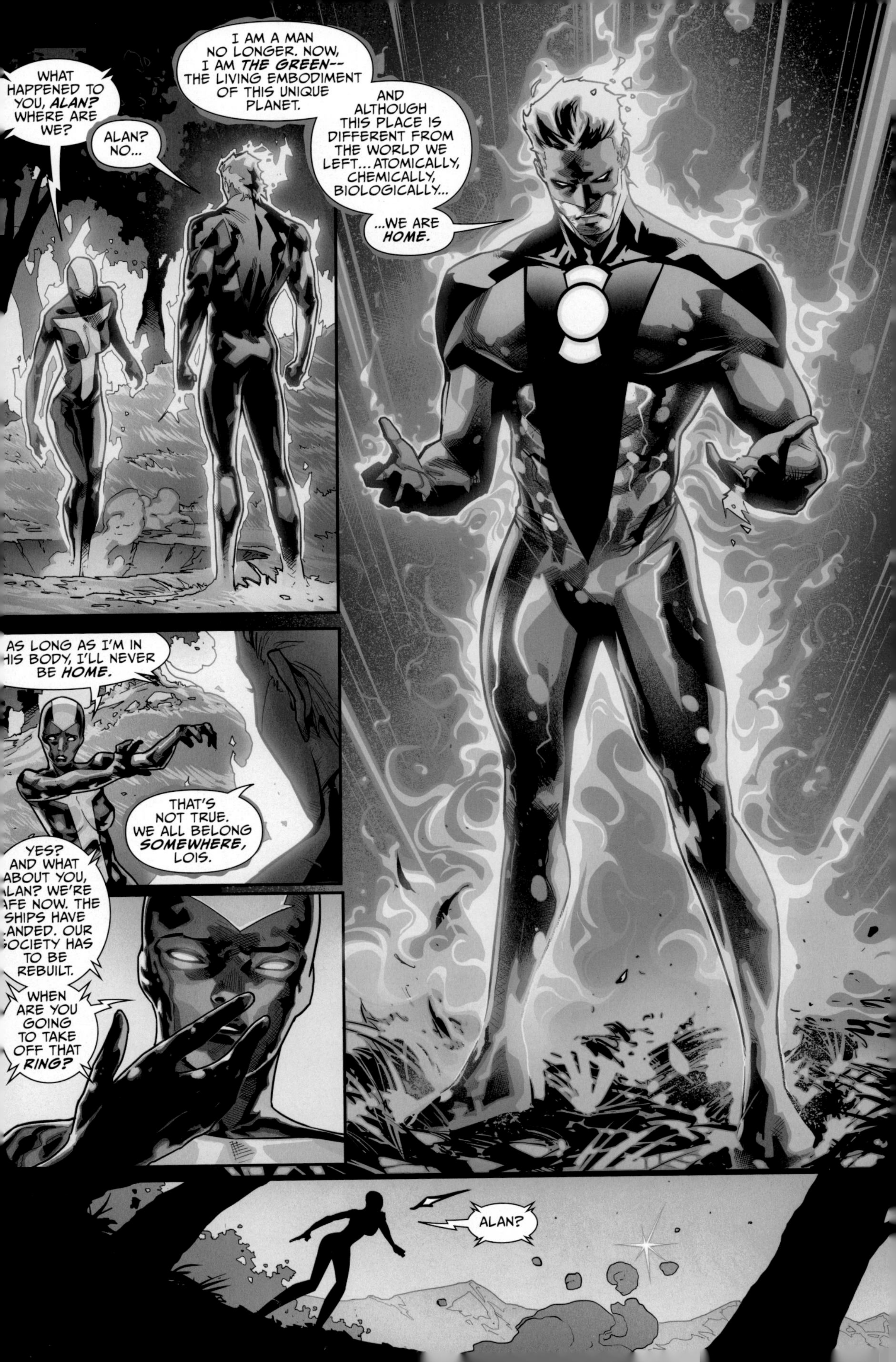
WHAT HAPPENED TO YOU, ALAN? WHERE ARE WE?
ALAN? NO...
I AM A MAN NO LONGER. NOW, I AM THE GREEN-- THE LIVING EMBODIMENT OF THIS UNIQUE PLANET.
AND ALTHOUGH THIS PLACE IS DIFFERENT FROM THE WORLD WE LEFT... ATOMICALLY, CHEMICALLY, BIOLOGICALLY...
...WE ARE HOME.
AS LONG AS I'M IN THIS BODY, I'LL NEVER BE HOME.
THAT'S NOT TRUE. WE ALL BELONG SOMEWHERE, LOIS.
YES? AND WHAT ABOUT YOU, ALAN? WE'RE SAFE NOW. THE SHIPS HAVE LANDED. OUR SOCIETY HAS TO BE REBUILT.
WHEN ARE YOU GOING TO TAKE OFF THAT RING?
ALAN?

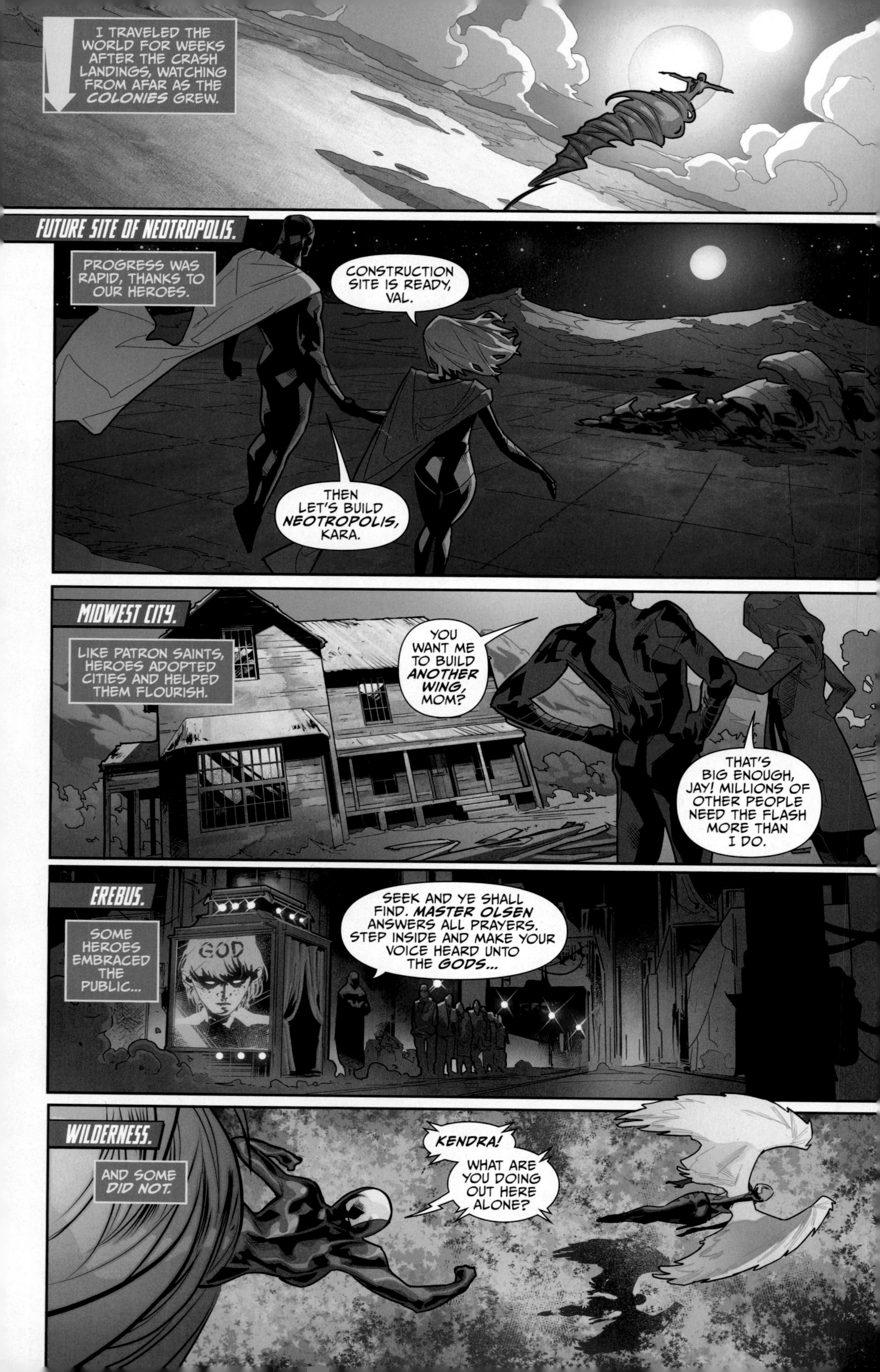

I TRAVELED THE WORLD FOR WEEKS AFTER THE CRASH LANDINGS, WATCHING FROM AFAR AS THE COLONIES GREW.
FUTURE SITE OF NEOTROPOLIS.
PROGRESS WAS RAPID, THANKS TO OUR HEROES.
CONSTRUCTION SITE IS READY, VAL.
THEN LET'S BUILD NEOTROPOLIS, KARA.
MIDWEST CITY.
LIKE PATRON SAINTS, HEROES ADOPTED CITIES AND HELPED THEM FLOURISH.
YOU WANT ME TO BUILD ANOTHER WING, MOM?
THAT'S BIG ENOUGH, JAY! MILLIONS OF OTHER PEOPLE NEED THE FLASH MORE THAN I DO.
EREBUS.
SOME HEROES EMBRACED THE PUBLIC...
GOD
SEEK AND YE SHALL FIND. MASTER OLSEN ANSWERS ALL PRAYERS. STEP INSIDE AND MAKE YOUR VOICE HEARD UNTO THE GODS...
WILDERNESS.
AND SOME DID NOT.
KENDRA!
WHAT ARE YOU DOING OUT HERE ALONE?

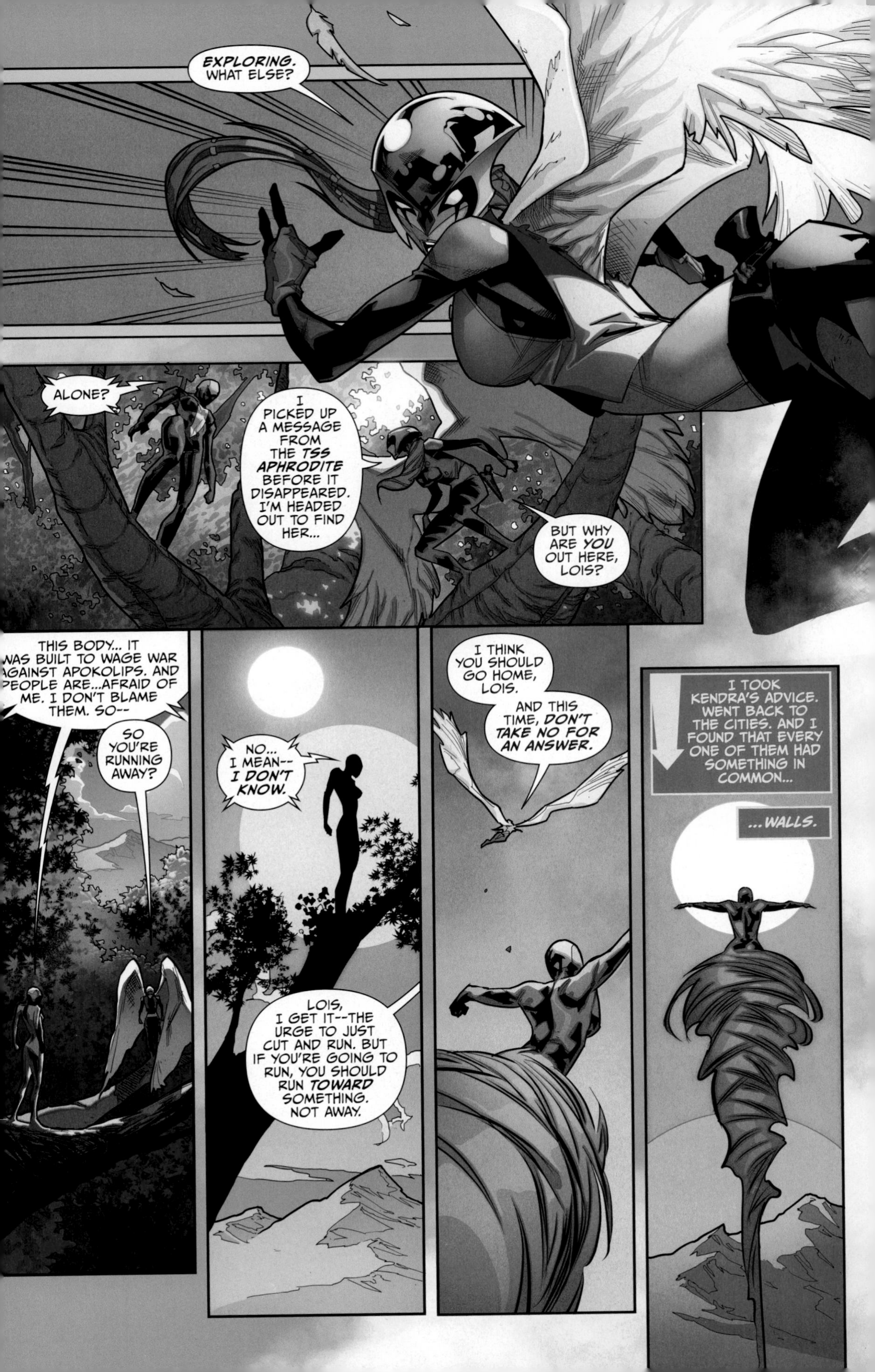
EXPLORING. WHAT ELSE?
ALONE?
I PICKED UP A MESSAGE FROM THE TSS APHRODITE BEFORE IT DISAPPEARED. I'M HEADED OUT TO FIND HER...
BUT WHY ARE YOU OUT HERE, LOIS?
THIS BODY... IT WAS BUILT TO WAGE WAR AGAINST APOKOLIPS. AND PEOPLE ARE...AFRAID OF ME. I DON'T BLAME THEM. SO--
SO YOU'RE RUNNING AWAY?
NO... I MEAN-- I DON'T KNOW.
LOIS, I GET IT--THE URGE TO JUST CUT AND RUN. BUT IF YOU'RE GOING TO RUN, YOU SHOULD RUN TOWARD SOMETHING. NOT AWAY.
I THINK YOU SHOULD GO HOME, LOIS.
AND THIS TIME, DON'T TAKE NO FOR AN ANSWER.
I TOOK KENDRA'S ADVICE. WENT BACK TO THE CITIES. AND I FOUND THAT EVERY ONE OF THEM HAD SOMETHING IN COMMON...
...WALLS.

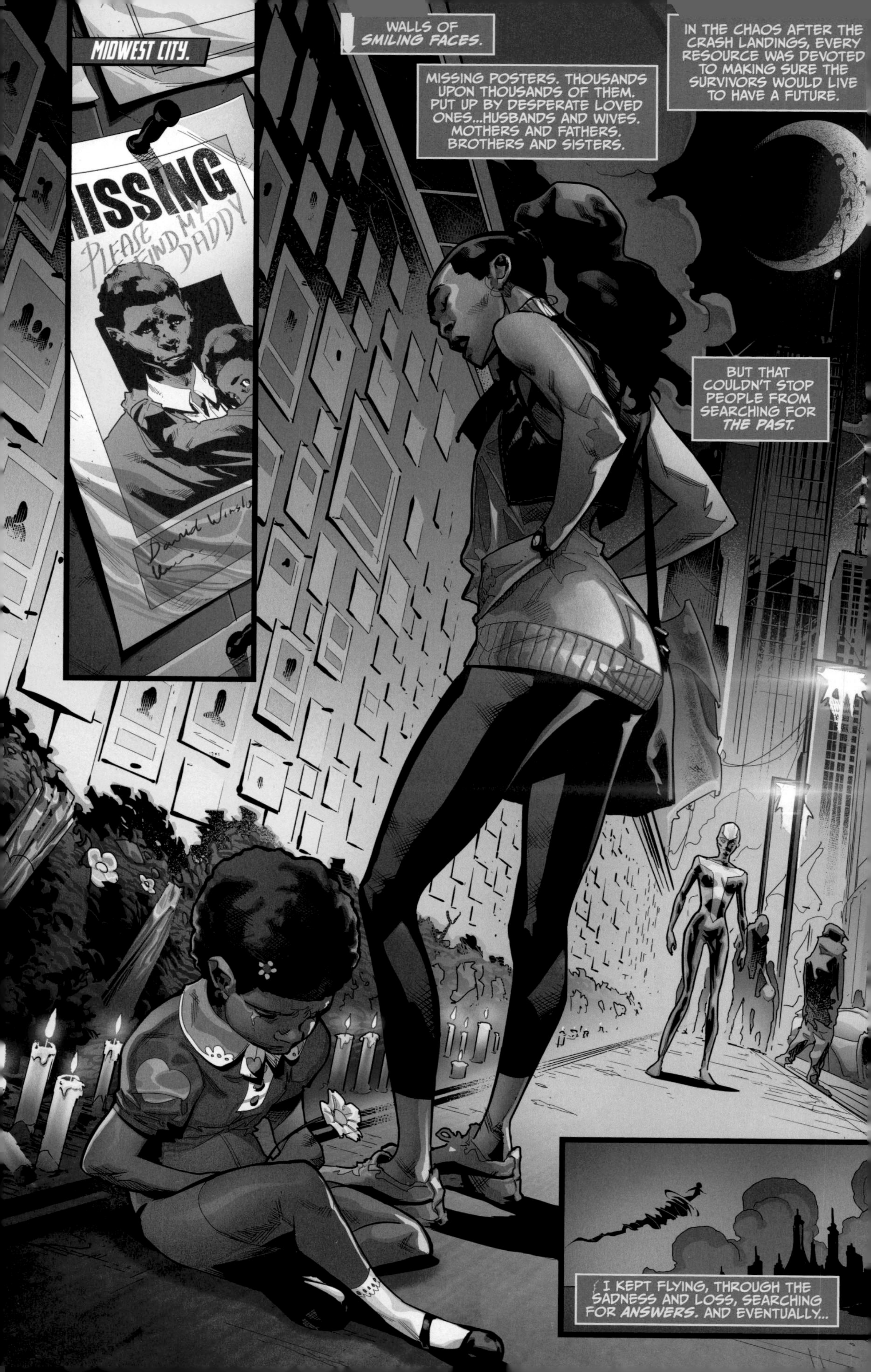
MIDWEST CITY.
MISSING
PLEASE FIND MY DADDY
WALLS OF SMILING FACES.
MISSING POSTERS. THOUSANDS UPON THOUSANDS OF THEM. PUT UP BY DESPERATE LOVED ONES...HUSBANDS AND WIVES. MOTHERS AND FATHERS. BROTHERS AND SISTERS.
IN THE CHAOS AFTER THE CRASH LANDINGS, EVERY RESOURCE WAS DEVOTED TO MAKING SURE THE SURVIVORS WOULD LIVE TO HAVE A FUTURE.
BUT THAT COULDN'T STOP PEOPLE FROM SEARCHING FOR THE PAST.
I KEPT FLYING, THROUGH THE SADNESS AND LOSS, SEARCHING FOR ANSWERS. AND EVENTUALLY...

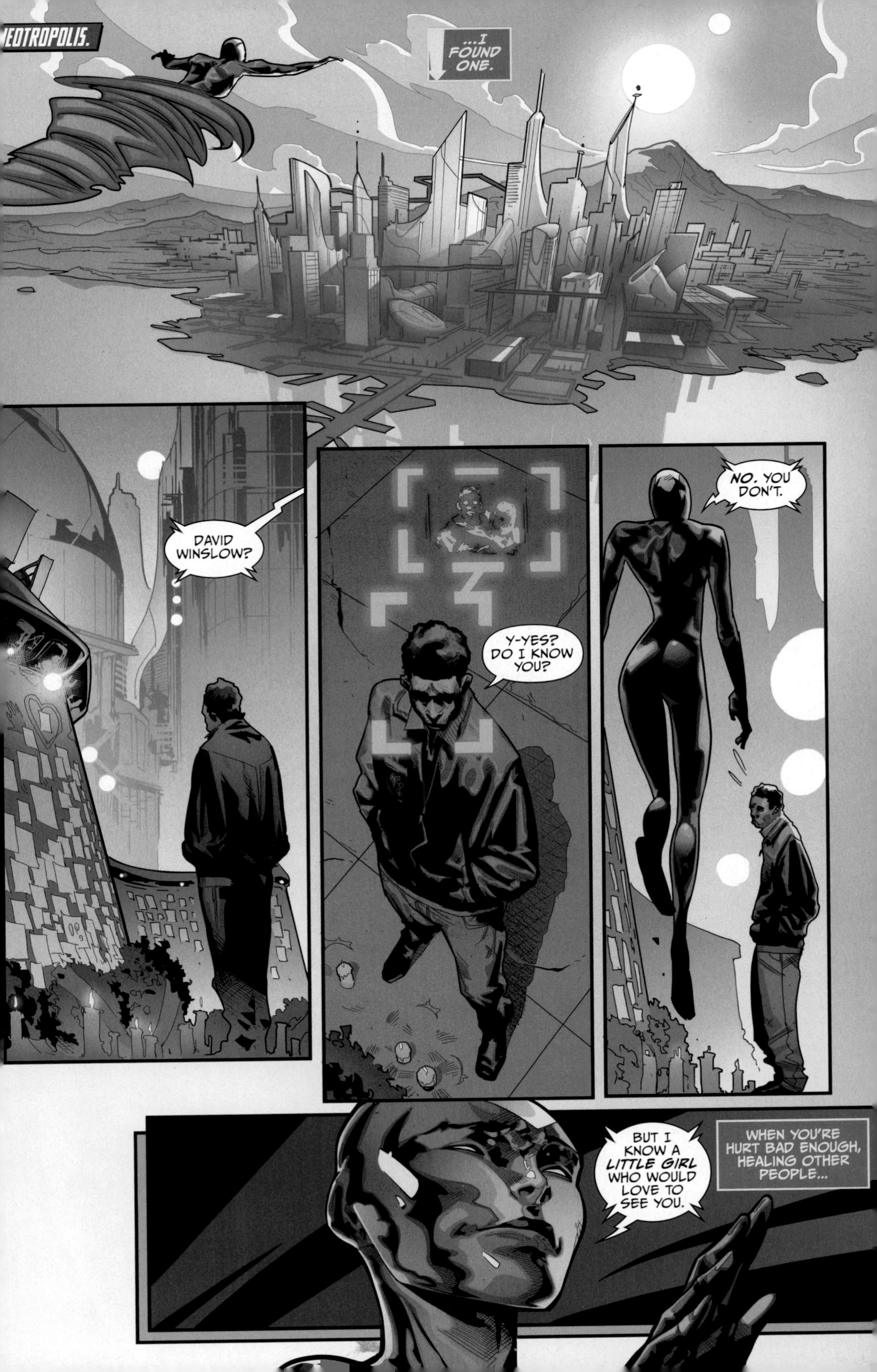
EOTROPOLIS.
...I FOUND ONE.
DAVID WINSLOW?
Y-YES? DO I KNOW YOU?
NO. YOU DON'T.
BUT I KNOW A LITTLE GIRL WHO WOULD LOVE TO SEE YOU.
WHEN YOU'RE HURT BAD ENOUGH, HEALING OTHER PEOPLE...

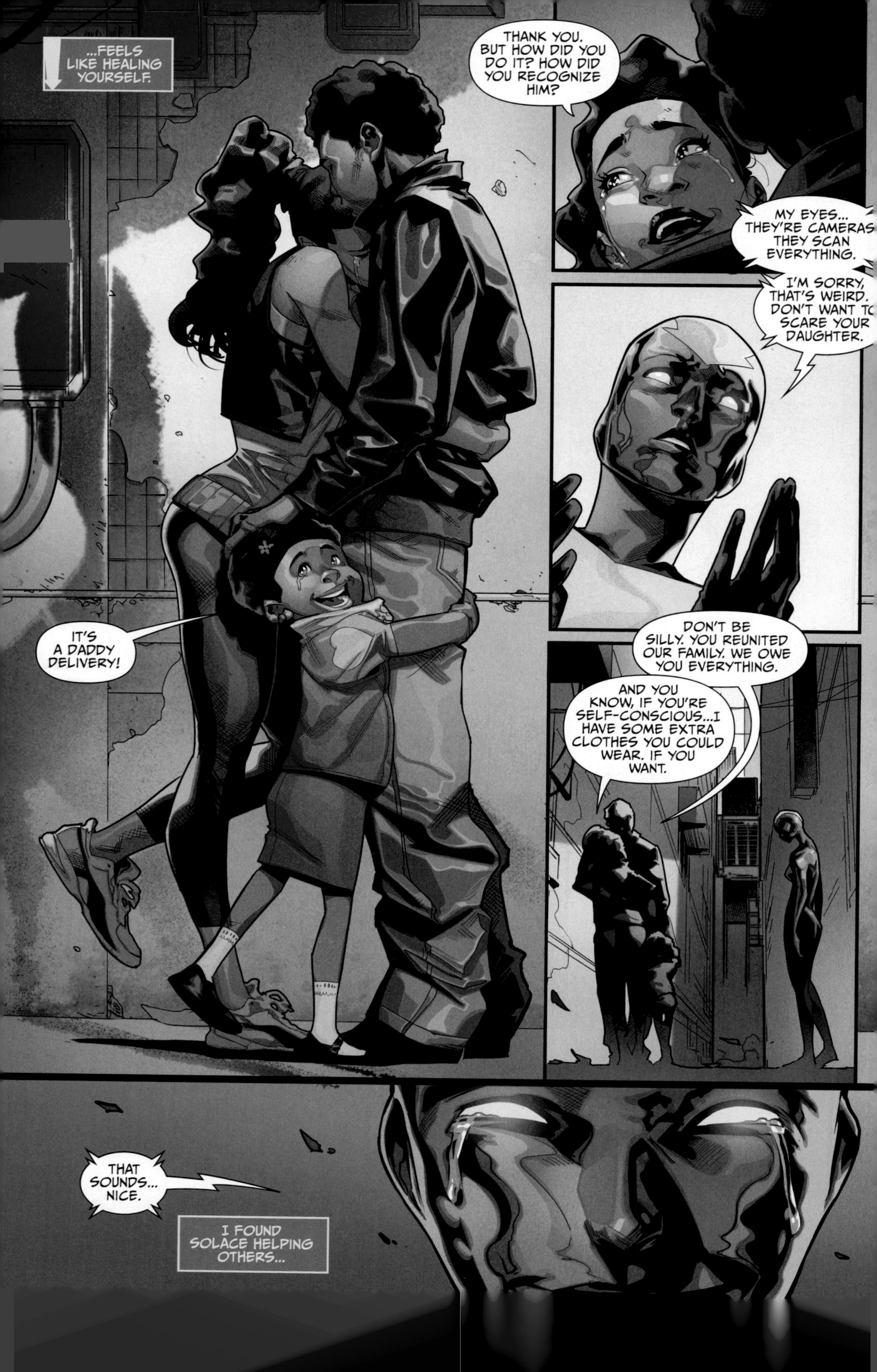
...FEELS LIKE HEALING YOURSELF.
THANK YOU. BUT HOW DID YOU DO IT? HOW DID YOU RECOGNIZE HIM?
MY EYES... THEY'RE CAMERAS. THEY SCAN EVERYTHING.
I'M SORRY, THAT'S WEIRD. DON'T WANT TO SCARE YOUR DAUGHTER.
IT'S A DADDY DELIVERY!
DON'T BE SILLY. YOU REUNITED OUR FAMILY. WE OWE YOU EVERYTHING.
AND YOU KNOW, IF YOU'RE SELF-CONSCIOUS...I HAVE SOME EXTRA CLOTHES YOU COULD WEAR. IF YOU WANT.
THAT SOUNDS... NICE.
I FOUND SOLACE HELPING OTHERS...

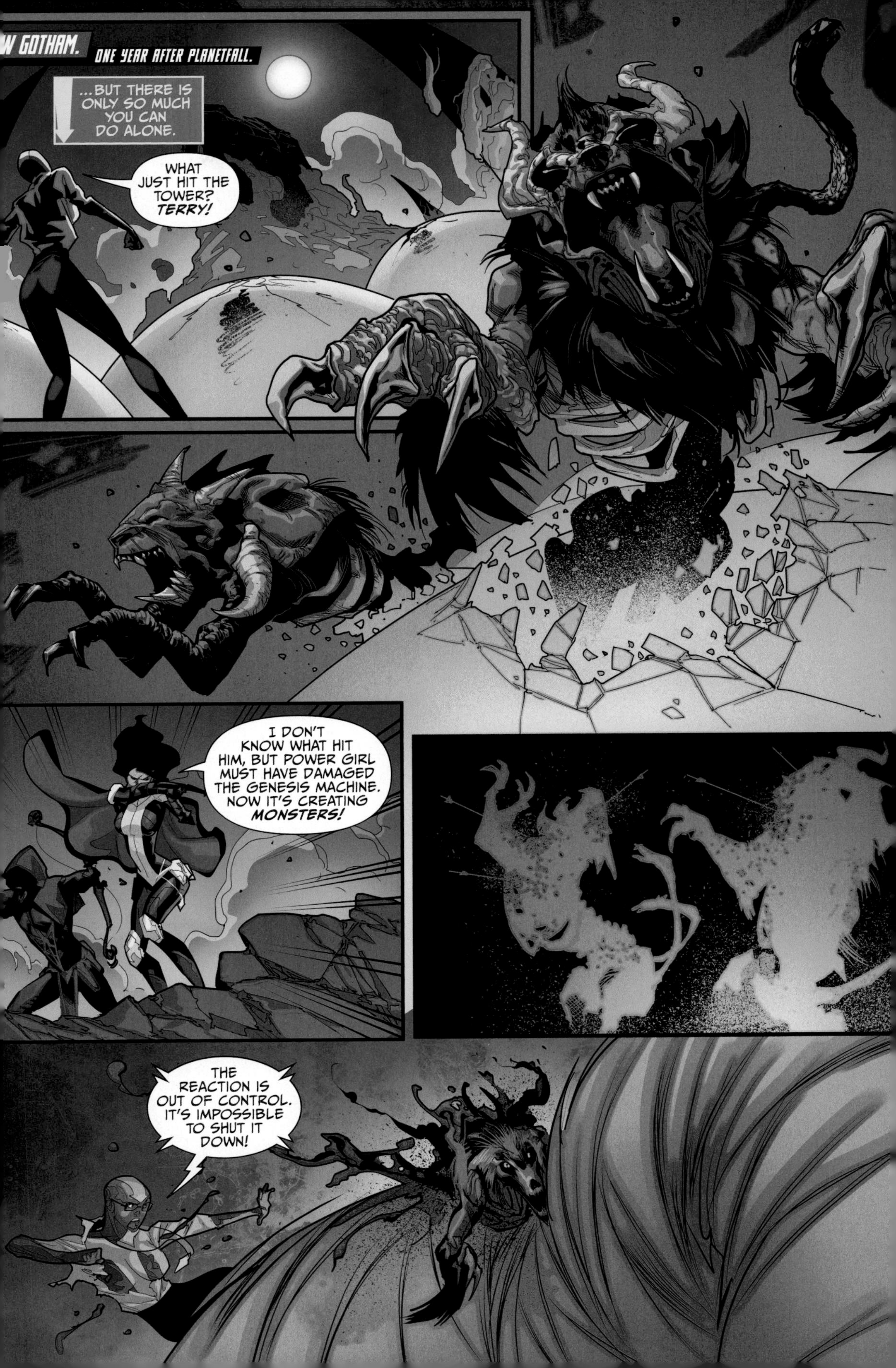
W GOTHAM.
ONE YEAR AFTER PLANETFALL.
...BUT THERE IS ONLY SO MUCH YOU CAN DO ALONE.
WHAT JUST HIT THE TOWER? TERRY!
I DON'T KNOW WHAT HIT HIM, BUT POWER GIRL MUST HAVE DAMAGED THE GENESIS MACHINE. NOW IT'S CREATING MONSTERS!
THE REACTION IS OUT OF CONTROL. IT'S IMPOSSIBLE TO SHUT IT DOWN!

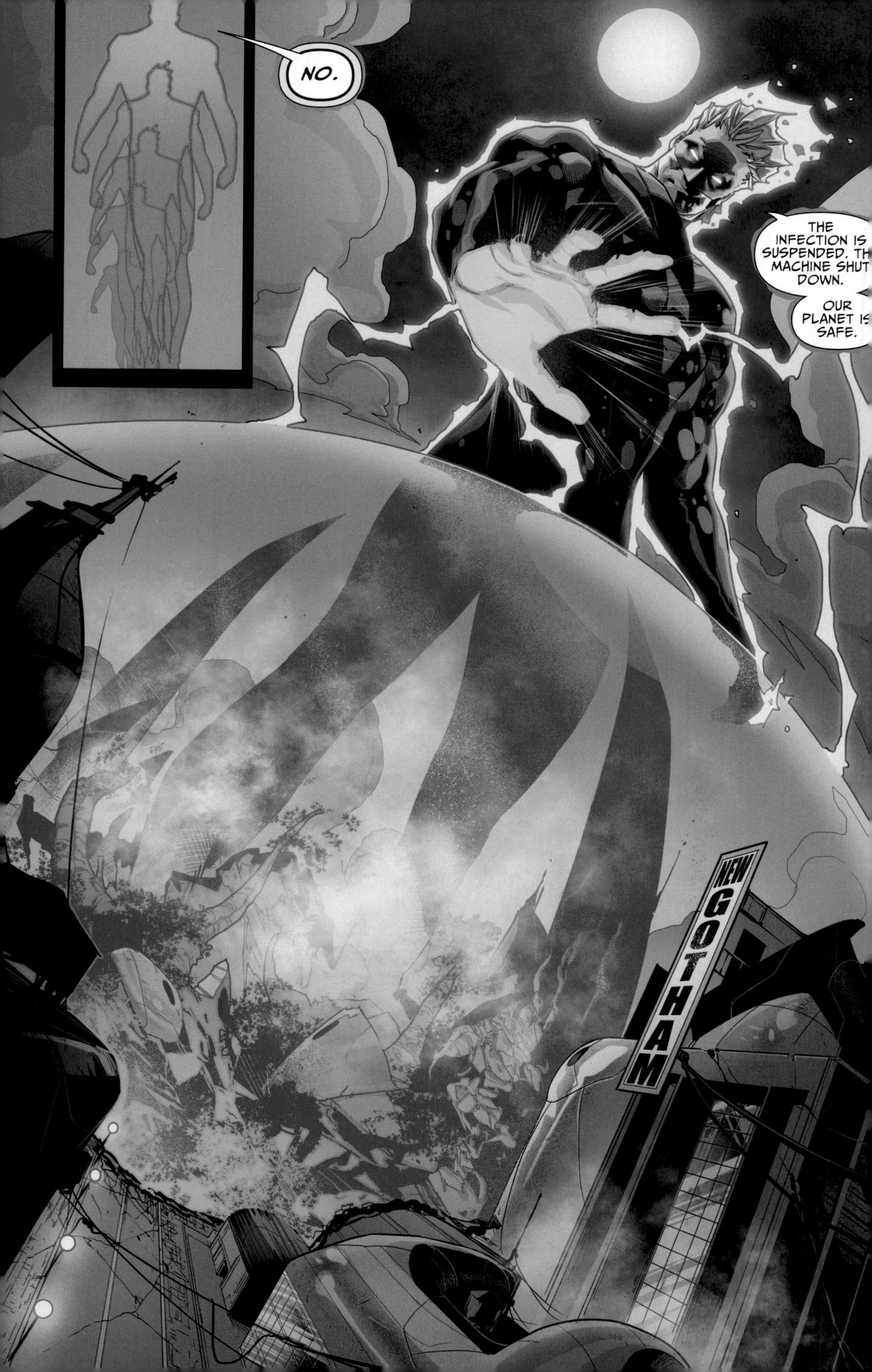
NO.
THE INFECTION IS SUSPENDED. TH MACHINE SHUT DOWN.
OUR PLANET IS SAFE.
NEW GOTHAM

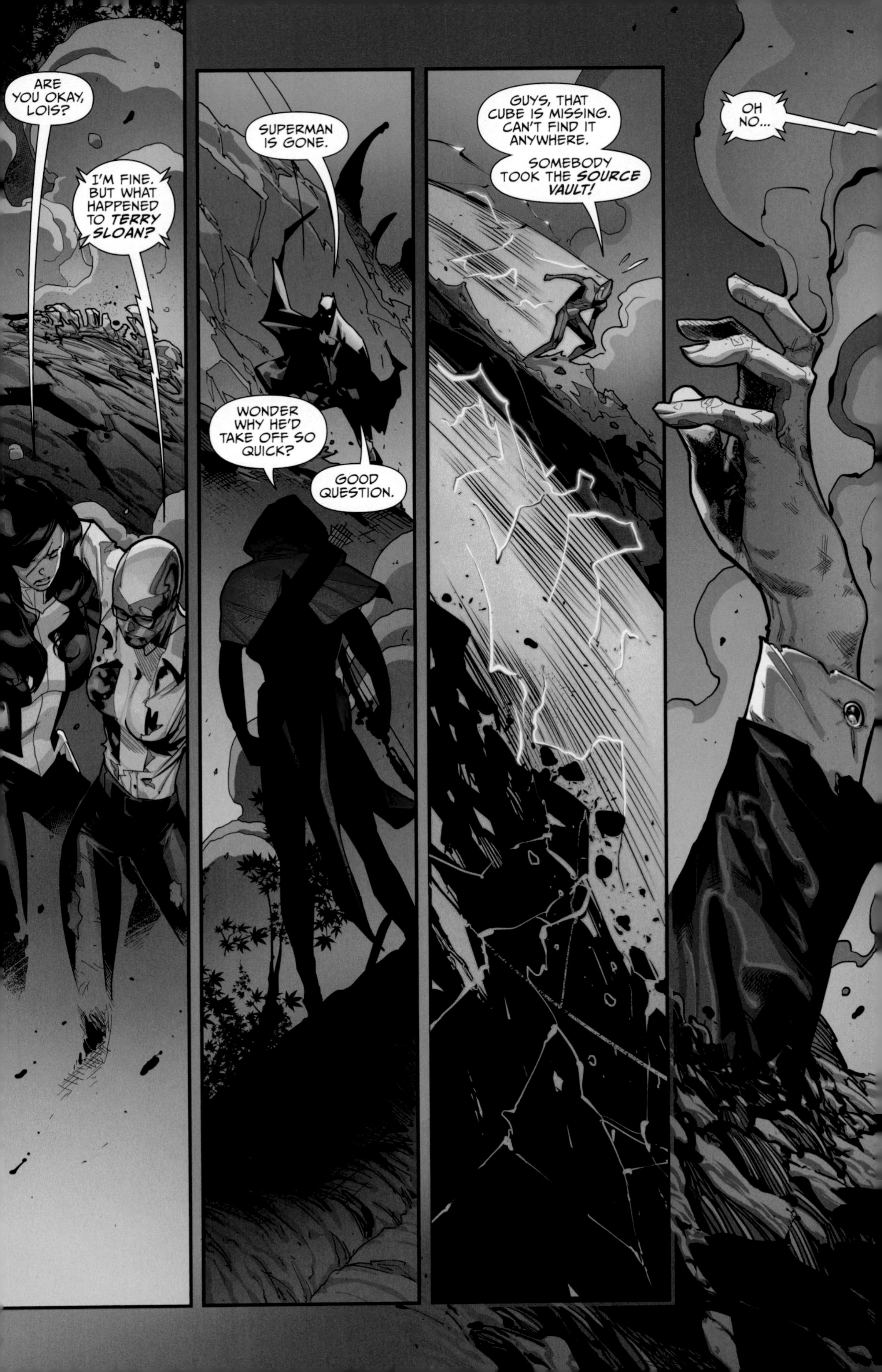
ARE YOU OKAY, LOIS?
I'M FINE. BUT WHAT HAPPENED TO TERRY SLOAN?
SUPERMAN IS GONE.
WONDER WHY HE'D TAKE OFF SO QUICK?
GOOD QUESTION.
GUYS, THAT CUBE IS MISSING. CAN'T FIND IT ANYWHERE.
SOMEBODY TOOK THE SOURCE VAULT!
OH NO...

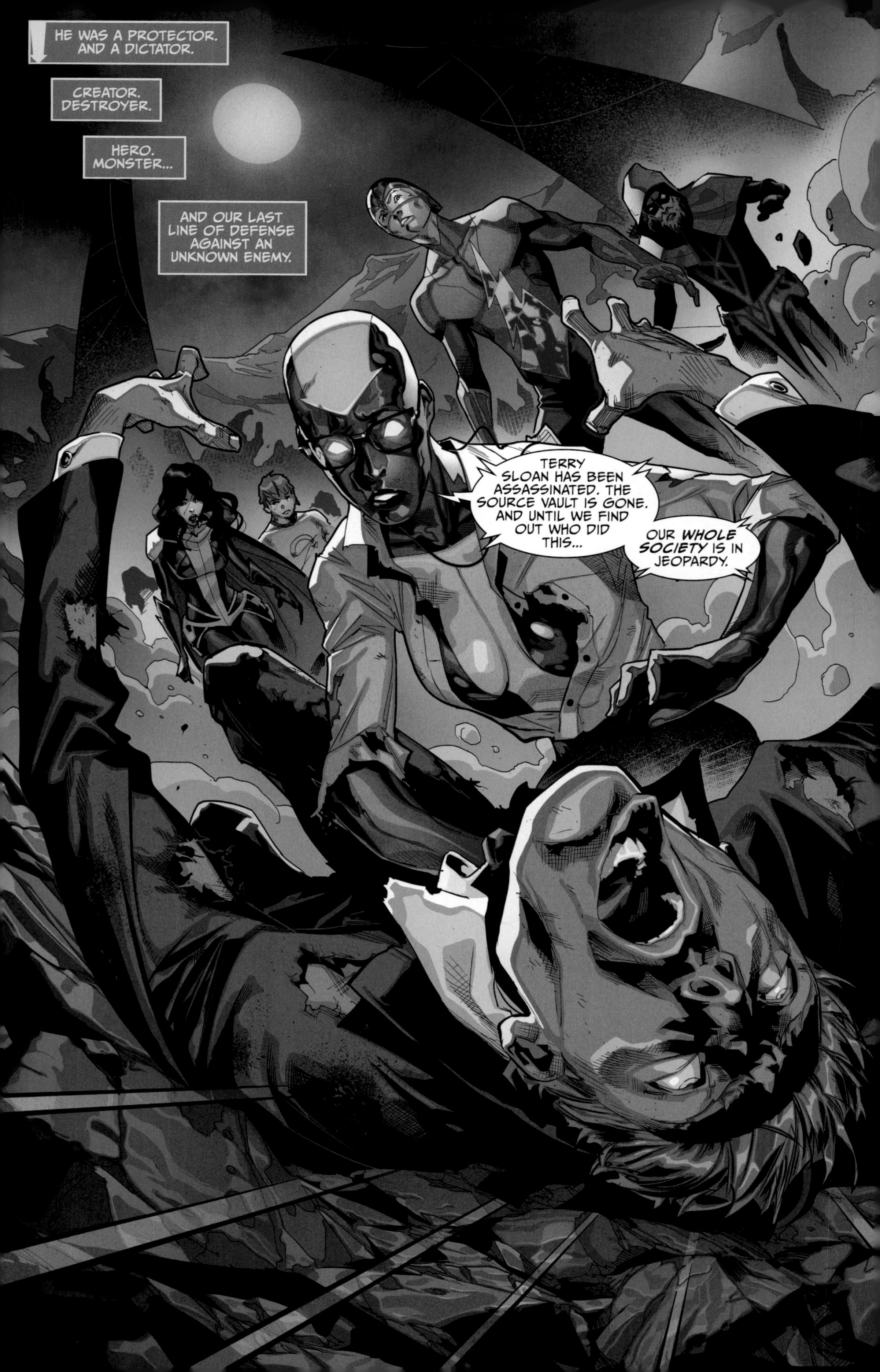
HE WAS A PROTECTOR. AND A DICTATOR.
CREATOR. DESTROYER.
HERO. MONSTER...
AND OUR LAST LINE OF DEFENSE AGAINST AN UNKNOWN ENEMY.
TERRY SLOAN HAS BEEN ASSASSINATED. THE SOURCE VAULT IS GONE. AND UNTIL WE FIND OUT WHO DID THIS...
OUR *WHOLE SOCIETY* IS IN JEOPARDY.

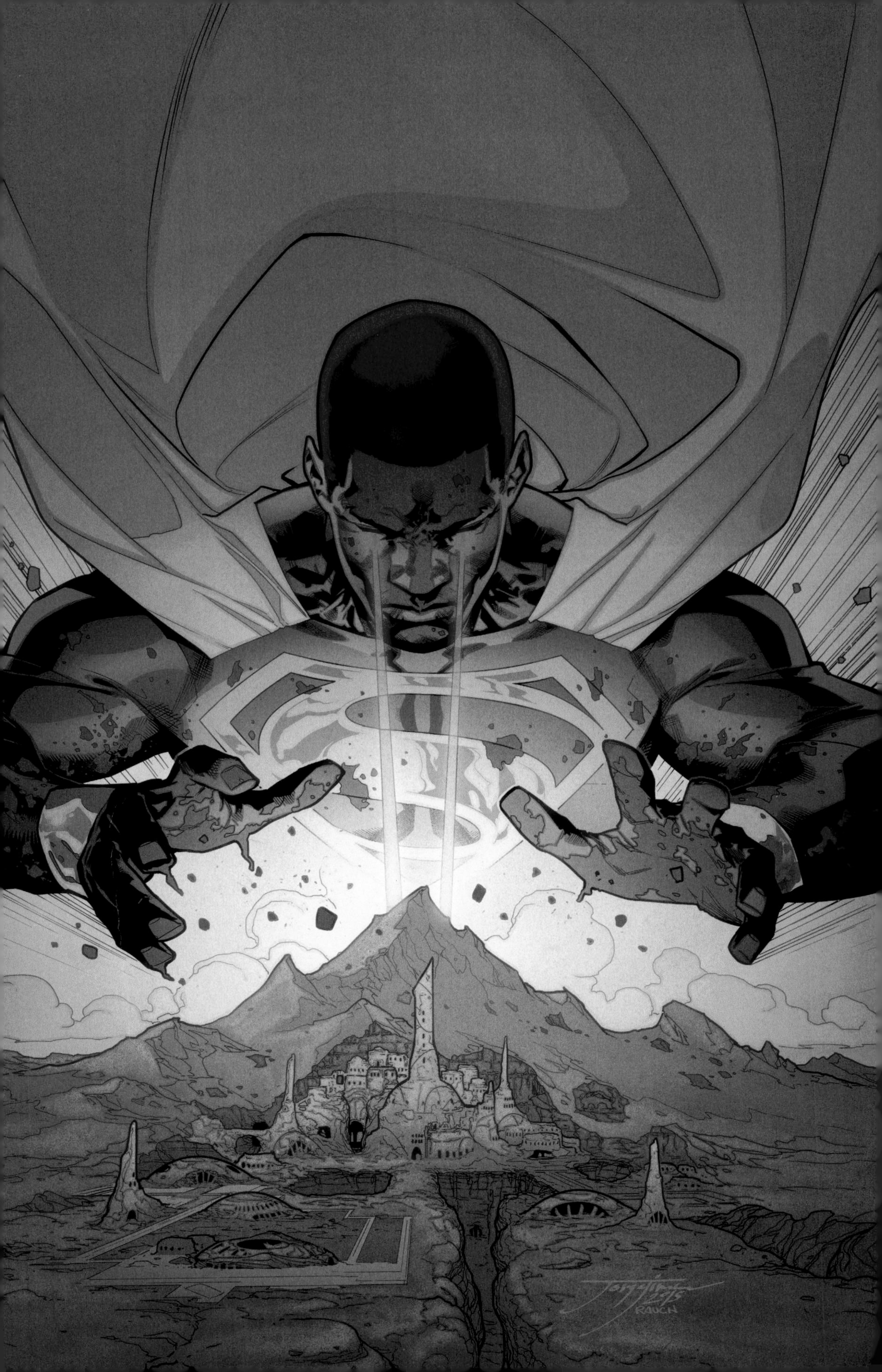

NEXUS

DANIEL H. WILSON writer **JORGE JIMENEZ** artist **ALEJANDRO SANCHEZ** colorist **TRAVIS LANHAM PATRICK BROSSEAU** letterers cover by **JIMENEZ & RAUCH**

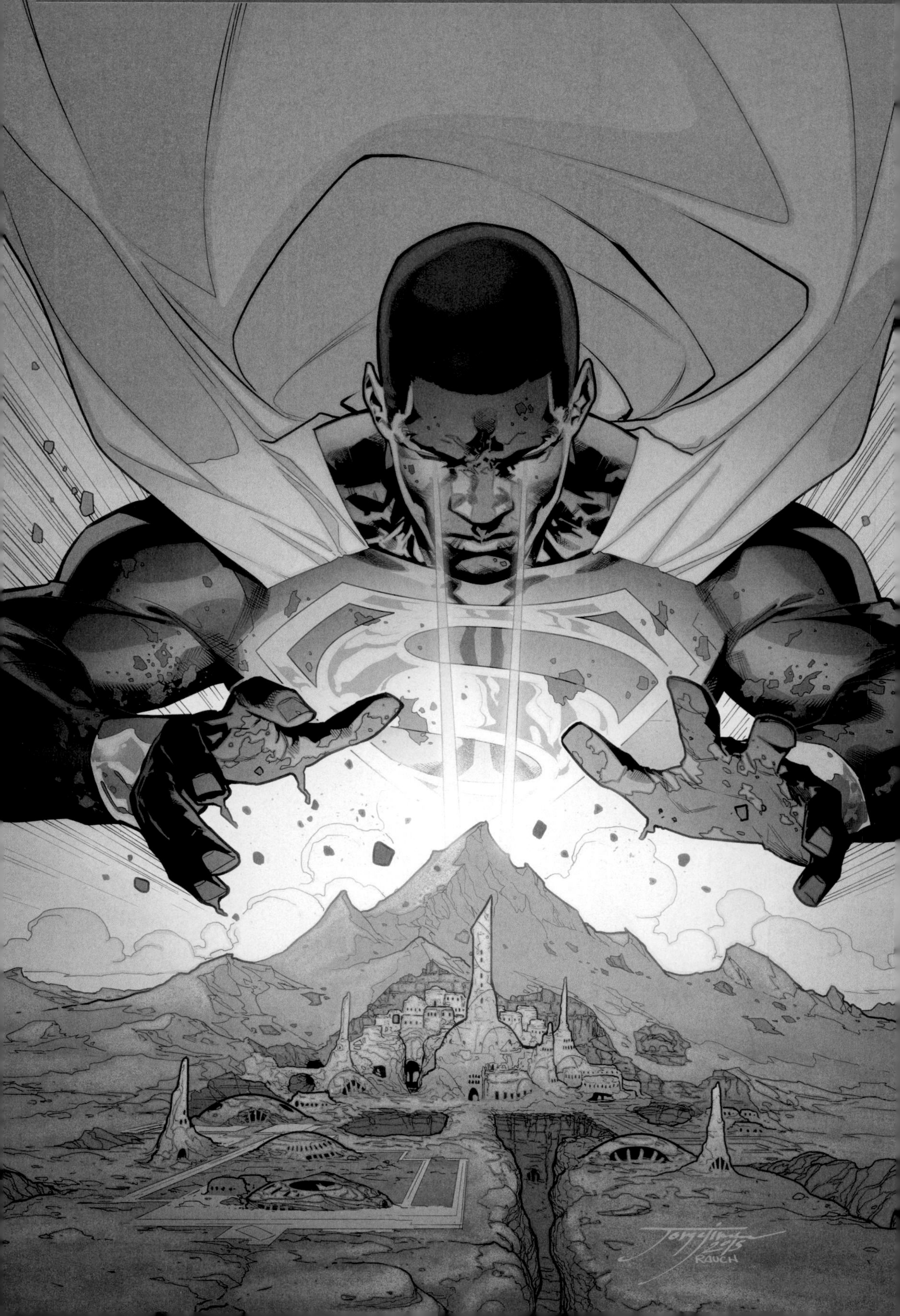

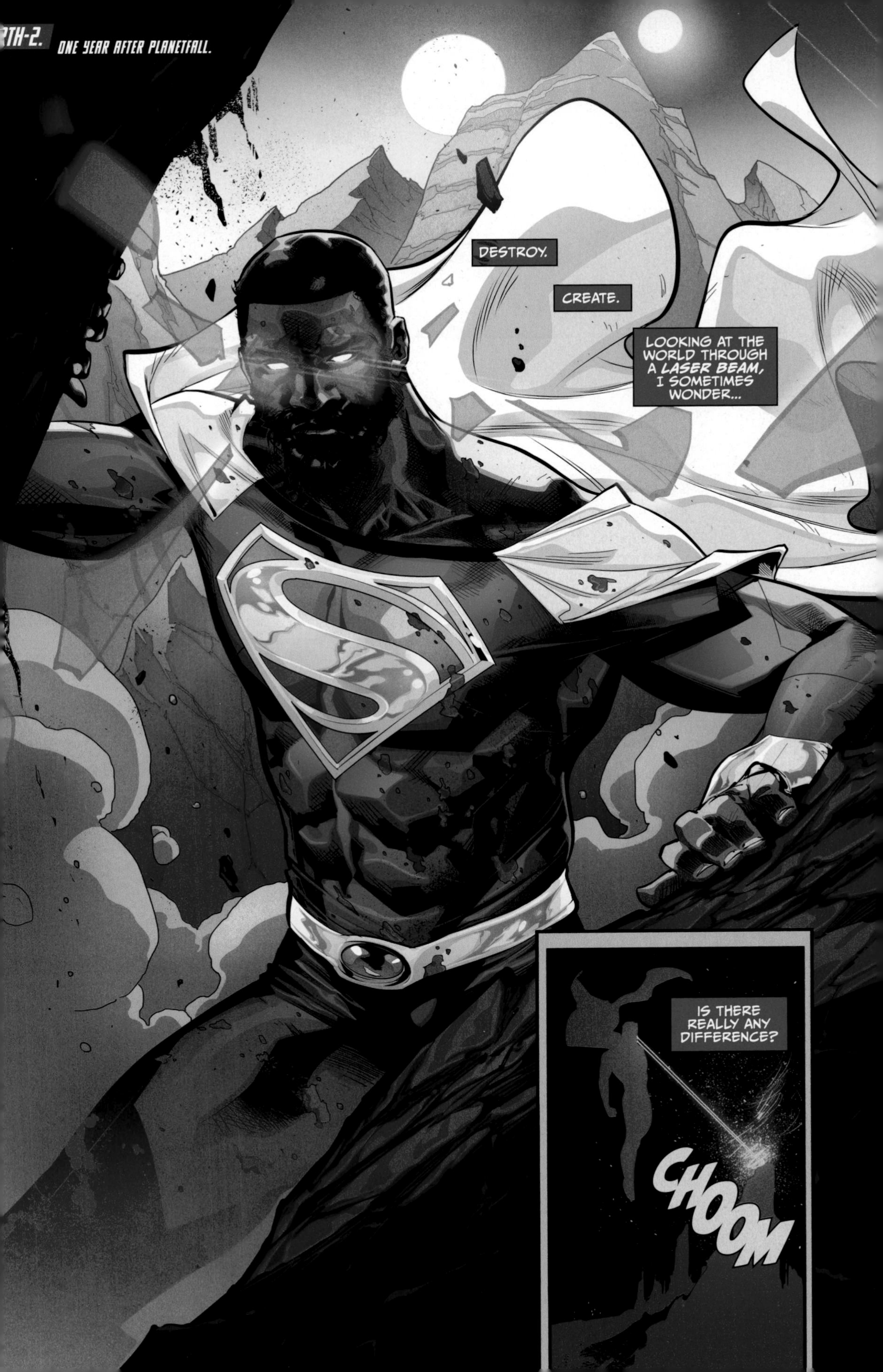
RTH-2. ONE YEAR AFTER PLANETFALL.
DESTROY.
CREATE.
LOOKING AT THE WORLD THROUGH A LASER BEAM, I SOMETIMES WONDER...
IS THERE REALLY ANY DIFFERENCE?
CHOOM

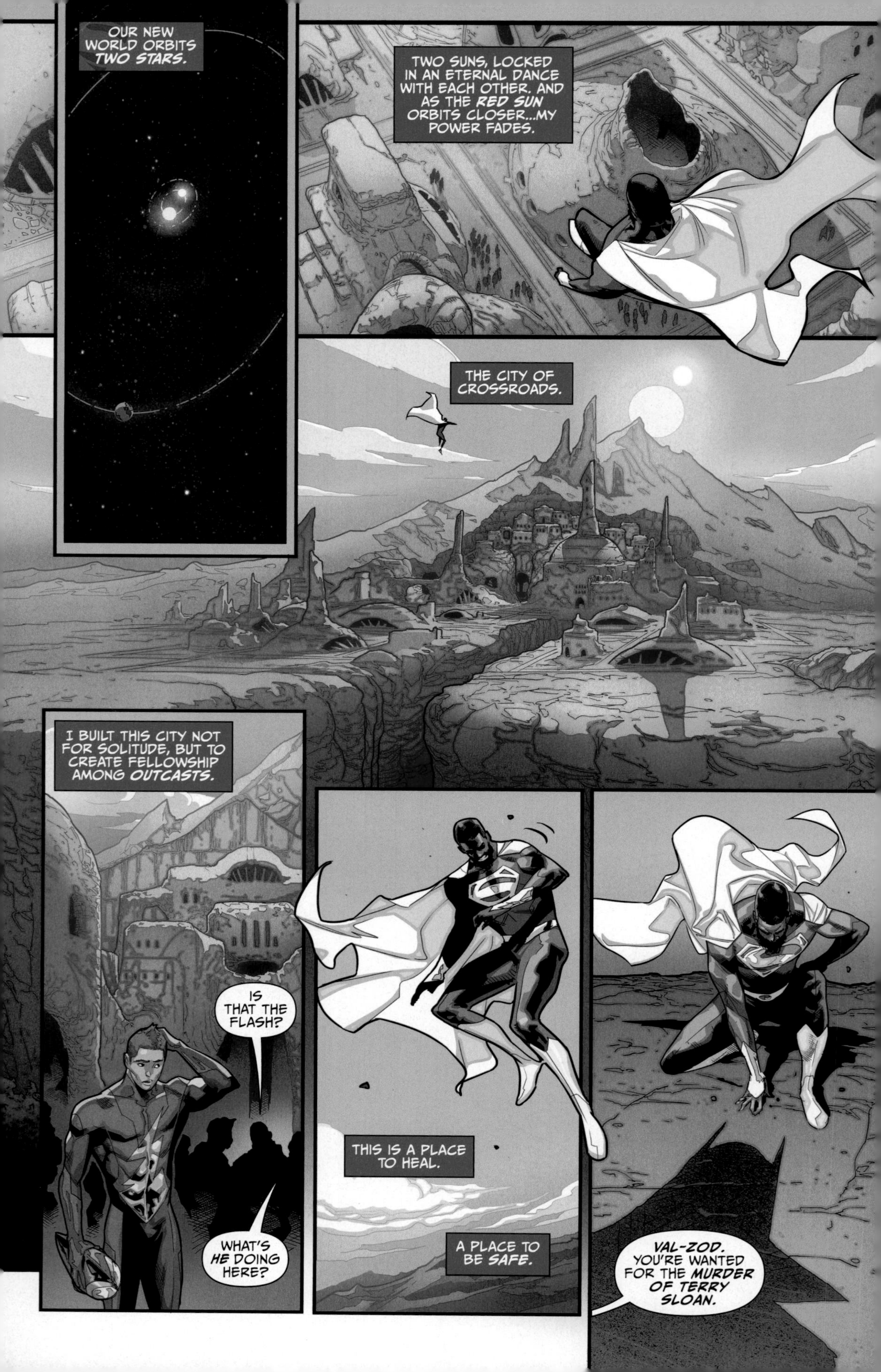
OUR NEW WORLD ORBITS TWO STARS.
TWO SUNS, LOCKED IN AN ETERNAL DANCE WITH EACH OTHER. AND AS THE RED SUN ORBITS CLOSER...MY POWER FADES.
THE CITY OF CROSSROADS.
I BUILT THIS CITY NOT FOR SOLITUDE, BUT TO CREATE FELLOWSHIP AMONG OUTCASTS.
IS THAT THE FLASH?
WHAT'S HE DOING HERE?
THIS IS A PLACE TO HEAL.
A PLACE TO BE SAFE.
VAL-ZOD. YOU'RE WANTED FOR THE MURDER OF TERRY SLOAN.

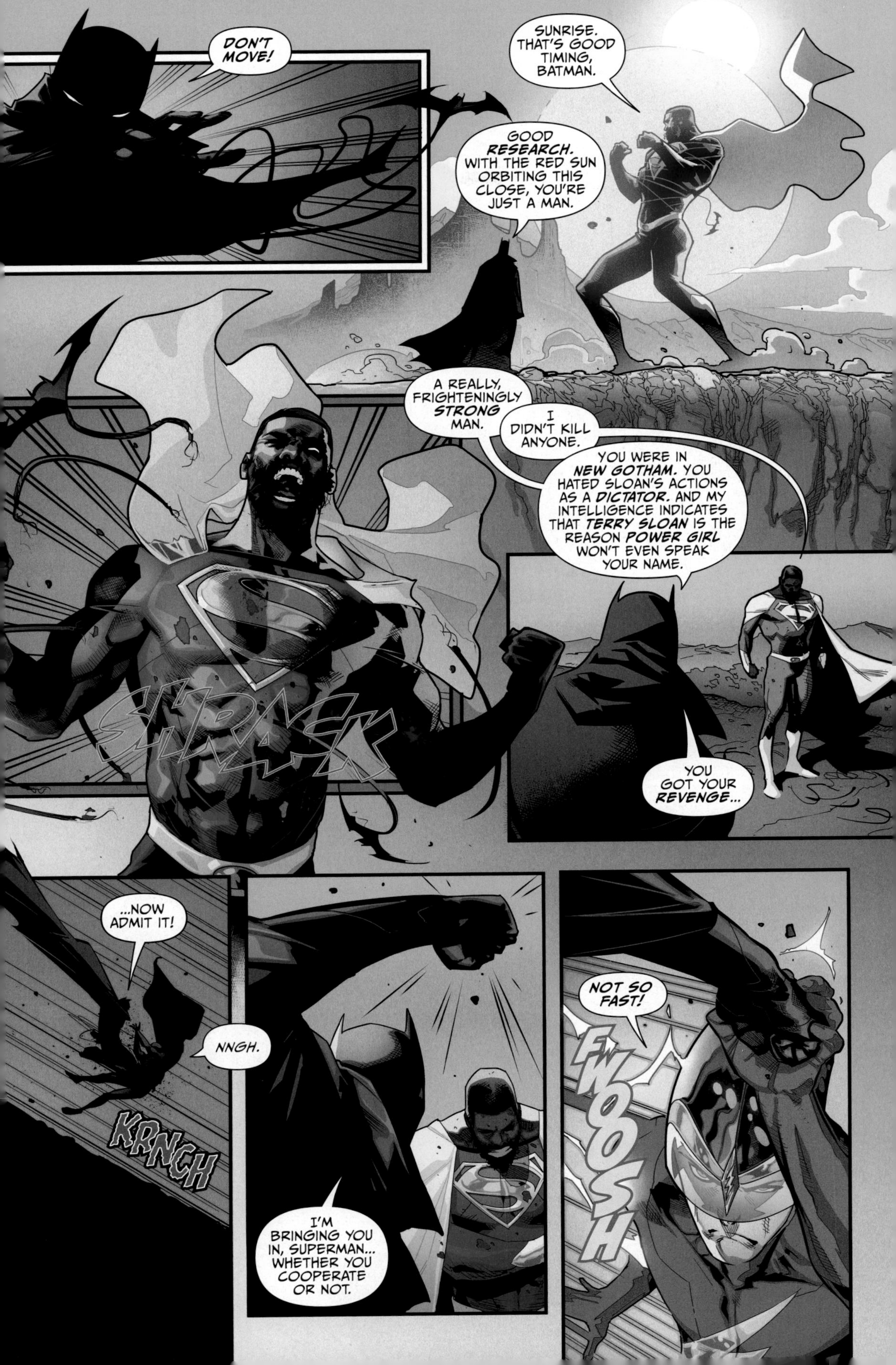
DON'T MOVE!
SUNRISE. THAT'S GOOD TIMING, BATMAN.
GOOD RESEARCH. WITH THE RED SUN ORBITING THIS CLOSE, YOU'RE JUST A MAN.
A REALLY, FRIGHTENINGLY STRONG MAN.
I DIDN'T KILL ANYONE.
YOU WERE IN NEW GOTHAM. YOU HATED SLOAN'S ACTIONS AS A DICTATOR. AND MY INTELLIGENCE INDICATES THAT TERRY SLOAN IS THE REASON POWER GIRL WON'T EVEN SPEAK YOUR NAME.
SHRACK
YOU GOT YOUR REVENGE...
...NOW ADMIT IT!
NNGH.
KRNCH
I'M BRINGING YOU IN, SUPERMAN... WHETHER YOU COOPERATE OR NOT.
NOT SO FAST!
FWOOSH

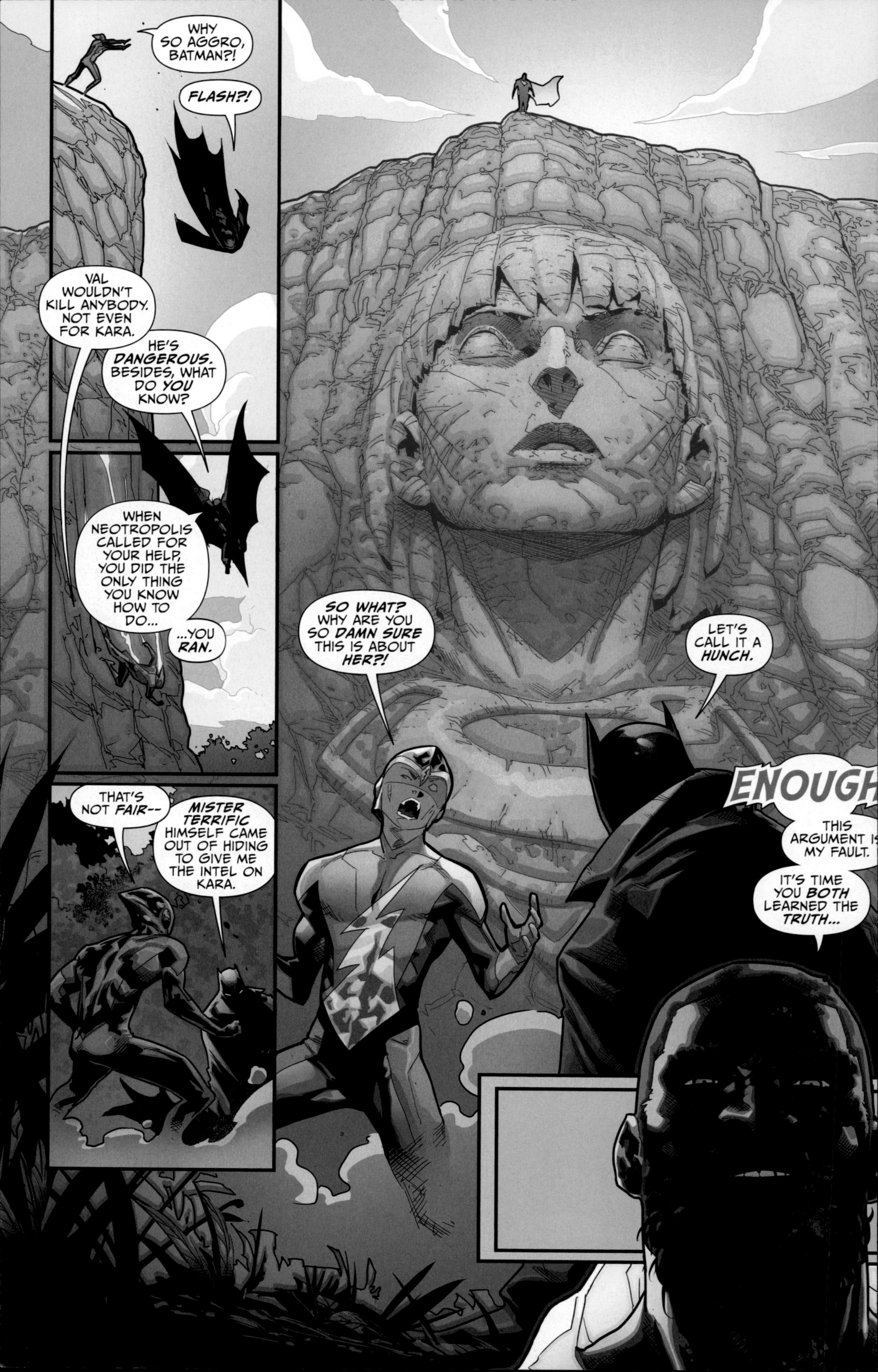
WHY SO AGGRO, BATMAN?!
FLASH?!
VAL WOULDN'T KILL ANYBODY. NOT EVEN FOR KARA.
HE'S DANGEROUS. BESIDES, WHAT DO YOU KNOW?
WHEN NEOTROPOLIS CALLED FOR YOUR HELP, YOU DID THE ONLY THING YOU KNOW HOW TO DO...
...YOU RAN.
THAT'S NOT FAIR--
MISTER TERRIFIC HIMSELF CAME OUT OF HIDING TO GIVE ME THE INTEL ON KARA.
SO WHAT? WHY ARE YOU SO DAMN SURE THIS IS ABOUT HER?!
LET'S CALL IT A HUNCH.
ENOUGH
THIS ARGUMENT IS MY FAULT.
IT'S TIME YOU BOTH LEARNED THE TRUTH...

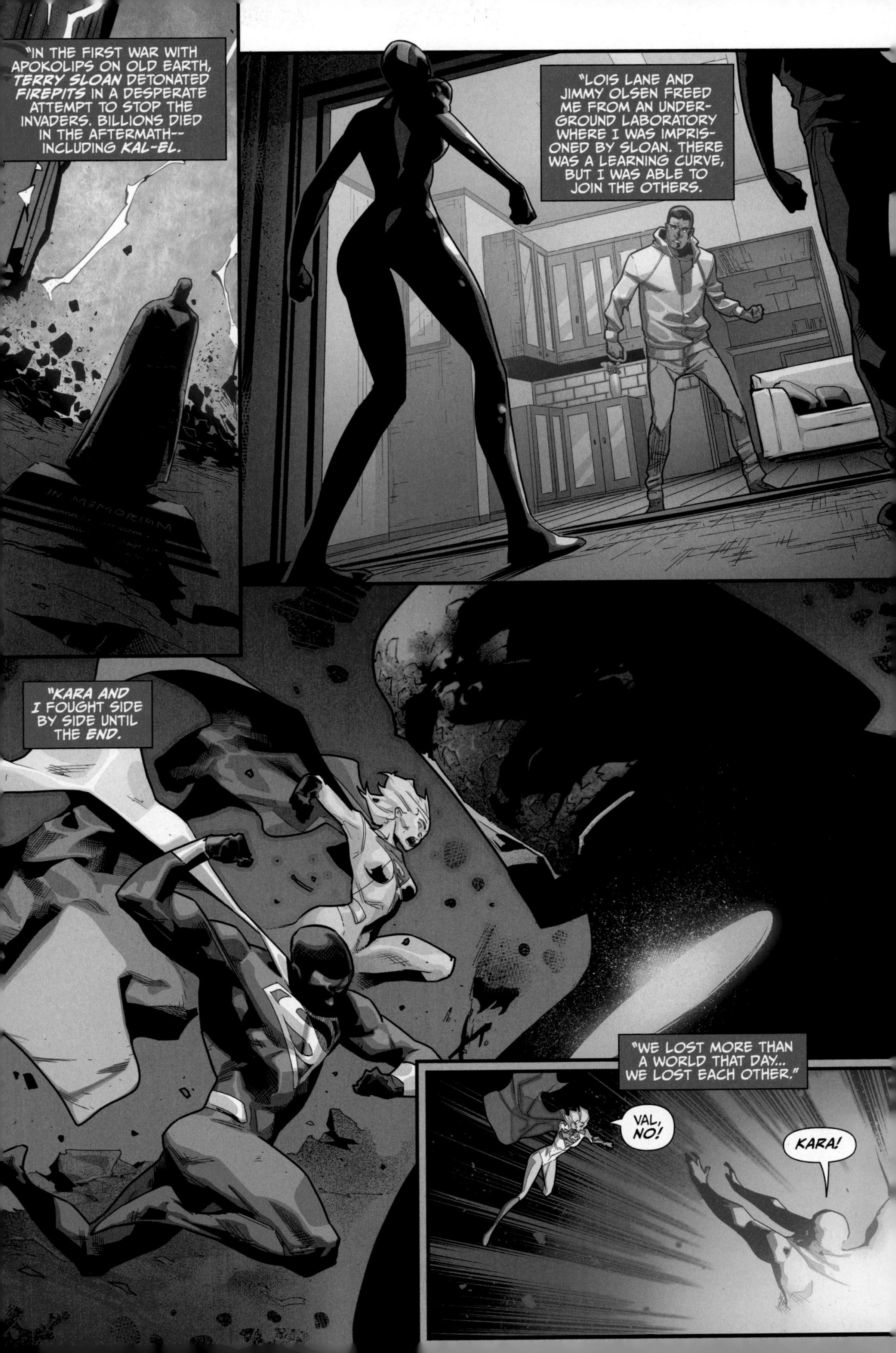
"IN THE FIRST WAR WITH APOKOLIPS ON OLD EARTH, TERRY SLOAN DETONATED FIREPITS IN A DESPERATE ATTEMPT TO STOP THE INVADERS. BILLIONS DIED IN THE AFTERMATH-- INCLUDING KAL-EL.
IN MEMORIAM
"LOIS LANE AND JIMMY OLSEN FREED ME FROM AN UNDER-GROUND LABORATORY WHERE I WAS IMPRIS-ONED BY SLOAN. THERE WAS A LEARNING CURVE, BUT I WAS ABLE TO JOIN THE OTHERS.
"KARA AND I FOUGHT SIDE BY SIDE UNTIL THE END.
"WE LOST MORE THAN A WORLD THAT DAY... WE LOST EACH OTHER."
VAL, NO!
KARA!

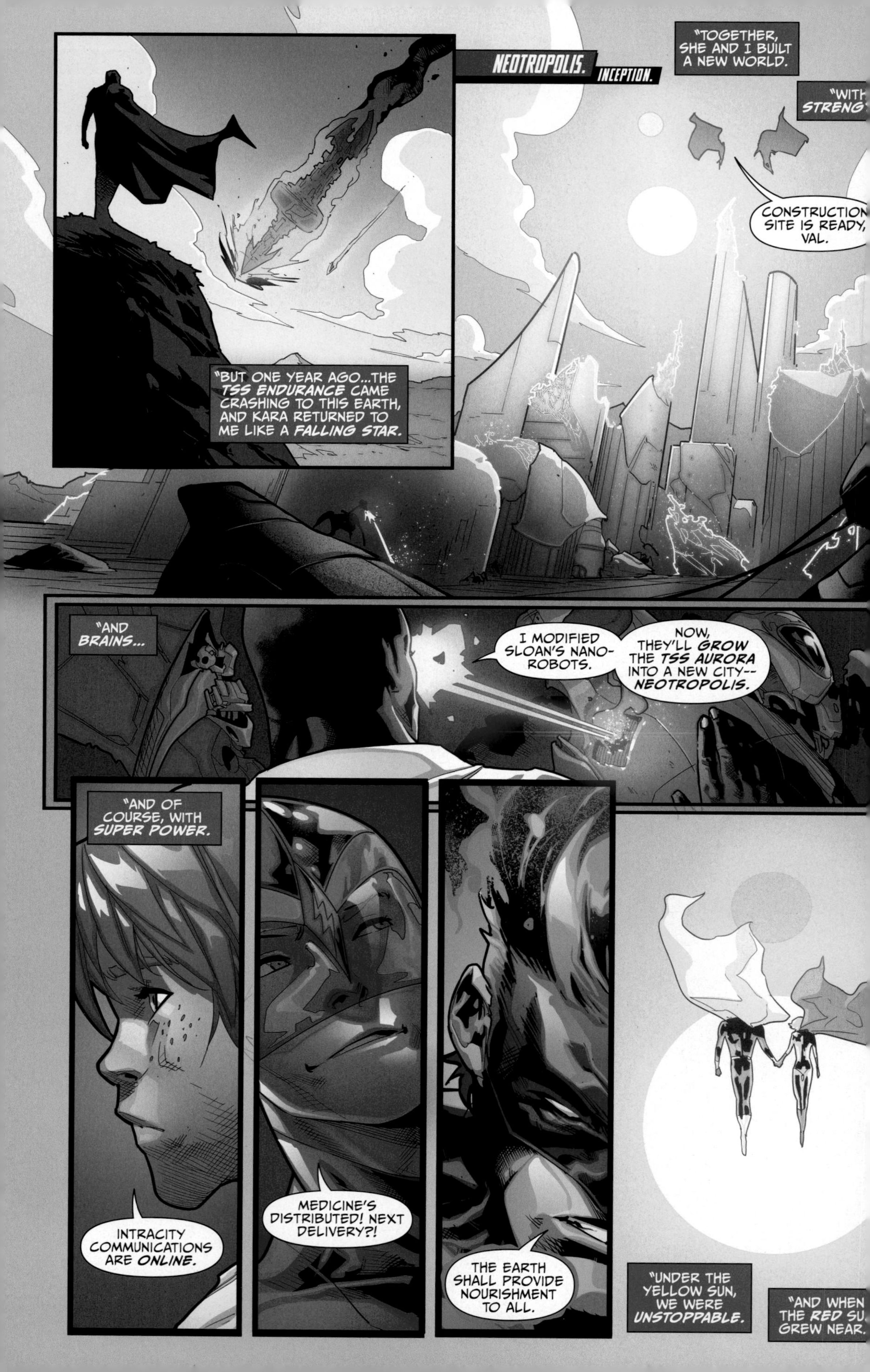
NEOTROPOLIS. INCEPTION.
"BUT ONE YEAR AGO...THE TSS ENDURANCE CAME CRASHING TO THIS EARTH, AND KARA RETURNED TO ME LIKE A FALLING STAR.
"TOGETHER, SHE AND I BUILT A NEW WORLD.
"WITH STRENG
CONSTRUCTION SITE IS READY, VAL.
"AND BRAINS...
I MODIFIED SLOAN'S NANO-ROBOTS.
NOW, THEY'LL GROW THE TSS AURORA INTO A NEW CITY--NEOTROPOLIS.
"AND OF COURSE, WITH SUPER POWER.
INTRACITY COMMUNICATIONS ARE ONLINE.
MEDICINE'S DISTRIBUTED! NEXT DELIVERY?!
THE EARTH SHALL PROVIDE NOURISHMENT TO ALL.
"UNDER THE YELLOW SUN, WE WERE UNSTOPPABLE.
"AND WHEN THE RED SU GREW NEAR.

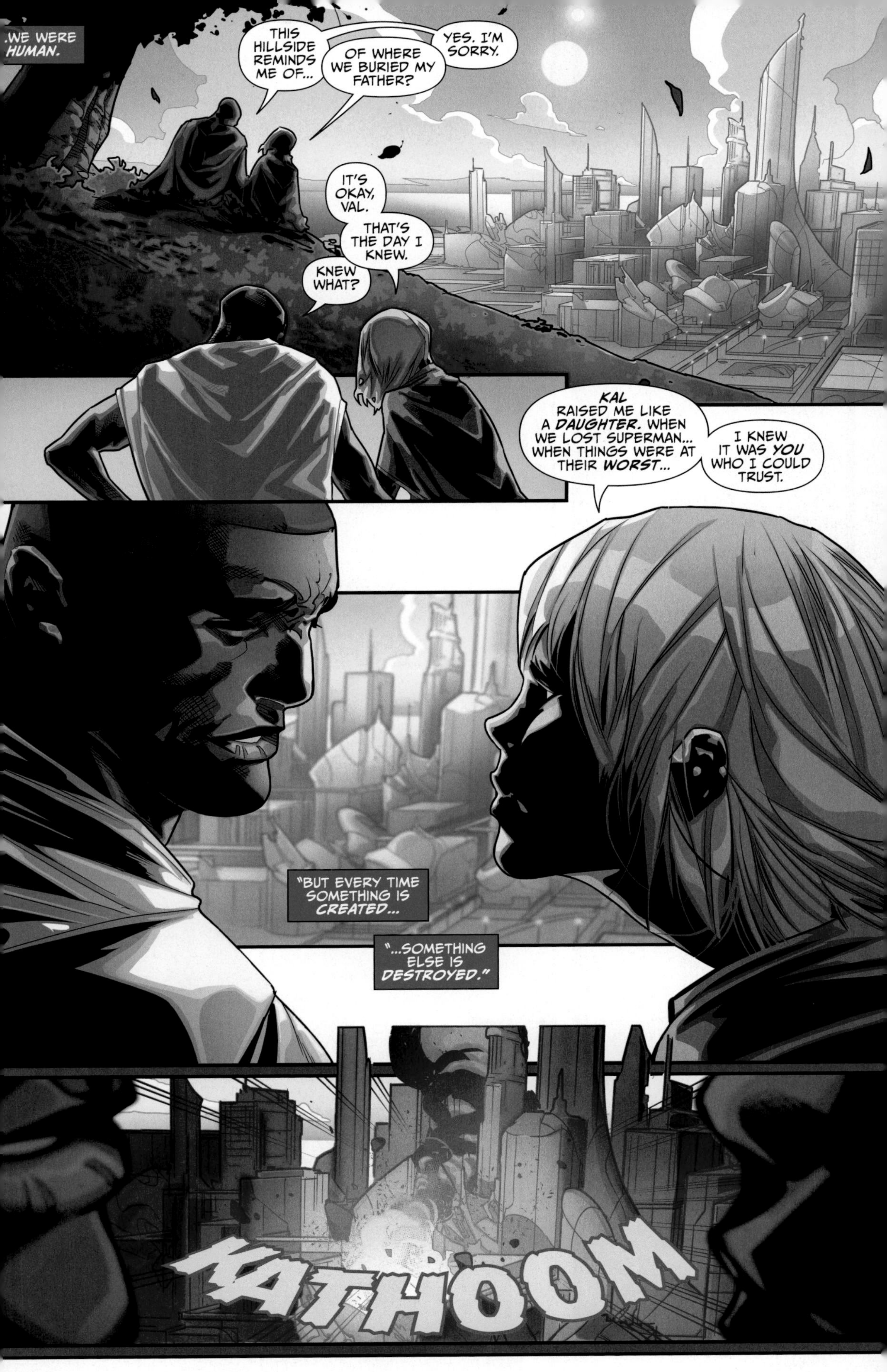
.WE WERE HUMAN.
THIS HILLSIDE REMINDS ME OF...
OF WHERE WE BURIED MY FATHER?
YES. I'M SORRY.
IT'S OKAY, VAL.
THAT'S THE DAY I KNEW.
KNEW WHAT?
KAL RAISED ME LIKE A DAUGHTER. WHEN WE LOST SUPERMAN... WHEN THINGS WERE AT THEIR WORST...
I KNEW IT WAS YOU WHO I COULD TRUST.
"BUT EVERY TIME SOMETHING IS CREATED...
"...SOMETHING ELSE IS DESTROYED."
KATHOOM

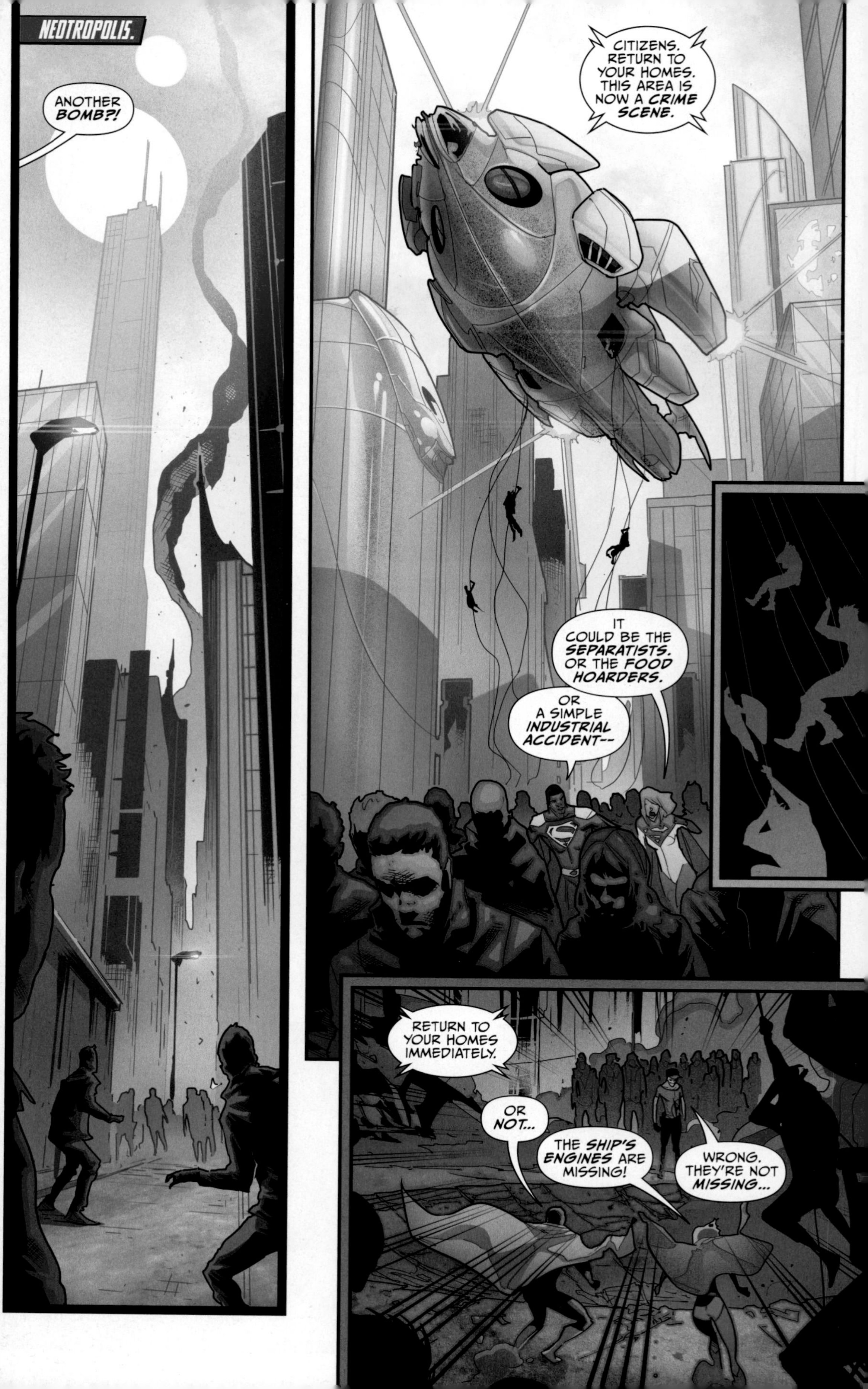
NEOTROPOLIS.
ANOTHER BOMB?!
CITIZENS. RETURN TO YOUR HOMES. THIS AREA IS NOW A CRIME SCENE.
IT COULD BE THE SEPARATISTS. OR THE FOOD HOARDERS.
OR A SIMPLE INDUSTRIAL ACCIDENT--
RETURN TO YOUR HOMES IMMEDIATELY.
OR NOT...
THE SHIP'S ENGINES ARE MISSING!
WRONG. THEY'RE NOT MISSING...

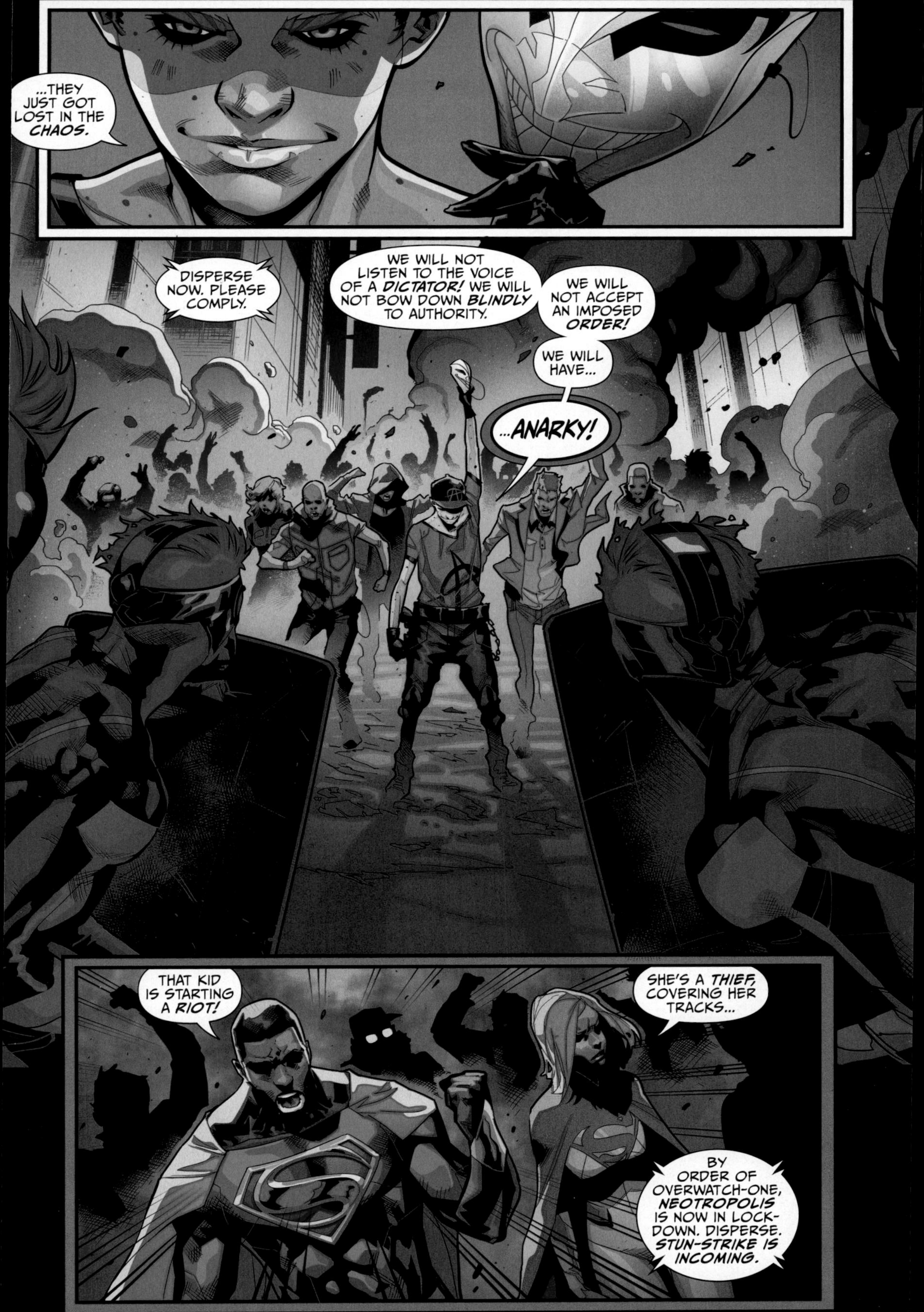
...THEY JUST GOT LOST IN THE *CHAOS.*
DISPERSE NOW. PLEASE COMPLY.
WE WILL NOT LISTEN TO THE VOICE OF A *DICTATOR!* WE WILL NOT BOW DOWN *BLINDLY* TO AUTHORITY.
WE WILL NOT ACCEPT AN IMPOSED *ORDER!*
WE WILL HAVE...
...ANARKY!
THAT KID IS STARTING A *RIOT!*
SHE'S A *THIEF,* COVERING HER TRACKS...
BY ORDER OF OVERWATCH-ONE, ***NEOTROPOLIS*** IS NOW IN LOCK-DOWN. DISPERSE. ***STUN-STRIKE IS INCOMING.***

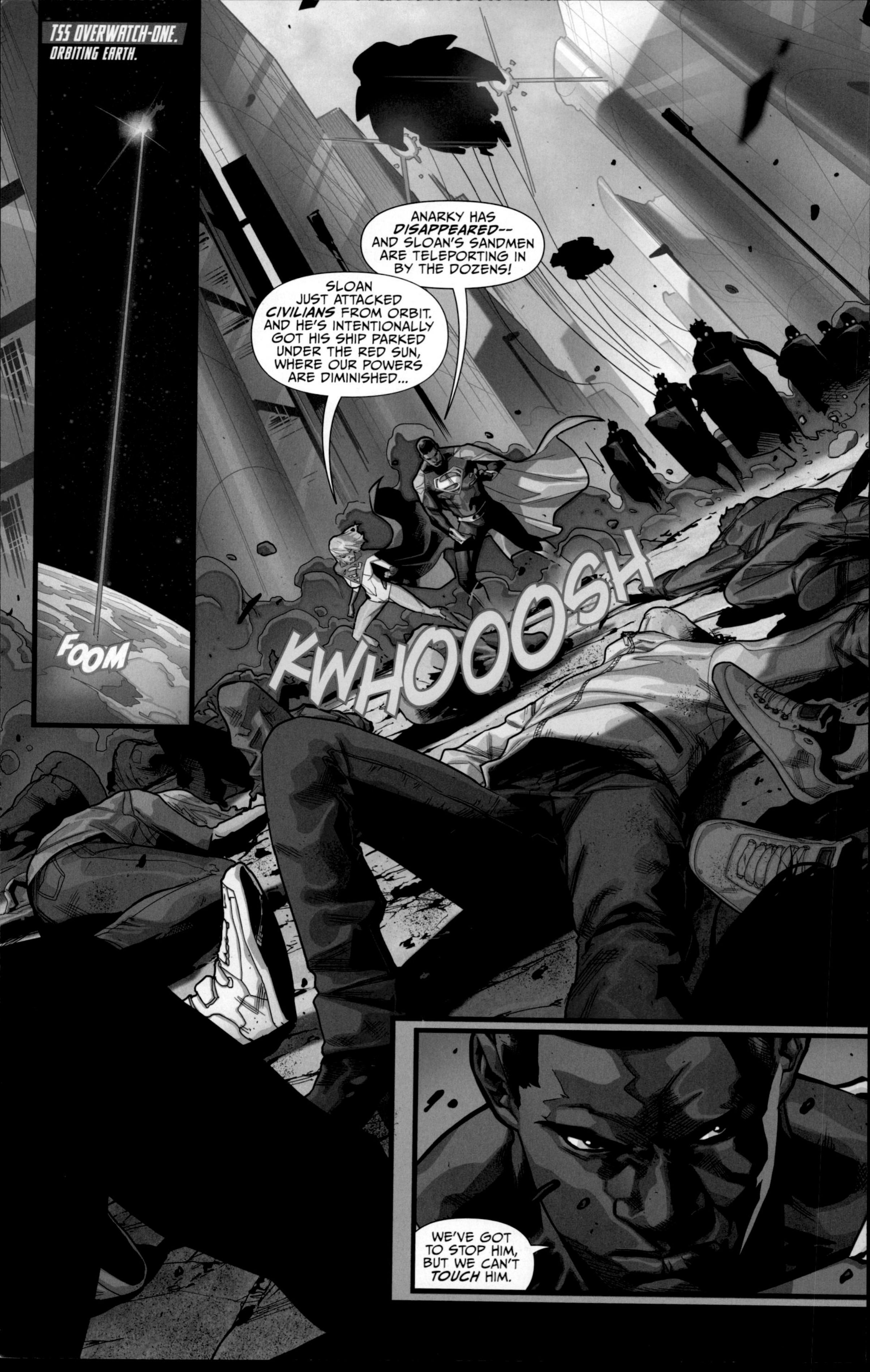
TSS OVERWATCH-ONE.
ORBITING EARTH.
FOOM
ANARKY HAS DISAPPEARED-- AND SLOAN'S SANDMEN ARE TELEPORTING IN BY THE DOZENS!
SLOAN JUST ATTACKED CIVILIANS FROM ORBIT. AND HE'S INTENTIONALLY GOT HIS SHIP PARKED UNDER THE RED SUN, WHERE OUR POWERS ARE DIMINISHED...
KWHOOOOSH
WE'VE GOT TO STOP HIM, BUT WE CAN'T TOUCH HIM.

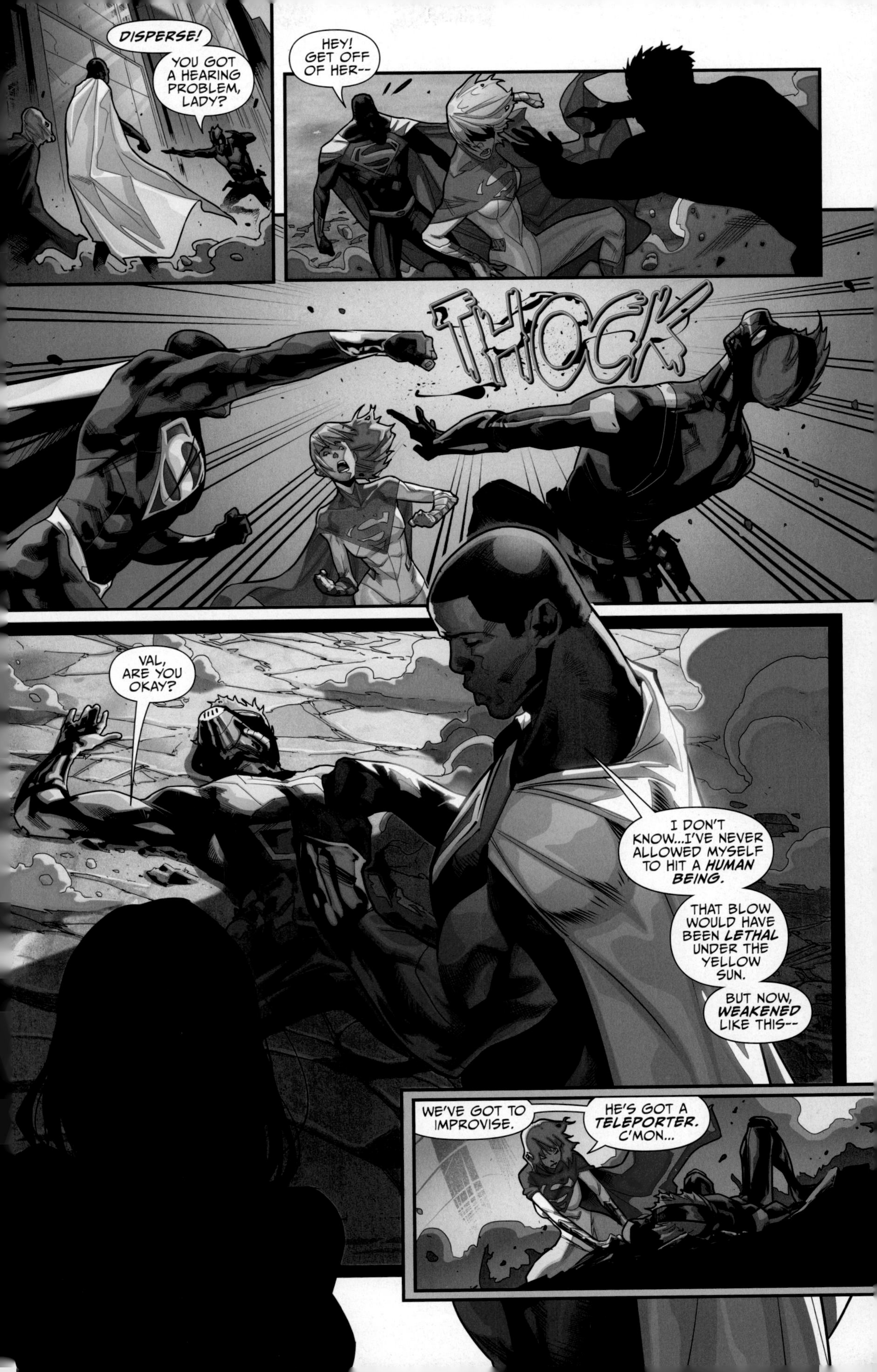
DISPERSE!
YOU GOT A HEARING PROBLEM, LADY?
HEY! GET OFF OF HER--
THOCK
VAL, ARE YOU OKAY?
I DON'T KNOW...I'VE NEVER ALLOWED MYSELF TO HIT A HUMAN BEING.
THAT BLOW WOULD HAVE BEEN LETHAL UNDER THE YELLOW SUN.
BUT NOW, WEAKENED LIKE THIS--
WE'VE GOT TO IMPROVISE.
HE'S GOT A TELEPORTER. C'MON...

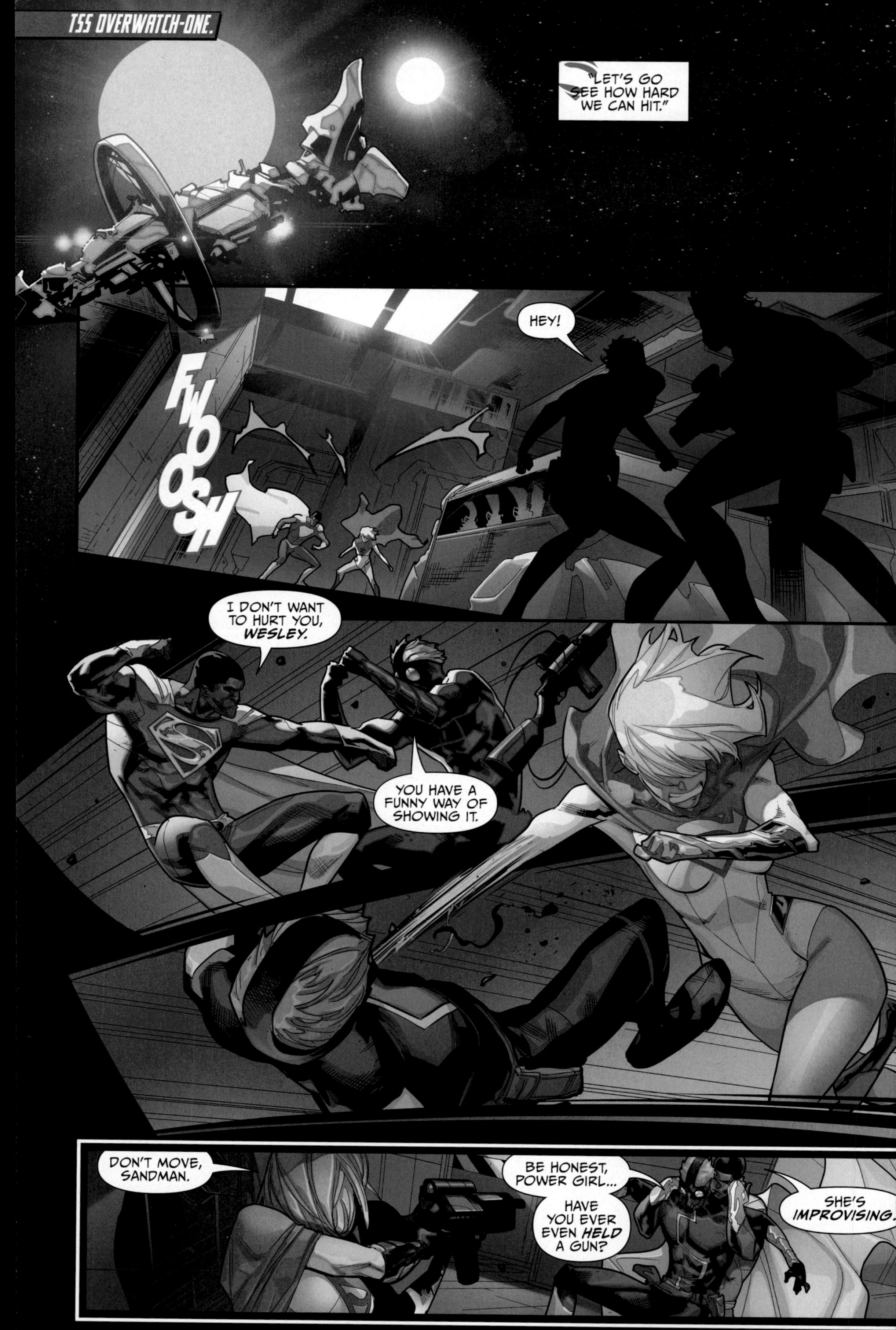
TSS OVERWATCH-ONE.
"LET'S GO SEE HOW HARD WE CAN HIT."
FWOOOSH
HEY!
I DON'T WANT TO HURT YOU, WESLEY.
YOU HAVE A FUNNY WAY OF SHOWING IT.
DON'T MOVE, SANDMAN.
BE HONEST, POWER GIRL...
HAVE YOU EVER EVEN HELD A GUN?
SHE'S IMPROVISING.

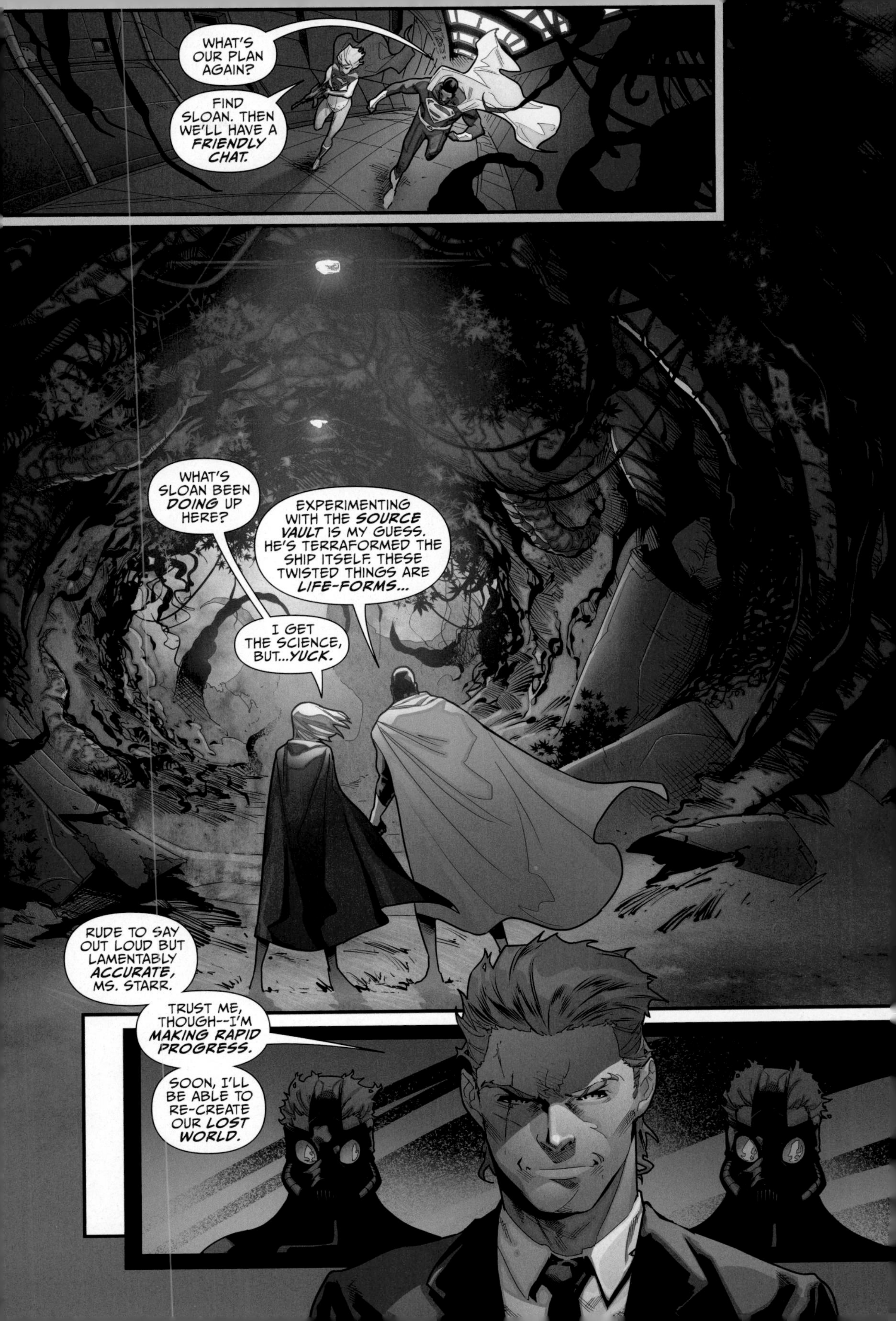
WHAT'S OUR PLAN AGAIN?
FIND SLOAN. THEN WE'LL HAVE A FRIENDLY CHAT.
WHAT'S SLOAN BEEN DOING UP HERE?
EXPERIMENTING WITH THE SOURCE VAULT IS MY GUESS. HE'S TERRAFORMED THE SHIP ITSELF. THESE TWISTED THINGS ARE LIFE-FORMS...
I GET THE SCIENCE, BUT...YUCK.
RUDE TO SAY OUT LOUD BUT LAMENTABLY ACCURATE, MS. STARR.
TRUST ME, THOUGH--I'M MAKING RAPID PROGRESS.
SOON, I'LL BE ABLE TO RE-CREATE OUR LOST WORLD.

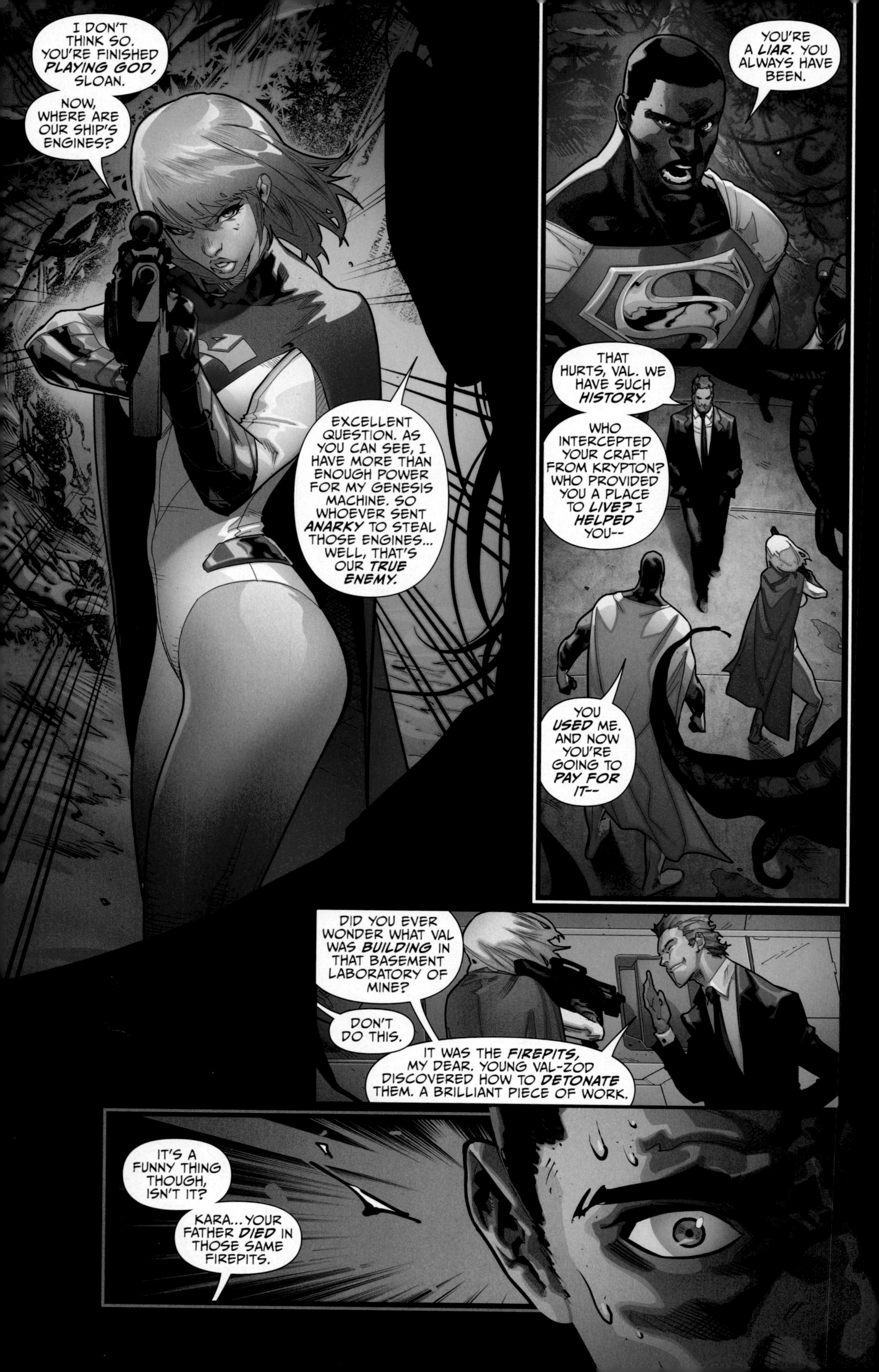

I DON'T THINK SO. YOU'RE FINISHED *PLAYING GOD*, SLOAN.
NOW, WHERE ARE OUR SHIP'S ENGINES?
EXCELLENT QUESTION. AS YOU CAN SEE, I HAVE MORE THAN ENOUGH POWER FOR MY GENESIS MACHINE. SO WHOEVER SENT *ANARKY* TO STEAL THOSE ENGINES... WELL, THAT'S OUR *TRUE ENEMY.*
YOU'RE A *LIAR.* YOU ALWAYS HAVE BEEN.
THAT HURTS, VAL. WE HAVE SUCH *HISTORY.*
WHO INTERCEPTED YOUR CRAFT FROM KRYPTON? WHO PROVIDED YOU A PLACE TO *LIVE?* I *HELPED* YOU--
YOU *USED* ME. AND NOW YOU'RE GOING TO *PAY FOR IT--*
DID YOU EVER WONDER WHAT VAL WAS *BUILDING* IN THAT BASEMENT LABORATORY OF MINE?
DON'T DO THIS.
IT WAS THE *FIREPITS,* MY DEAR. YOUNG VAL-ZOD DISCOVERED HOW TO *DETONATE* THEM. A BRILLIANT PIECE OF WORK.
IT'S A FUNNY THING THOUGH, ISN'T IT?
KARA...YOUR FATHER *DIED* IN THOSE SAME FIREPITS.

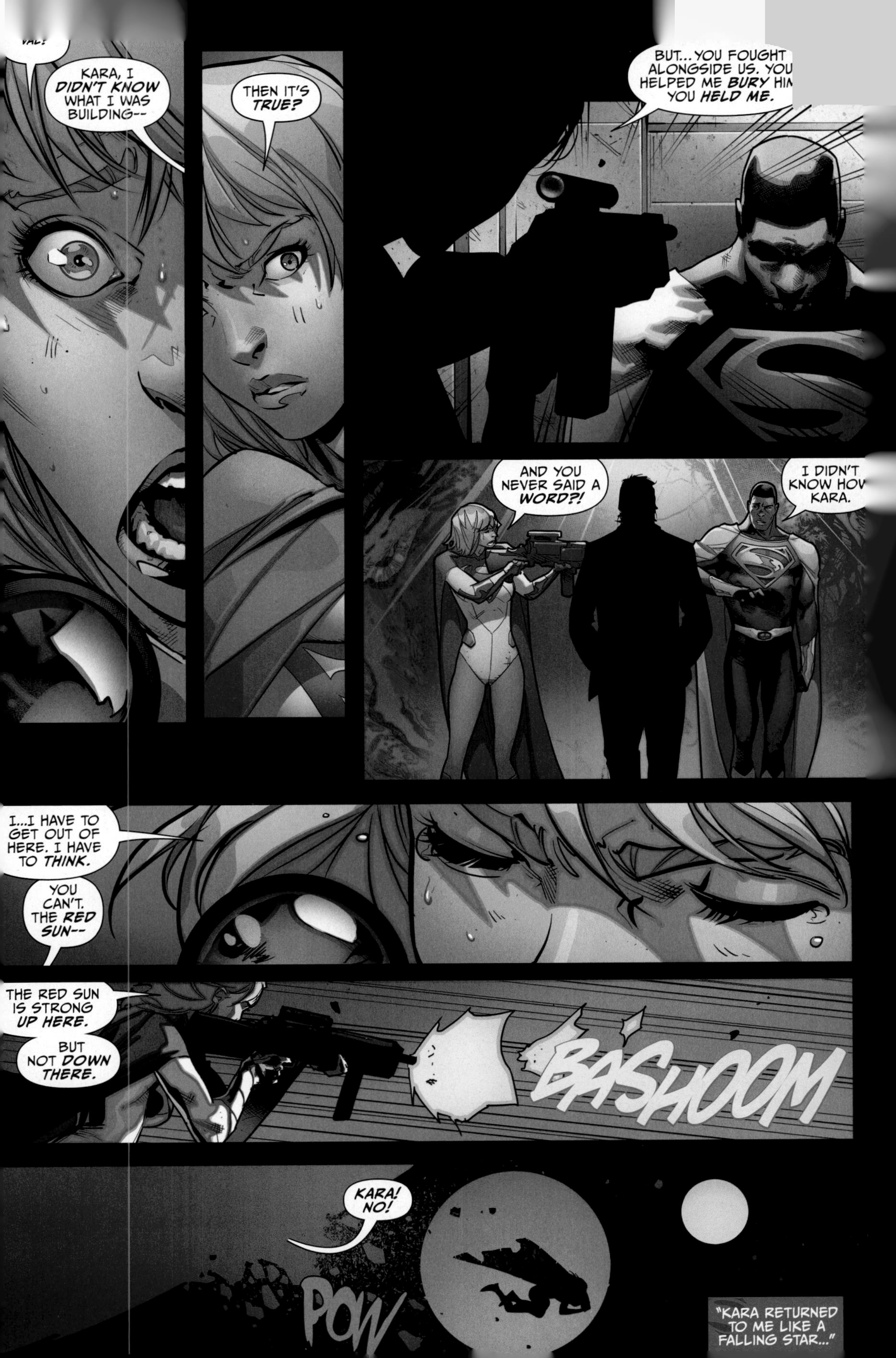
VAL!
KARA, I DIDN'T KNOW WHAT I WAS BUILDING--
THEN IT'S TRUE?
BUT...YOU FOUGHT ALONGSIDE US. YOU HELPED ME BURY HIM. YOU HELD ME.
AND YOU NEVER SAID A WORD?!
I DIDN'T KNOW HOW, KARA.
I...I HAVE TO GET OUT OF HERE. I HAVE TO THINK.
YOU CAN'T. THE RED SUN--
THE RED SUN IS STRONG UP HERE.
BUT NOT DOWN THERE.
BASHOOM
KARA! NO!
POW
"KARA RETURNED TO ME LIKE A FALLING STAR..."

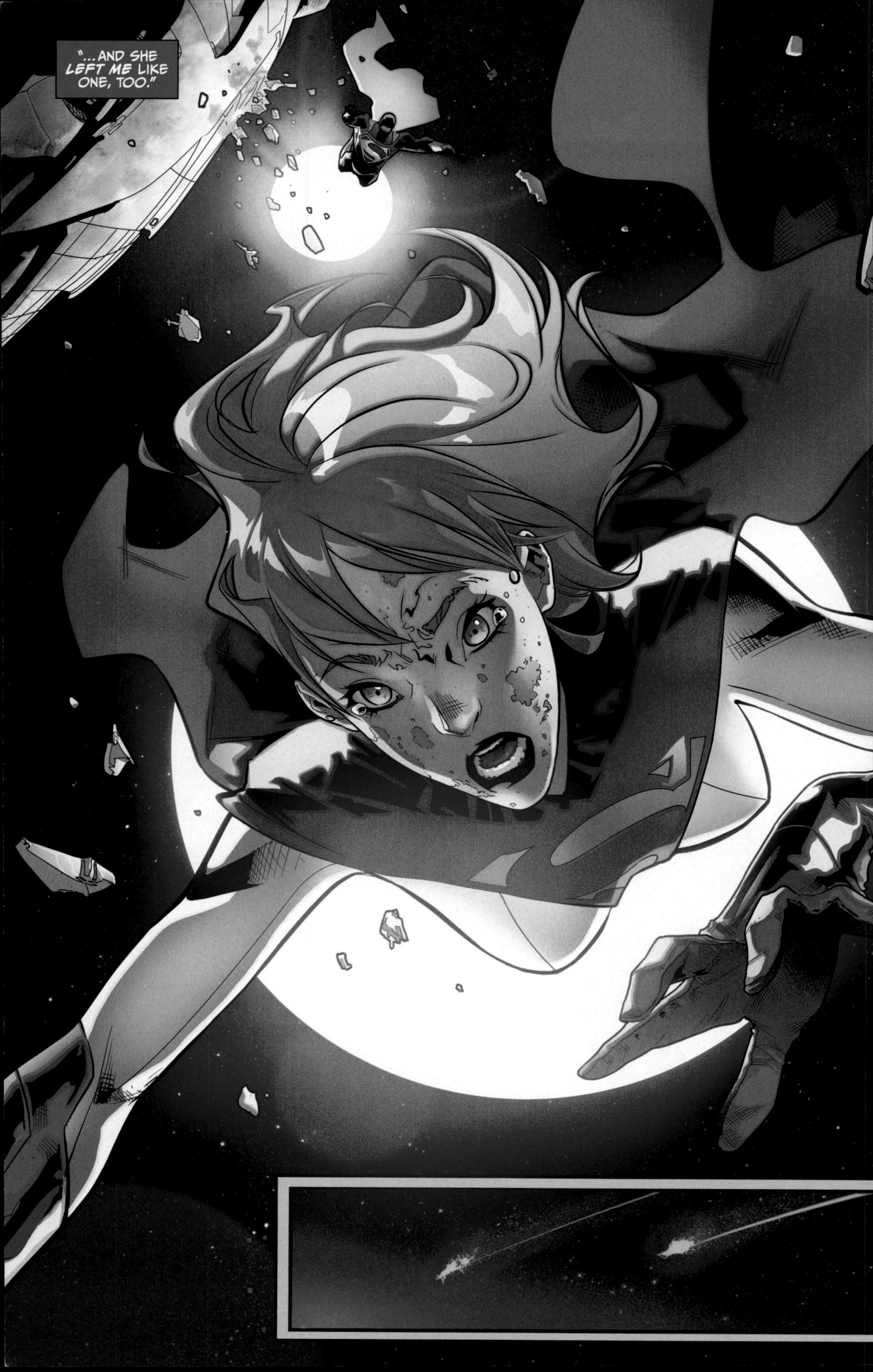
"...AND SHE LEFT ME LIKE ONE, TOO."

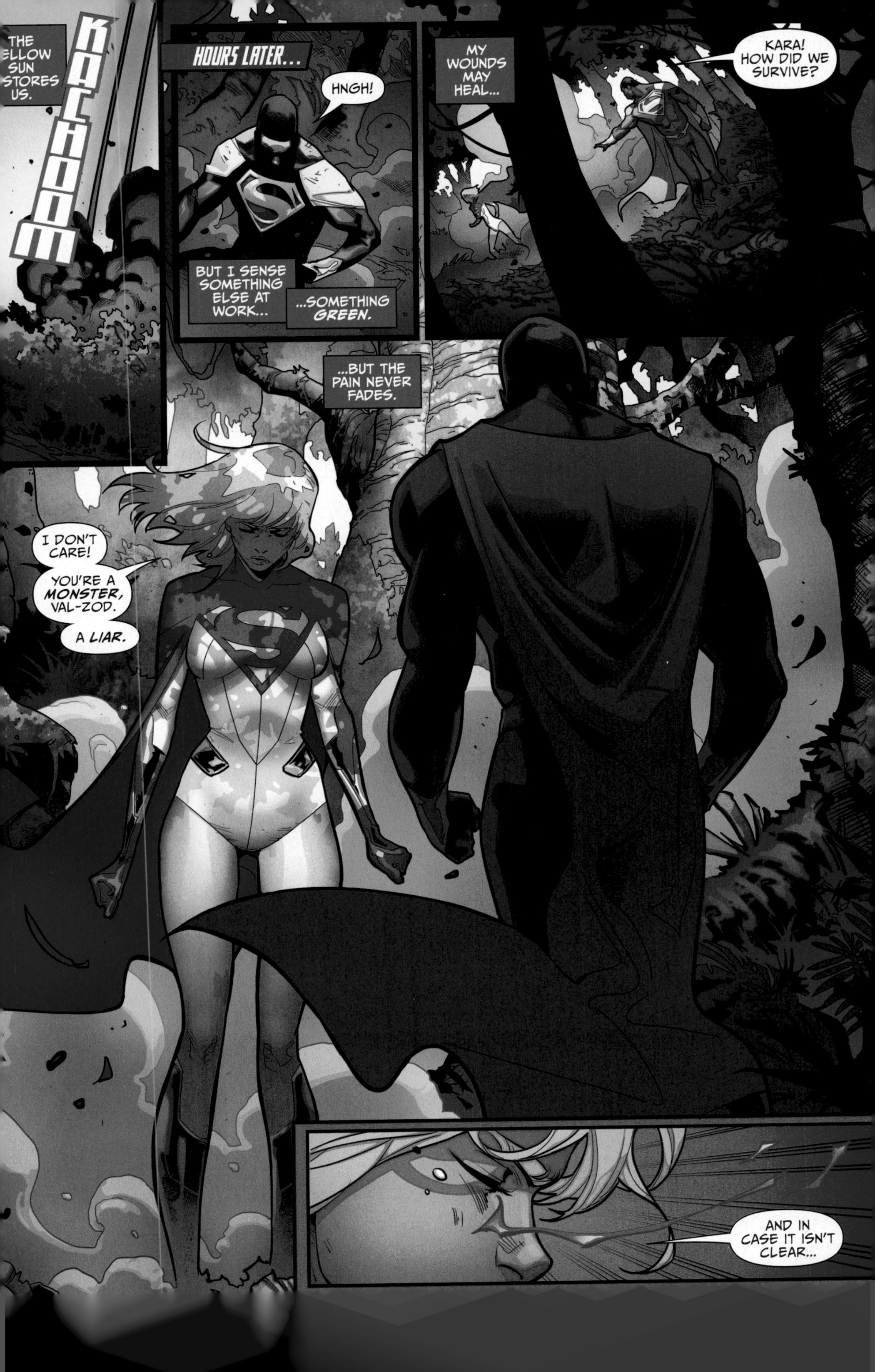

THE ELLOW SUN STORES US.
KACHOOM
HOURS LATER...
HNGH!
BUT I SENSE SOMETHING ELSE AT WORK...
...SOMETHING GREEN.
MY WOUNDS MAY HEAL...
KARA! HOW DID WE SURVIVE?
...BUT THE PAIN NEVER FADES.
I DON'T CARE!
YOU'RE A MONSTER, VAL-ZOD.
A LIAR.
AND IN CASE IT ISN'T CLEAR...

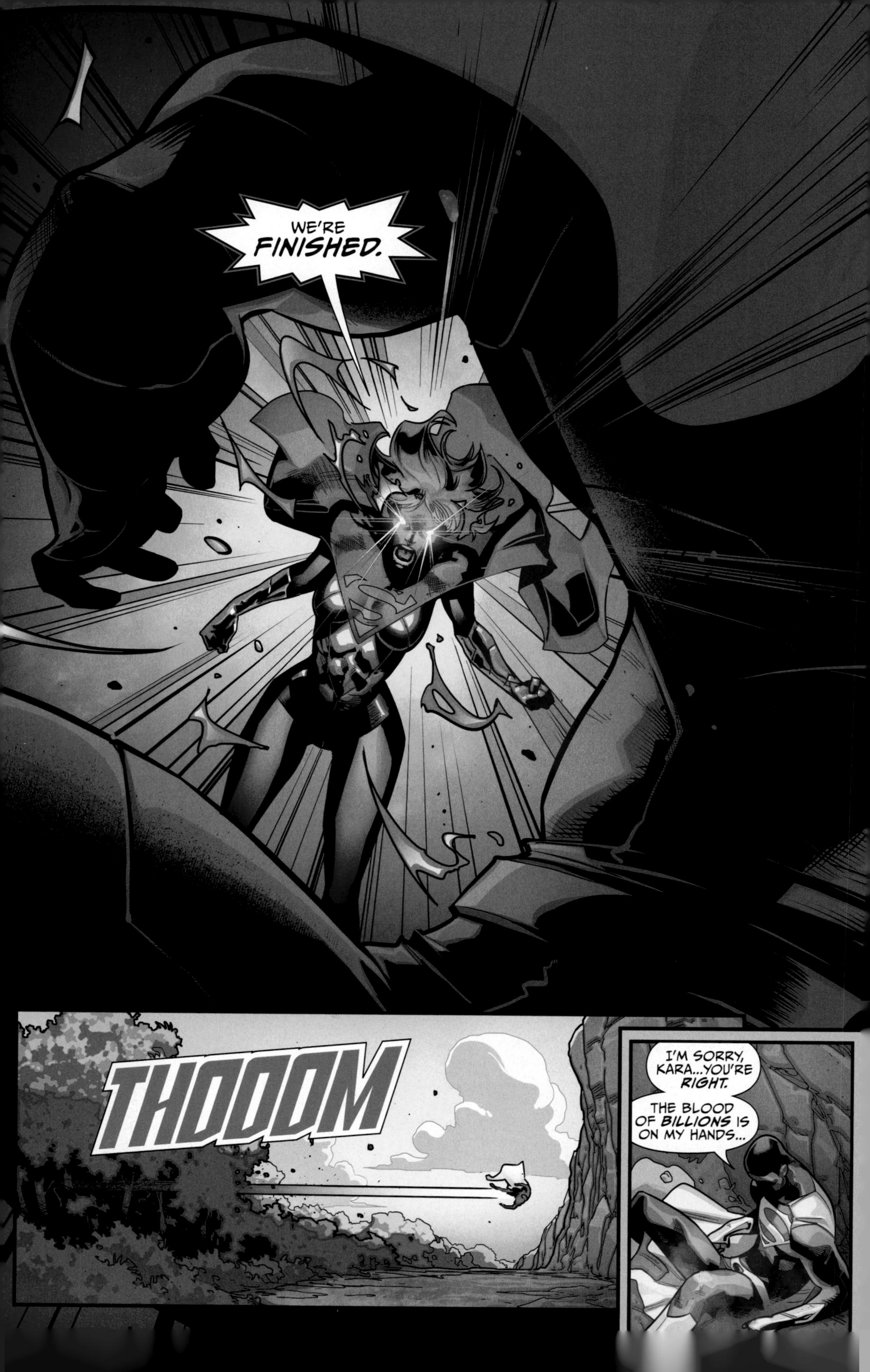
WE'RE FINISHED.
THOOOM
I'M SORRY, KARA...YOU'RE RIGHT.
THE BLOOD OF BILLIONS IS ON MY HANDS...

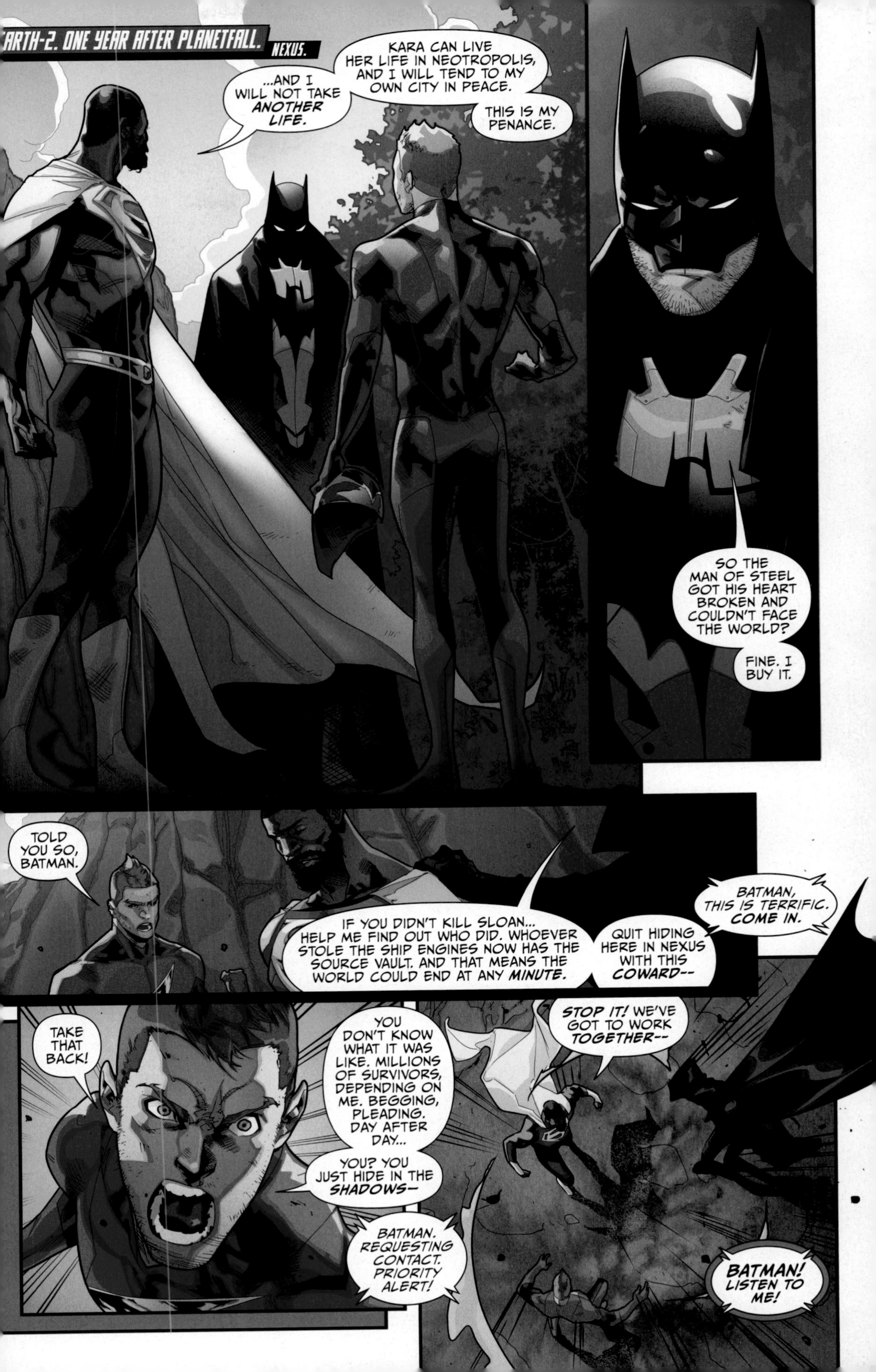

EARTH-2. ONE YEAR AFTER PLANETFALL.
NEXUS.
...AND I WILL NOT TAKE ANOTHER LIFE.
KARA CAN LIVE HER LIFE IN NEOTROPOLIS, AND I WILL TEND TO MY OWN CITY IN PEACE.
THIS IS MY PENANCE.
SO THE MAN OF STEEL GOT HIS HEART BROKEN AND COULDN'T FACE THE WORLD?
FINE. I BUY IT.
TOLD YOU SO, BATMAN.
IF YOU DIDN'T KILL SLOAN... HELP ME FIND OUT WHO DID. WHOEVER STOLE THE SHIP ENGINES NOW HAS THE SOURCE VAULT. AND THAT MEANS THE WORLD COULD END AT ANY MINUTE.
QUIT HIDING HERE IN NEXUS WITH THIS COWARD--
BATMAN, THIS IS TERRIFIC. COME IN.
TAKE THAT BACK!
YOU DON'T KNOW WHAT IT WAS LIKE. MILLIONS OF SURVIVORS, DEPENDING ON ME. BEGGING, PLEADING. DAY AFTER DAY...
YOU? YOU JUST HIDE IN THE SHADOWS—
BATMAN. REQUESTING CONTACT. PRIORITY ALERT!
STOP IT! WE'VE GOT TO WORK TOGETHER--
BATMAN! LISTEN TO ME!

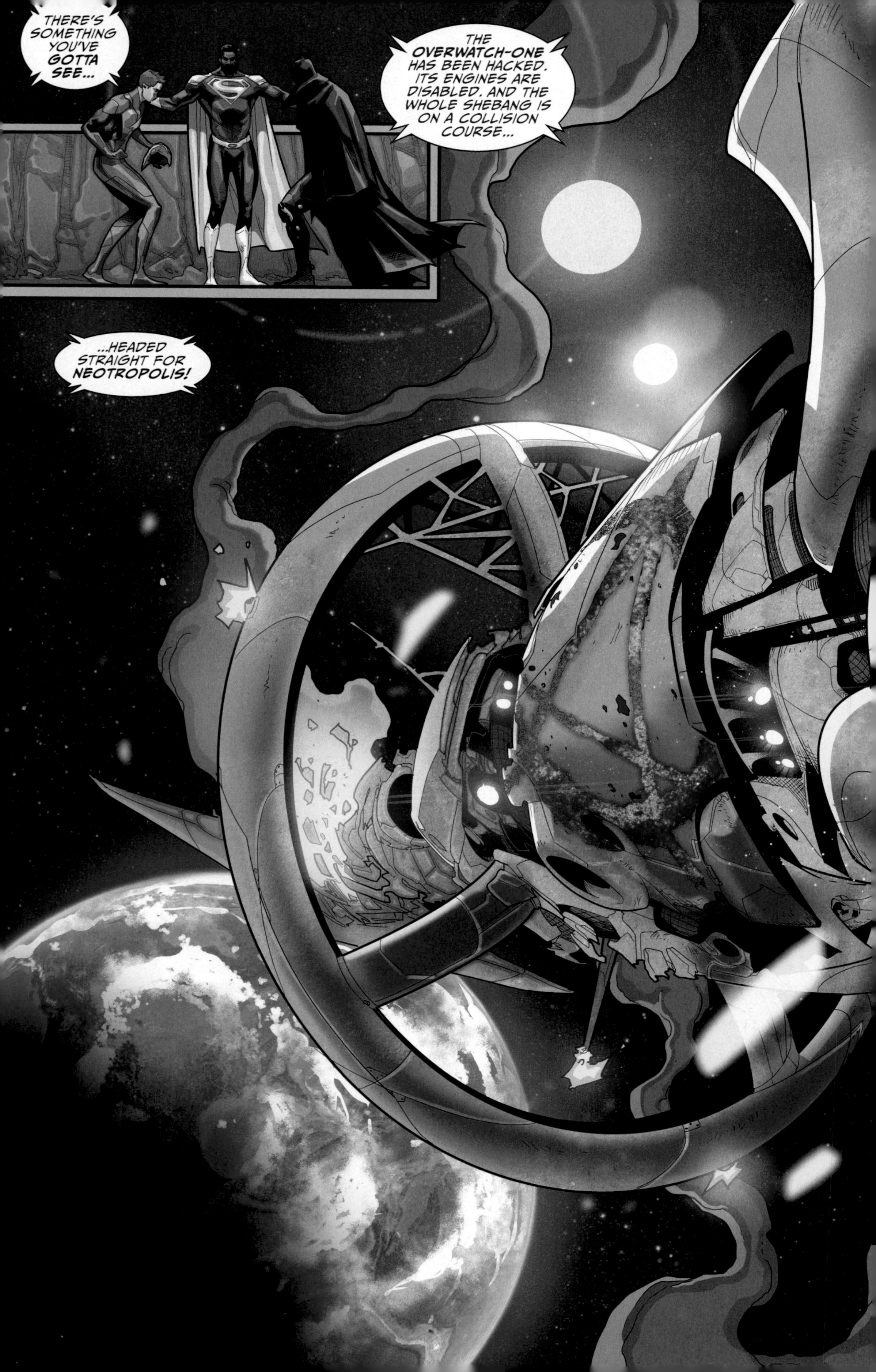
THERE'S SOMETHING YOU'VE GOTTA SEE...
THE OVERWATCH-ONE HAS BEEN HACKED. ITS ENGINES ARE DISABLED. AND THE WHOLE SHEBANG IS ON A COLLISION COURSE...
...HEADED STRAIGHT FOR NEOTROPOLIS!

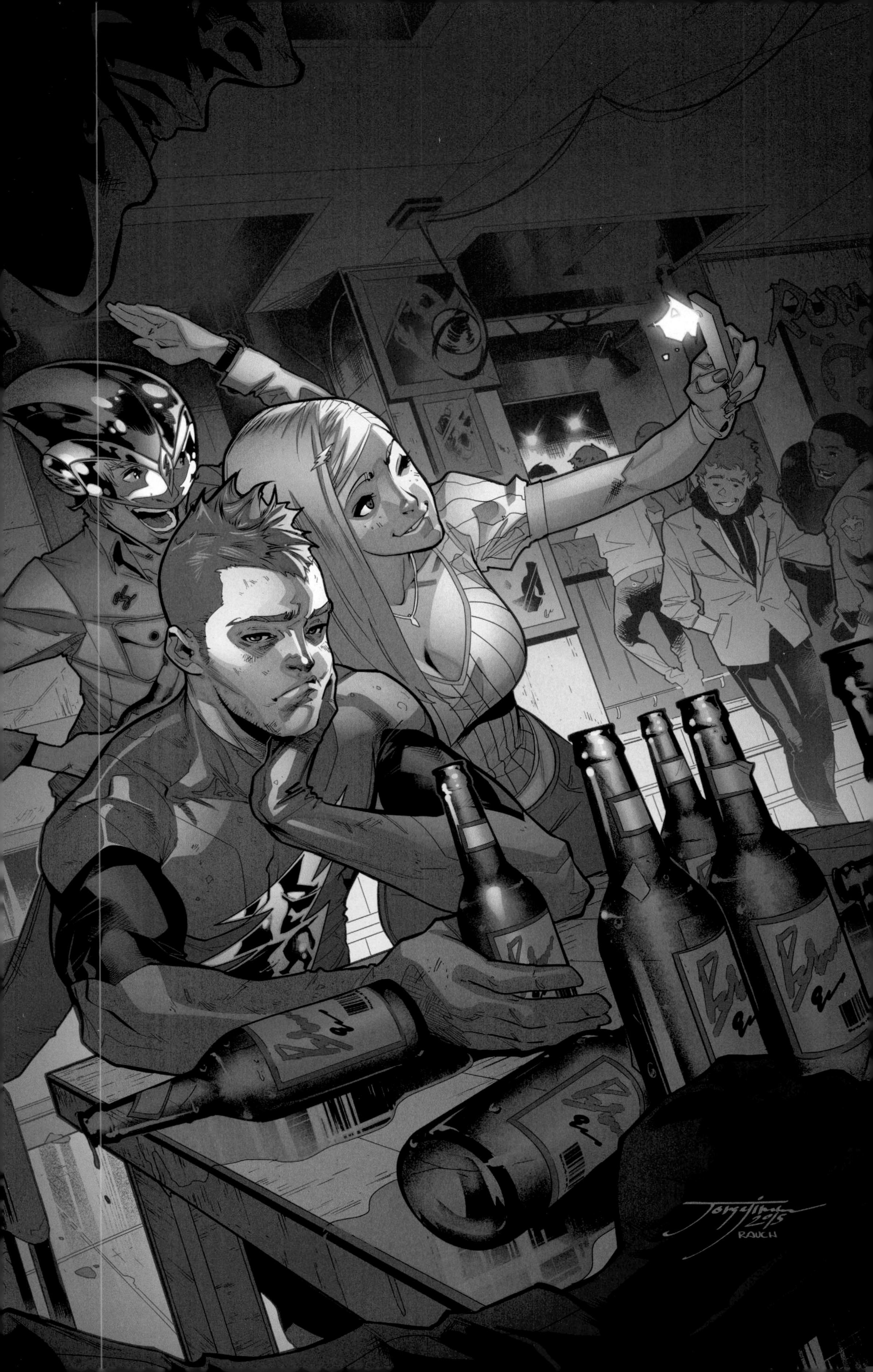
RAUCH

FAME

DANIEL H. WILSON writer JORGE JIMENEZ artist ALEJANDRO SANCHEZ colorist TRAVIS LANHAM letterer cover by JIMENEZ & RAUCH

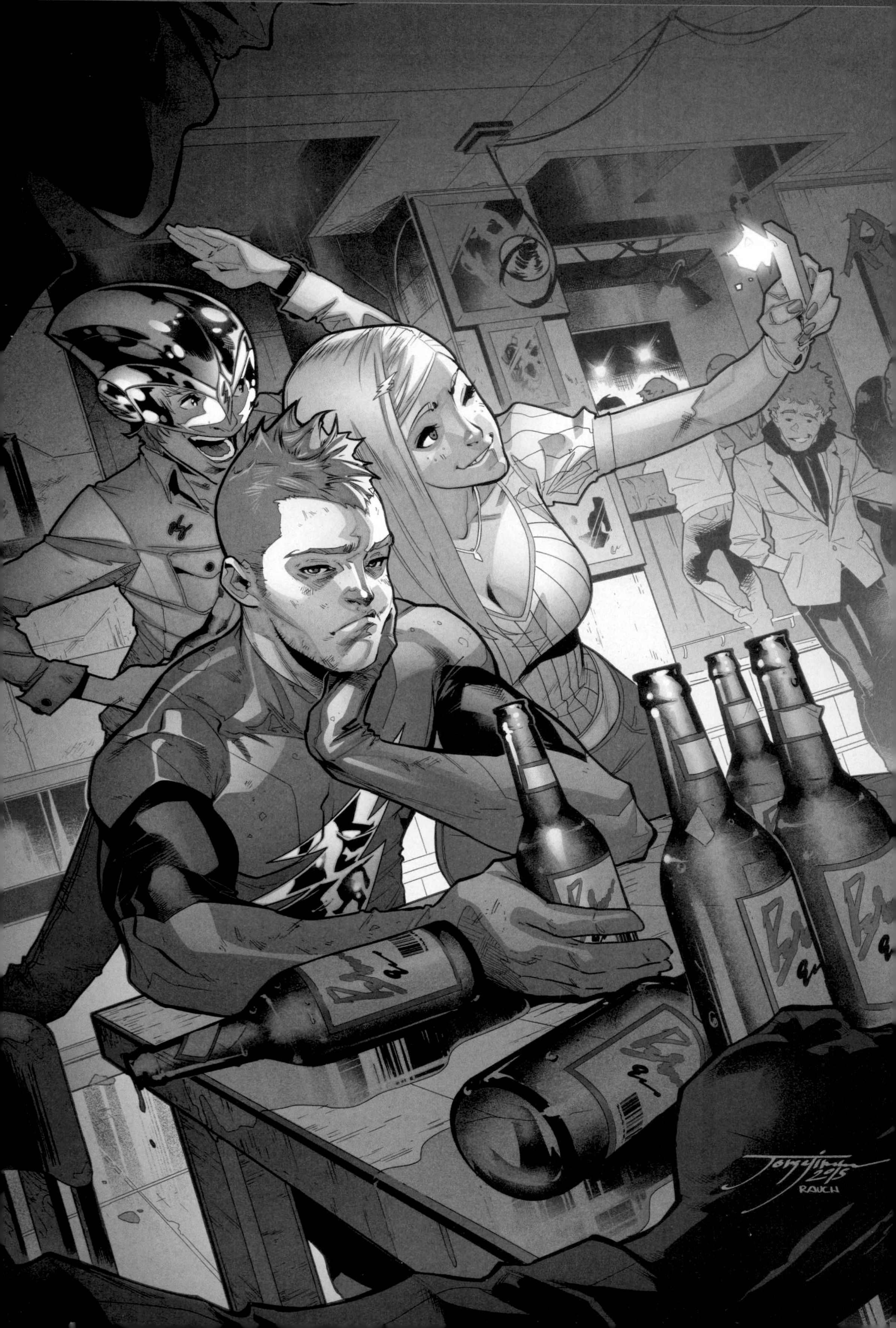

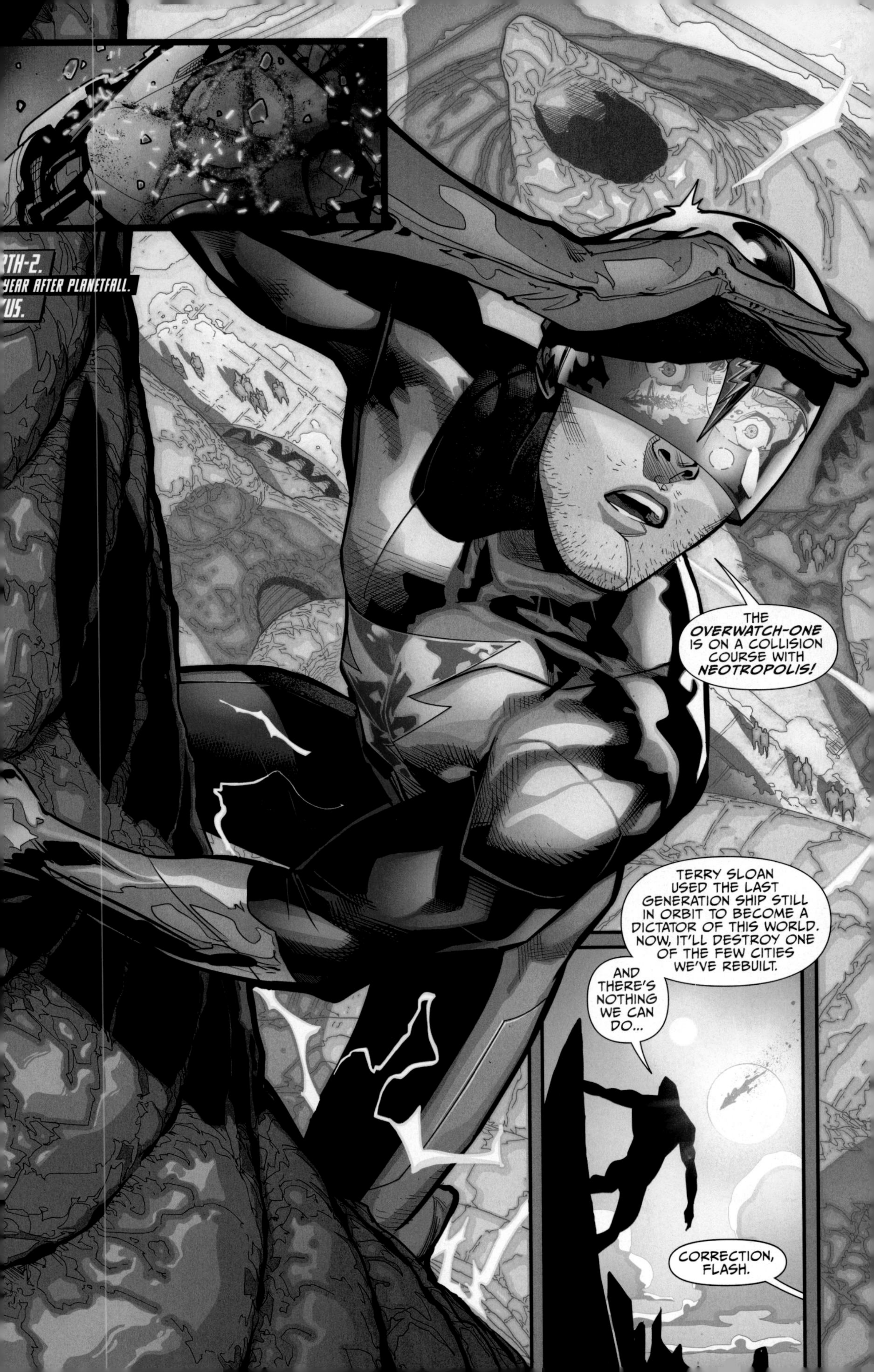
RTH-2.
YEAR AFTER PLANETFALL.
US.
THE OVERWATCH-ONE IS ON A COLLISION COURSE WITH NEOTROPOLIS!
TERRY SLOAN USED THE LAST GENERATION SHIP STILL IN ORBIT TO BECOME A DICTATOR OF THIS WORLD. NOW, IT'LL DESTROY ONE OF THE FEW CITIES WE'VE REBUILT.
AND THERE'S NOTHING WE CAN DO...
CORRECTION, FLASH.

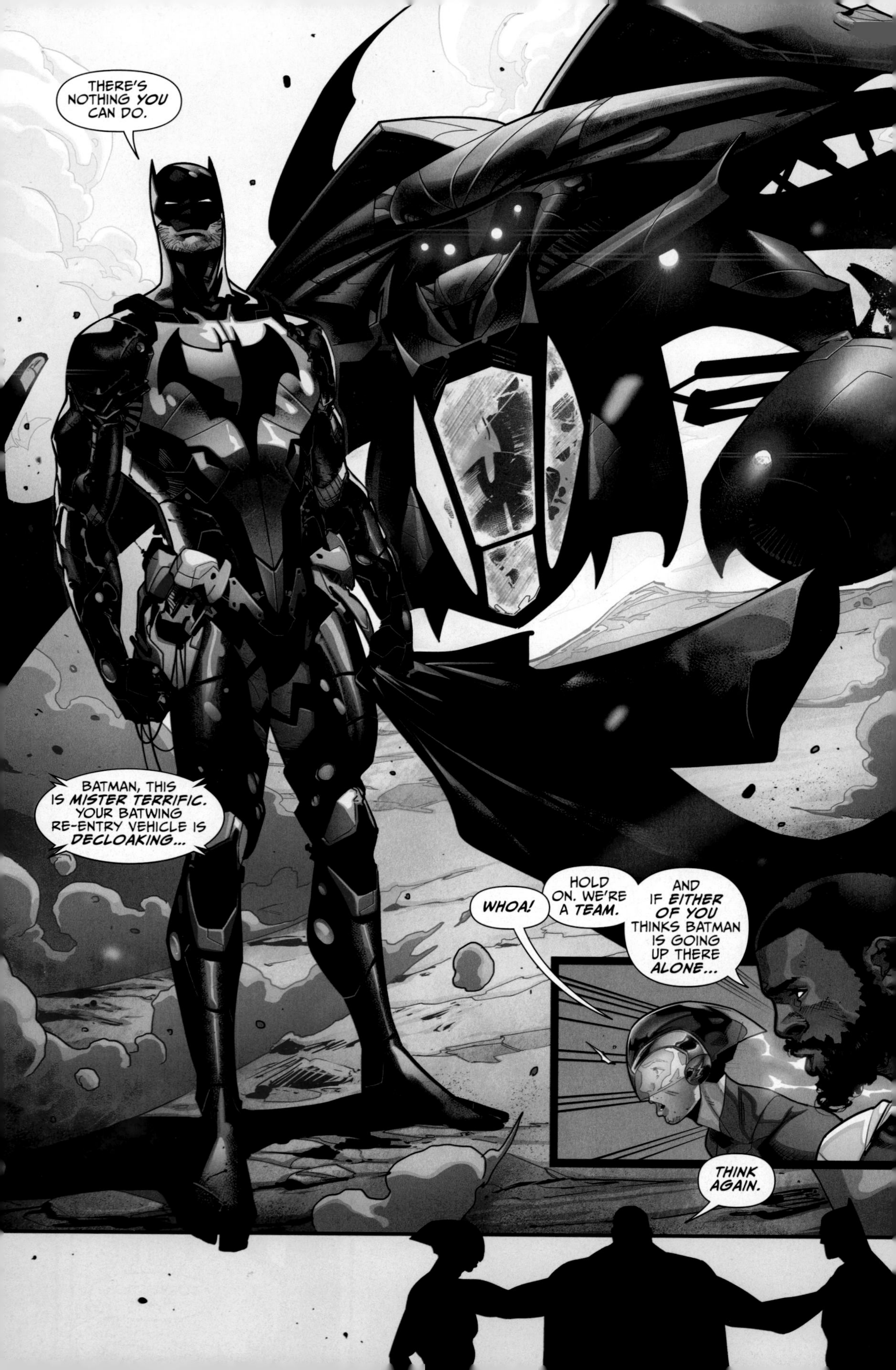

THERE'S NOTHING YOU CAN DO.
BATMAN, THIS IS MISTER TERRIFIC. YOUR BATWING RE-ENTRY VEHICLE IS DECLOAKING...
WHOA!
HOLD ON. WE'RE A TEAM.
AND IF EITHER OF YOU THINKS BATMAN IS GOING UP THERE ALONE...
THINK AGAIN.

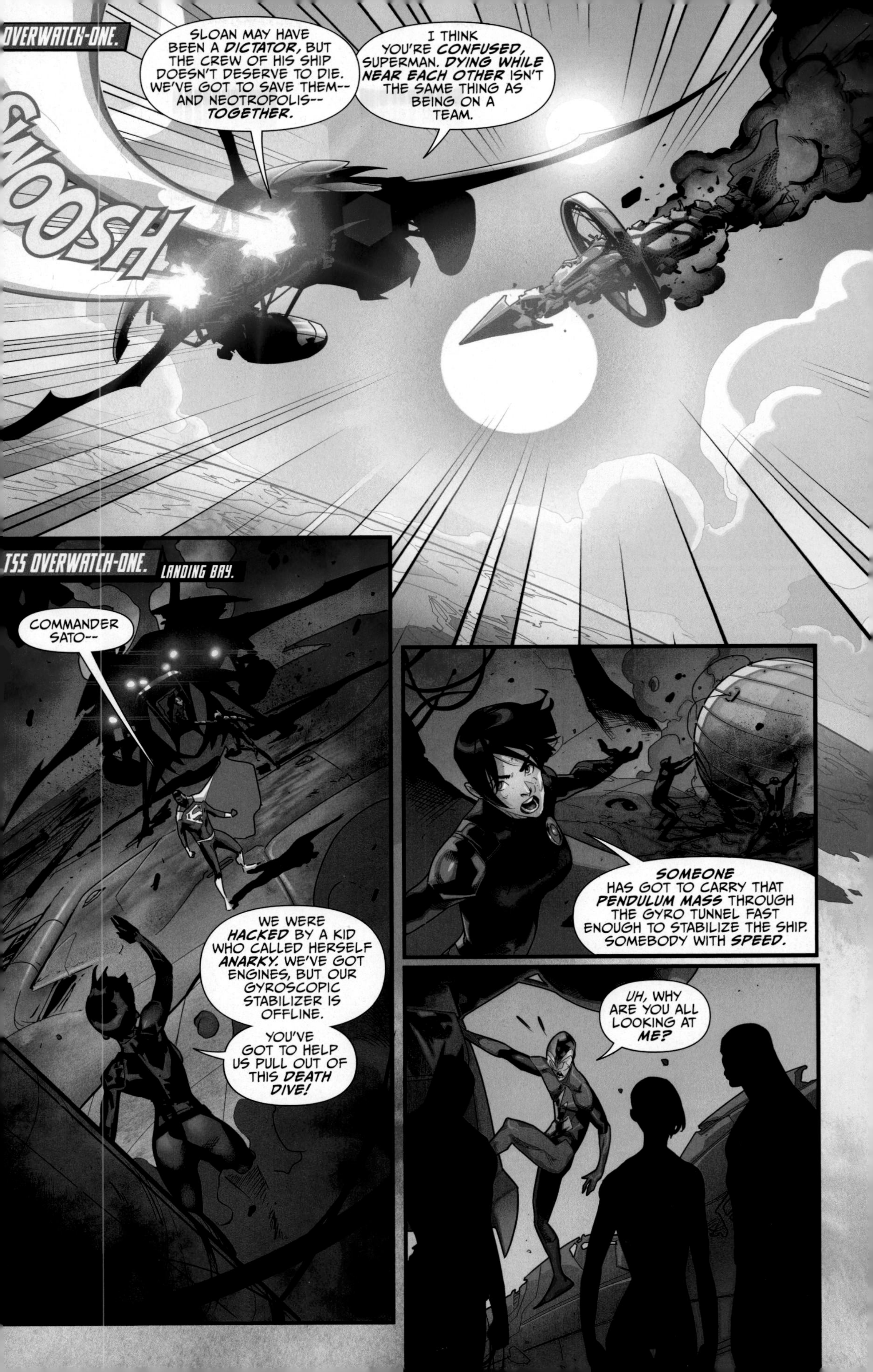
OVERWATCH-ONE.
SLOAN MAY HAVE BEEN A DICTATOR, BUT THE CREW OF HIS SHIP DOESN'T DESERVE TO DIE. WE'VE GOT TO SAVE THEM-- AND NEOTROPOLIS-- TOGETHER.
I THINK YOU'RE CONFUSED, SUPERMAN. DYING WHILE NEAR EACH OTHER ISN'T THE SAME THING AS BEING ON A TEAM.
SWOOSH
TSS OVERWATCH-ONE. LANDING BAY.
COMMANDER SATO--
WE WERE HACKED BY A KID WHO CALLED HERSELF ANARKY. WE'VE GOT ENGINES, BUT OUR GYROSCOPIC STABILIZER IS OFFLINE.
YOU'VE GOT TO HELP US PULL OUT OF THIS DEATH DIVE!
SOMEONE HAS GOT TO CARRY THAT PENDULUM MASS THROUGH THE GYRO TUNNEL FAST ENOUGH TO STABILIZE THE SHIP. SOMEBODY WITH SPEED.
UH, WHY ARE YOU ALL LOOKING AT ME?

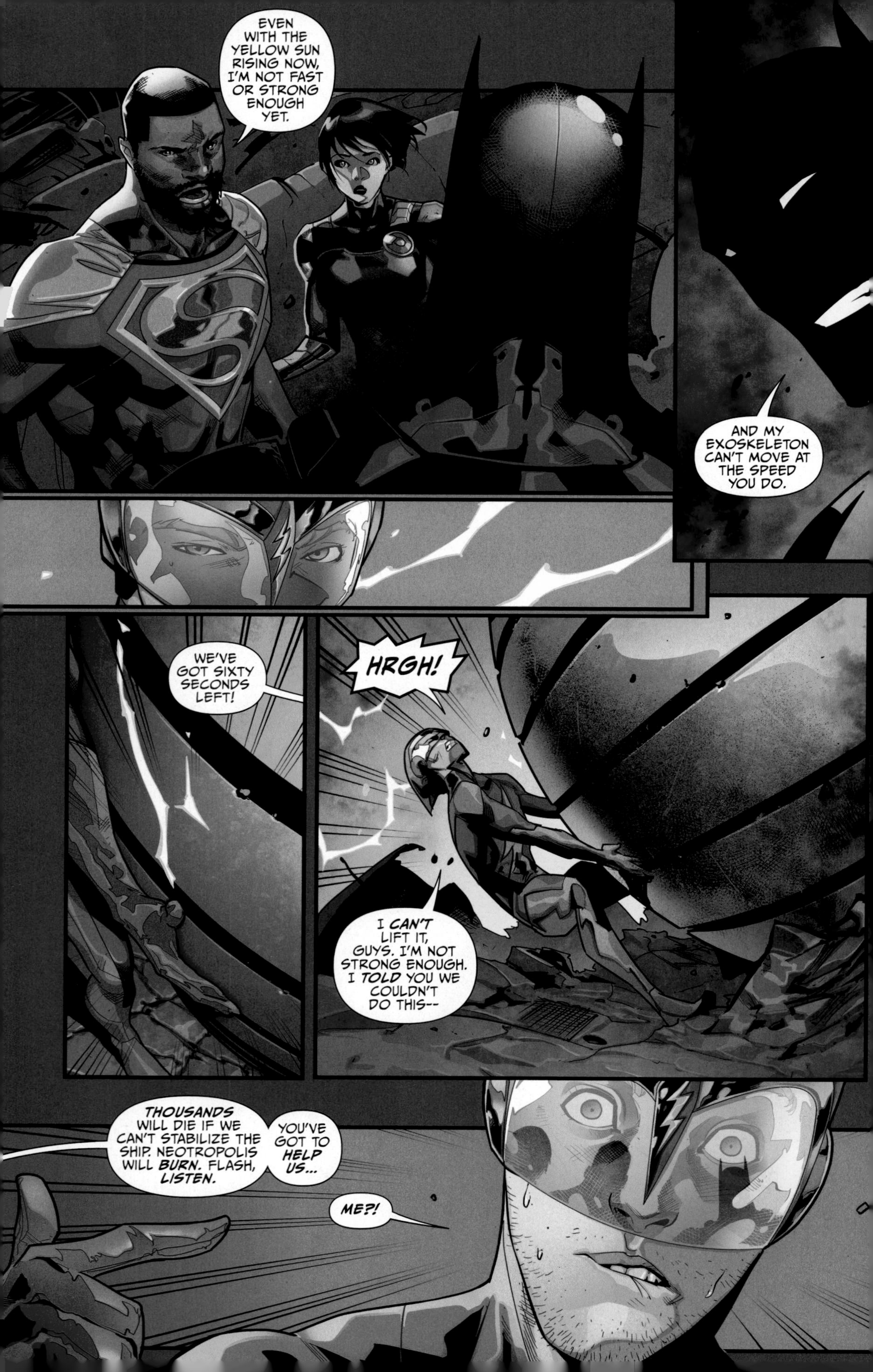
EVEN WITH THE YELLOW SUN RISING NOW, I'M NOT FAST OR STRONG ENOUGH YET.
AND MY EXOSKELETON CAN'T MOVE AT THE SPEED YOU DO.
WE'VE GOT SIXTY SECONDS LEFT!
HRGH!
I CAN'T LIFT IT, GUYS. I'M NOT STRONG ENOUGH. I TOLD YOU WE COULDN'T DO THIS--
THOUSANDS WILL DIE IF WE CAN'T STABILIZE THE SHIP. NEOTROPOLIS WILL BURN. FLASH, LISTEN.
YOU'VE GOT TO HELP US...
ME?!

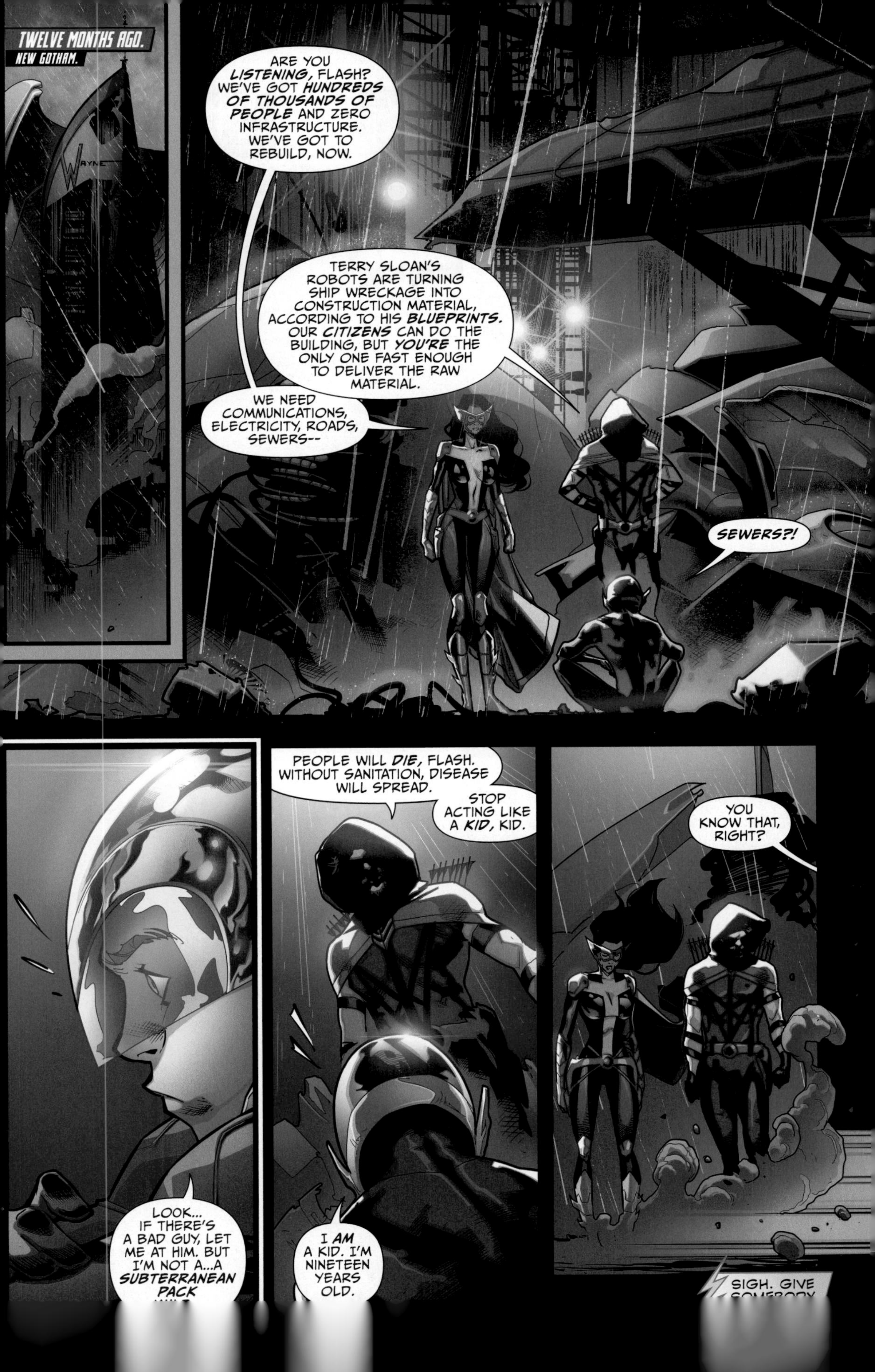
TWELVE MONTHS AGO.
NEW GOTHAM.
ARE YOU LISTENING, FLASH? WE'VE GOT HUNDREDS OF THOUSANDS OF PEOPLE AND ZERO INFRASTRUCTURE. WE'VE GOT TO REBUILD, NOW.
TERRY SLOAN'S ROBOTS ARE TURNING SHIP WRECKAGE INTO CONSTRUCTION MATERIAL, ACCORDING TO HIS BLUEPRINTS. OUR CITIZENS CAN DO THE BUILDING, BUT YOU'RE THE ONLY ONE FAST ENOUGH TO DELIVER THE RAW MATERIAL.
WE NEED COMMUNICATIONS, ELECTRICITY, ROADS, SEWERS--
SEWERS?!
LOOK... IF THERE'S A BAD GUY, LET ME AT HIM. BUT I'M NOT A...A SUBTERRANEAN PACK
PEOPLE WILL DIE, FLASH. WITHOUT SANITATION, DISEASE WILL SPREAD.
STOP ACTING LIKE A KID, KID.
I AM A KID. I'M NINETEEN YEARS OLD.
YOU KNOW THAT, RIGHT?
SIGH. GIVE

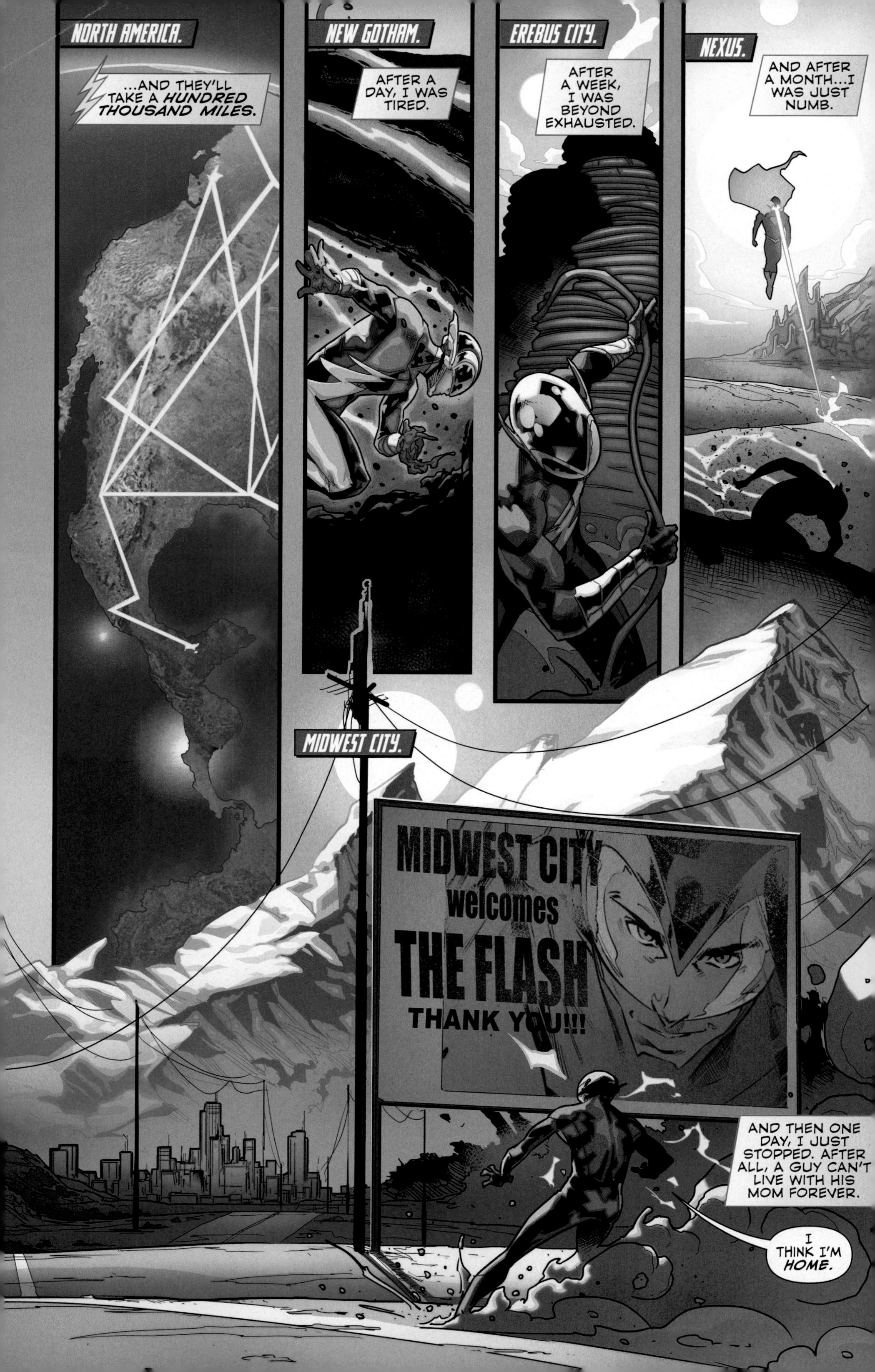
NORTH AMERICA.
...AND THEY'LL TAKE A HUNDRED THOUSAND MILES.
NEW GOTHAM.
AFTER A DAY, I WAS TIRED.
EREBUS CITY.
AFTER A WEEK, I WAS BEYOND EXHAUSTED.
NEXUS.
AND AFTER A MONTH...I WAS JUST NUMB.
MIDWEST CITY.
MIDWEST CITY welcomes THE FLASH THANK YOU!!!
AND THEN ONE DAY, I JUST STOPPED. AFTER ALL, A GUY CAN'T LIVE WITH HIS MOM FOREVER.
I THINK I'M HOME.

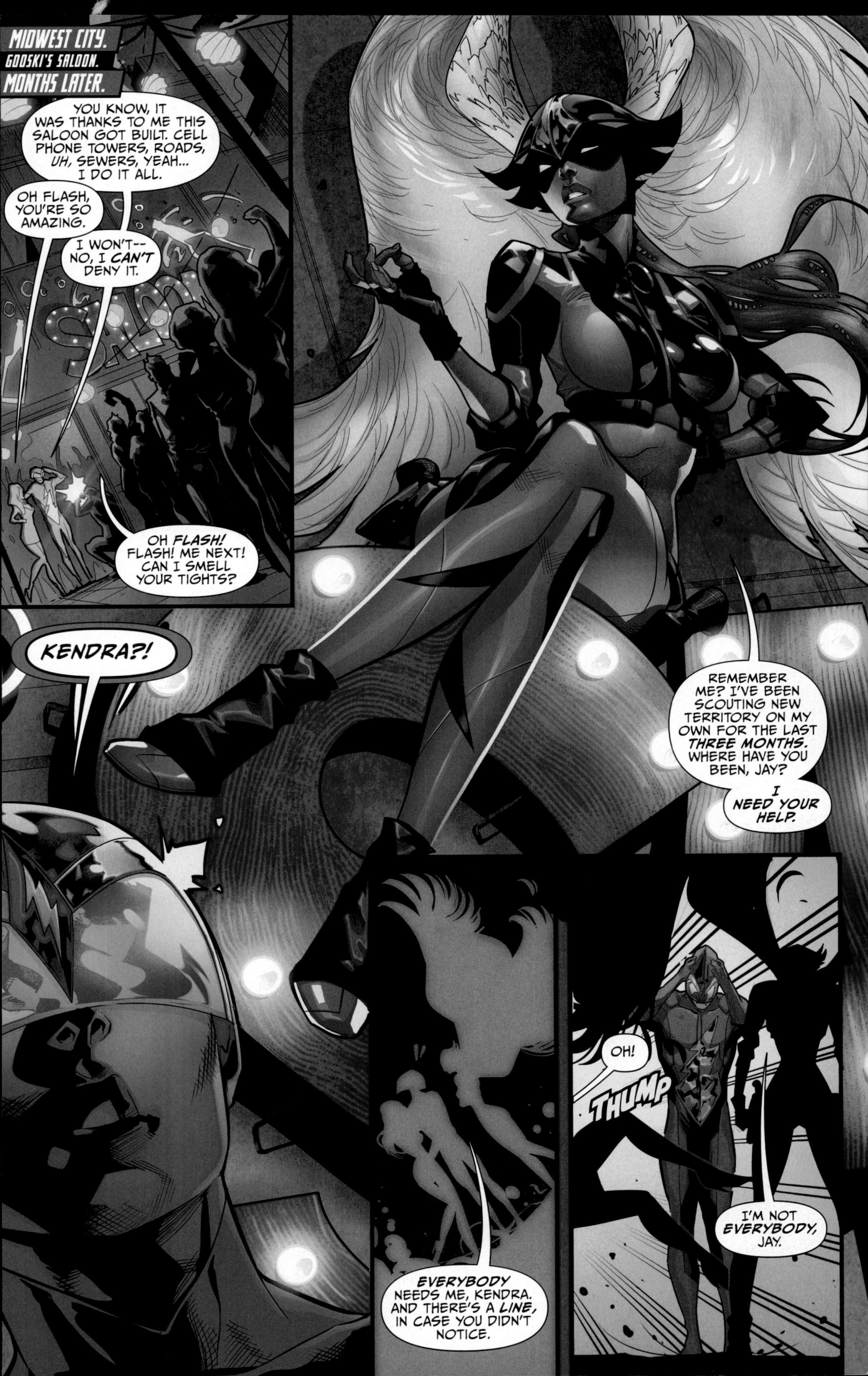
MIDWEST CITY.
GOOSKI'S SALOON.
MONTHS LATER.
YOU KNOW, IT WAS THANKS TO ME THIS SALOON GOT BUILT. CELL PHONE TOWERS, ROADS, *UH,* SEWERS, YEAH... I DO IT ALL.
OH FLASH, YOU'RE SO AMAZING.
I WON'T-- NO, I ***CAN'T*** DENY IT.
OH ***FLASH!*** FLASH! ME NEXT! CAN I SMELL YOUR TIGHTS?
KENDRA?!
REMEMBER ME? I'VE BEEN SCOUTING NEW TERRITORY ON MY OWN FOR THE LAST ***THREE MONTHS.*** WHERE HAVE YOU BEEN, JAY?
I NEED YOUR HELP.
EVERYBODY NEEDS ME, KENDRA. AND THERE'S A ***LINE,*** IN CASE YOU DIDN'T NOTICE.
OH!
THUMP
I'M NOT ***EVERYBODY,*** JAY.

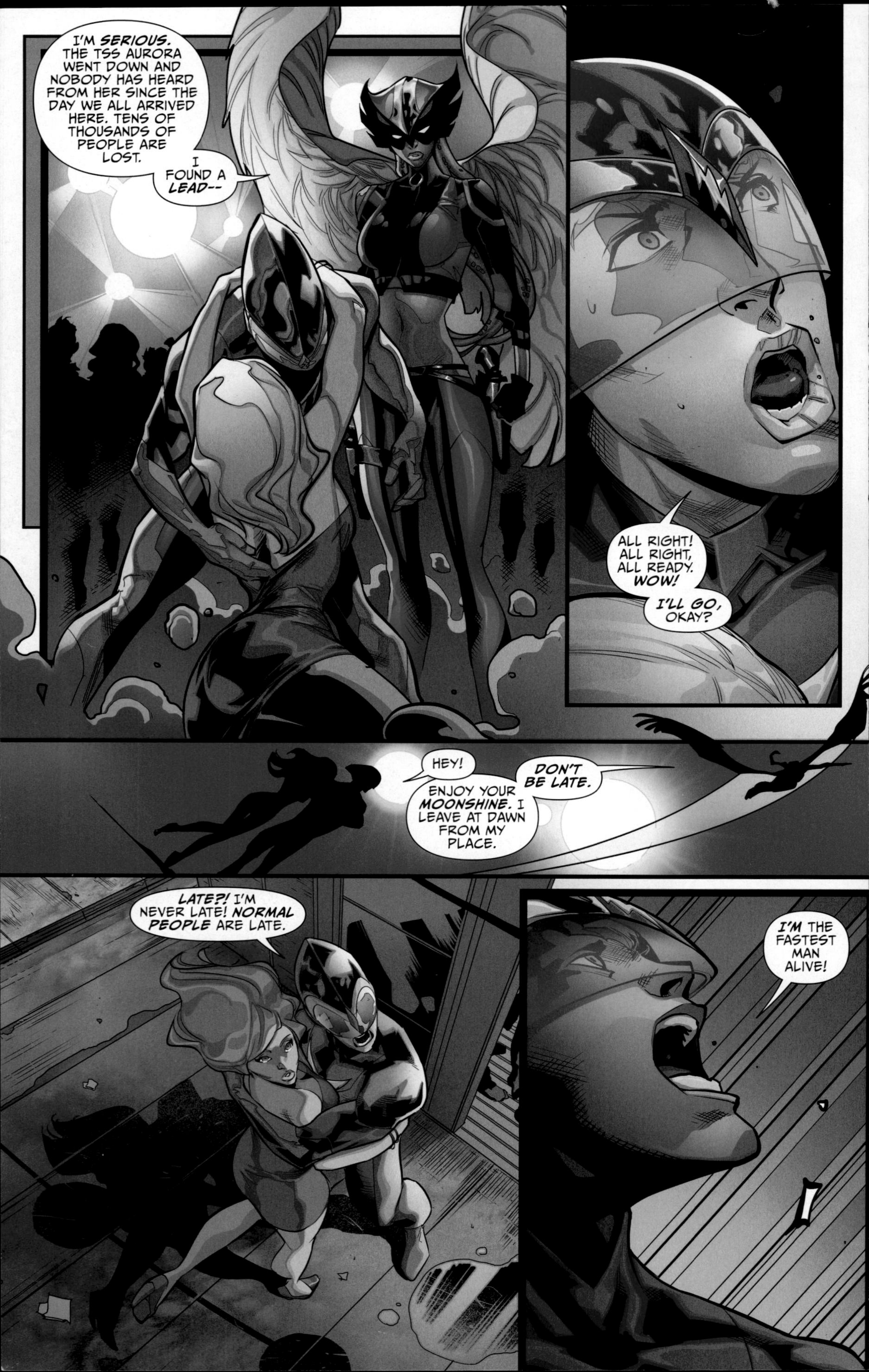
I'M SERIOUS. THE TSS AURORA WENT DOWN AND NOBODY HAS HEARD FROM HER SINCE THE DAY WE ALL ARRIVED HERE. TENS OF THOUSANDS OF PEOPLE ARE LOST.
I FOUND A LEAD--
ALL RIGHT! ALL RIGHT, ALL READY. WOW!
I'LL GO, OKAY?
HEY!
ENJOY YOUR MOONSHINE. I LEAVE AT DAWN FROM MY PLACE.
DON'T BE LATE.
LATE?! I'M NEVER LATE! NORMAL PEOPLE ARE LATE.
I'M THE FASTEST MAN ALIVE!

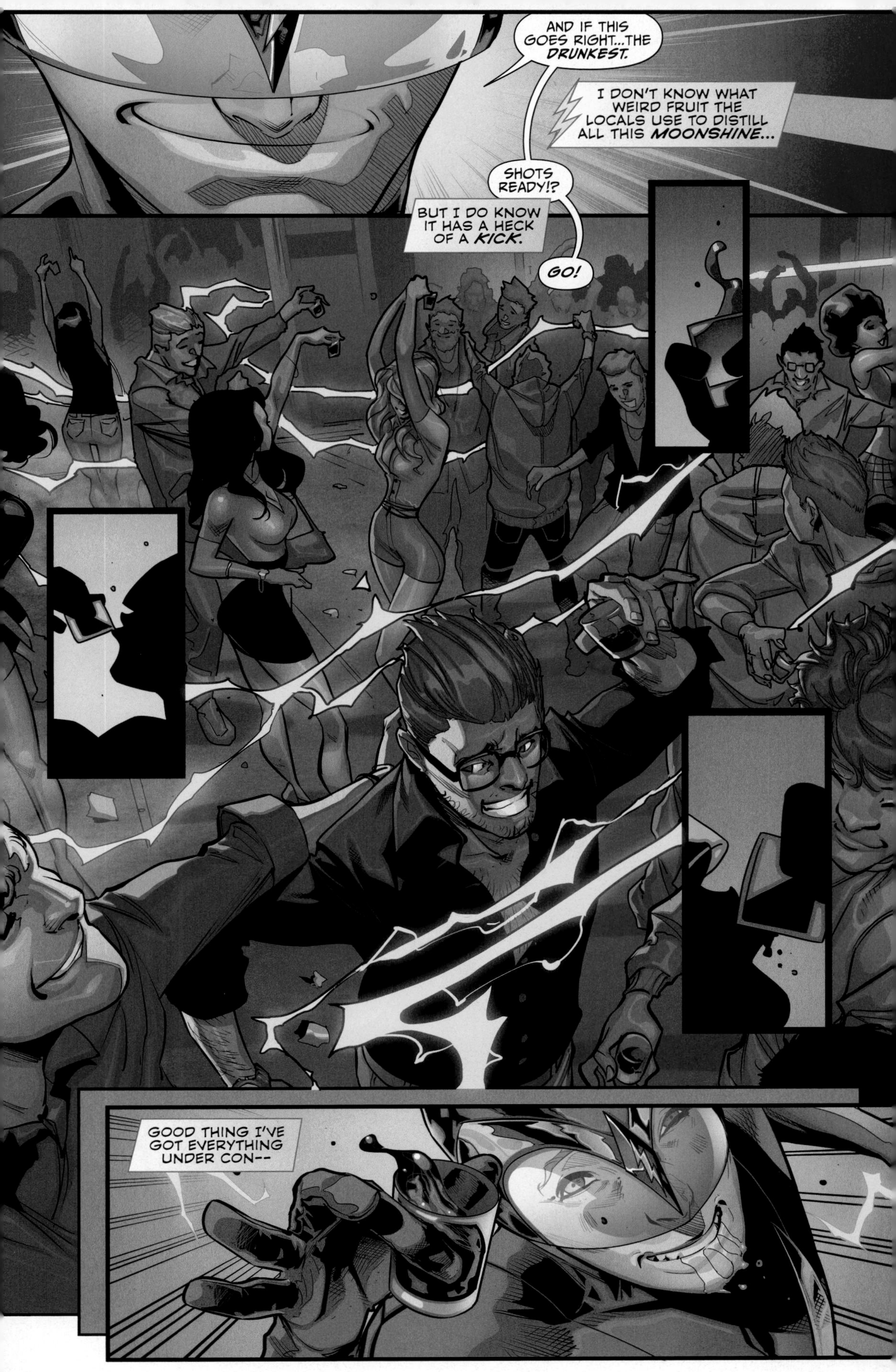
AND IF THIS GOES RIGHT...THE DRUNKEST.
I DON'T KNOW WHAT WEIRD FRUIT THE LOCALS USE TO DISTILL ALL THIS MOONSHINE...
SHOTS READY!?
BUT I DO KNOW IT HAS A HECK OF A KICK.
GO!
GOOD THING I'VE GOT EVERYTHING UNDER CON--

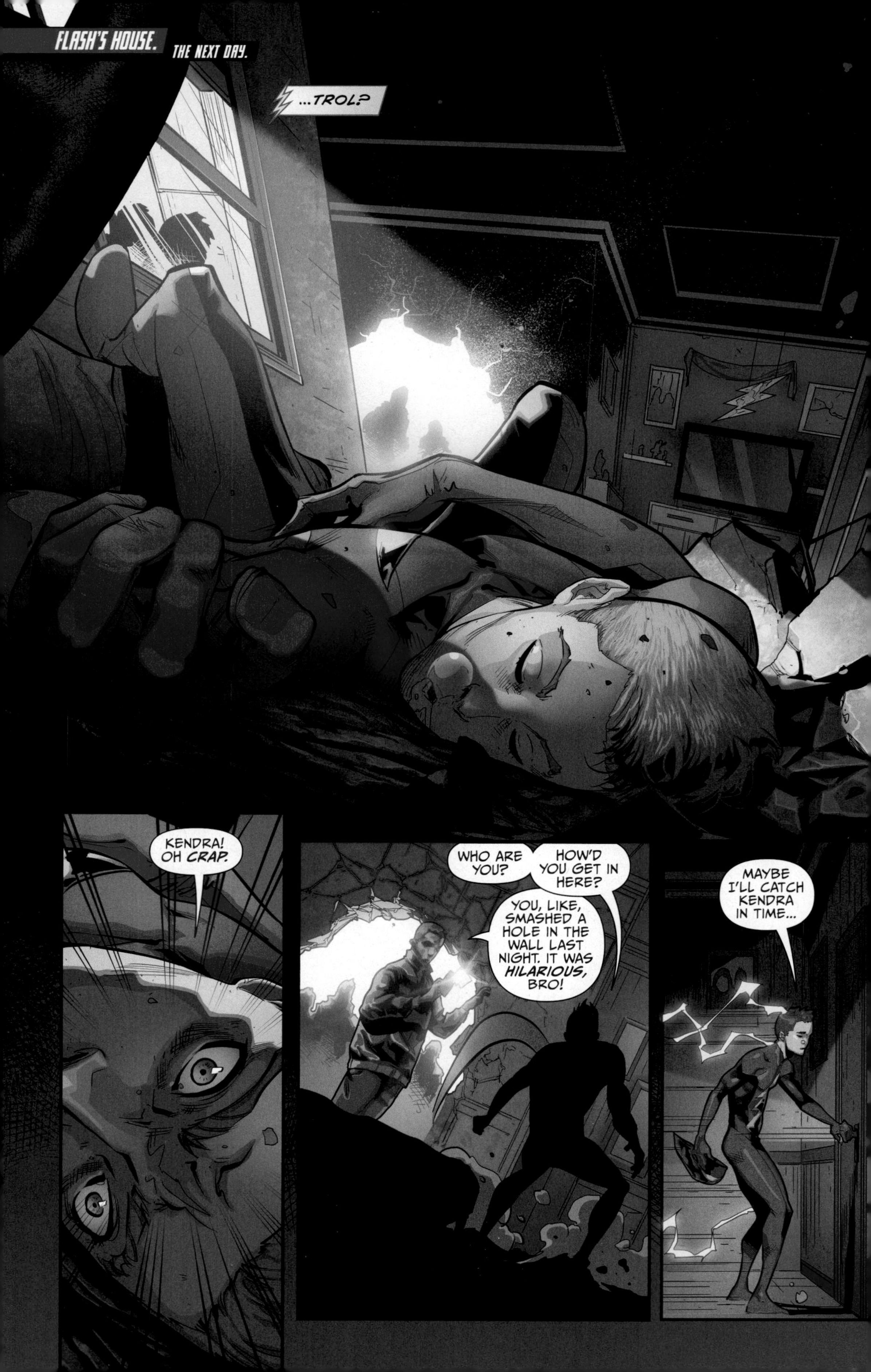
FLASH'S HOUSE.
THE NEXT DAY.
...TROL?
KENDRA! OH CRAP.
WHO ARE YOU?
HOW'D YOU GET IN HERE?
YOU, LIKE, SMASHED A HOLE IN THE WALL LAST NIGHT. IT WAS HILARIOUS, BRO!
MAYBE I'LL CATCH KENDRA IN TIME...

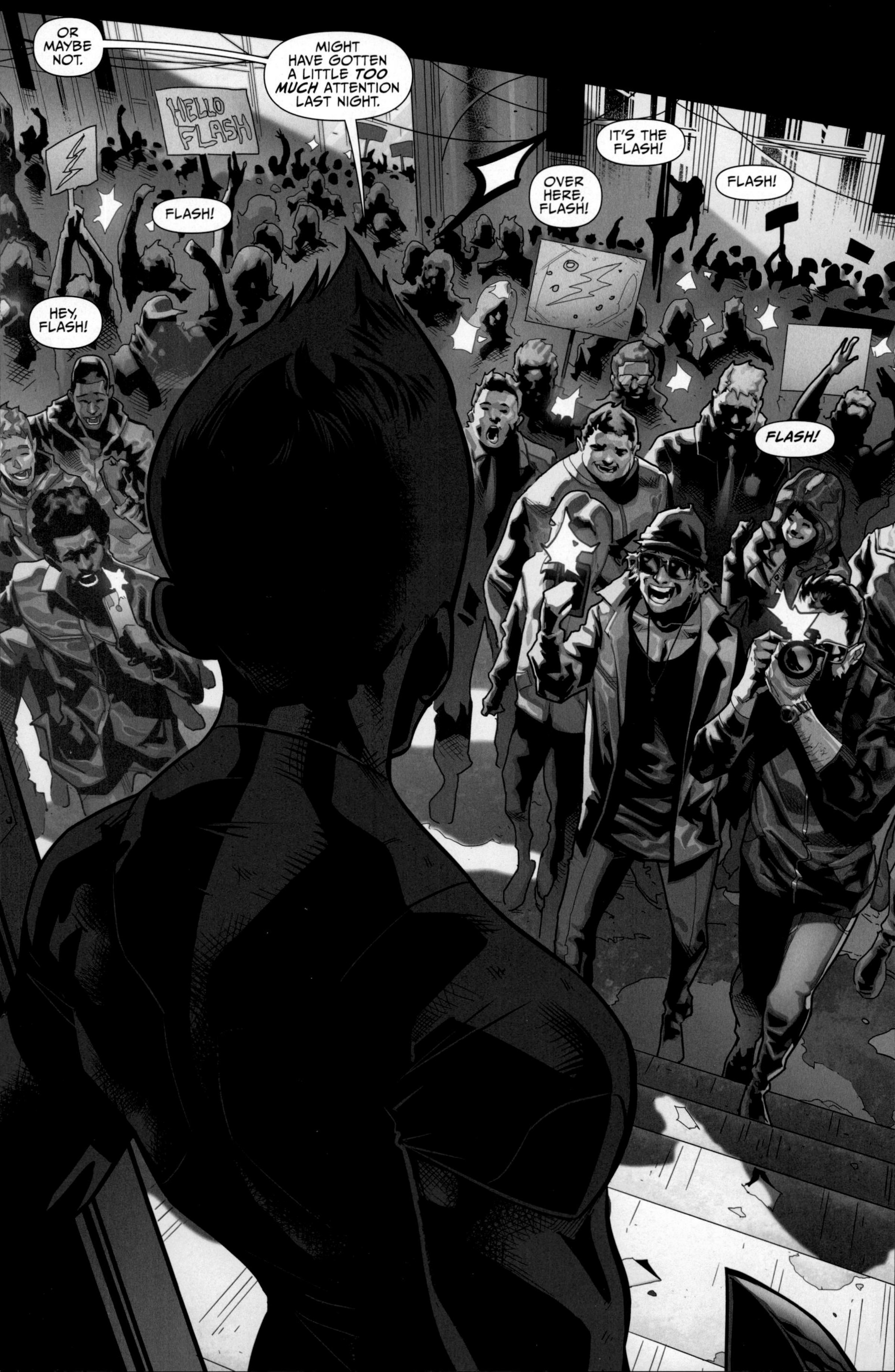
OR MAYBE NOT.
MIGHT HAVE GOTTEN A LITTLE *TOO MUCH* ATTENTION LAST NIGHT.
HELLO FLASH
IT'S THE FLASH!
FLASH!
OVER HERE, FLASH!
FLASH!
HEY, FLASH!
FLASH!

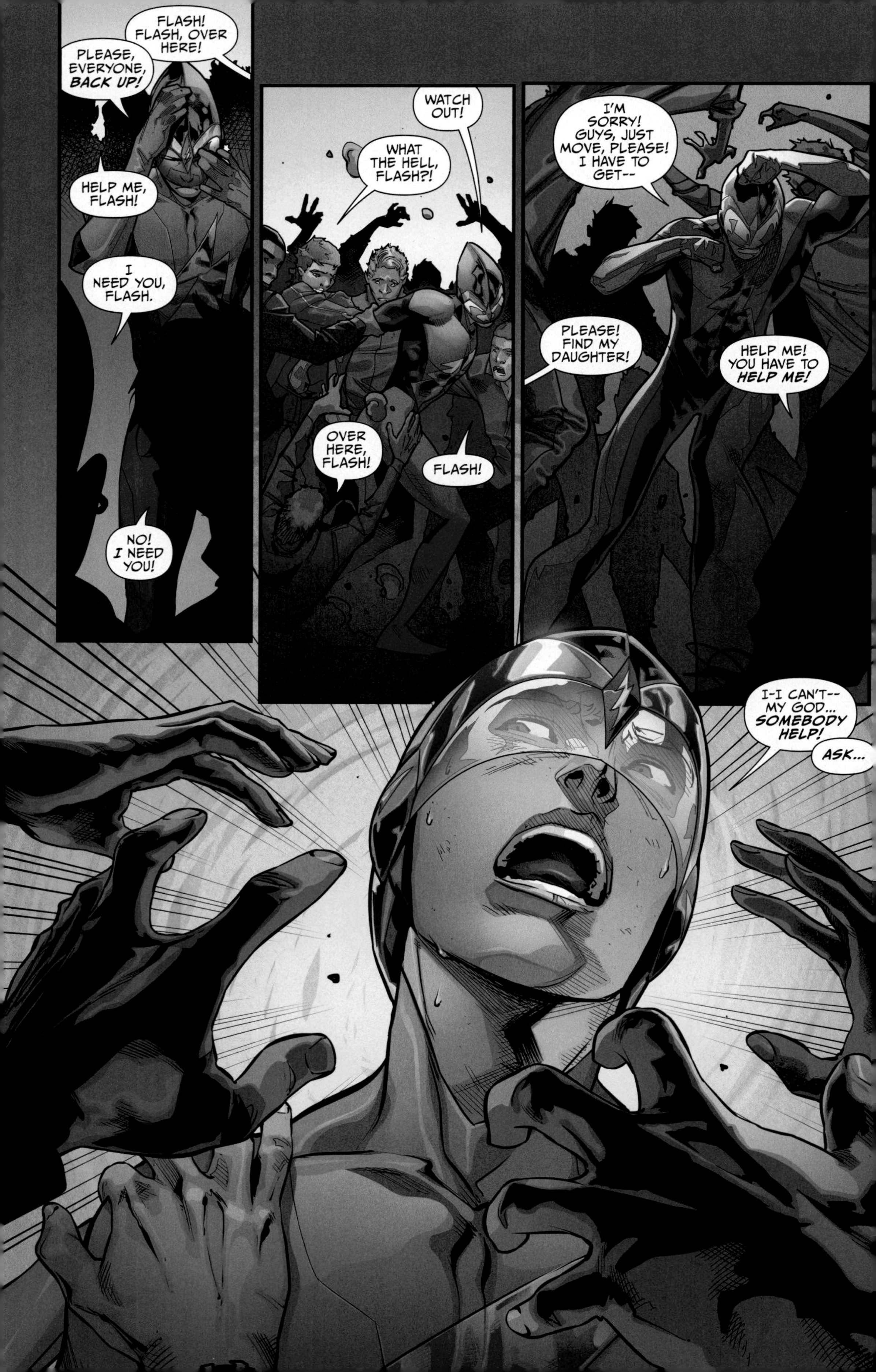
FLASH! FLASH, OVER HERE!
PLEASE, EVERYONE, BACK UP!
HELP ME, FLASH!
I NEED YOU, FLASH.
NO! I NEED YOU!
WATCH OUT!
WHAT THE HELL, FLASH?!
OVER HERE, FLASH!
FLASH!
I'M SORRY! GUYS, JUST MOVE, PLEASE! I HAVE TO GET--
PLEASE! FIND MY DAUGHTER!
HELP ME! YOU HAVE TO HELP ME!
I-I CAN'T-- MY GOD... SOMEBODY HELP!
ASK...

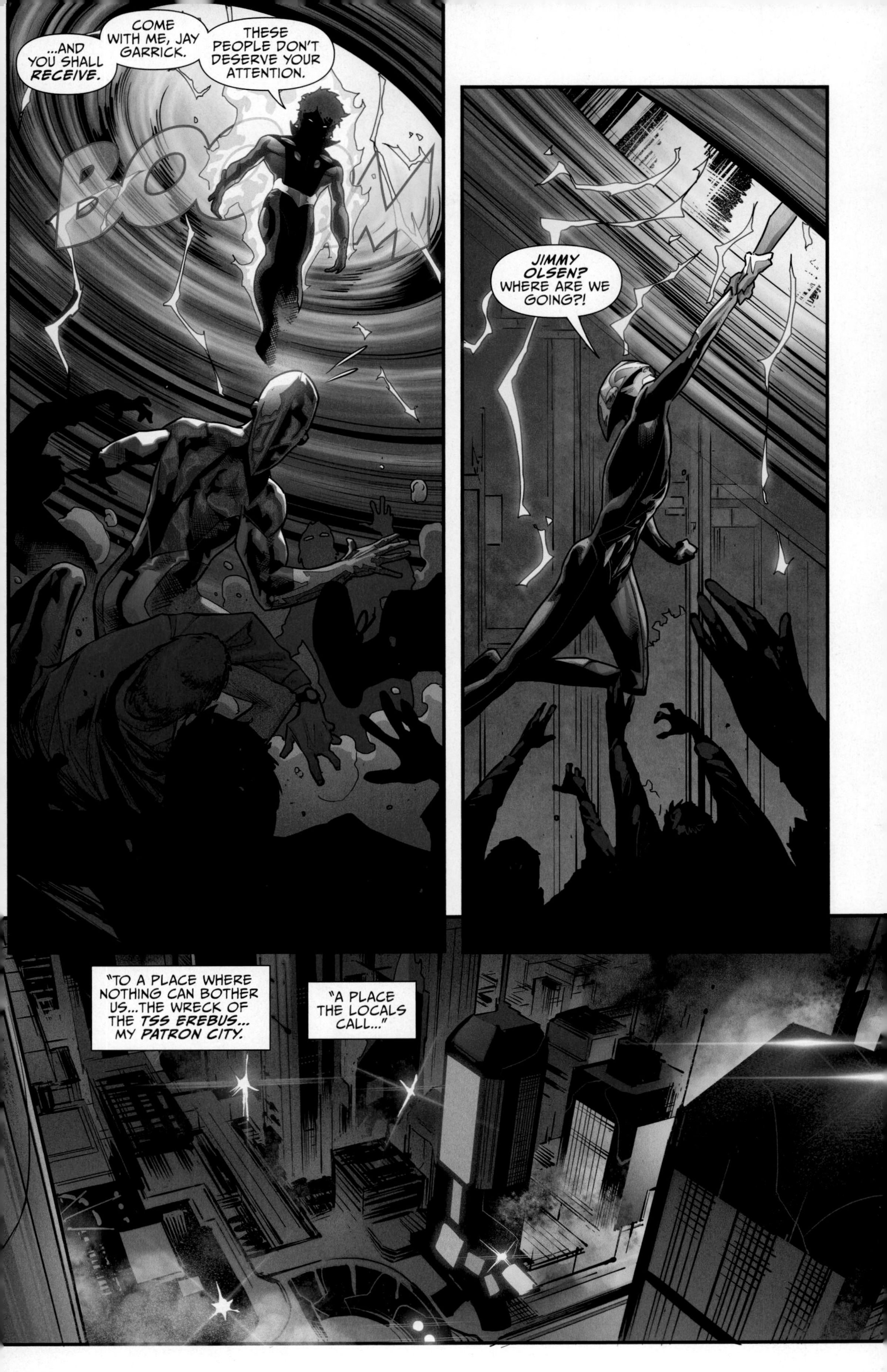
...AND YOU SHALL RECEIVE.
COME WITH ME, JAY GARRICK.
THESE PEOPLE DON'T DESERVE YOUR ATTENTION.
BOOM
JIMMY OLSEN? WHERE ARE WE GOING?!
"TO A PLACE WHERE NOTHING CAN BOTHER US...THE WRECK OF THE TSS EREBUS... MY PATRON CITY.
"A PLACE THE LOCALS CALL..."

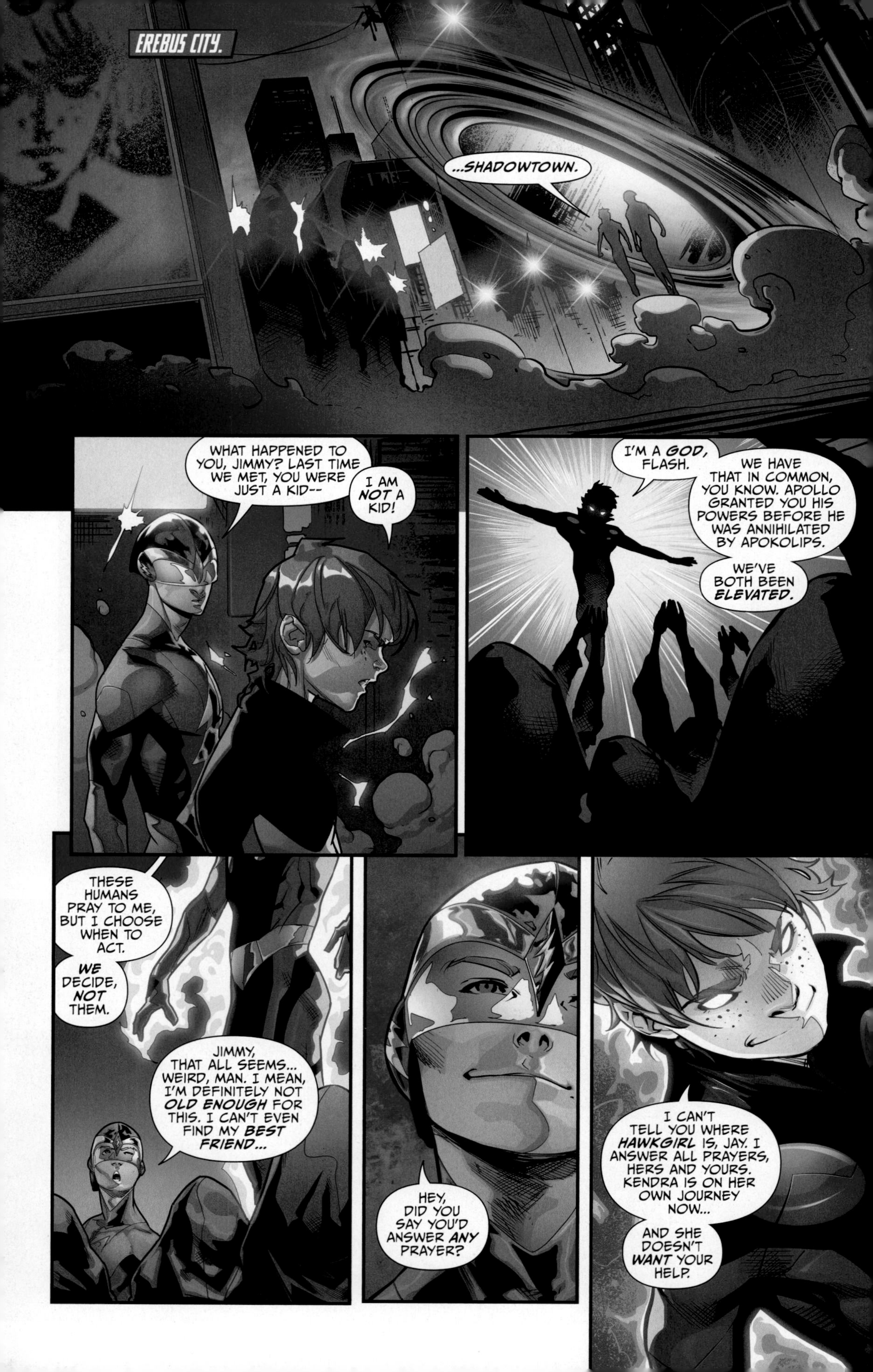
EREBUS CITY.
...SHADOWTOWN.
WHAT HAPPENED TO YOU, JIMMY? LAST TIME WE MET, YOU WERE JUST A KID--
I AM NOT A KID!
I'M A GOD, FLASH.
WE HAVE THAT IN COMMON, YOU KNOW. APOLLO GRANTED YOU HIS POWERS BEFORE HE WAS ANNIHILATED BY APOKOLIPS.
WE'VE BOTH BEEN ELEVATED.
THESE HUMANS PRAY TO ME, BUT I CHOOSE WHEN TO ACT.
WE DECIDE, NOT THEM.
JIMMY, THAT ALL SEEMS... WEIRD, MAN. I MEAN, I'M DEFINITELY NOT OLD ENOUGH FOR THIS. I CAN'T EVEN FIND MY BEST FRIEND...
HEY, DID YOU SAY YOU'D ANSWER ANY PRAYER?
I CAN'T TELL YOU WHERE HAWKGIRL IS, JAY. I ANSWER ALL PRAYERS, HERS AND YOURS. KENDRA IS ON HER OWN JOURNEY NOW...
AND SHE DOESN'T WANT YOUR HELP.

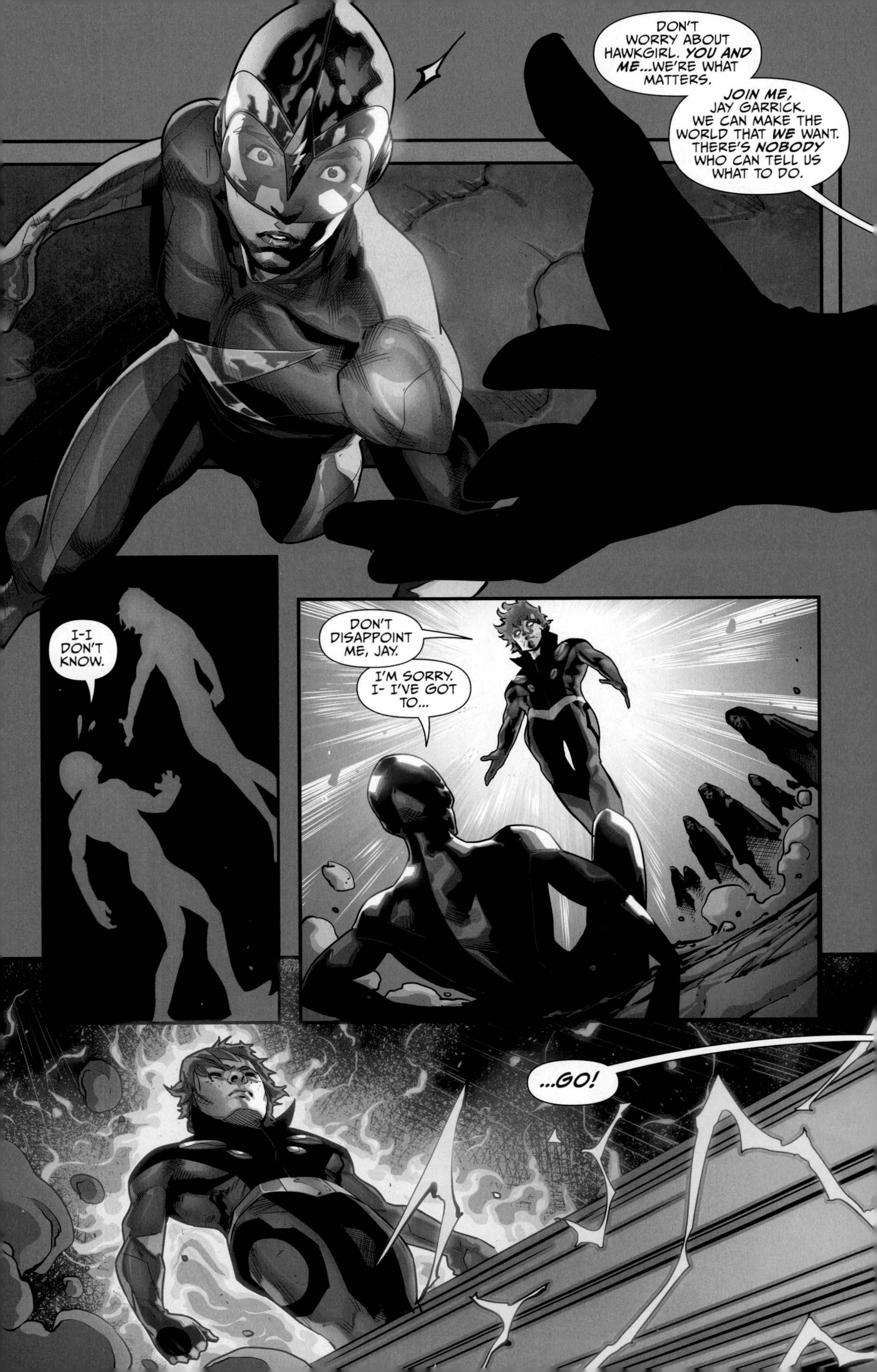
DON'T WORRY ABOUT HAWKGIRL. YOU AND ME...WE'RE WHAT MATTERS.
JOIN ME, JAY GARRICK. WE CAN MAKE THE WORLD THAT WE WANT. THERE'S NOBODY WHO CAN TELL US WHAT TO DO.
I-I DON'T KNOW.
DON'T DISAPPOINT ME, JAY.
I'M SORRY. I- I'VE GOT TO...
...GO!

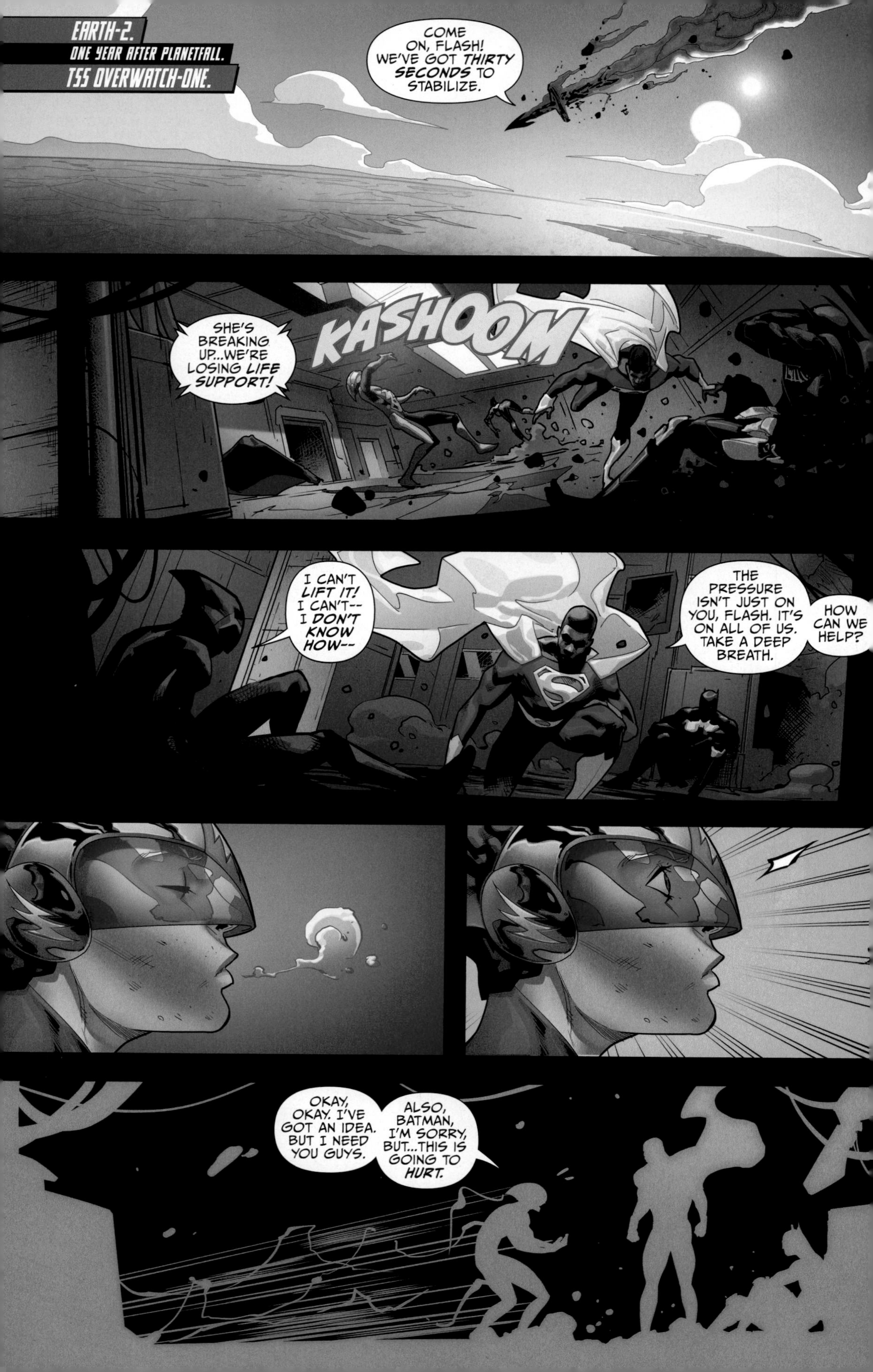
EARTH-2.
ONE YEAR AFTER PLANETFALL.
TSS OVERWATCH-ONE.
COME ON, FLASH! WE'VE GOT THIRTY SECONDS TO STABILIZE.
SHE'S BREAKING UP...WE'RE LOSING LIFE SUPPORT!
KASHOOM
I CAN'T LIFT IT! I CAN'T-- I DON'T KNOW HOW--
THE PRESSURE ISN'T JUST ON YOU, FLASH. IT'S ON ALL OF US. TAKE A DEEP BREATH.
HOW CAN WE HELP?
OKAY, OKAY. I'VE GOT AN IDEA. BUT I NEED YOU GUYS.
ALSO, BATMAN, I'M SORRY, BUT...THIS IS GOING TO HURT.

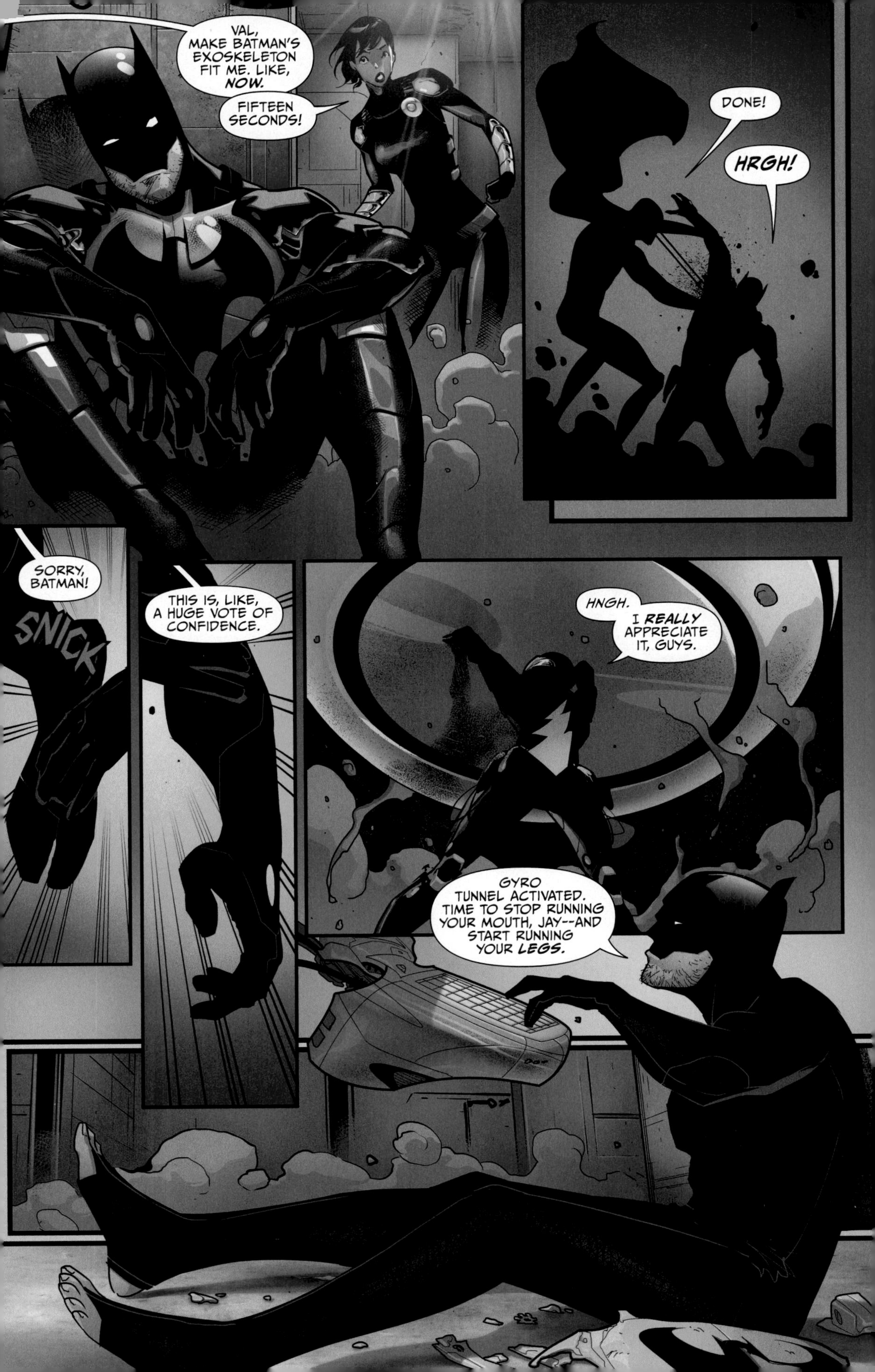
VAL, MAKE BATMAN'S EXOSKELETON FIT ME. LIKE, *NOW.*
FIFTEEN SECONDS!
DONE!
HRGH!
SORRY, BATMAN!
SNICK
THIS IS, LIKE, A HUGE VOTE OF CONFIDENCE.
HNGH.
I *REALLY* APPRECIATE IT, GUYS.
GYRO TUNNEL ACTIVATED. TIME TO STOP RUNNING YOUR MOUTH, JAY--AND START RUNNING YOUR *LEGS.*

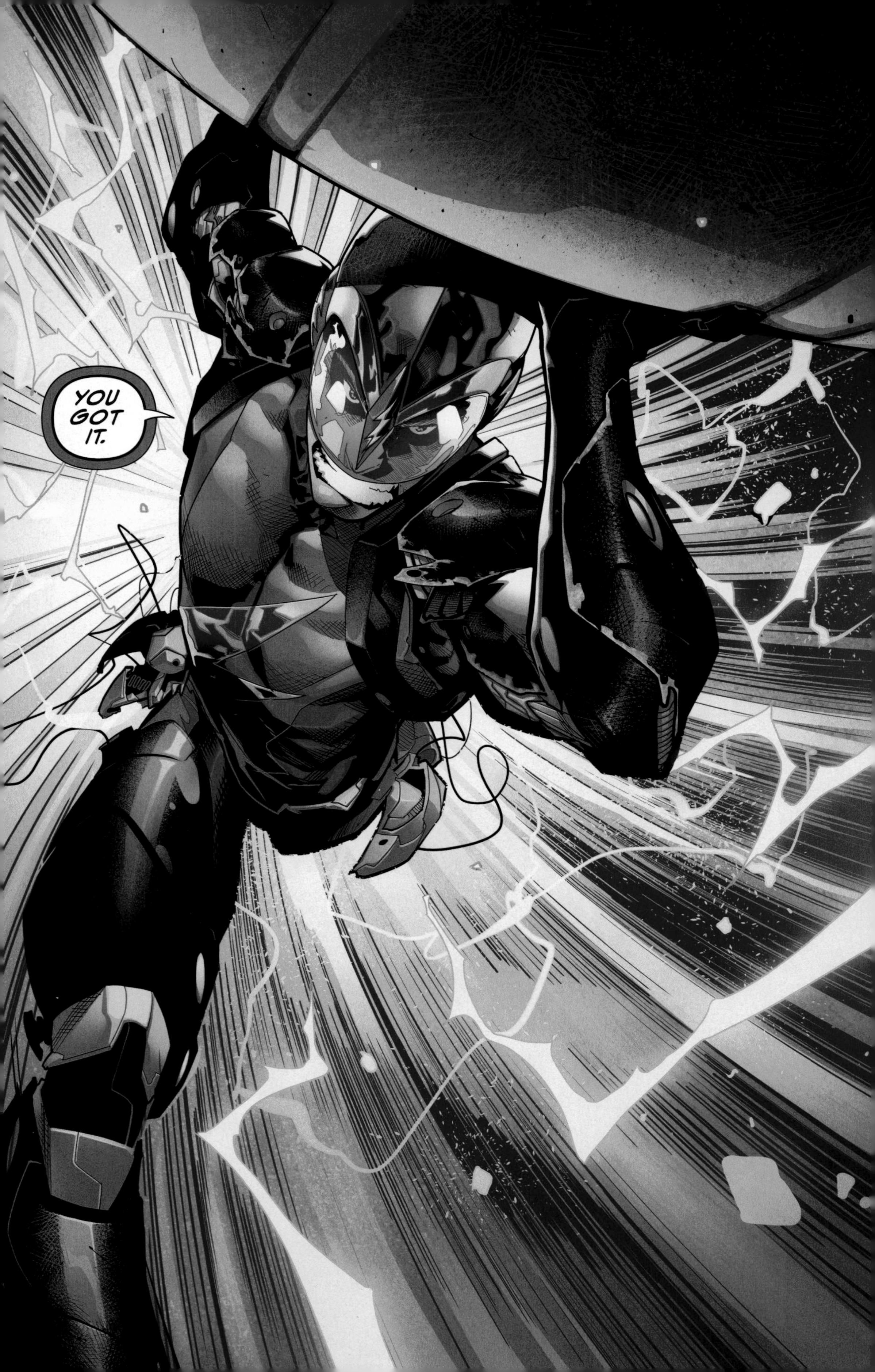
YOU GOT IT.

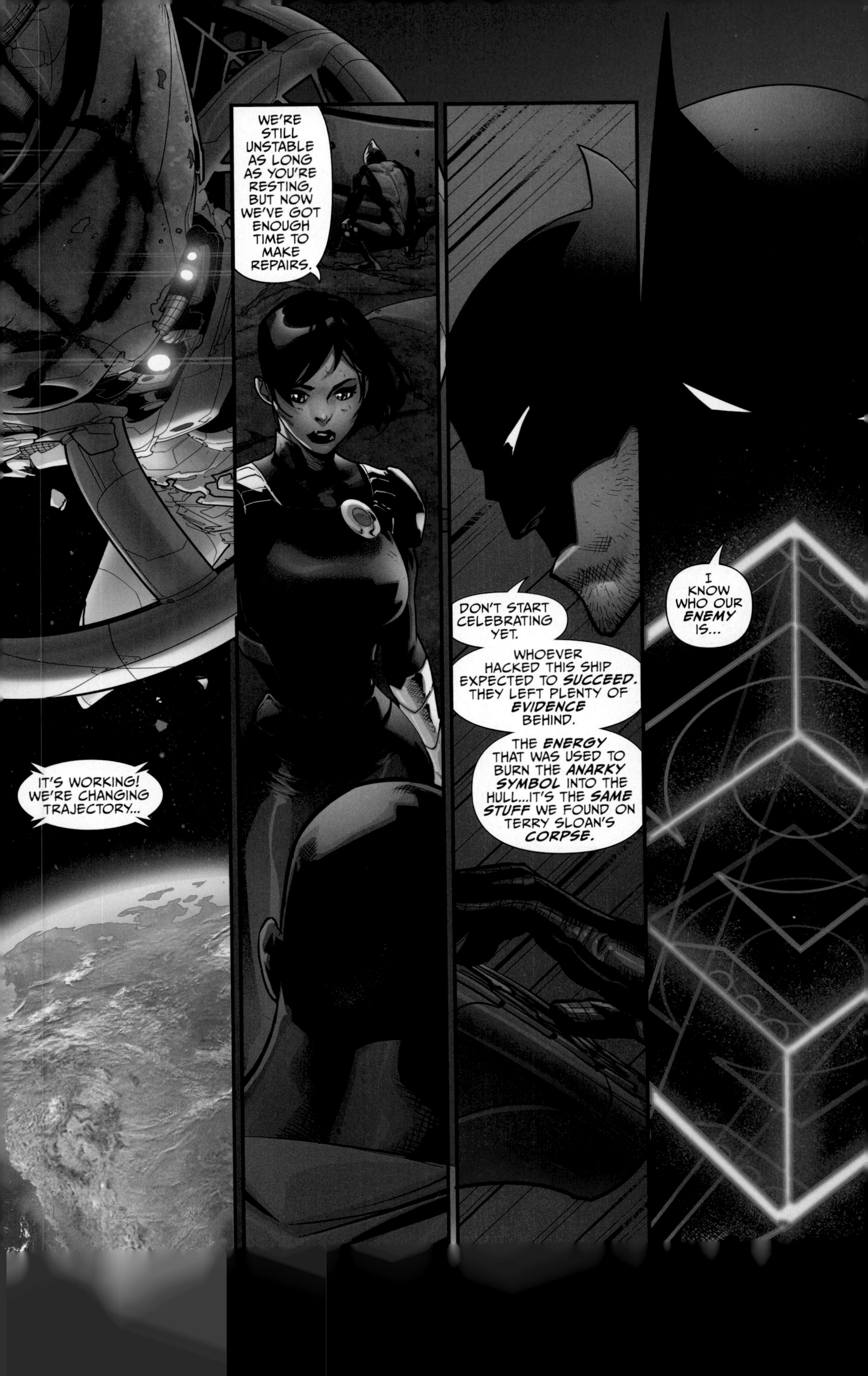
IT'S WORKING! WE'RE CHANGING TRAJECTORY...
WE'RE STILL UNSTABLE AS LONG AS YOU'RE RESTING, BUT NOW WE'VE GOT ENOUGH TIME TO MAKE REPAIRS.
DON'T START CELEBRATING YET.
WHOEVER HACKED THIS SHIP EXPECTED TO SUCCEED. THEY LEFT PLENTY OF EVIDENCE BEHIND.
THE ENERGY THAT WAS USED TO BURN THE ANARKY SYMBOL INTO THE HULL...IT'S THE SAME STUFF WE FOUND ON TERRY SLOAN'S CORPSE.
I KNOW WHO OUR ENEMY IS...

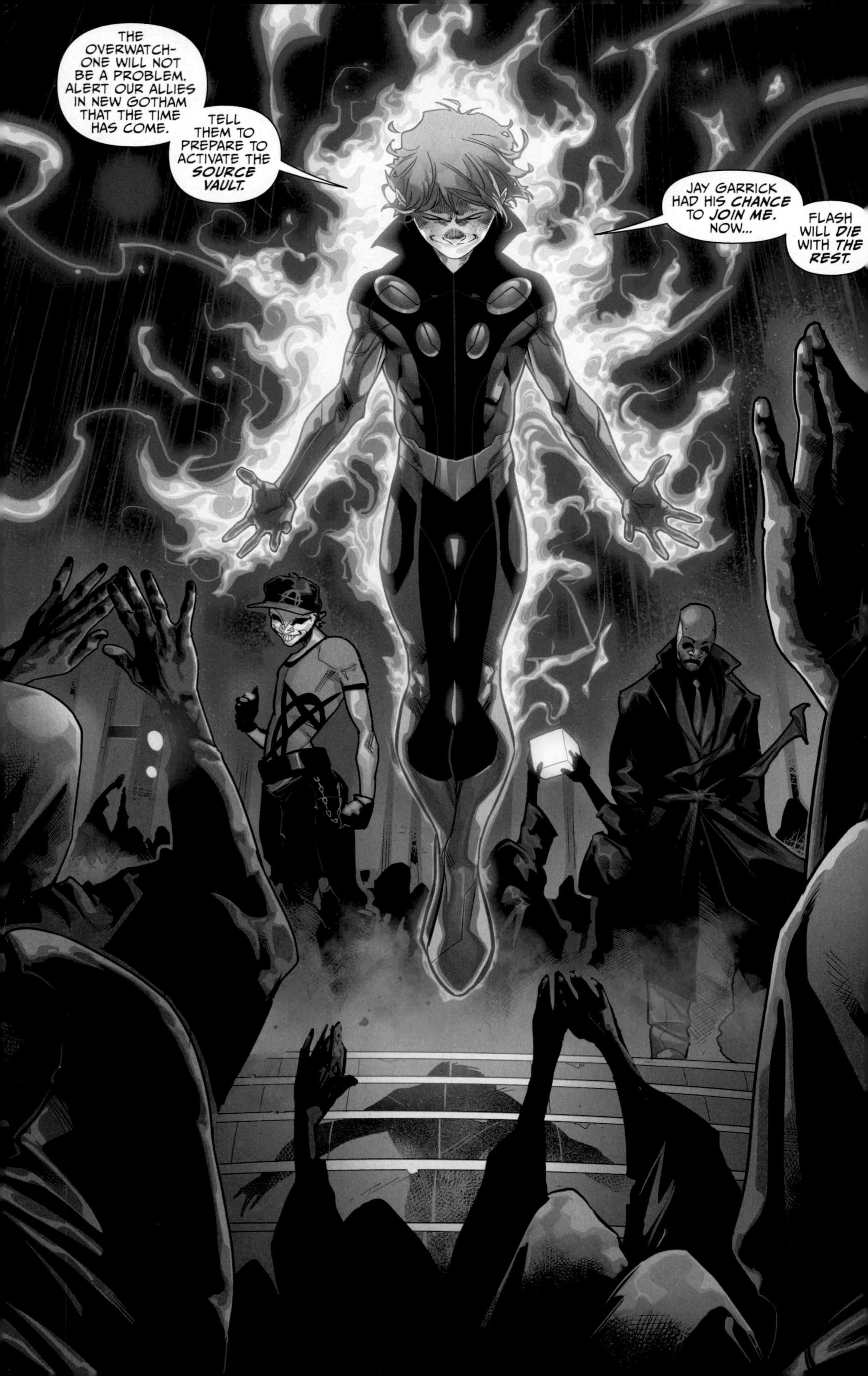
THE OVERWATCH-ONE WILL NOT BE A PROBLEM. ALERT OUR ALLIES IN NEW GOTHAM THAT THE TIME HAS COME.
TELL THEM TO PREPARE TO ACTIVATE THE SOURCE VAULT.
JAY GARRICK HAD HIS CHANCE TO JOIN ME. NOW...
FLASH WILL DIE WITH THE REST.

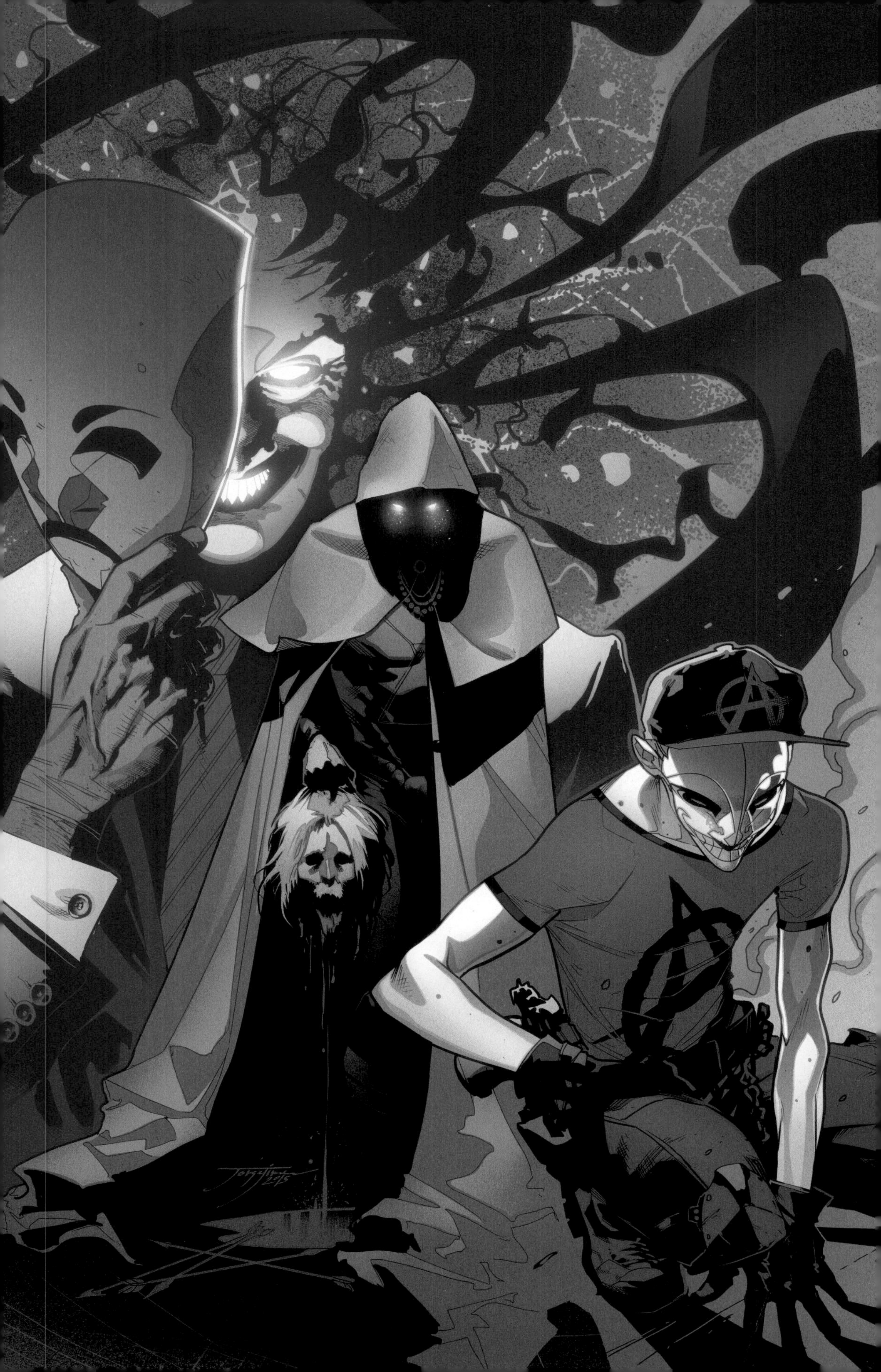

GODHOOD

DANIEL H. WILSON writer **ALISSON BORGES** artist **ALEJANDRO SANCHEZ BLOND** colorists **TRAVIS LANHAM** letterer cover by **JIMENEZ & RAUCH**

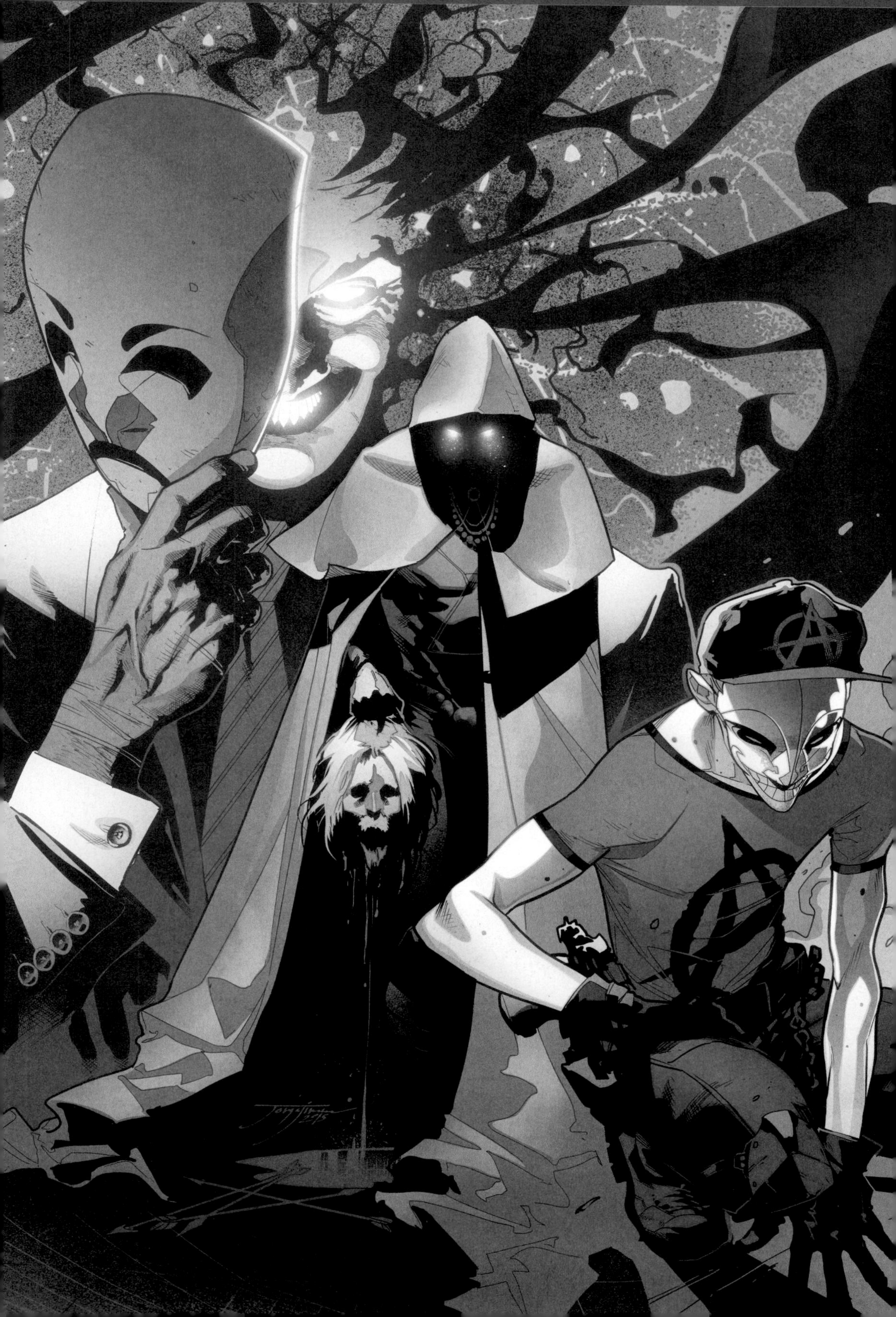

RTH-2.
YEAR AFTER PLANETFALL.
EBUS CITY.
ONCE, I WAS JIMMY OLSEN...A SMART KID WITH A TALENT FOR HACKING. BUT THE WAR WITH APOKOLIPS CHANGED ALL THAT.
PREPARE YOURSELVES FOR A FIGHT. THE YELLOW SUN IS IN PHASE.
NOW, I HAVE UNIMAGINABLE POWER.
AND ONCE I ACTIVATE THE GENESIS MACHINE, I WILL TERRAFORM THIS PLANET AND TAKE CONTROL OF EVERY ATOM.
NOTHING IS BEYOND MY ABILITY. AND SO I CALL MYSELF...
...DOCTOR IMPOSSIBLE.
AND AN ANGRY KRYPTONIAN IS ON HIS WAY.

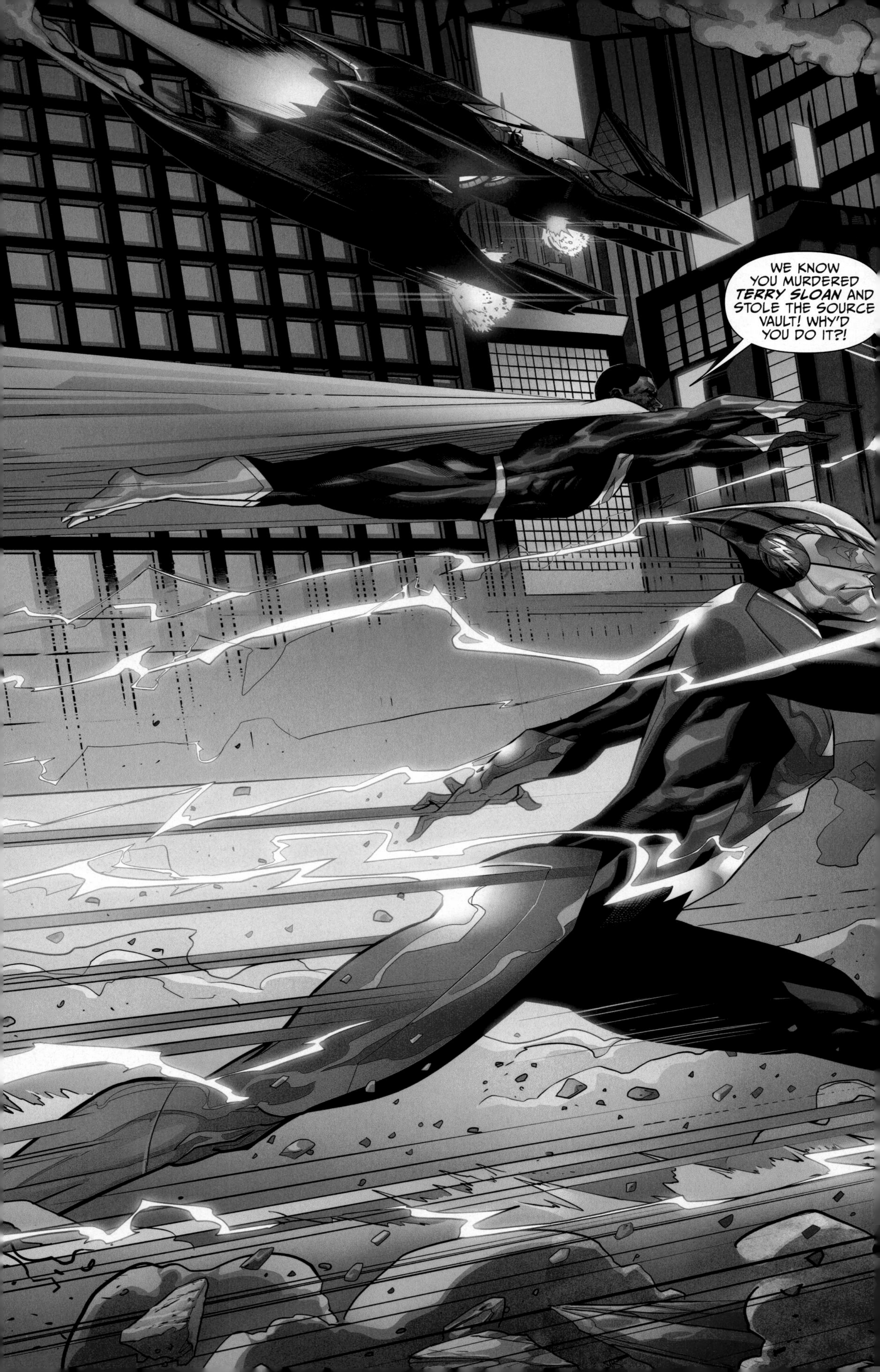
WE KNOW YOU MURDERED TERRY SLOAN AND STOLE THE SOURCE VAULT! WHY'D YOU DO IT?!

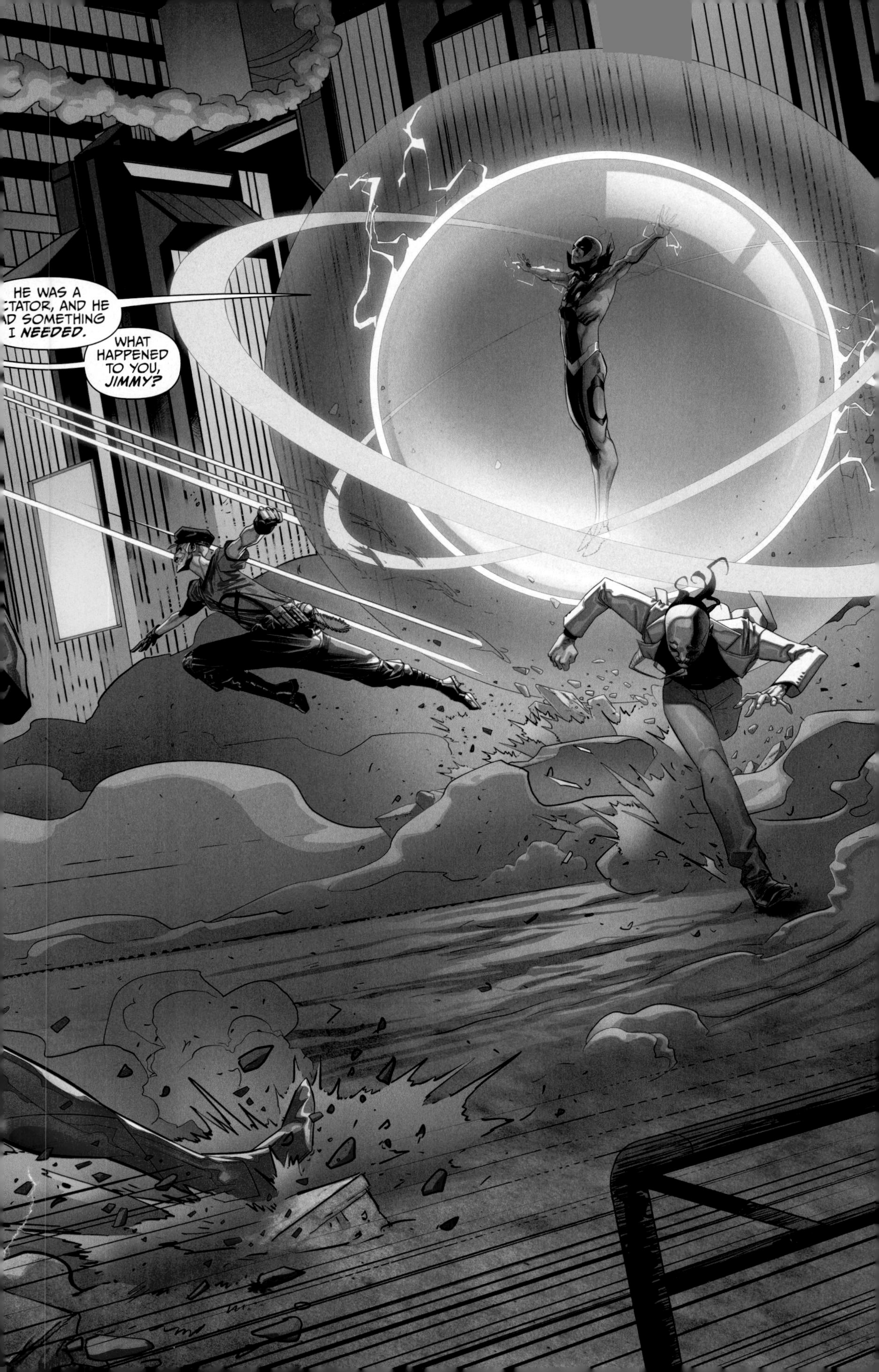
HE WAS A
CTATOR, AND HE
AD SOMETHING
I NEEDED.
WHAT HAPPENED TO YOU, JIMMY?

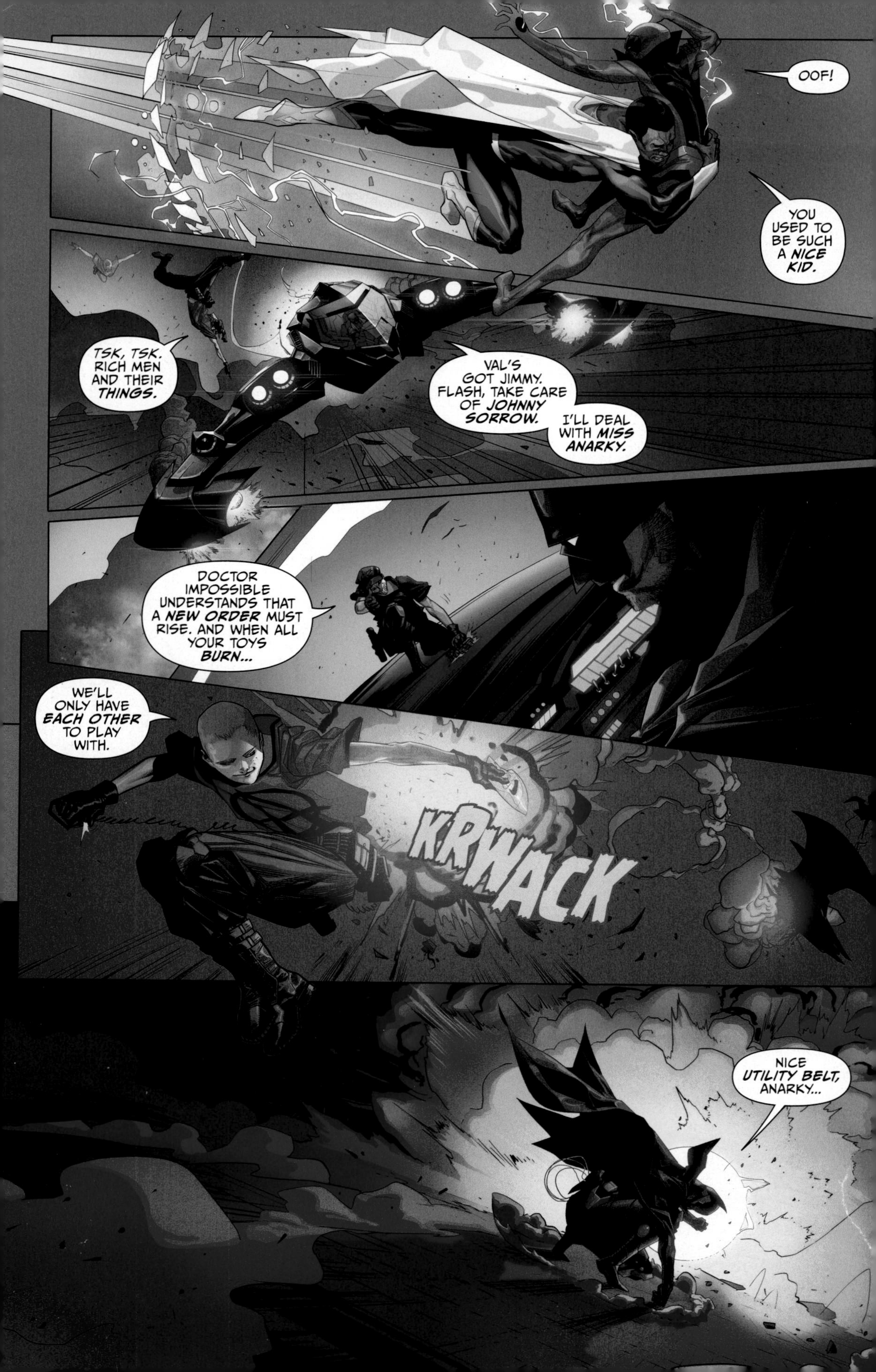
OOF!
YOU USED TO BE SUCH A NICE KID.
TSK, TSK. RICH MEN AND THEIR THINGS.
VAL'S GOT JIMMY. FLASH, TAKE CARE OF JOHNNY SORROW.
I'LL DEAL WITH MISS ANARKY.
DOCTOR IMPOSSIBLE UNDERSTANDS THAT A NEW ORDER MUST RISE. AND WHEN ALL YOUR TOYS BURN...
WE'LL ONLY HAVE EACH OTHER TO PLAY WITH.
KRWACK
NICE UTILITY BELT, ANARKY...

...I'VE GOT ONE, TOO!
JOHNNY SORROW, HUH?
LET'S TURN THAT FROWN UPSIDE DOWN.
YOU'RE FIGHTING ON THE WRONG SIDE, BOY. DOCTOR IMPOSSIBLE IS ALL-POWERFUL.
SO GO AHEAD AND GIVE ME YOUR--
THWACK
SORRY, DIDN'T CATCH THAT. WHAT WERE YOU SAYING?
I SAID...
GIVE ME YOUR BEST SHOT. HAH HAH HAH!
WAAAGH!

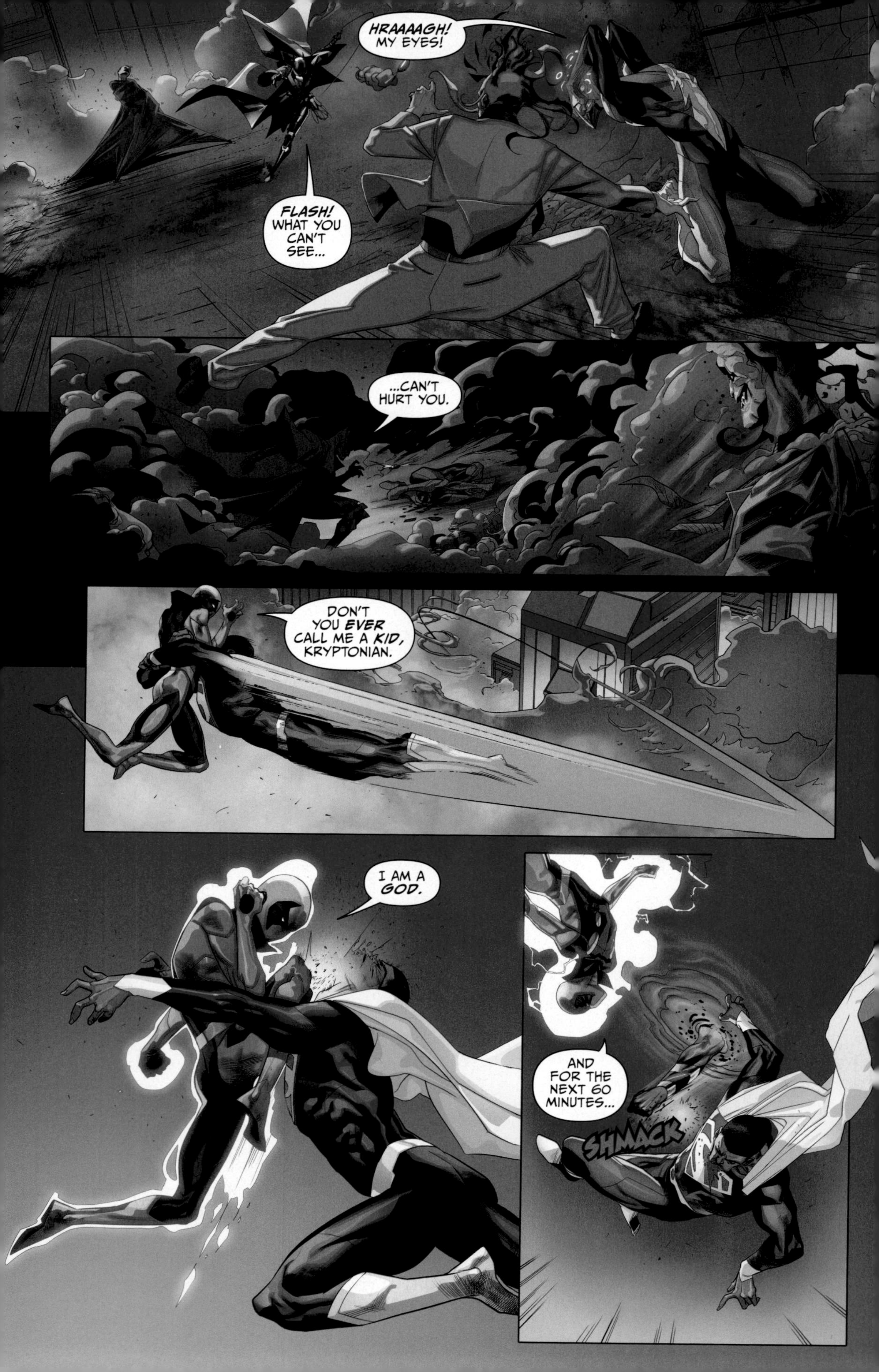

HRAAAAGH! MY EYES!
FLASH! WHAT YOU CAN'T SEE...
...CAN'T HURT YOU.
DON'T YOU EVER CALL ME A KID, KRYPTONIAN.
I AM A GOD.
AND FOR THE NEXT 60 MINUTES...
SHMACK

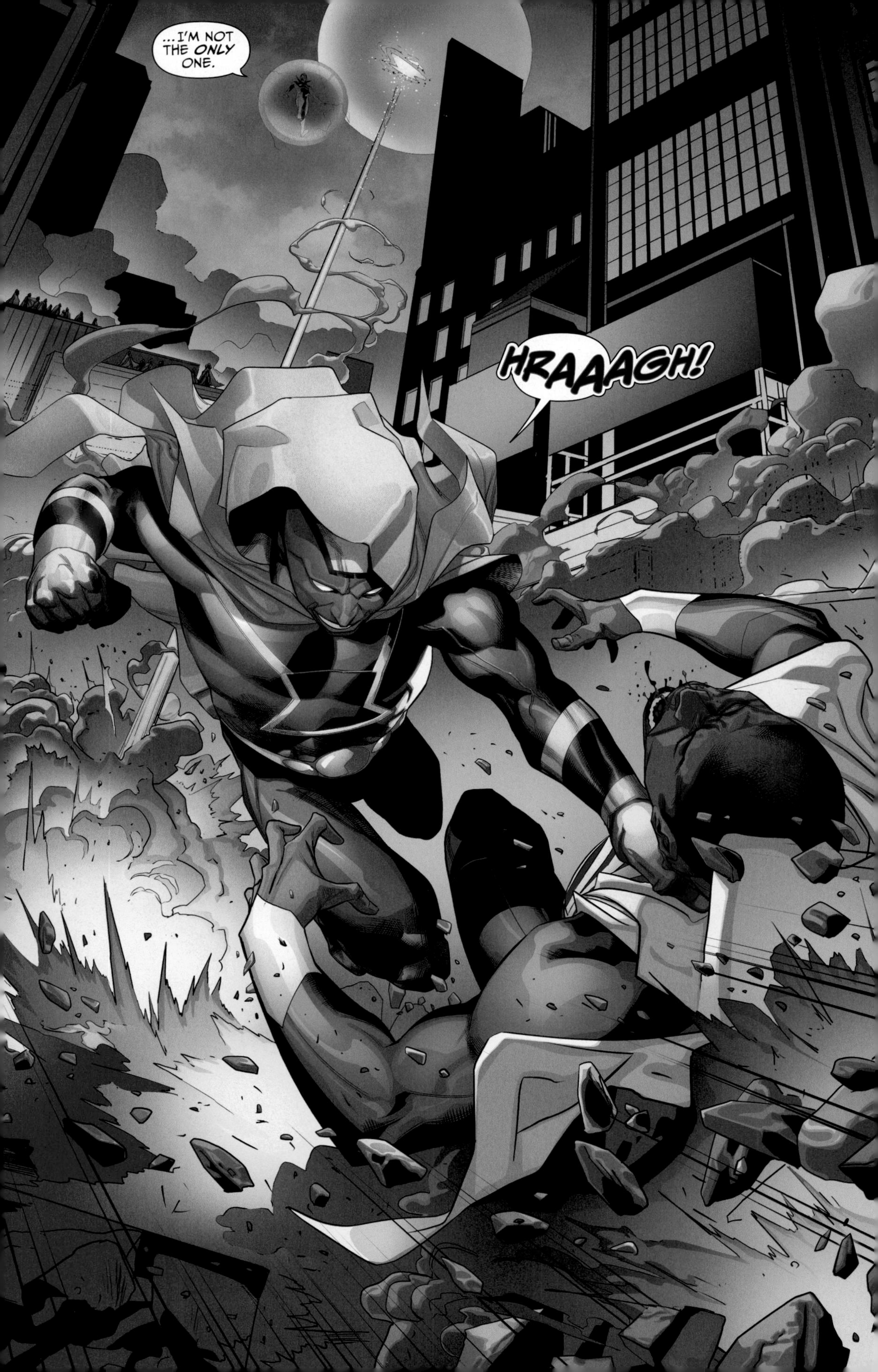
...I'M NOT THE ONLY ONE.
HRAAAGH!

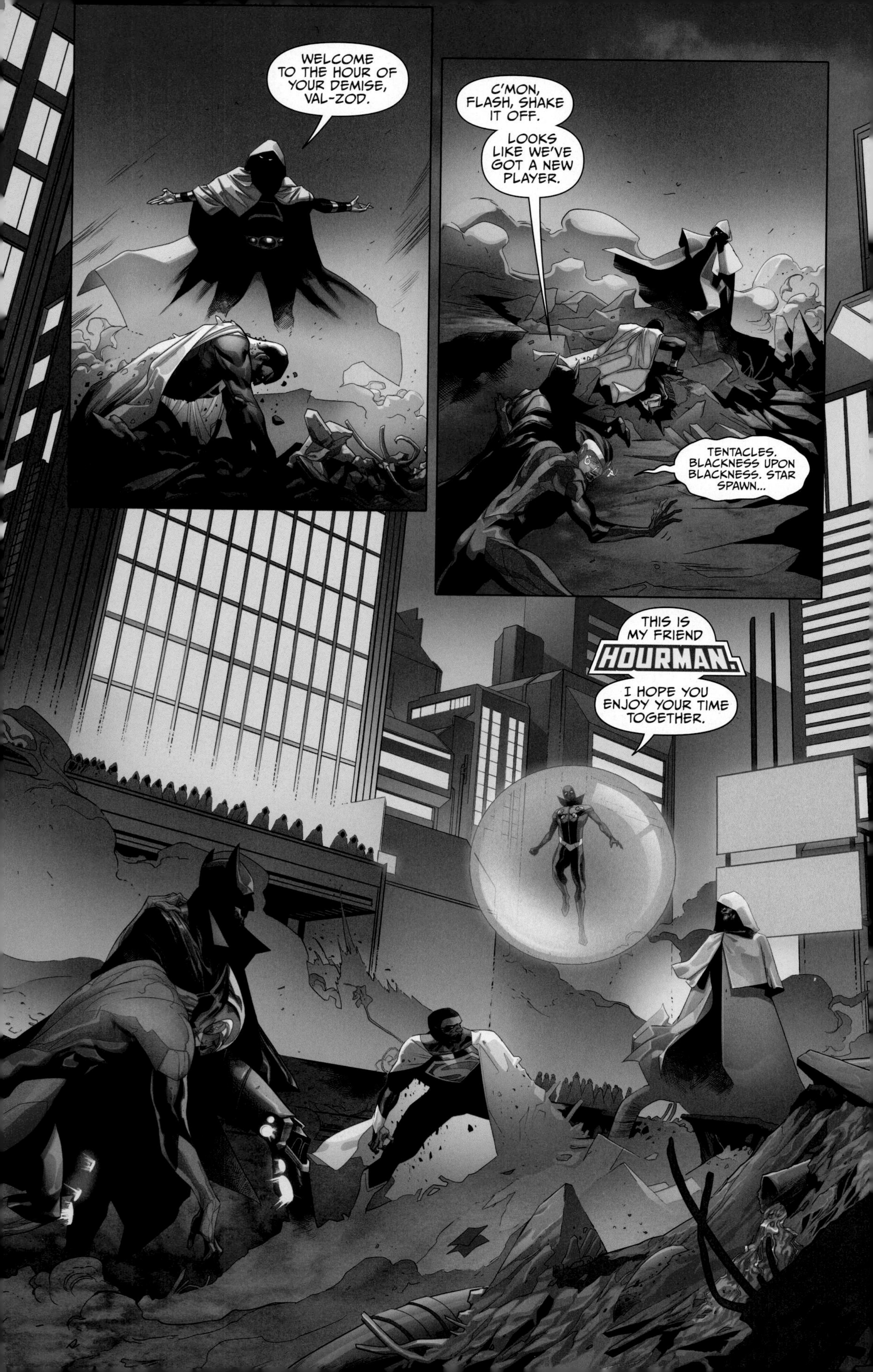
WELCOME TO THE HOUR OF YOUR DEMISE, VAL-ZOD.
C'MON, FLASH, SHAKE IT OFF.
LOOKS LIKE WE'VE GOT A NEW PLAYER.
TENTACLES. BLACKNESS UPON BLACKNESS. STAR SPAWN...
THIS IS MY FRIEND HOURMAN.
I HOPE YOU ENJOY YOUR TIME TOGETHER.

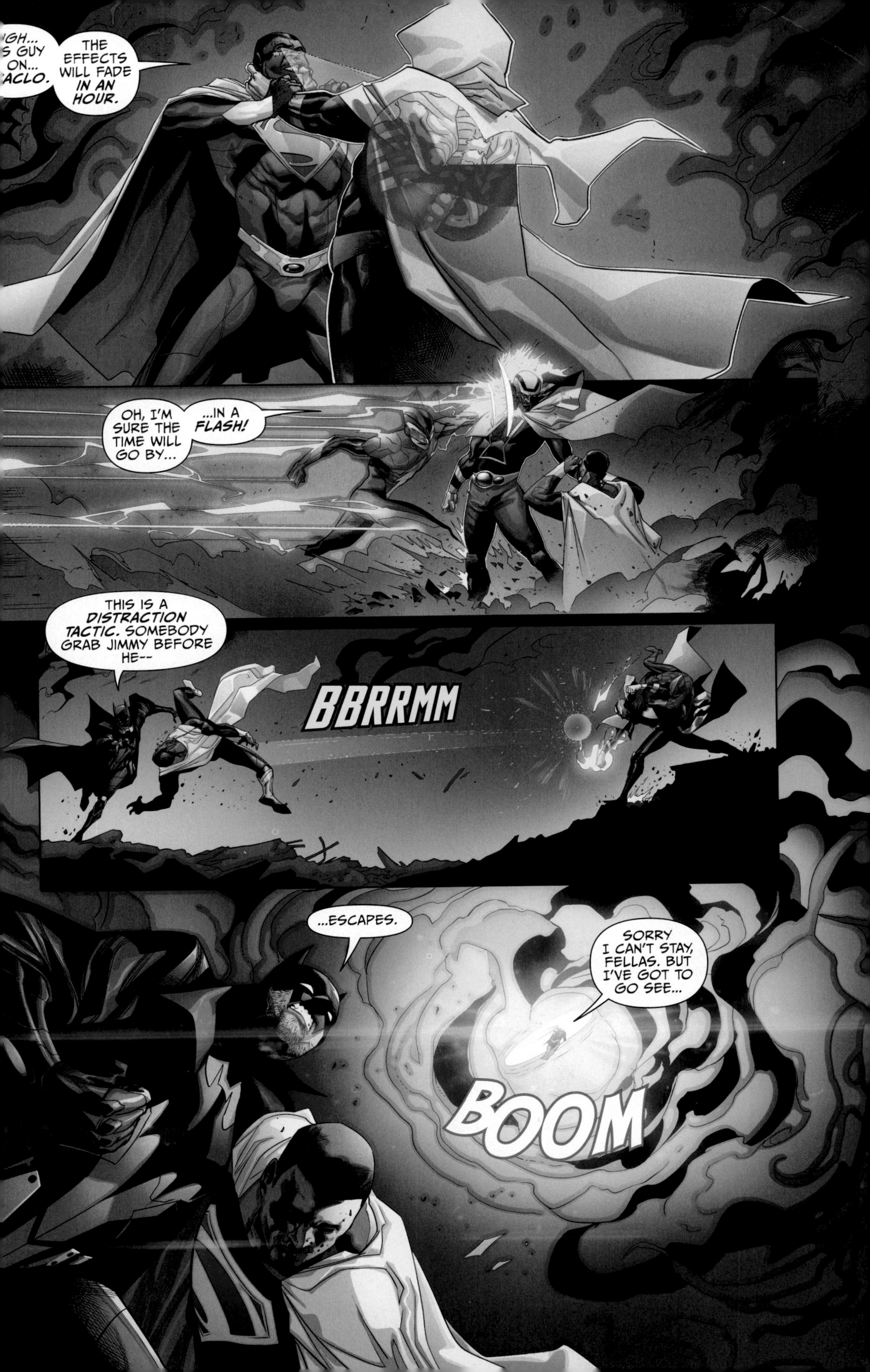

THE EFFECTS WILL FADE IN AN HOUR.
OH, I'M SURE THE TIME WILL GO BY...
...IN A FLASH!
THIS IS A DISTRACTION TACTIC. SOMEBODY GRAB JIMMY BEFORE HE--
BBRRMM
...ESCAPES.
SORRY I CAN'T STAY, FELLAS. BUT I'VE GOT TO GO SEE...
BOOM

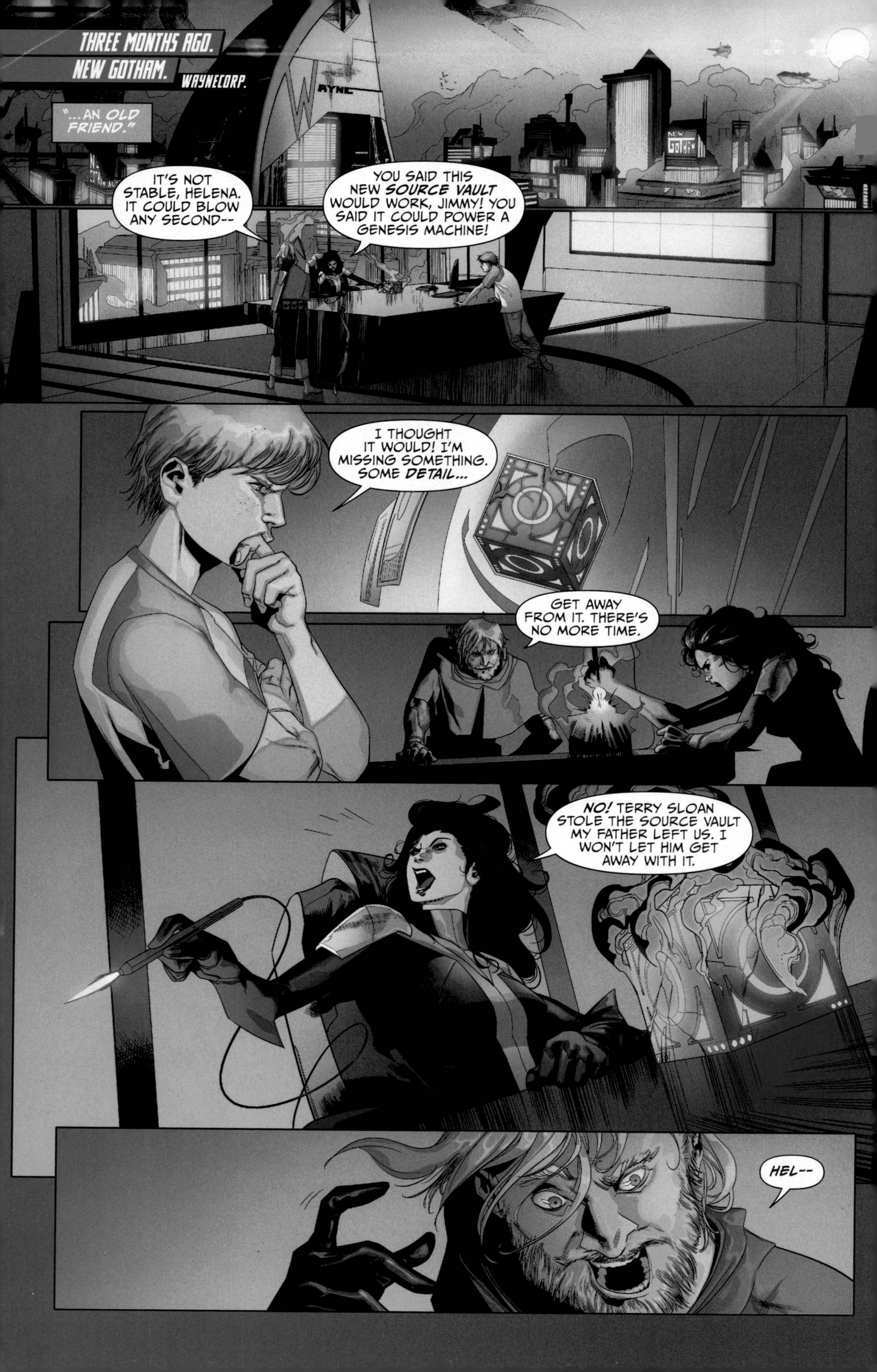
THREE MONTHS AGO.
NEW GOTHAM.
WAYNECORP.
"...AN OLD FRIEND."
IT'S NOT STABLE, HELENA. IT COULD BLOW ANY SECOND--
YOU SAID THIS NEW SOURCE VAULT WOULD WORK, JIMMY! YOU SAID IT COULD POWER A GENESIS MACHINE!
I THOUGHT IT WOULD! I'M MISSING SOMETHING. SOME DETAIL...
GET AWAY FROM IT. THERE'S NO MORE TIME.
NO! TERRY SLOAN STOLE THE SOURCE VAULT MY FATHER LEFT US. I WON'T LET HIM GET AWAY WITH IT.
HEL--

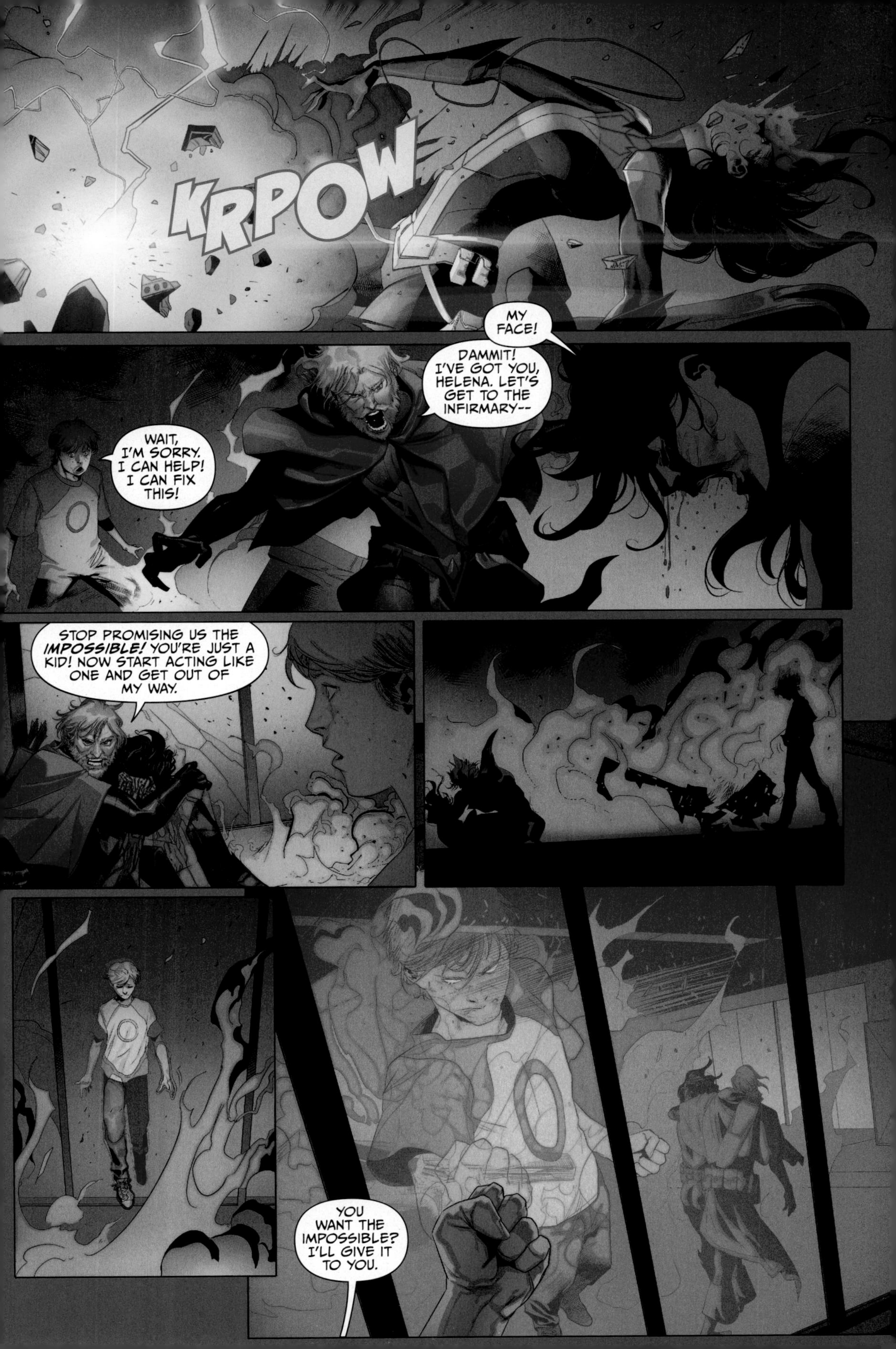
KRPOW
MY FACE!
DAMMIT! I'VE GOT YOU, HELENA. LET'S GET TO THE INFIRMARY--
WAIT, I'M SORRY. I CAN HELP! I CAN FIX THIS!
STOP PROMISING US THE *IMPOSSIBLE!* YOU'RE JUST A KID! NOW START ACTING LIKE ONE AND GET OUT OF MY WAY.
YOU WANT THE IMPOSSIBLE? I'LL GIVE IT TO YOU.

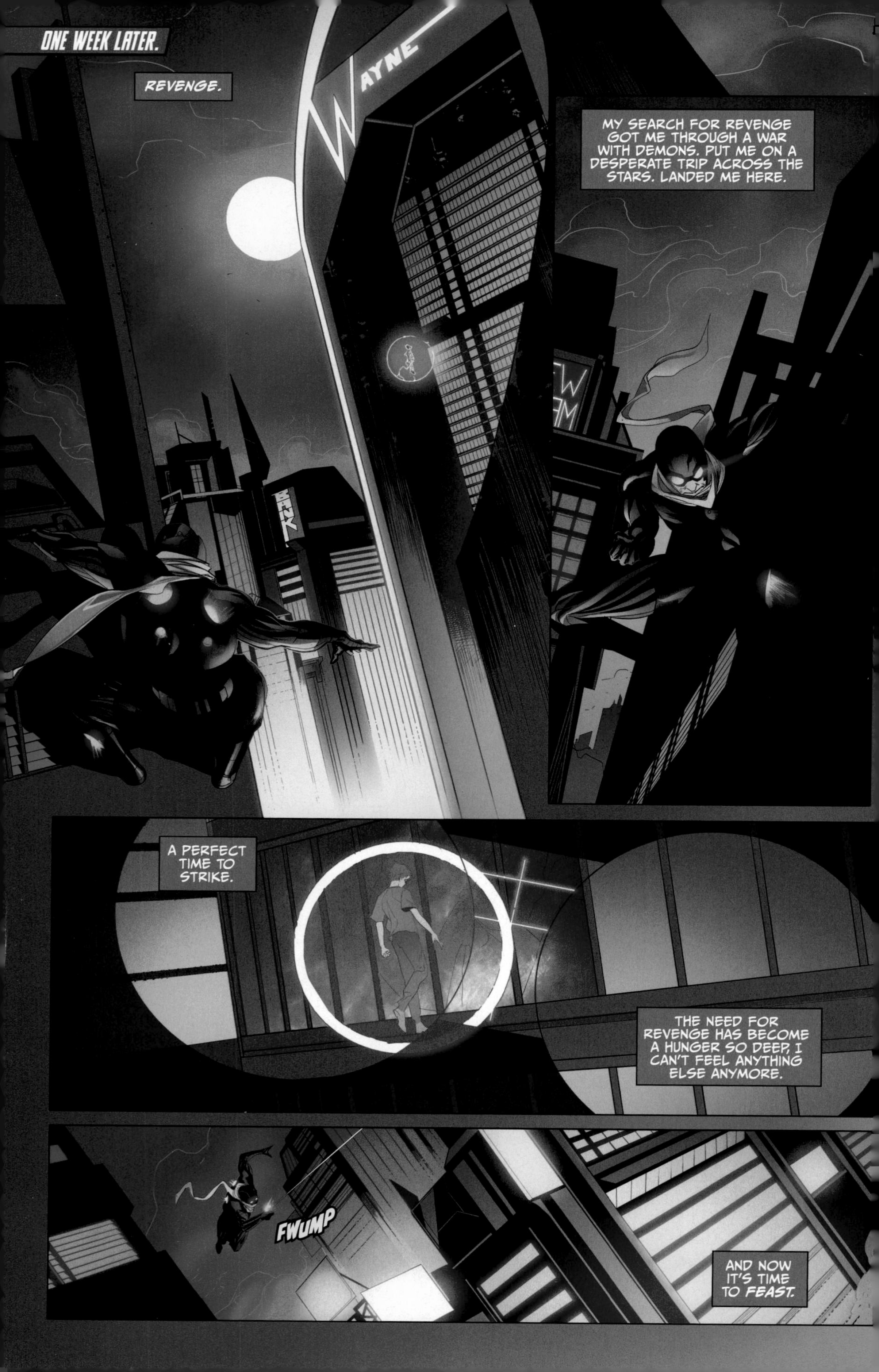

ONE WEEK LATER.
REVENGE.
WAYNE
BANK
MY SEARCH FOR REVENGE GOT ME THROUGH A WAR WITH DEMONS. PUT ME ON A DESPERATE TRIP ACROSS THE STARS. LANDED ME HERE.
A PERFECT TIME TO STRIKE.
THE NEED FOR REVENGE HAS BECOME A HUNGER SO DEEP, I CAN'T FEEL ANYTHING ELSE ANYMORE.
FWUMP
AND NOW IT'S TIME TO *FEAST.*

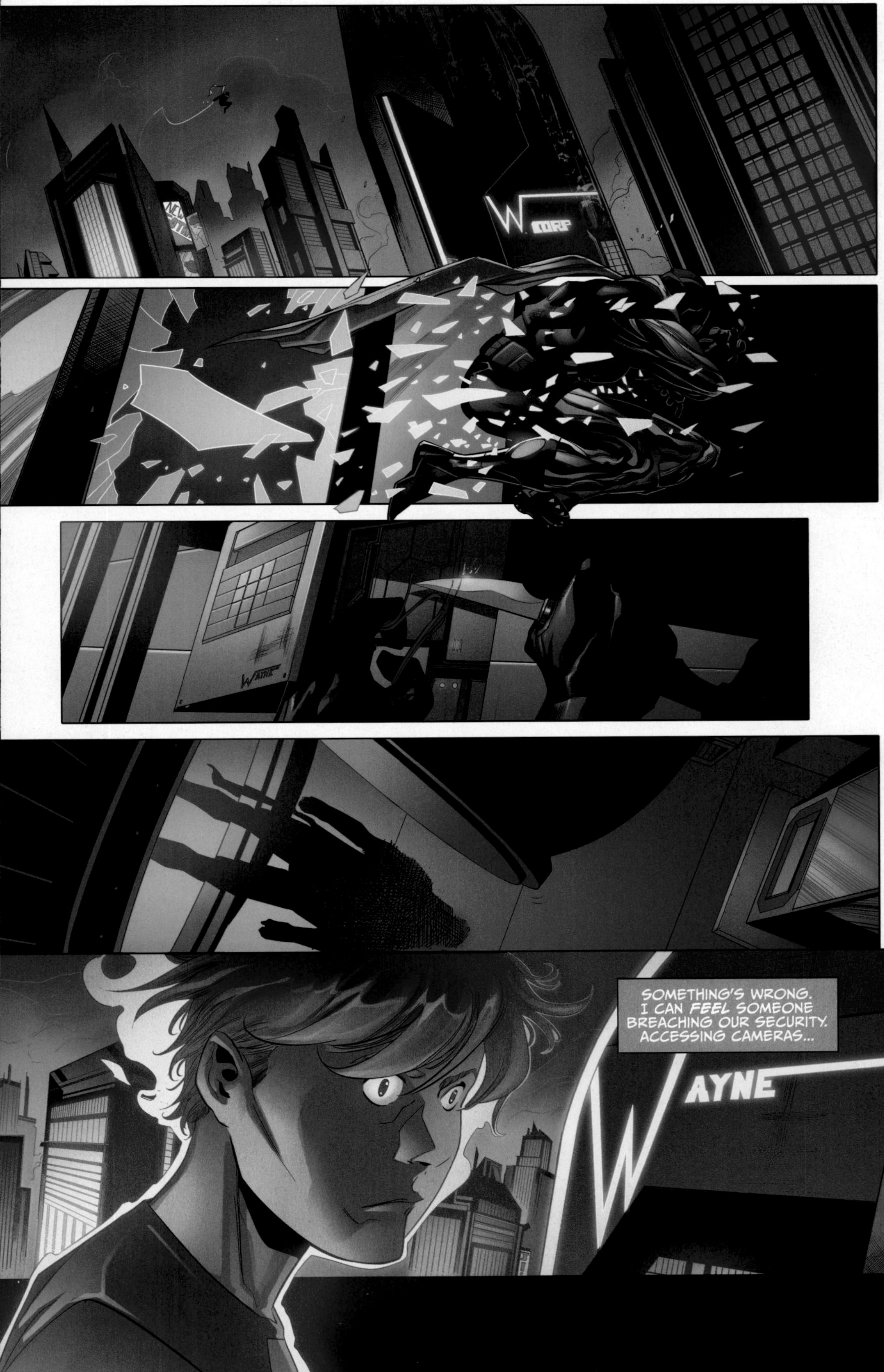
W CORP
SOMETHING'S WRONG. I CAN *FEEL* SOMEONE BREACHING OUR SECURITY. ACCESSING CAMERAS...
AYNE

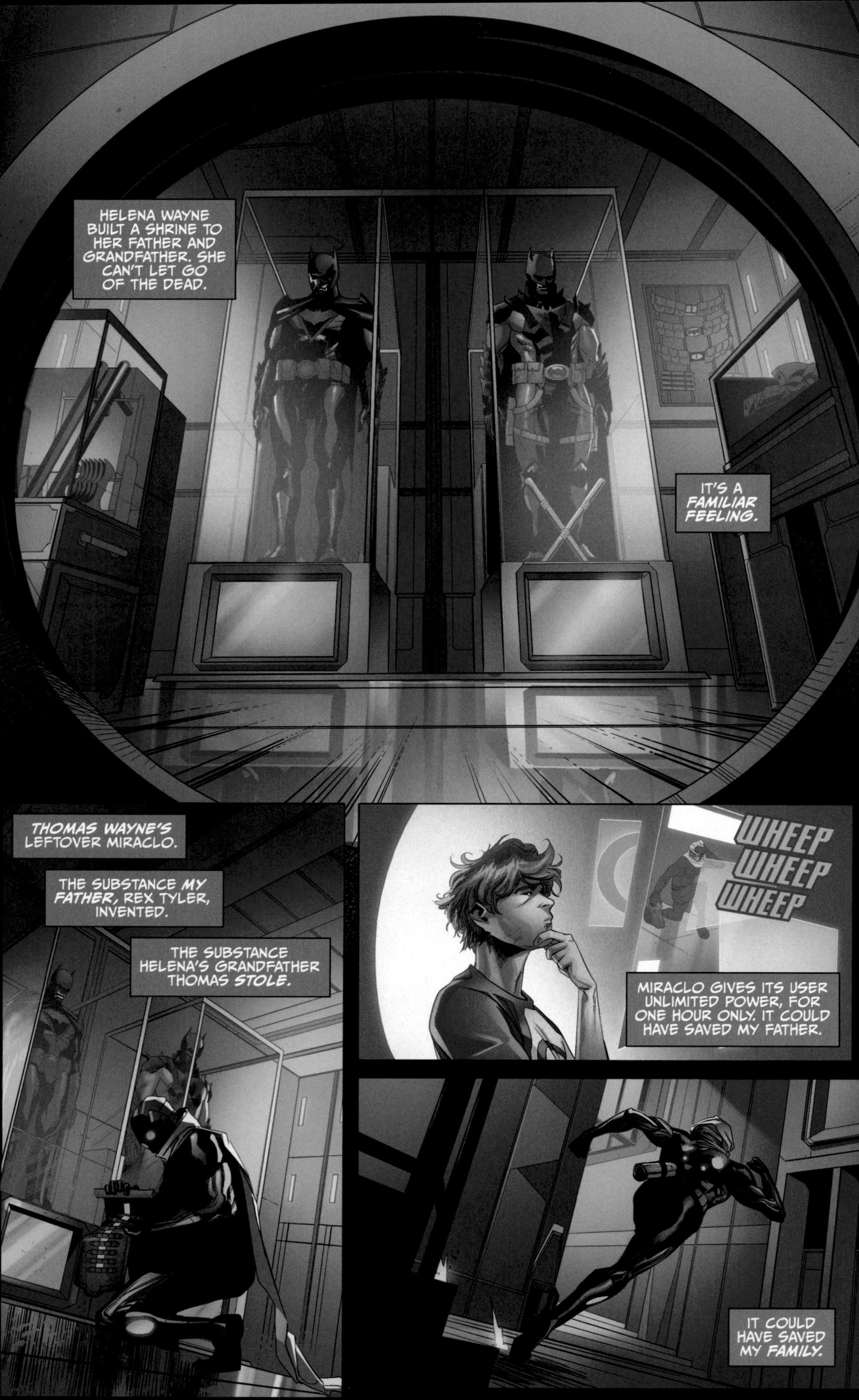
HELENA WAYNE BUILT A SHRINE TO HER FATHER AND GRANDFATHER. SHE CAN'T LET GO OF THE DEAD.
IT'S A *FAMILIAR FEELING.*
THOMAS WAYNE'S LEFTOVER MIRACLO.
THE SUBSTANCE *MY FATHER,* REX TYLER, INVENTED.
THE SUBSTANCE HELENA'S GRANDFATHER THOMAS *STOLE.*
WHEEP WHEEP WHEEP
MIRACLO GIVES ITS USER UNLIMITED POWER, FOR ONE HOUR ONLY. IT COULD HAVE SAVED MY FATHER.
IT COULD HAVE SAVED MY *FAMILY.*

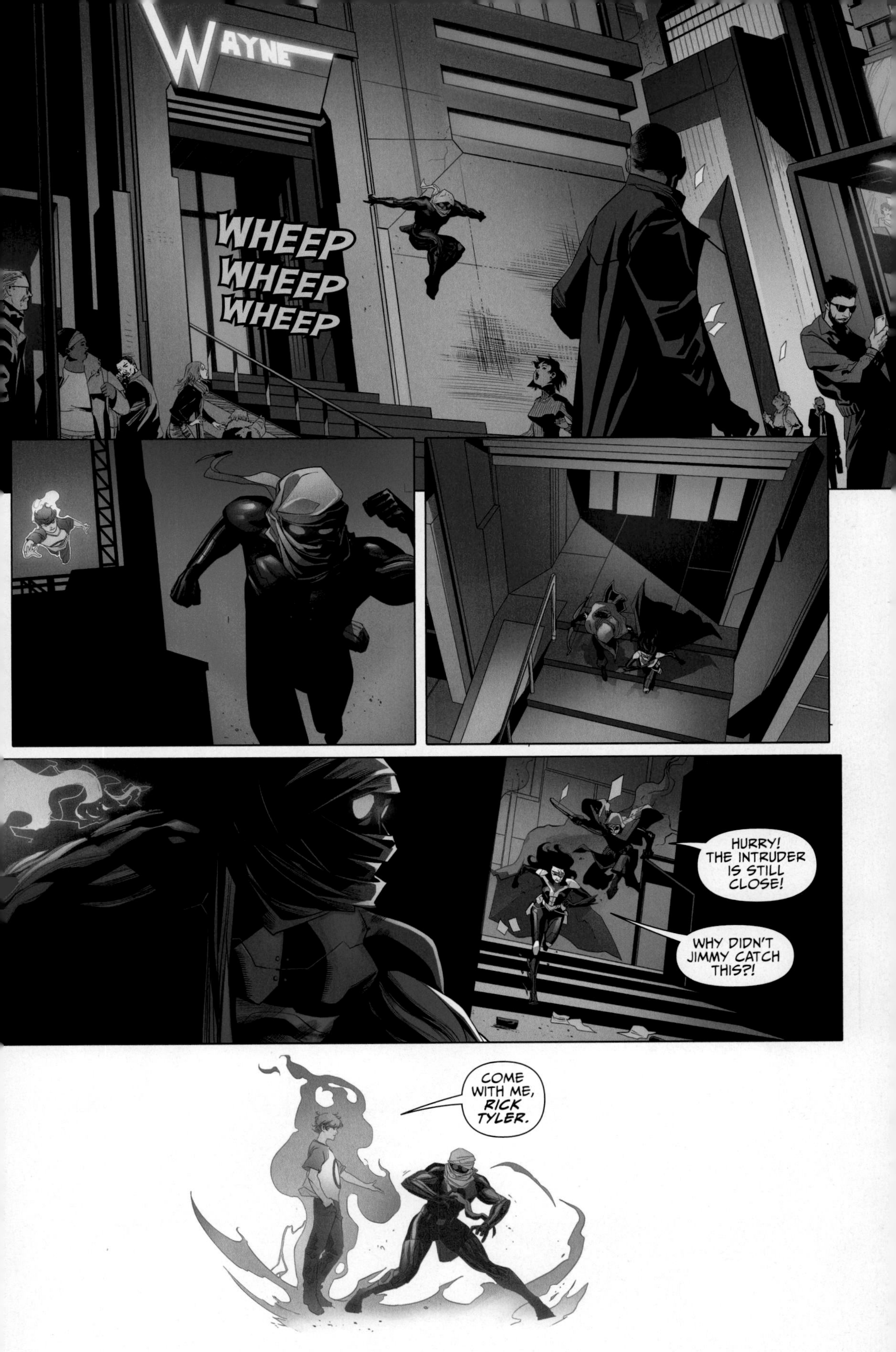
WAYNE
WHEEP WHEEP WHEEP
HURRY! THE INTRUDER IS STILL CLOSE!
WHY DIDN'T JIMMY CATCH THIS?!
COME WITH ME, RICK TYLER.

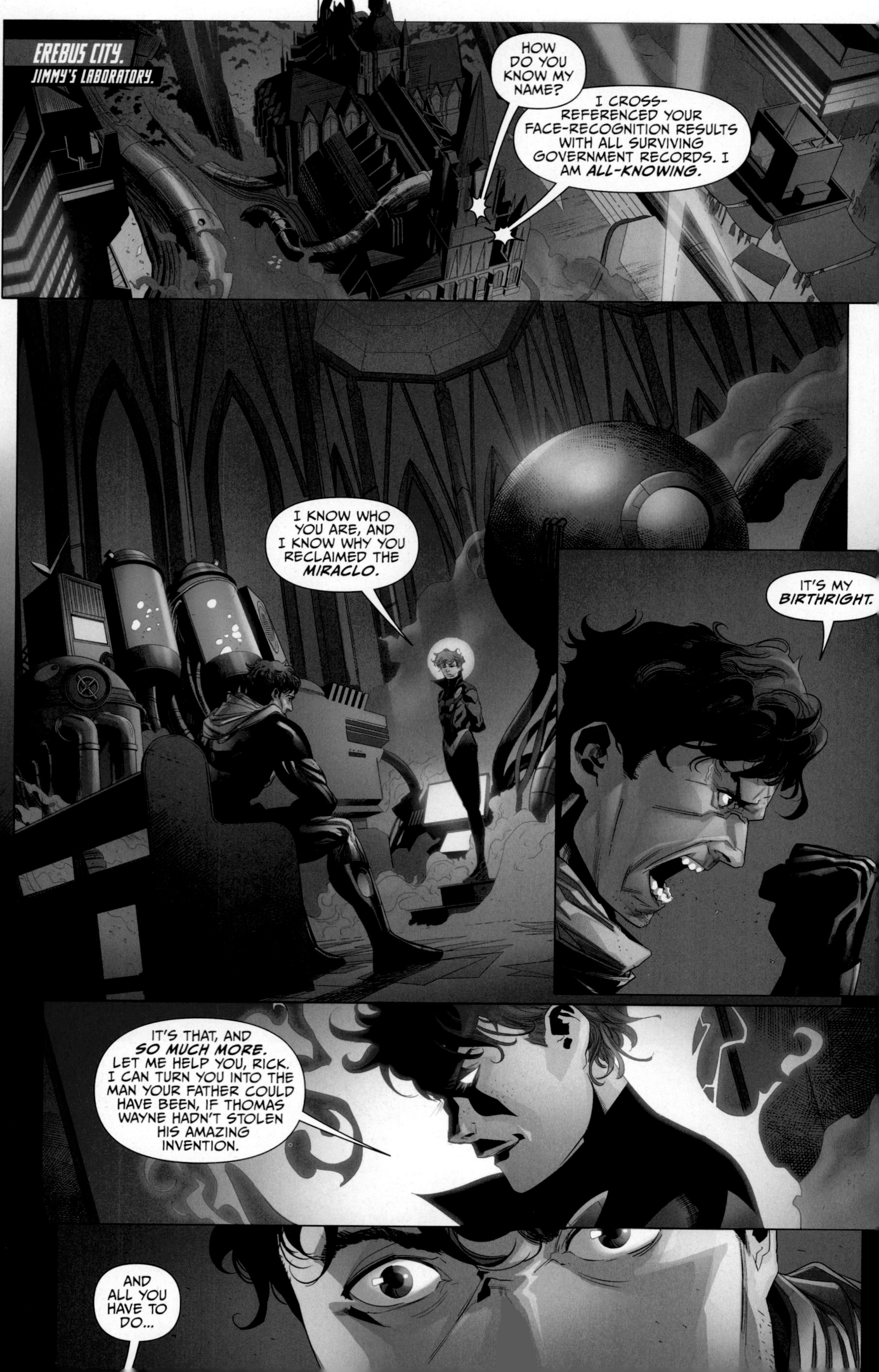
EREBUS CITY.
JIMMY'S LABORATORY.
HOW DO YOU KNOW MY NAME?
I CROSS-REFERENCED YOUR FACE-RECOGNITION RESULTS WITH ALL SURVIVING GOVERNMENT RECORDS. I AM ALL-KNOWING.
I KNOW WHO YOU ARE, AND I KNOW WHY YOU RECLAIMED THE MIRACLO.
IT'S MY BIRTHRIGHT.
IT'S THAT, AND SO MUCH MORE. LET ME HELP YOU, RICK. I CAN TURN YOU INTO THE MAN YOUR FATHER COULD HAVE BEEN, IF THOMAS WAYNE HADN'T STOLEN HIS AMAZING INVENTION.
AND ALL YOU HAVE TO DO...

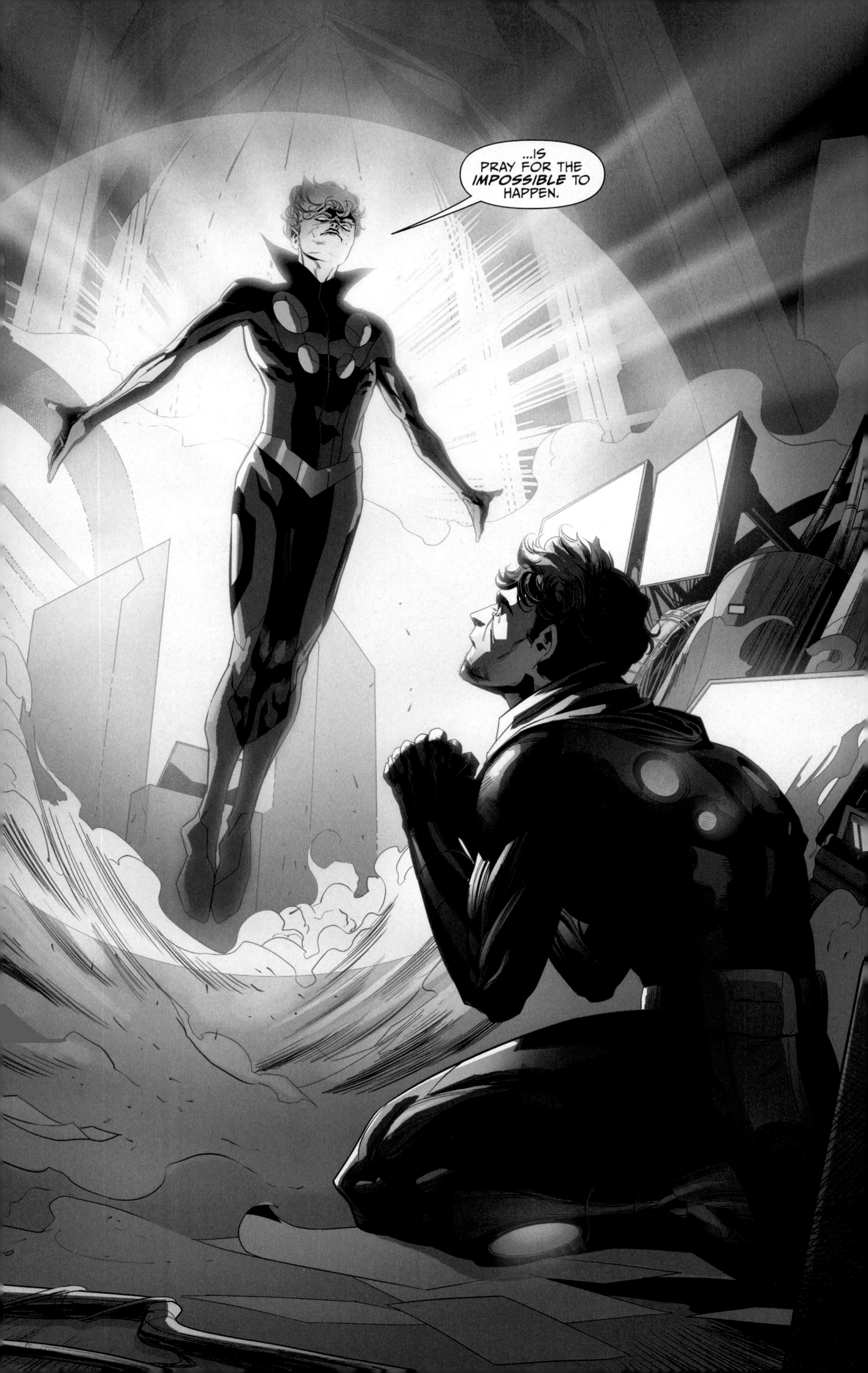
...IS PRAY FOR THE IMPOSSIBLE TO HAPPEN.

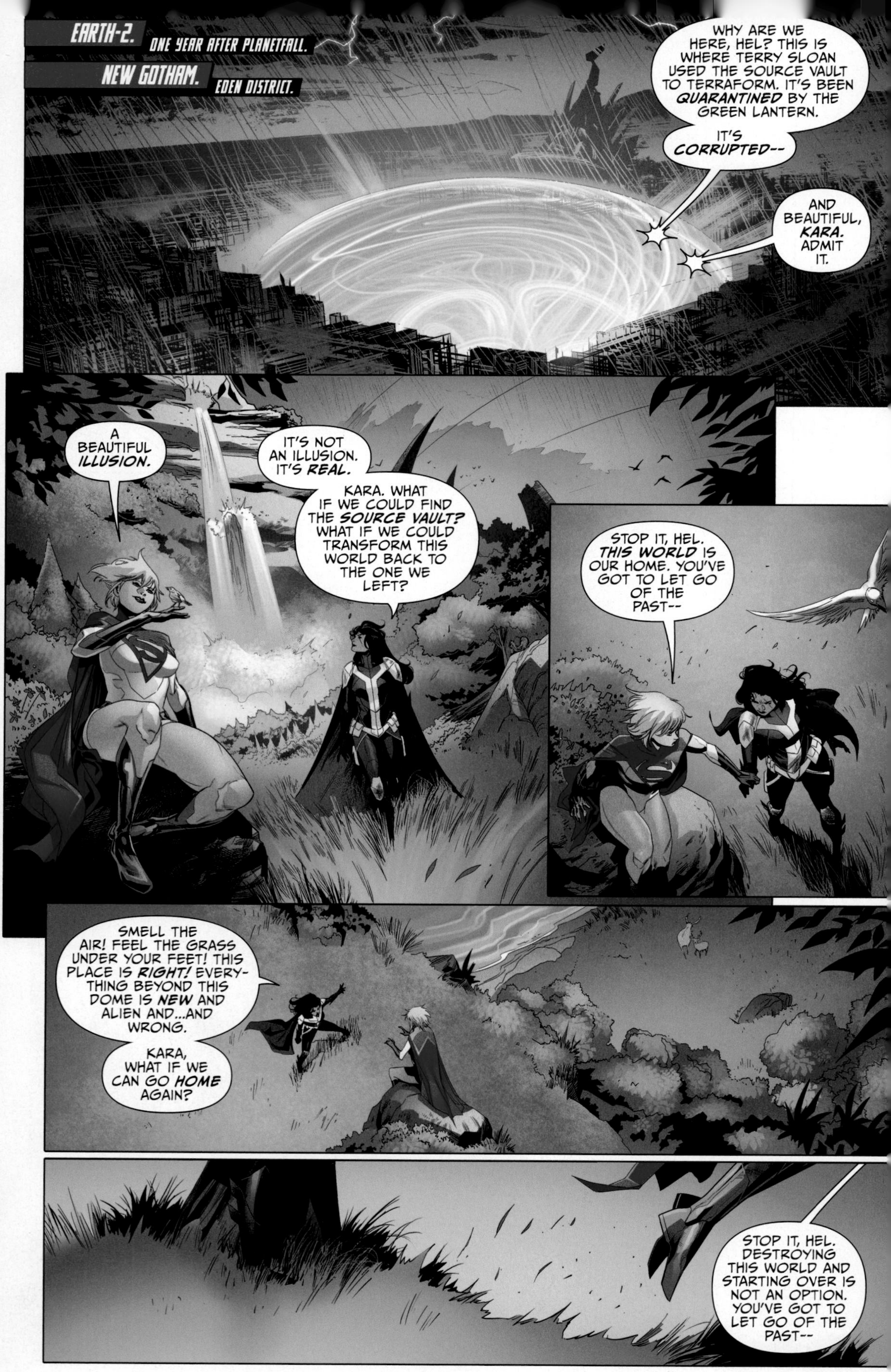
EARTH-2. ONE YEAR AFTER PLANETFALL.
NEW GOTHAM. EDEN DISTRICT.
WHY ARE WE HERE, HEL? THIS IS WHERE TERRY SLOAN USED THE SOURCE VAULT TO TERRAFORM. IT'S BEEN QUARANTINED BY THE GREEN LANTERN.
IT'S CORRUPTED--
AND BEAUTIFUL, KARA. ADMIT IT.
A BEAUTIFUL ILLUSION.
IT'S NOT AN ILLUSION. IT'S REAL.
KARA. WHAT IF WE COULD FIND THE SOURCE VAULT? WHAT IF WE COULD TRANSFORM THIS WORLD BACK TO THE ONE WE LEFT?
STOP IT, HEL. THIS WORLD IS OUR HOME. YOU'VE GOT TO LET GO OF THE PAST--
SMELL THE AIR! FEEL THE GRASS UNDER YOUR FEET! THIS PLACE IS RIGHT! EVERYTHING BEYOND THIS DOME IS NEW AND ALIEN AND...AND WRONG.
KARA, WHAT IF WE CAN GO HOME AGAIN?
STOP IT, HEL. DESTROYING THIS WORLD AND STARTING OVER IS NOT AN OPTION. YOU'VE GOT TO LET GO OF THE PAST--

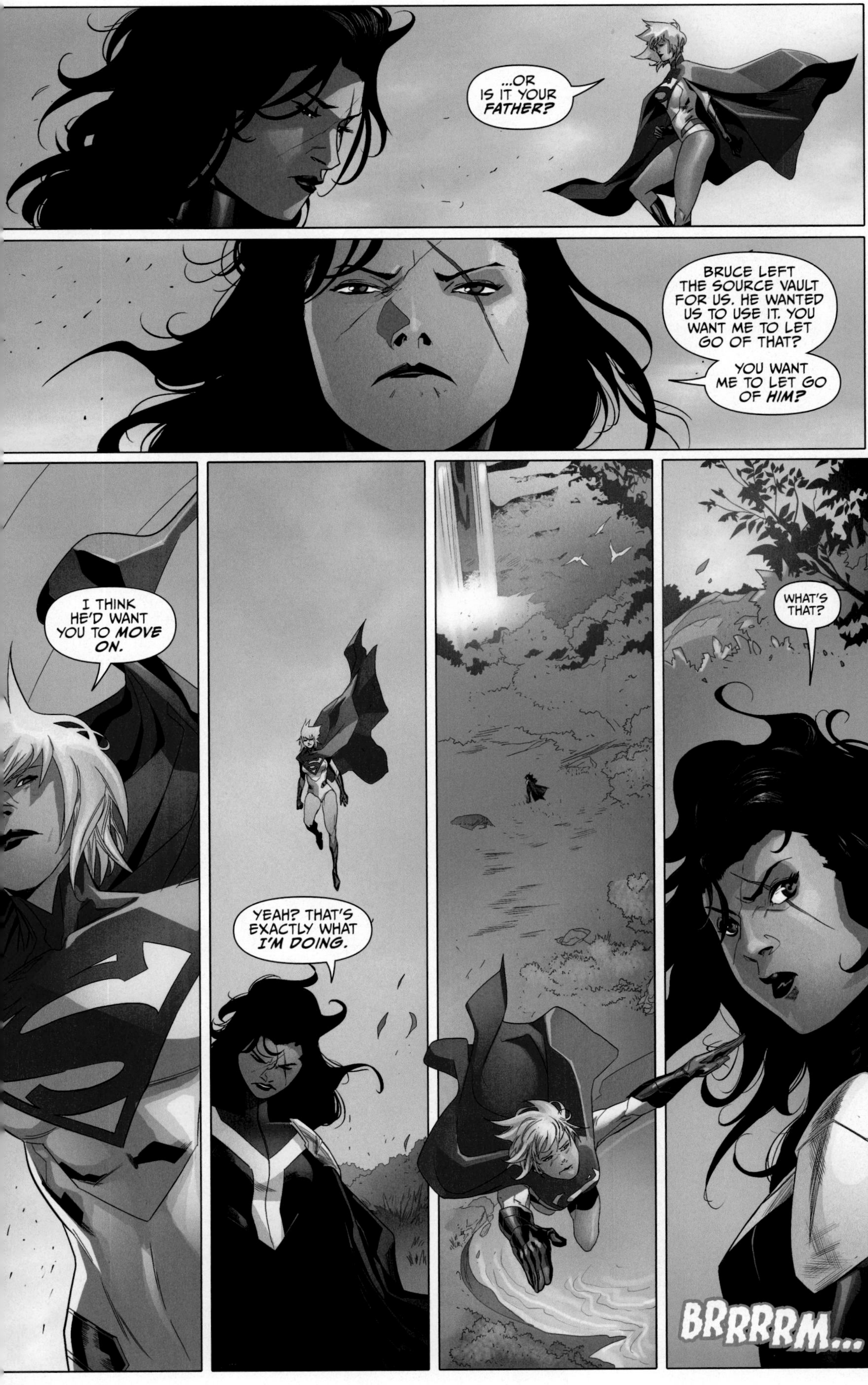
...OR IS IT YOUR *FATHER?*
BRUCE LEFT THE SOURCE VAULT FOR US. HE WANTED US TO USE IT. YOU WANT ME TO LET GO OF THAT?
YOU WANT ME TO LET GO OF *HIM?*
I THINK HE'D WANT YOU TO *MOVE ON.*
YEAH? THAT'S EXACTLY WHAT *I'M DOING.*
WHAT'S THAT?
BRRRRM...

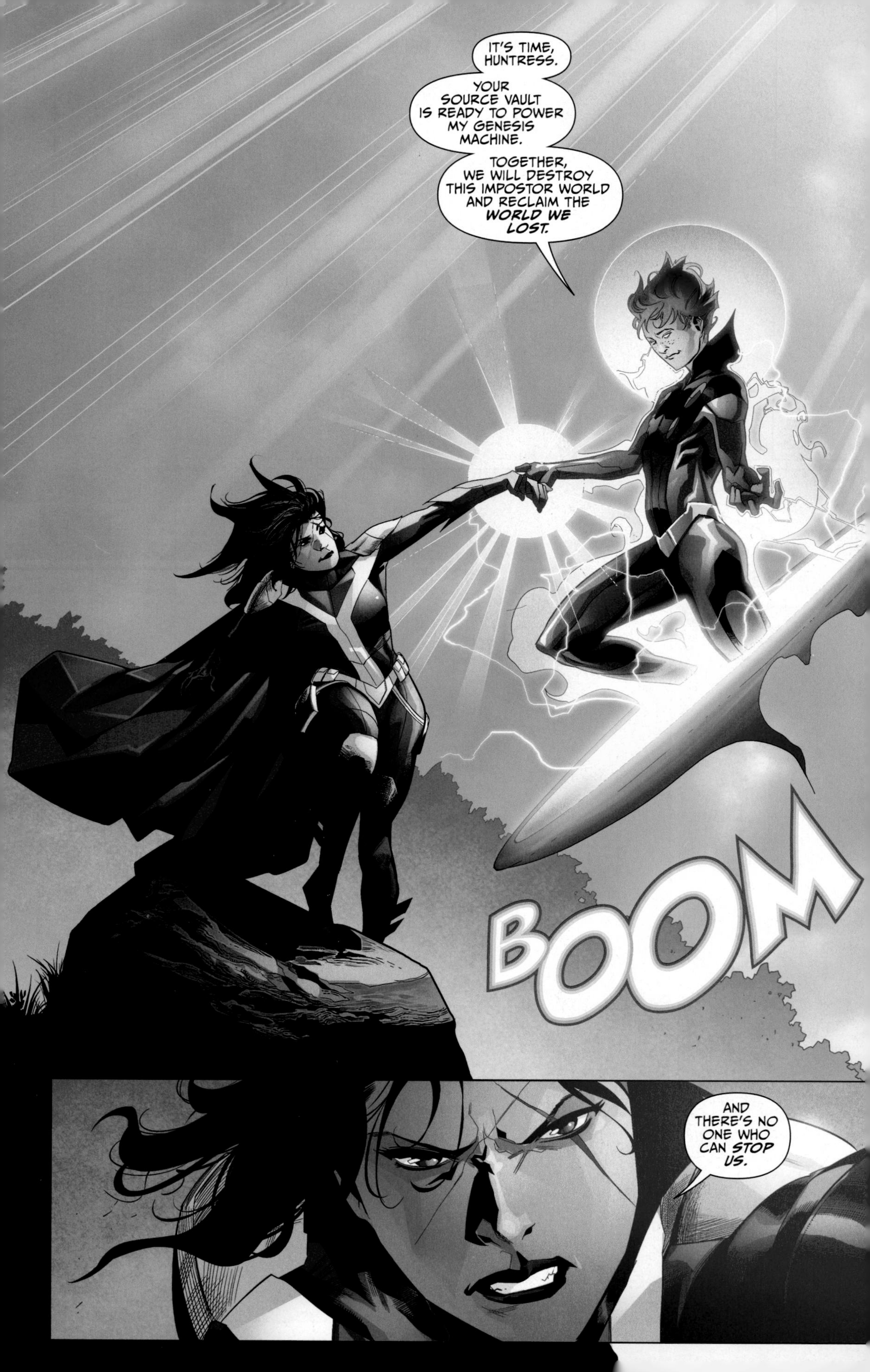
IT'S TIME, HUNTRESS.
YOUR SOURCE VAULT IS READY TO POWER MY GENESIS MACHINE.
TOGETHER, WE WILL DESTROY THIS IMPOSTOR WORLD AND RECLAIM THE WORLD WE LOST.
BOOM
AND THERE'S NO ONE WHO CAN STOP US.

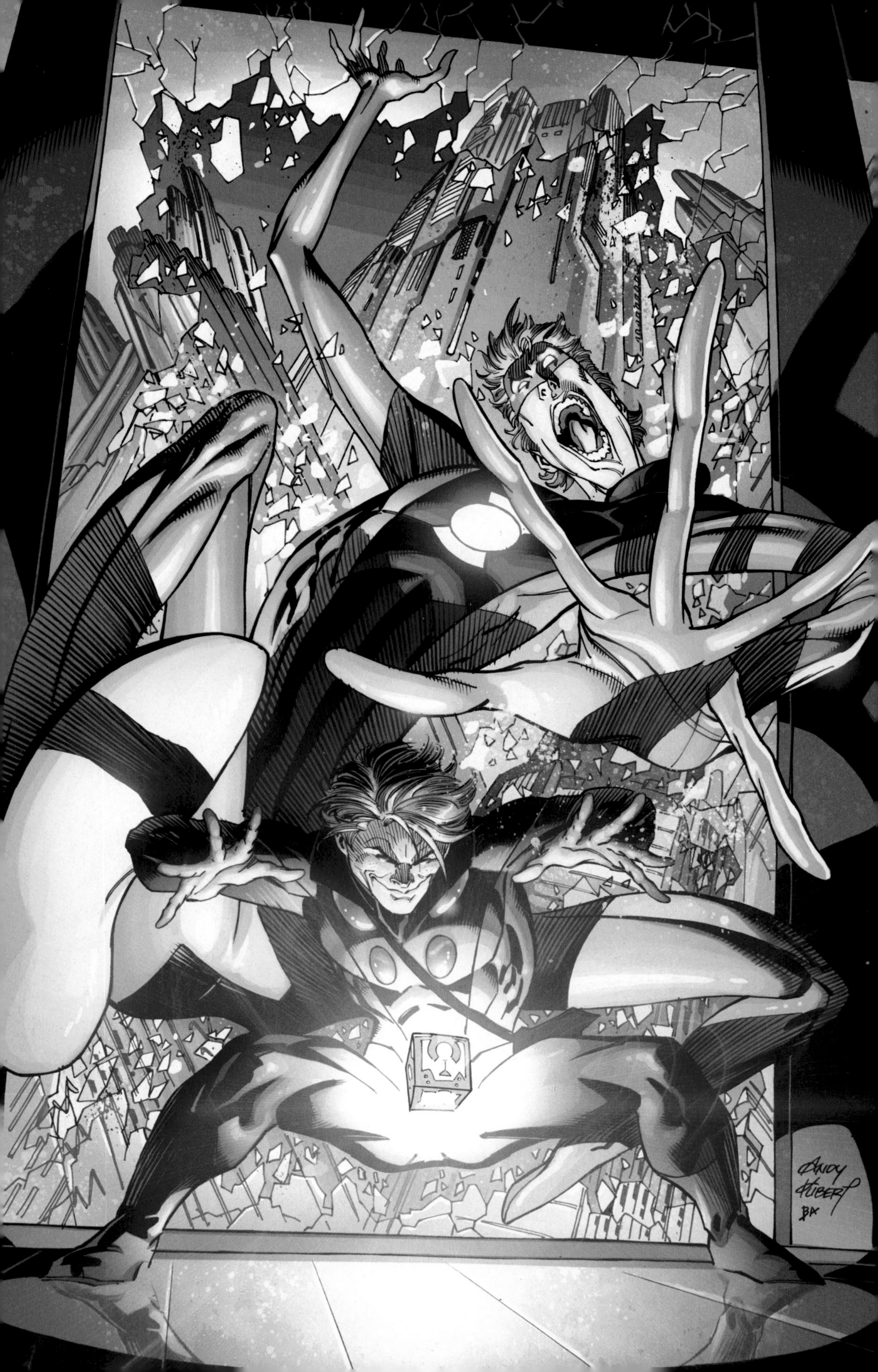
ANDY KUBERT
BA

JUSTICE

DANIEL H. WILSON writer JORGE JIMENEZ ALISSON BORGES artists ALEJANDRO SANCHEZ BLOND colorists TRAVIS LANHAM letterer cover by ANDY KUBERT & BRAD ANDERS

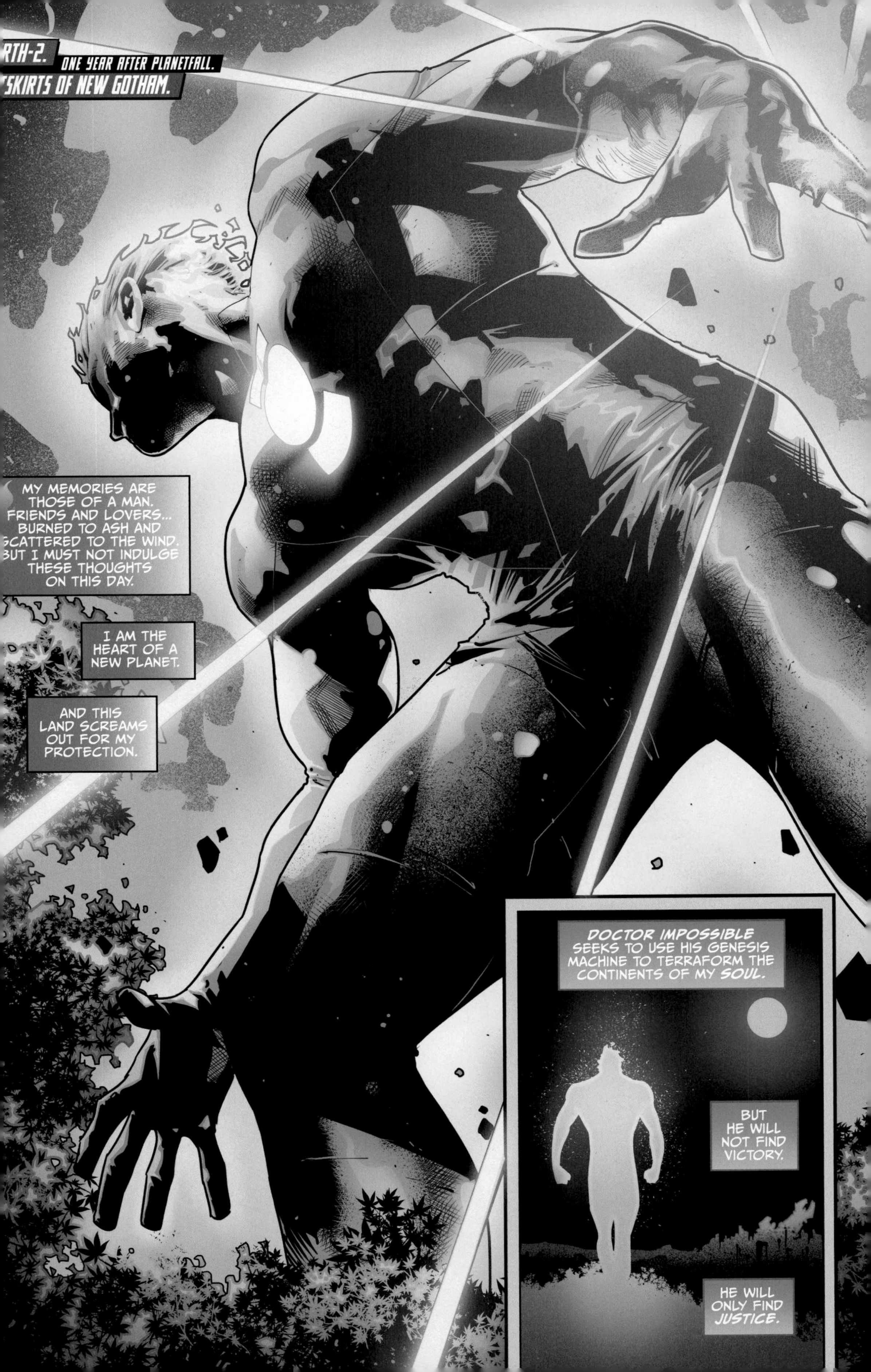

RTH-2. ONE YEAR AFTER PLANETFALL.
SKIRTS OF NEW GOTHAM.
MY MEMORIES ARE THOSE OF A MAN. FRIENDS AND LOVERS... BURNED TO ASH AND SCATTERED TO THE WIND. BUT I MUST NOT INDULGE THESE THOUGHTS ON THIS DAY.
I AM THE HEART OF A NEW PLANET.
AND THIS LAND SCREAMS OUT FOR MY PROTECTION.
DOCTOR IMPOSSIBLE SEEKS TO USE HIS GENESIS MACHINE TO TERRAFORM THE CONTINENTS OF MY SOUL.
BUT HE WILL NOT FIND VICTORY.
HE WILL ONLY FIND JUSTICE.

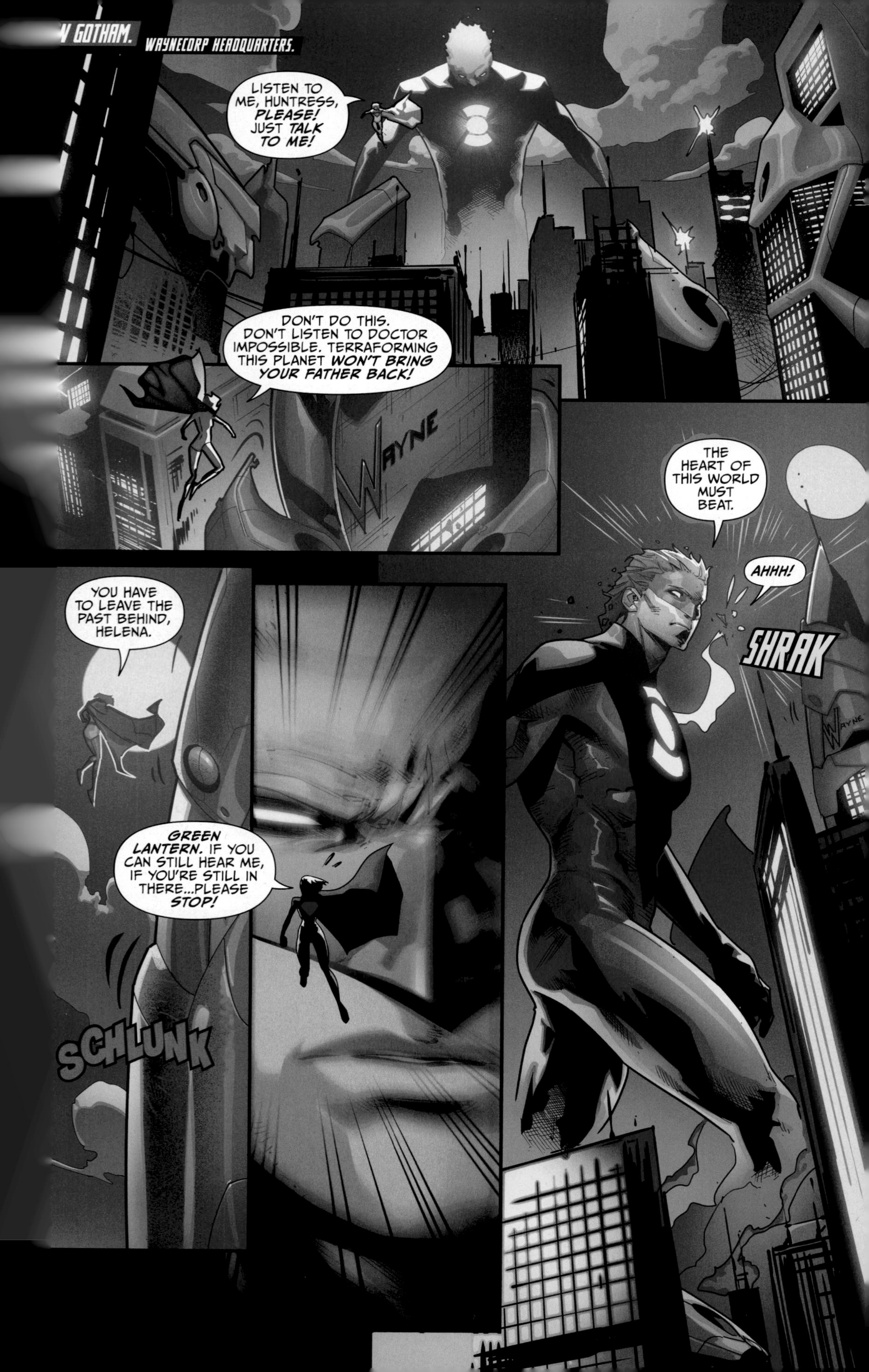
V GOTHAM.
WAYNECORP HEADQUARTERS.
LISTEN TO ME, HUNTRESS, PLEASE! JUST TALK TO ME!
DON'T DO THIS. DON'T LISTEN TO DOCTOR IMPOSSIBLE. TERRAFORMING THIS PLANET WON'T BRING YOUR FATHER BACK!
WAYNE
THE HEART OF THIS WORLD MUST BEAT.
YOU HAVE TO LEAVE THE PAST BEHIND, HELENA.
AHHH!
SHRAK
WAYNE
GREEN LANTERN. IF YOU CAN STILL HEAR ME, IF YOU'RE STILL IN THERE...PLEASE STOP!
SCHLUNK

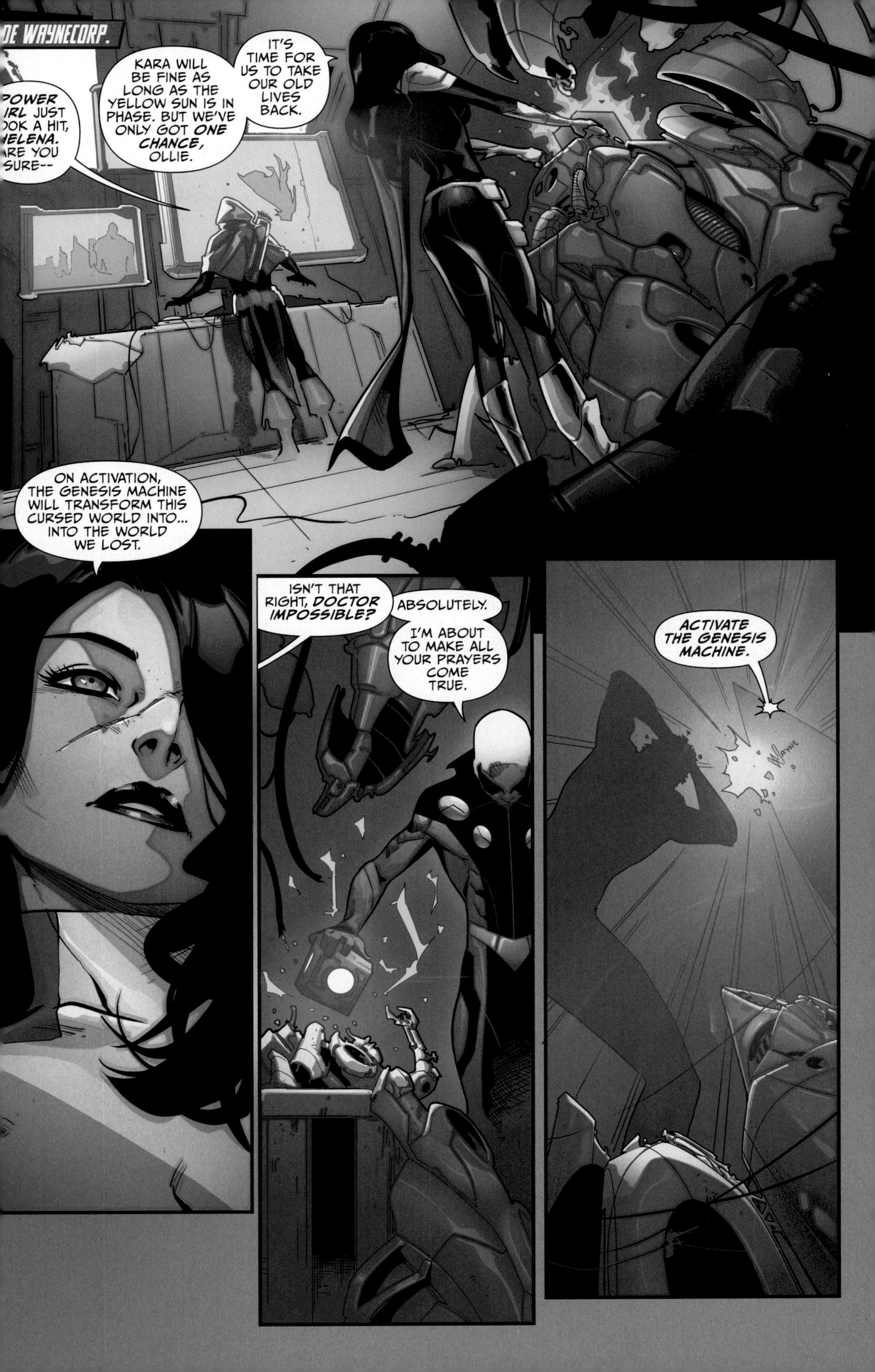

DE WAYNECORP.
POWER GIRL JUST TOOK A HIT, HELENA. ARE YOU SURE--
KARA WILL BE FINE AS LONG AS THE YELLOW SUN IS IN PHASE. BUT WE'VE ONLY GOT ONE CHANCE, OLLIE.
IT'S TIME FOR US TO TAKE OUR OLD LIVES BACK.
ON ACTIVATION, THE GENESIS MACHINE WILL TRANSFORM THIS CURSED WORLD INTO... INTO THE WORLD WE LOST.
ISN'T THAT RIGHT, DOCTOR IMPOSSIBLE?
ABSOLUTELY.
I'M ABOUT TO MAKE ALL YOUR PRAYERS COME TRUE.
ACTIVATE THE GENESIS MACHINE.

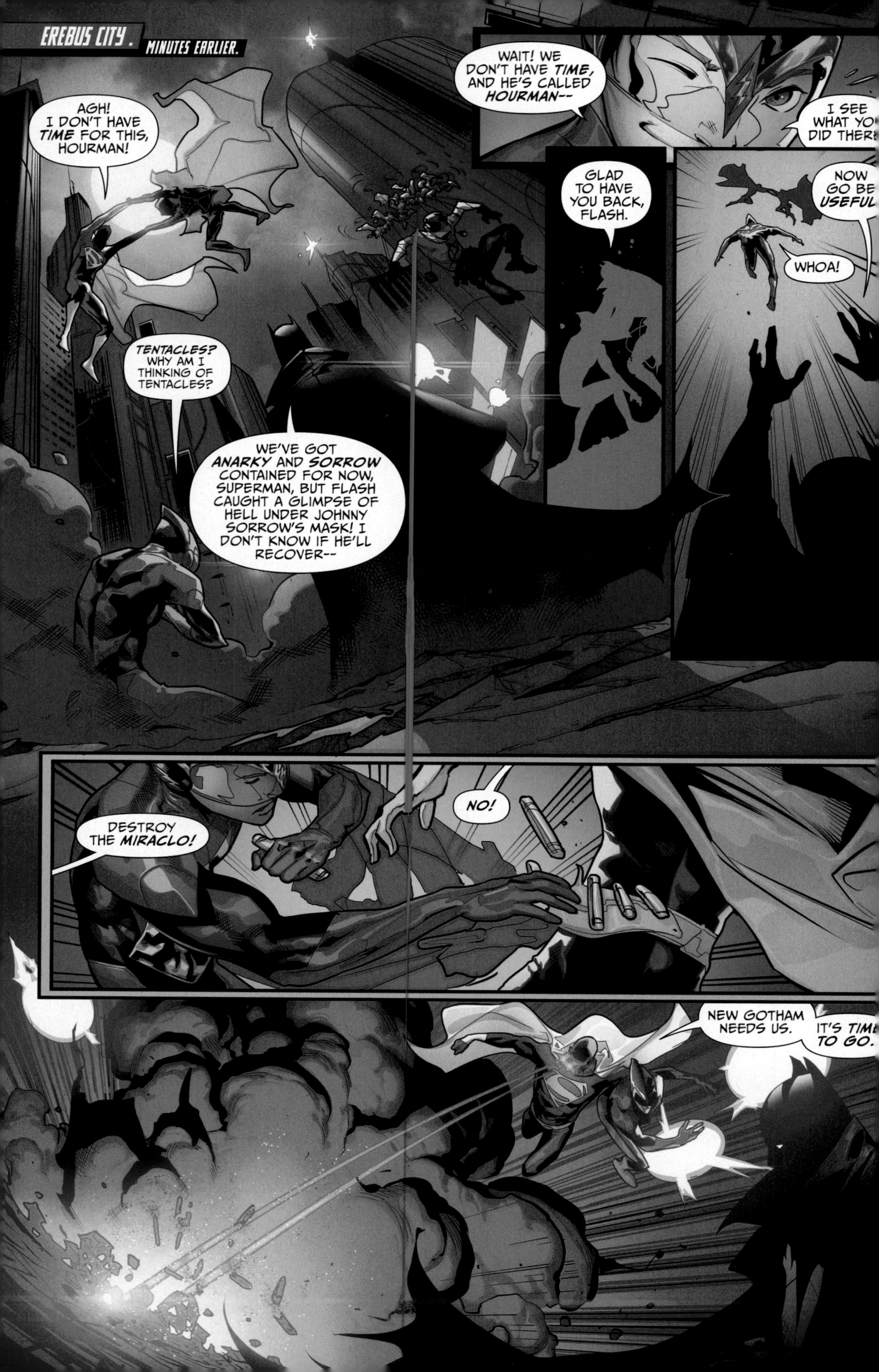
EREBUS CITY. MINUTES EARLIER.
AGH! I DON'T HAVE TIME FOR THIS, HOURMAN!
WAIT! WE DON'T HAVE TIME, AND HE'S CALLED HOURMAN--
I SEE WHAT YO DID THER
GLAD TO HAVE YOU BACK, FLASH.
NOW GO BE USEFUL
WHOA!
TENTACLES? WHY AM I THINKING OF TENTACLES?
WE'VE GOT ANARKY AND SORROW CONTAINED FOR NOW, SUPERMAN, BUT FLASH CAUGHT A GLIMPSE OF HELL UNDER JOHNNY SORROW'S MASK! I DON'T KNOW IF HE'LL RECOVER--
DESTROY THE MIRACLO!
NO!
NEW GOTHAM NEEDS US.
IT'S TIM TO GO.

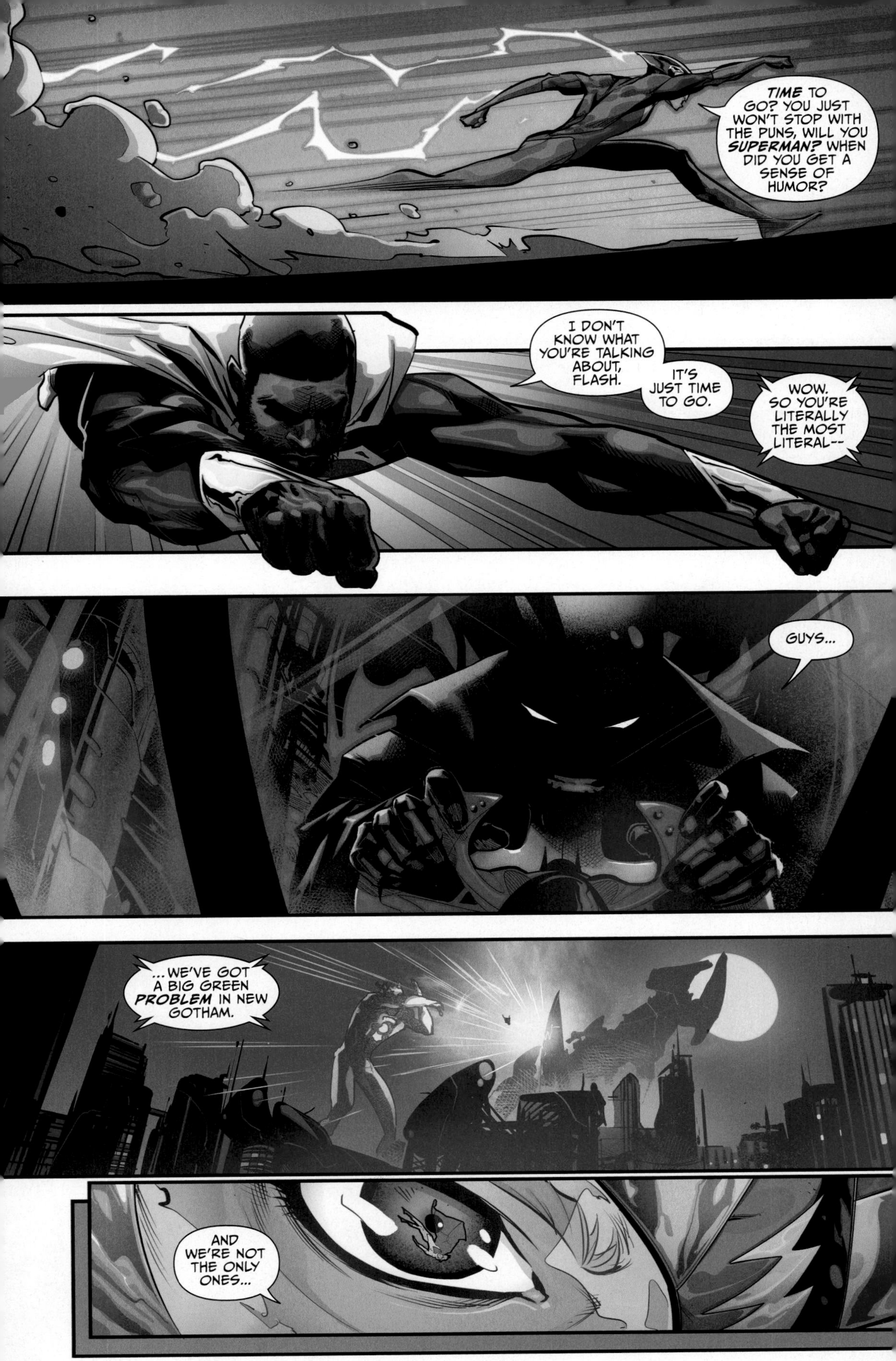
TIME TO GO? YOU JUST WON'T STOP WITH THE PUNS, WILL YOU SUPERMAN? WHEN DID YOU GET A SENSE OF HUMOR?
I DON'T KNOW WHAT YOU'RE TALKING ABOUT, FLASH.
IT'S JUST TIME TO GO.
WOW. SO YOU'RE LITERALLY THE MOST LITERAL--
GUYS...
...WE'VE GOT A BIG GREEN PROBLEM IN NEW GOTHAM.
AND WE'RE NOT THE ONLY ONES...

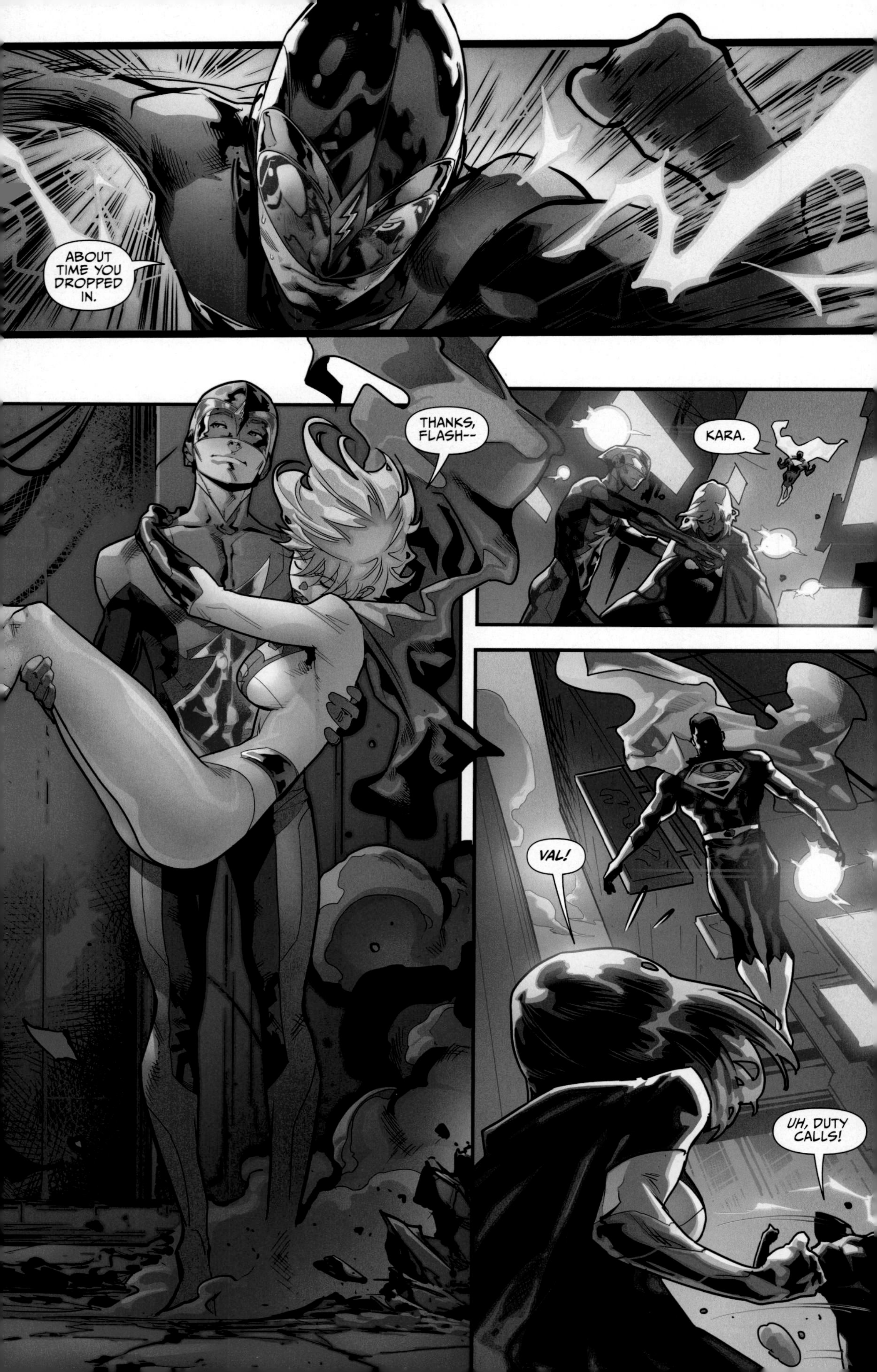
ABOUT TIME YOU DROPPED IN.
THANKS, FLASH--
KARA.
VAL!
UH, DUTY CALLS!

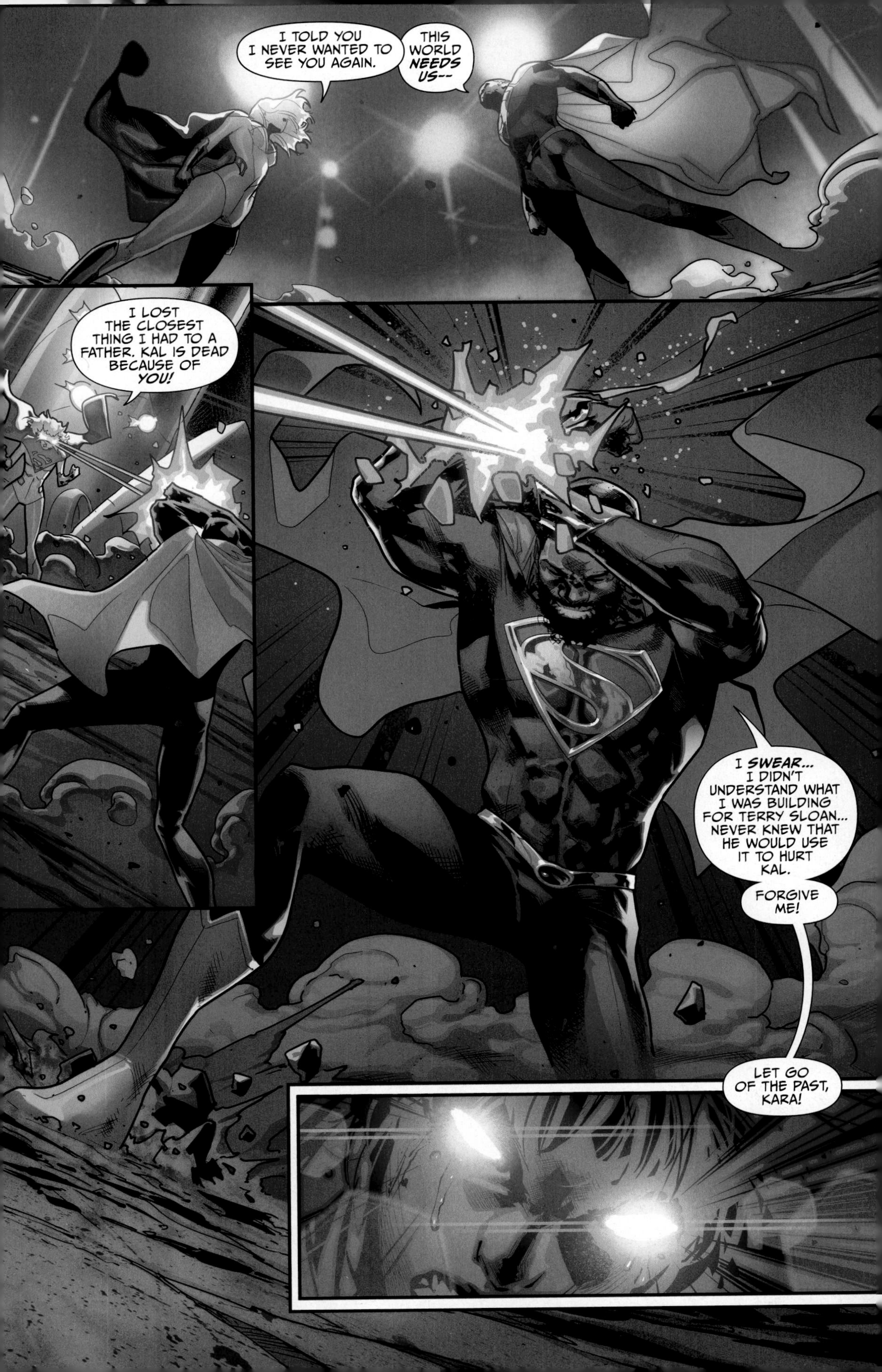
I TOLD YOU I NEVER WANTED TO SEE YOU AGAIN.
THIS WORLD NEEDS US--
I LOST THE CLOSEST THING I HAD TO A FATHER. KAL IS DEAD BECAUSE OF YOU!
I SWEAR... I DIDN'T UNDERSTAND WHAT I WAS BUILDING FOR TERRY SLOAN... NEVER KNEW THAT HE WOULD USE IT TO HURT KAL.
FORGIVE ME!
LET GO OF THE PAST, KARA!

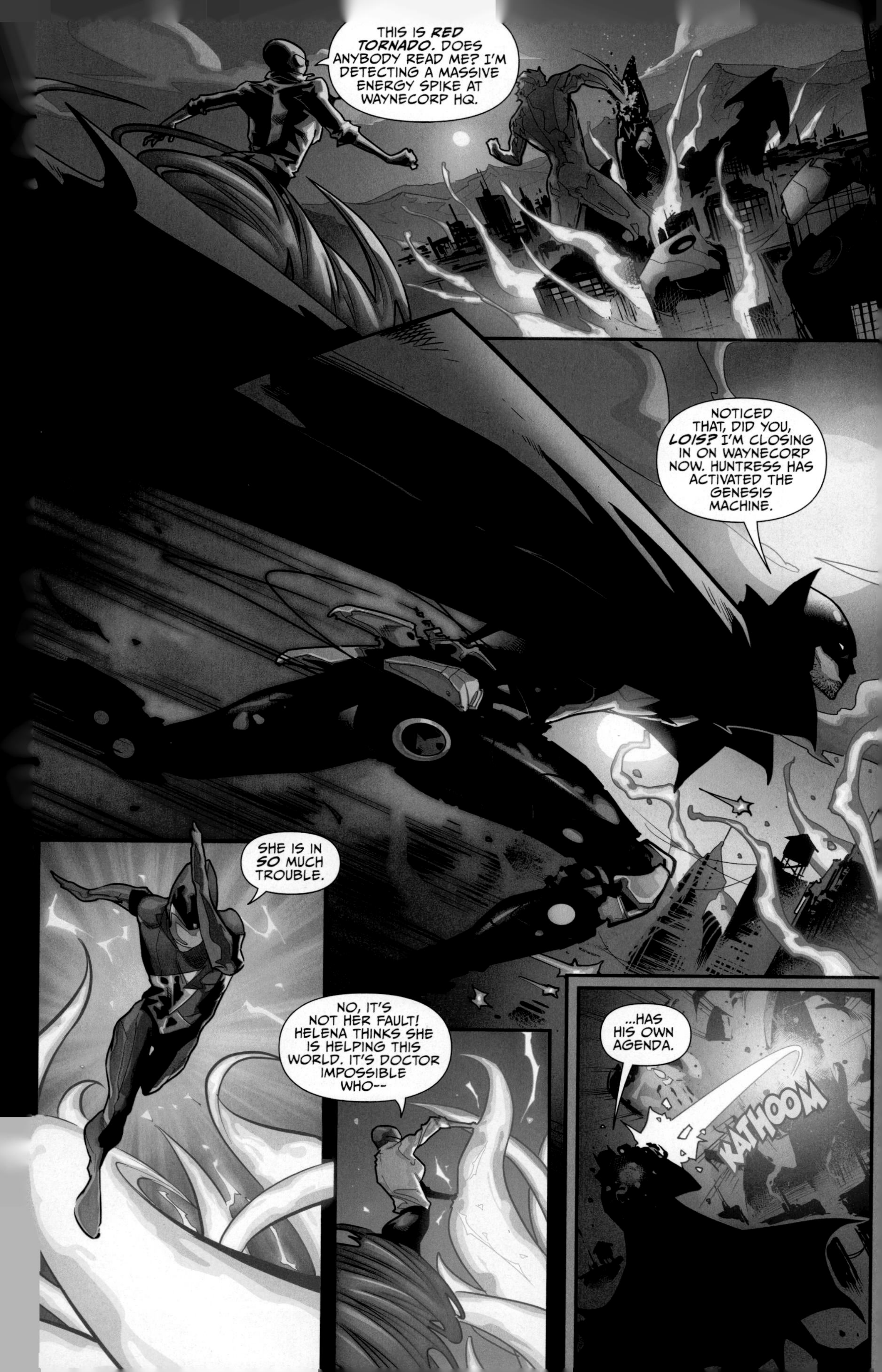
THIS IS RED TORNADO. DOES ANYBODY READ ME? I'M DETECTING A MASSIVE ENERGY SPIKE AT WAYNECORP HQ.
NOTICED THAT, DID YOU, LOIS? I'M CLOSING IN ON WAYNECORP NOW. HUNTRESS HAS ACTIVATED THE GENESIS MACHINE.
SHE IS IN SO MUCH TROUBLE.
NO, IT'S NOT HER FAULT! HELENA THINKS SHE IS HELPING THIS WORLD. IT'S DOCTOR IMPOSSIBLE WHO--
...HAS HIS OWN AGENDA.
KATHOOM

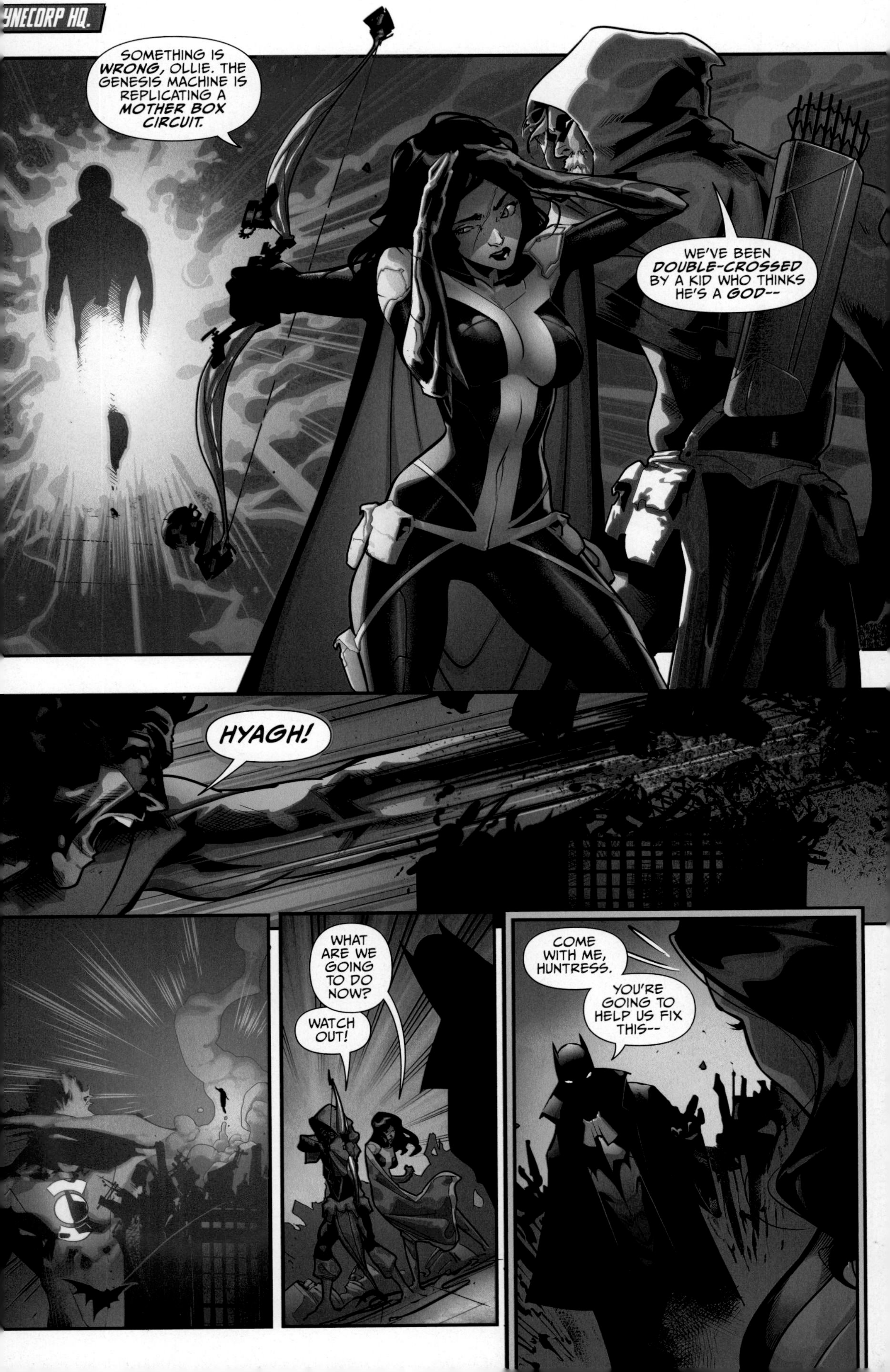

YNECORP HQ.
SOMETHING IS WRONG, OLLIE. THE GENESIS MACHINE IS REPLICATING A MOTHER BOX CIRCUIT.
WE'VE BEEN DOUBLE-CROSSED BY A KID WHO THINKS HE'S A GOD--
HYAGH!
WHAT ARE WE GOING TO DO NOW?
WATCH OUT!
COME WITH ME, HUNTRESS.
YOU'RE GOING TO HELP US FIX THIS--

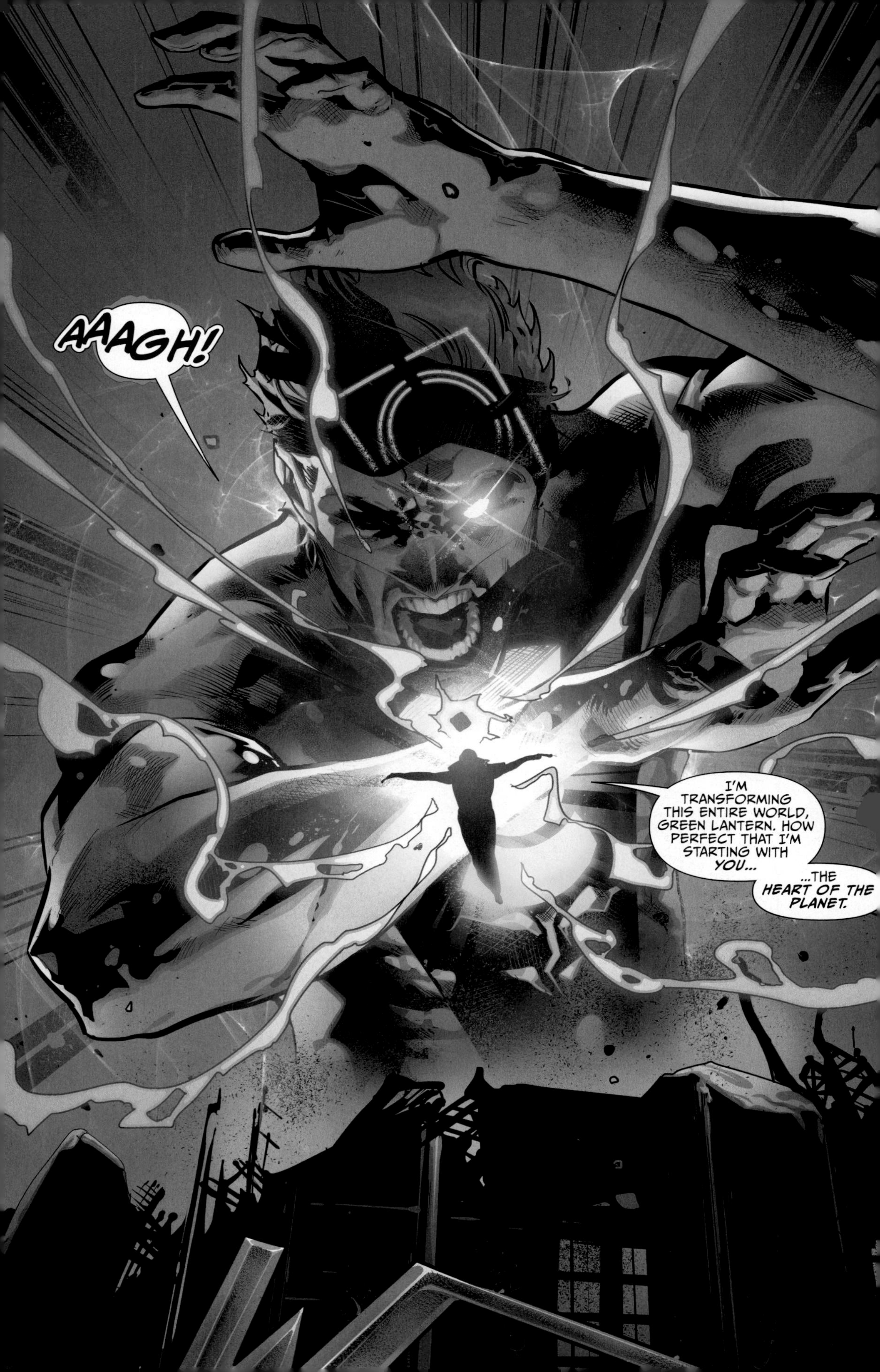
AAAGH!
I'M TRANSFORMING THIS ENTIRE WORLD, GREEN LANTERN. HOW PERFECT THAT I'M STARTING WITH YOU...
...THE HEART OF THE PLANET.

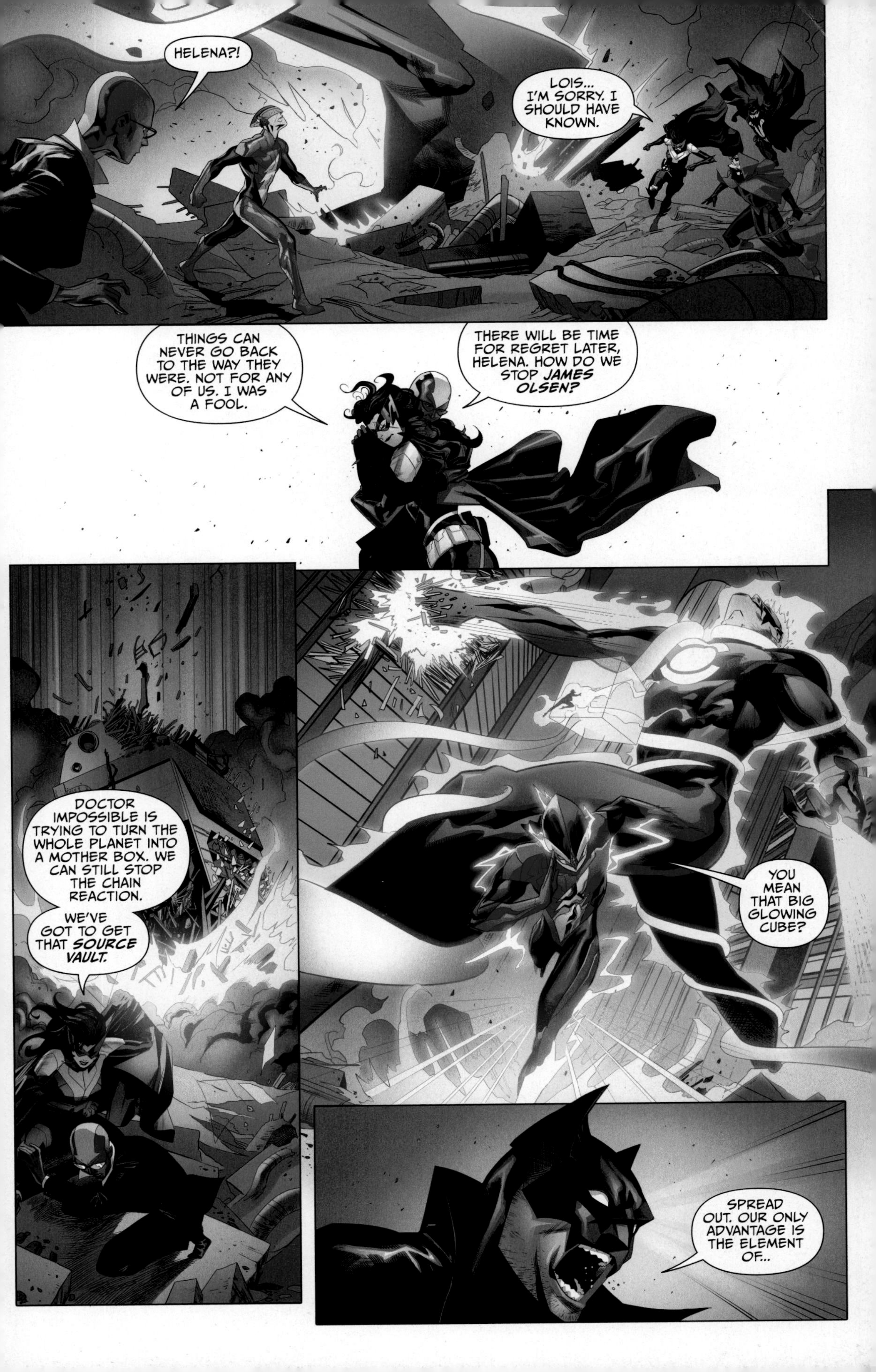
HELENA?!
LOIS... I'M SORRY. I SHOULD HAVE KNOWN.
THINGS CAN NEVER GO BACK TO THE WAY THEY WERE. NOT FOR ANY OF US. I WAS A FOOL.
THERE WILL BE TIME FOR REGRET LATER, HELENA. HOW DO WE STOP JAMES OLSEN?
DOCTOR IMPOSSIBLE IS TRYING TO TURN THE WHOLE PLANET INTO A MOTHER BOX. WE CAN STILL STOP THE CHAIN REACTION.
WE'VE GOT TO GET THAT SOURCE VAULT.
YOU MEAN THAT BIG GLOWING CUBE?
SPREAD OUT. OUR ONLY ADVANTAGE IS THE ELEMENT OF...

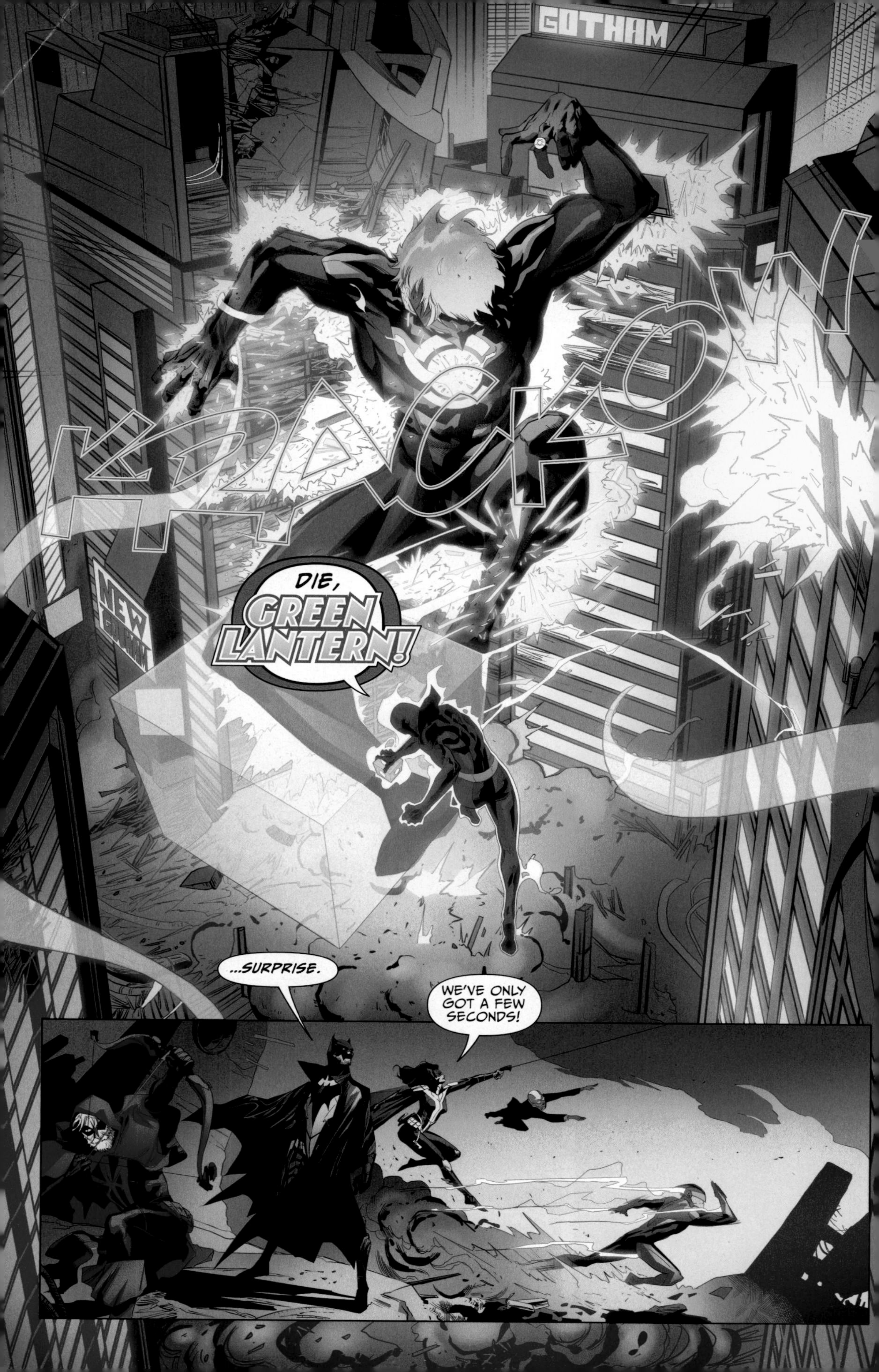
GOTHAM
KRACKOOM
DIE, GREEN LANTERN!
NEW GOTHAM
...SURPRISE.
WE'VE ONLY GOT A FEW SECONDS!

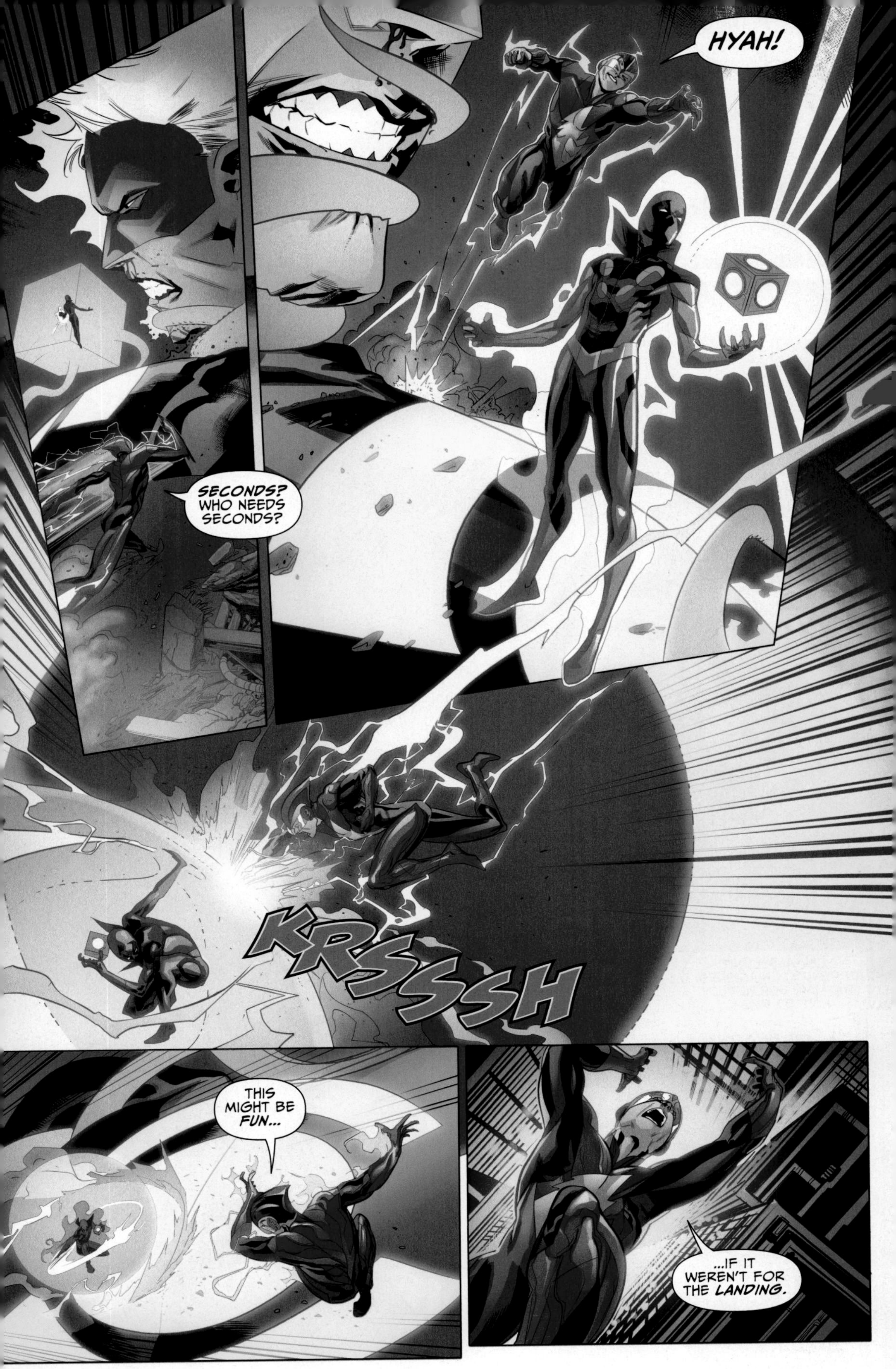
HYAH!
SECONDS? WHO NEEDS SECONDS?
KRSSSSH
THIS MIGHT BE FUN...
...IF IT WEREN'T FOR THE LANDING.

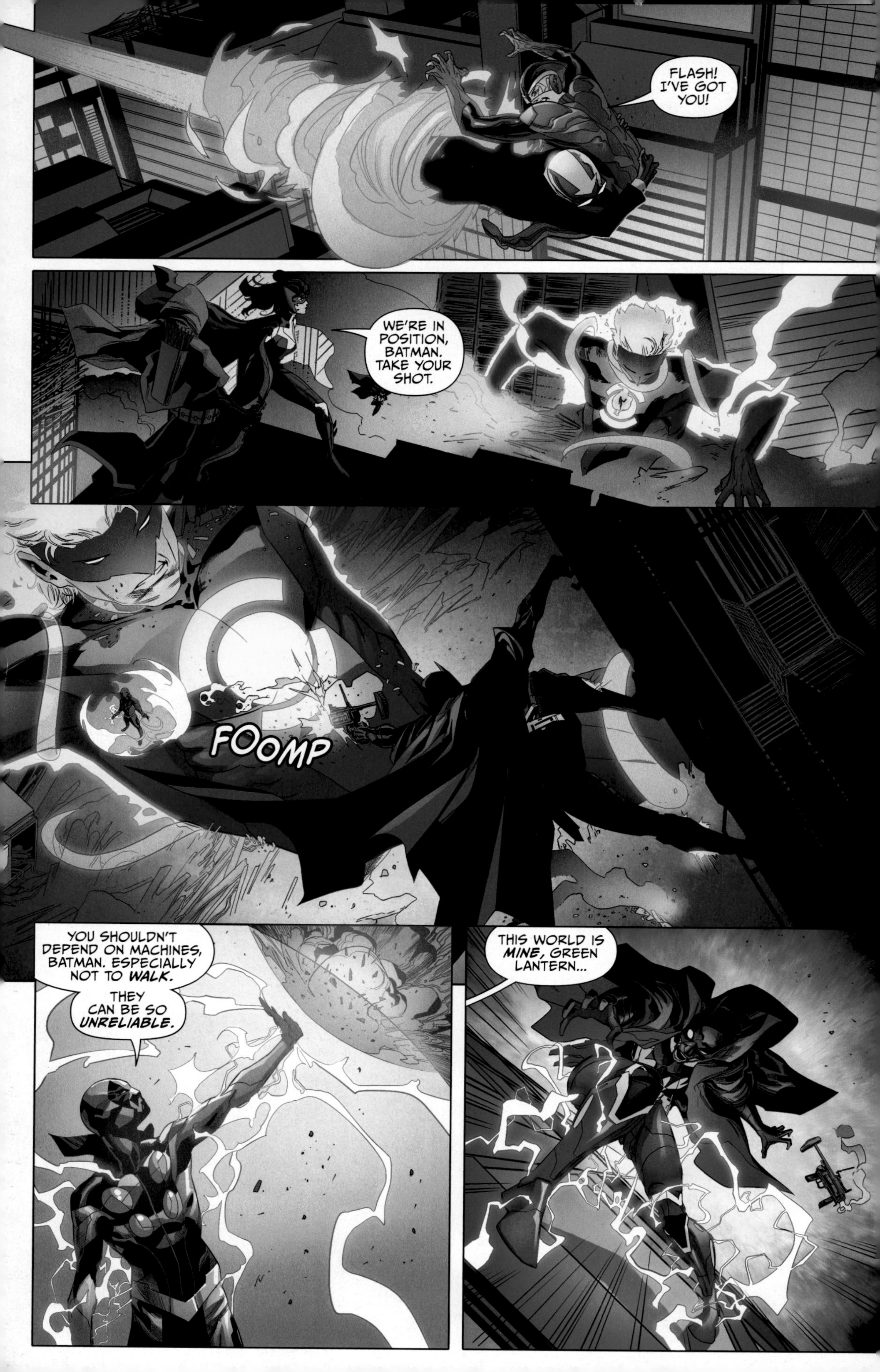
FLASH! I'VE GOT YOU!
WE'RE IN POSITION, BATMAN. TAKE YOUR SHOT.
FOOMP
YOU SHOULDN'T DEPEND ON MACHINES, BATMAN. ESPECIALLY NOT TO WALK.
THEY CAN BE SO UNRELIABLE.
THIS WORLD IS MINE, GREEN LANTERN...

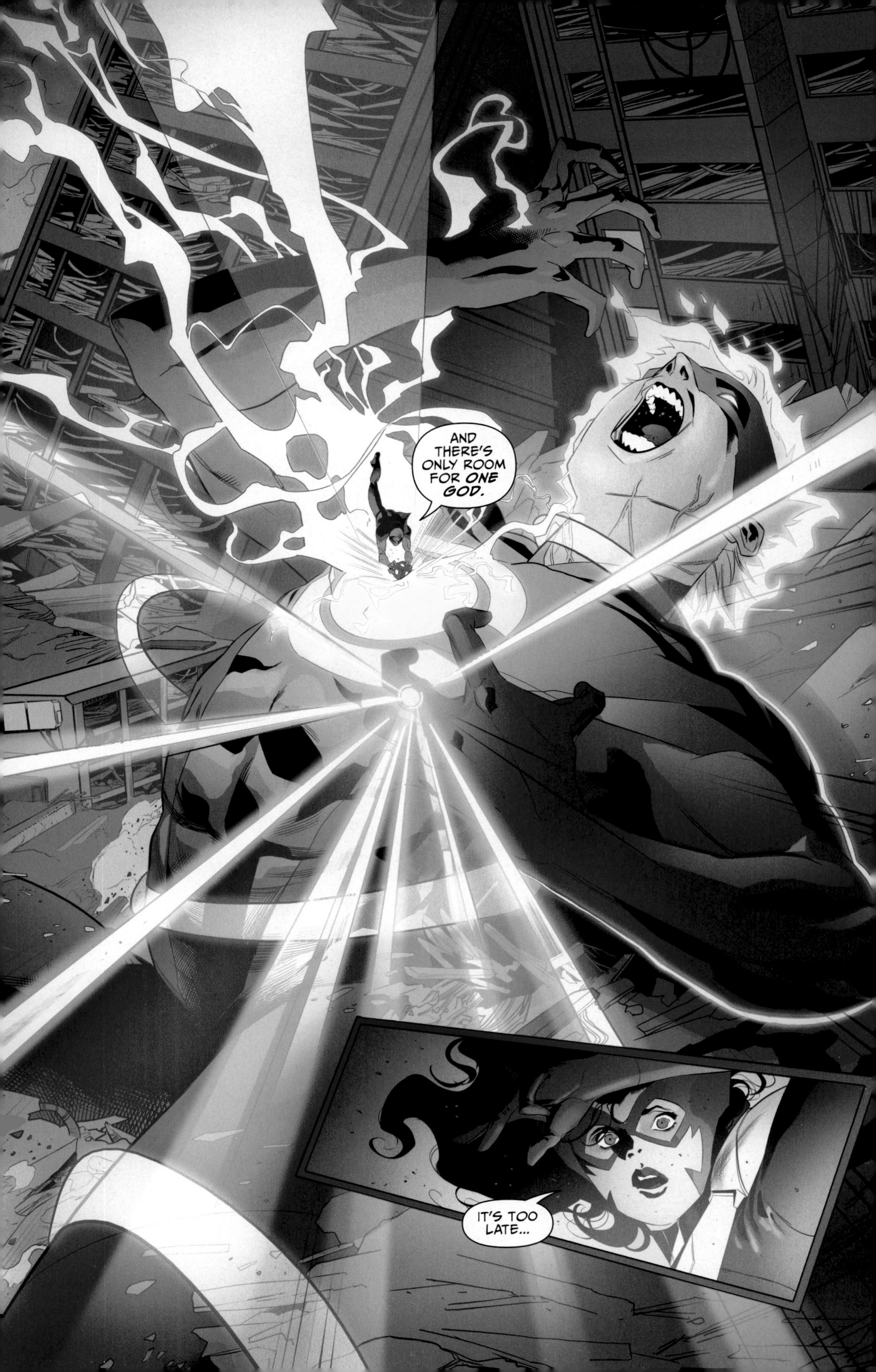
AND THERE'S ONLY ROOM FOR ONE GOD.
IT'S TOO LATE...

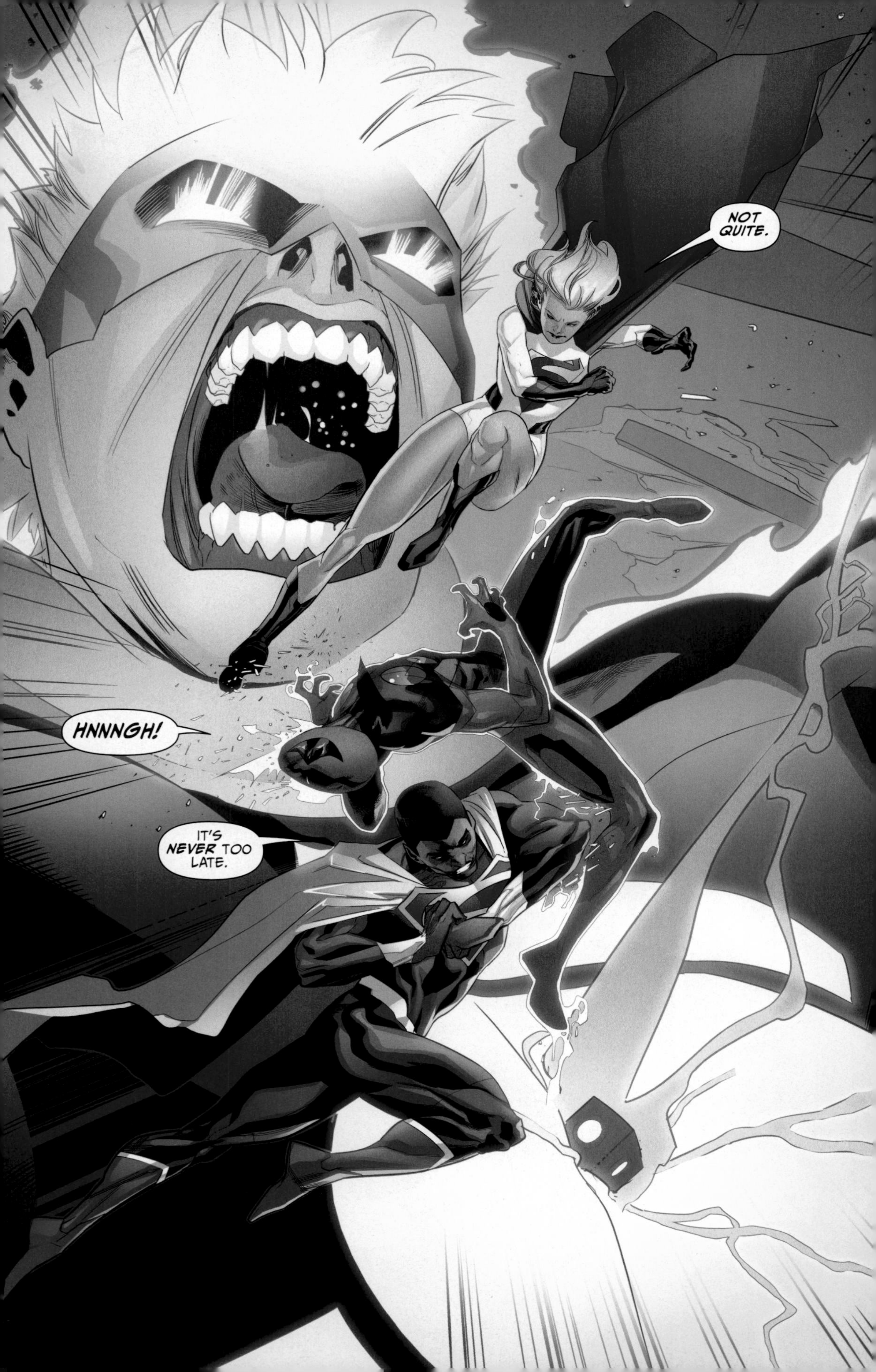
NOT QUITE.
HNNNGH!
IT'S NEVER TOO LATE.

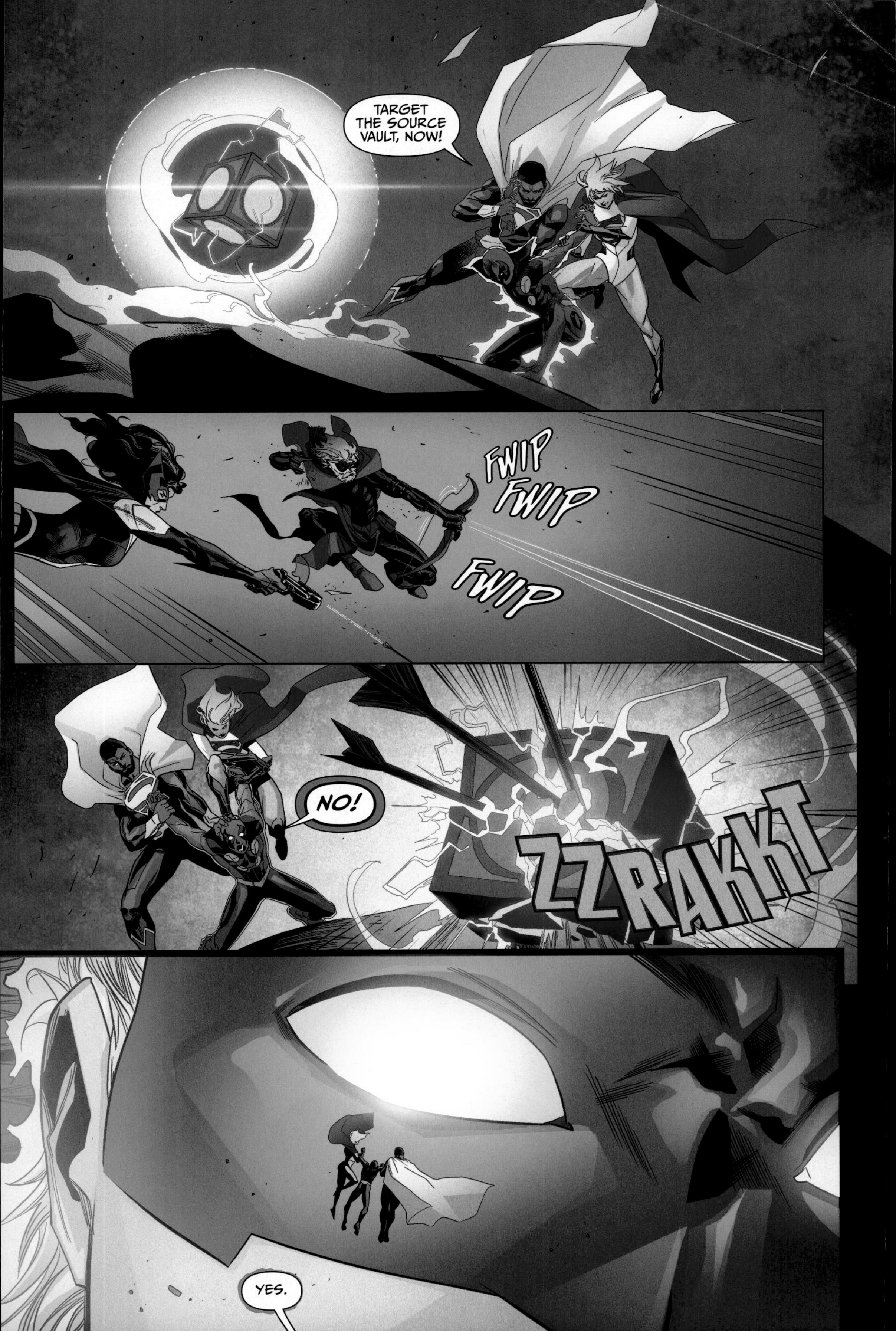

TARGET THE SOURCE VAULT, NOW!
FWIP
FWIP
FWIP
NO!
ZZRAKKT
YES.

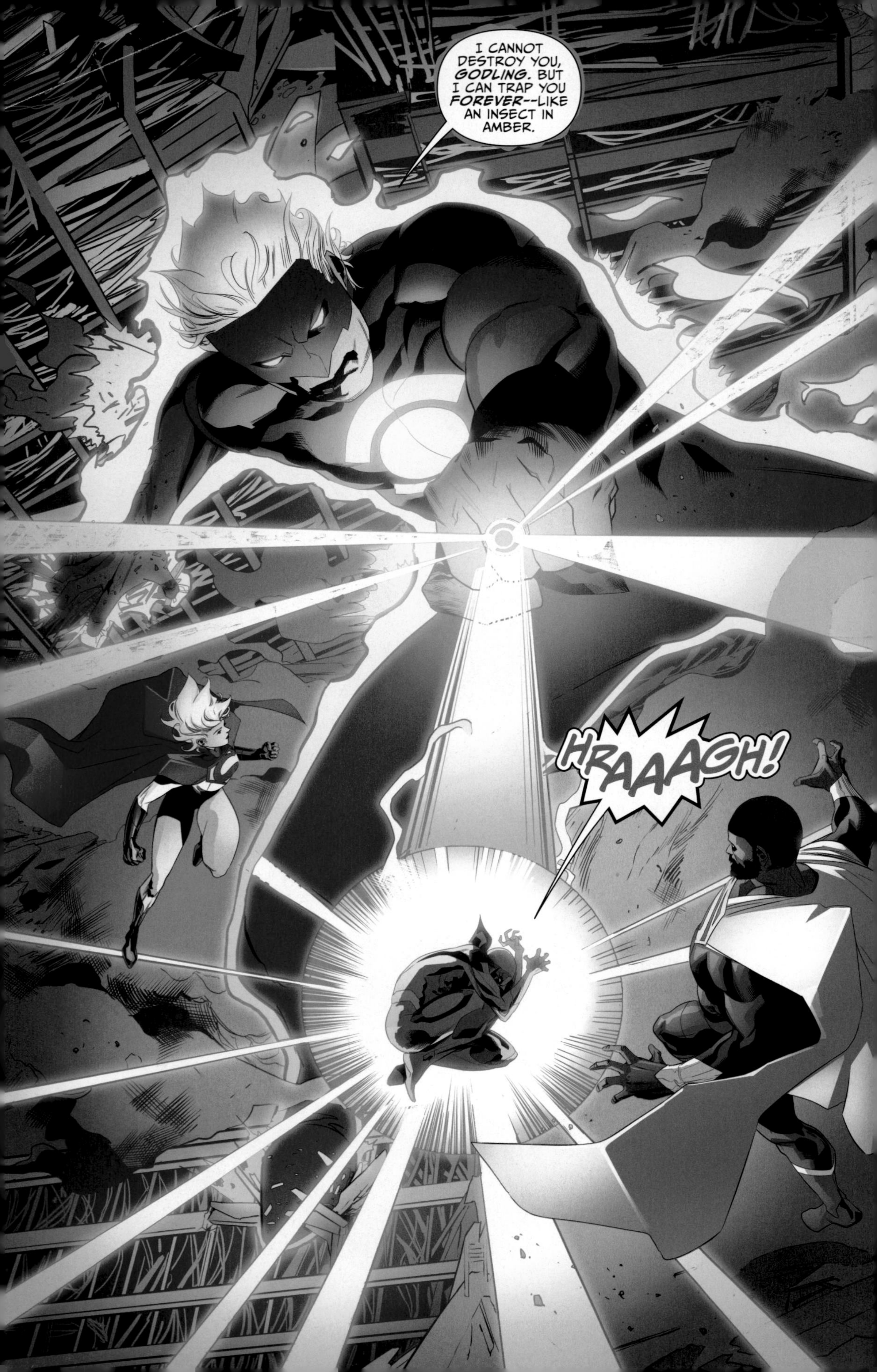
I CANNOT DESTROY YOU, GODLING. BUT I CAN TRAP YOU FOREVER--LIKE AN INSECT IN AMBER.
HRAAAGH!

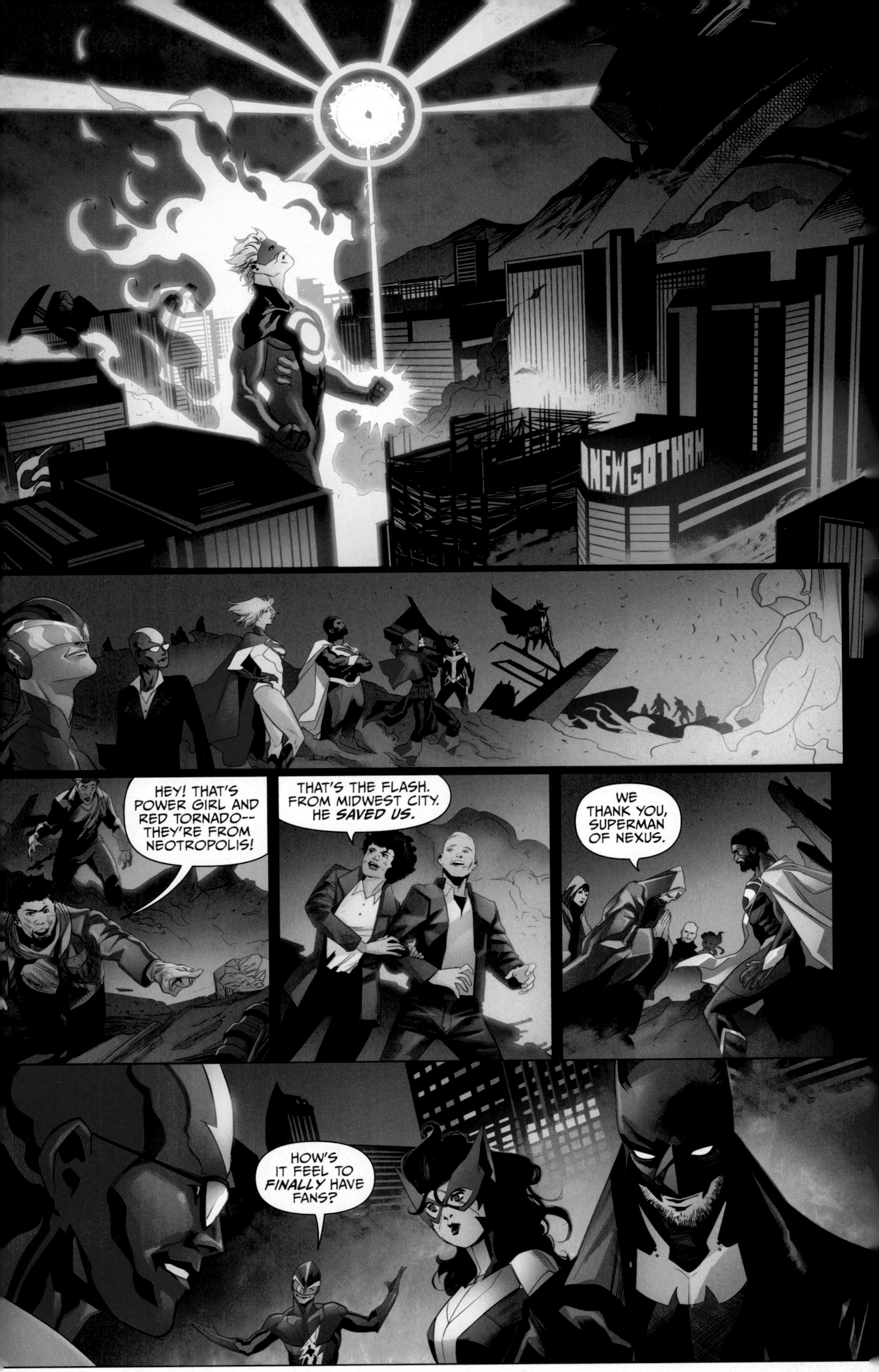
NEW GOTHAM
HEY! THAT'S POWER GIRL AND RED TORNADO-- THEY'RE FROM NEOTROPOLIS!
THAT'S THE FLASH. FROM MIDWEST CITY. HE SAVED US.
WE THANK YOU, SUPERMAN OF NEXUS.
HOW'S IT FEEL TO FINALLY HAVE FANS?

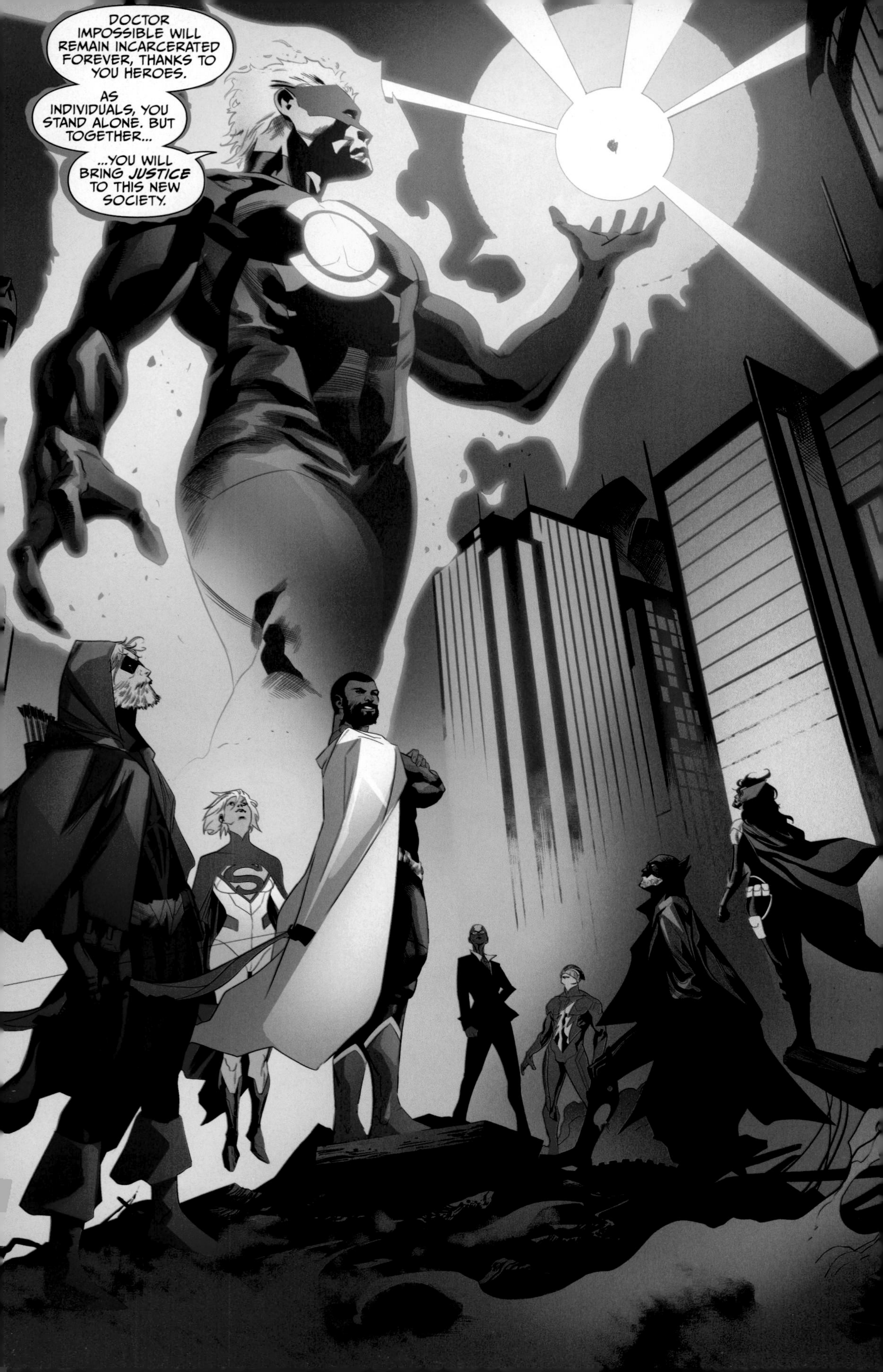
DOCTOR IMPOSSIBLE WILL REMAIN INCARCERATED FOREVER, THANKS TO YOU HEROES.
AS INDIVIDUALS, YOU STAND ALONE. BUT TOGETHER...
...YOU WILL BRING JUSTICE TO THIS NEW SOCIETY.

EARTH 2: SOCIETY #1 Variant Cover by
PAULO SIQUEIRA, CAM SMITH & HI-FI

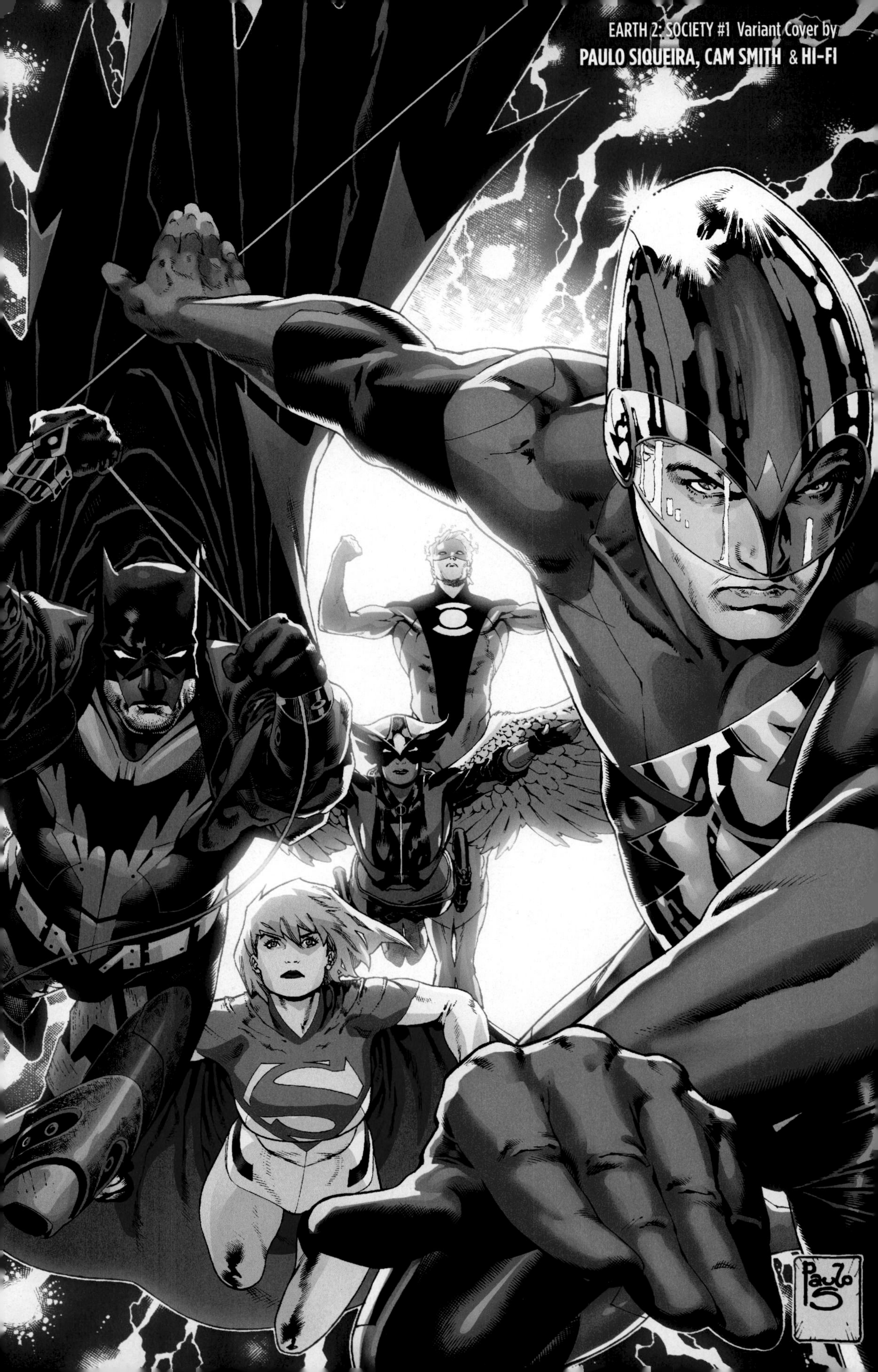

EARTH 2: SOCIETY #2 Variant Cover by
ANDY KUBERT & BRAD ANDERSON

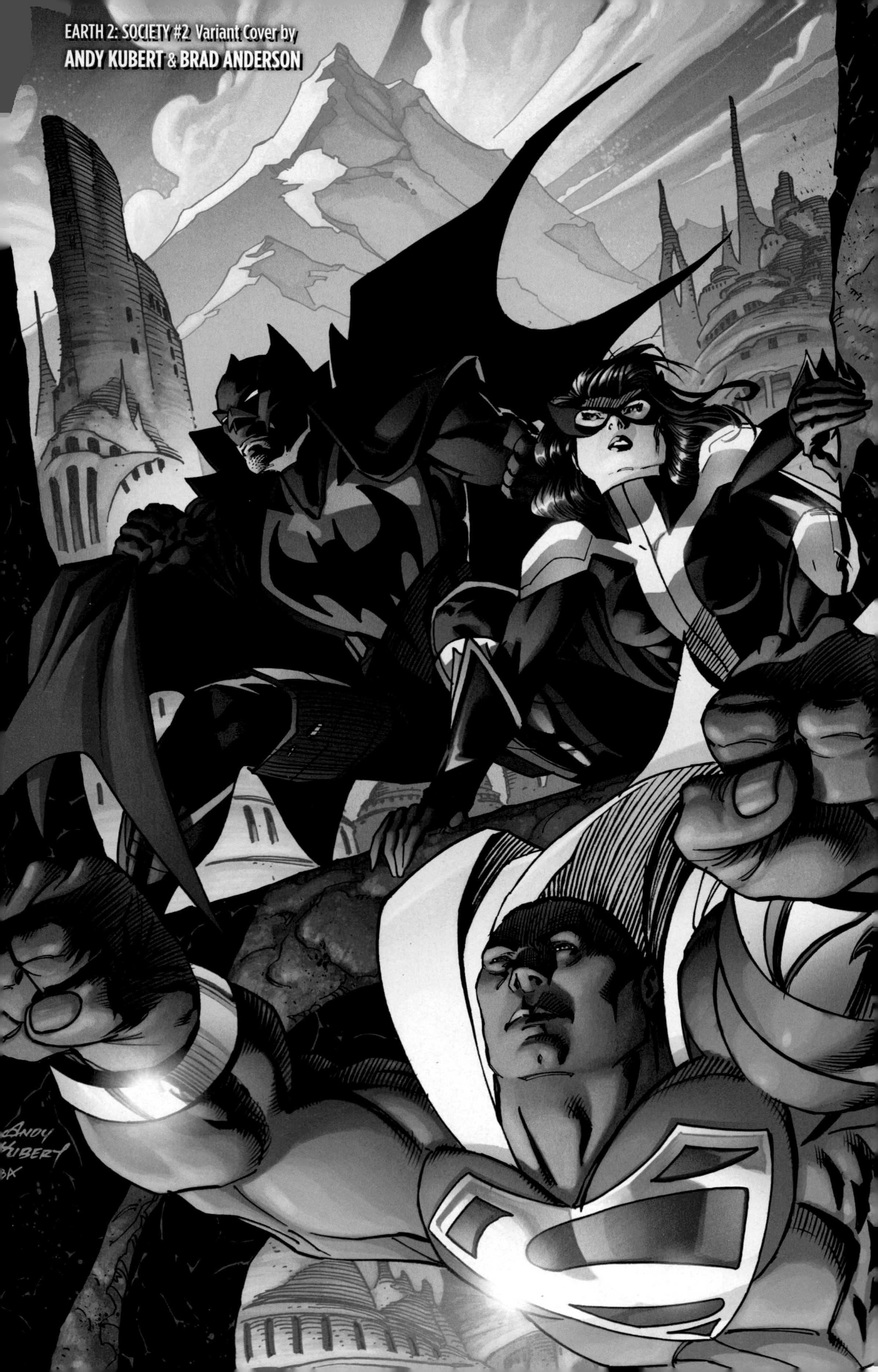
ANDY KUBERT

EARTH 2: SOCIETY #3 Variant Cover by
ETHAN VAN SCIVER & ANDREW DALHOUSE

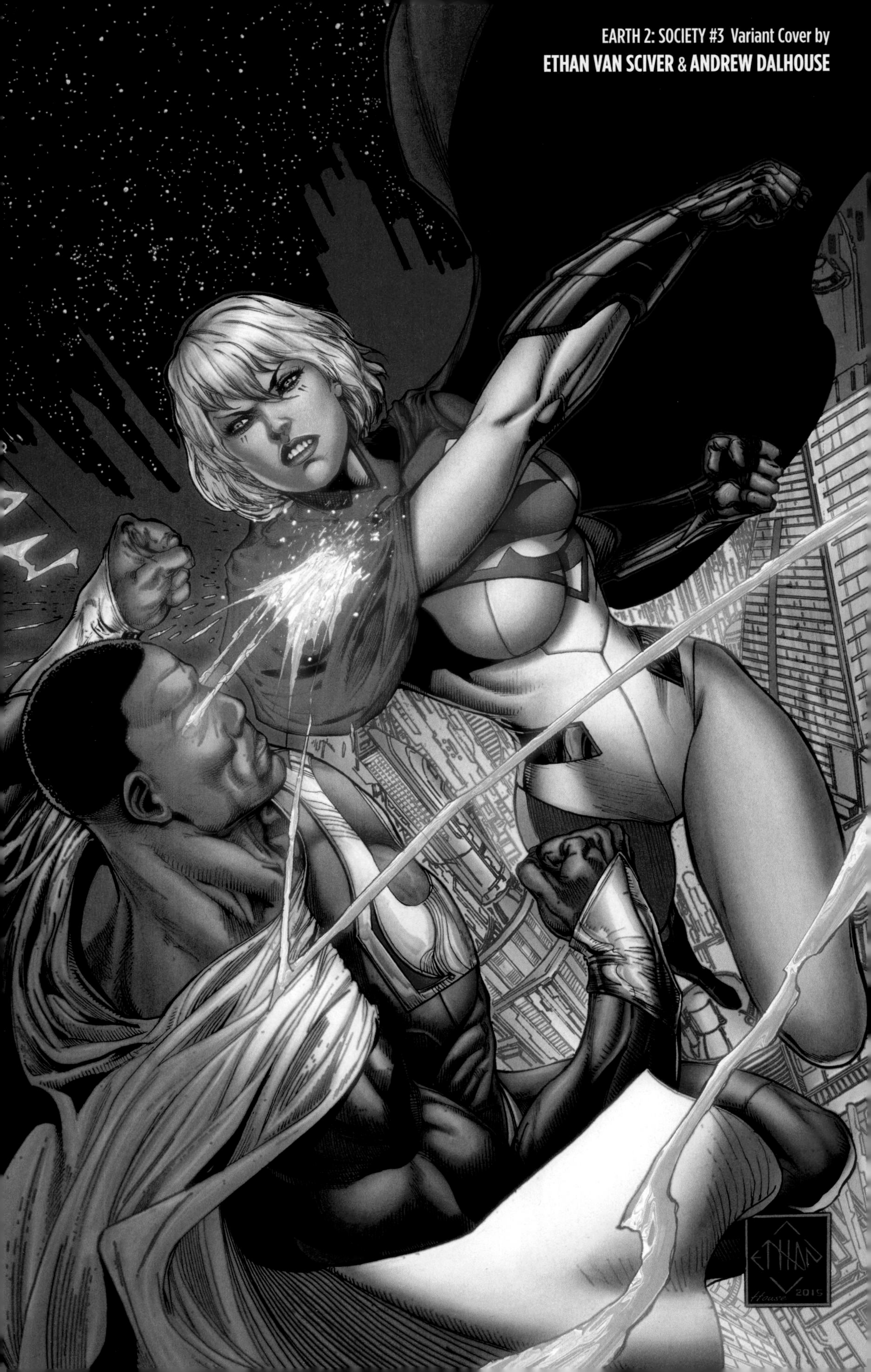

CHARACTER DESIGNS BY
JORGE JIMENEZ

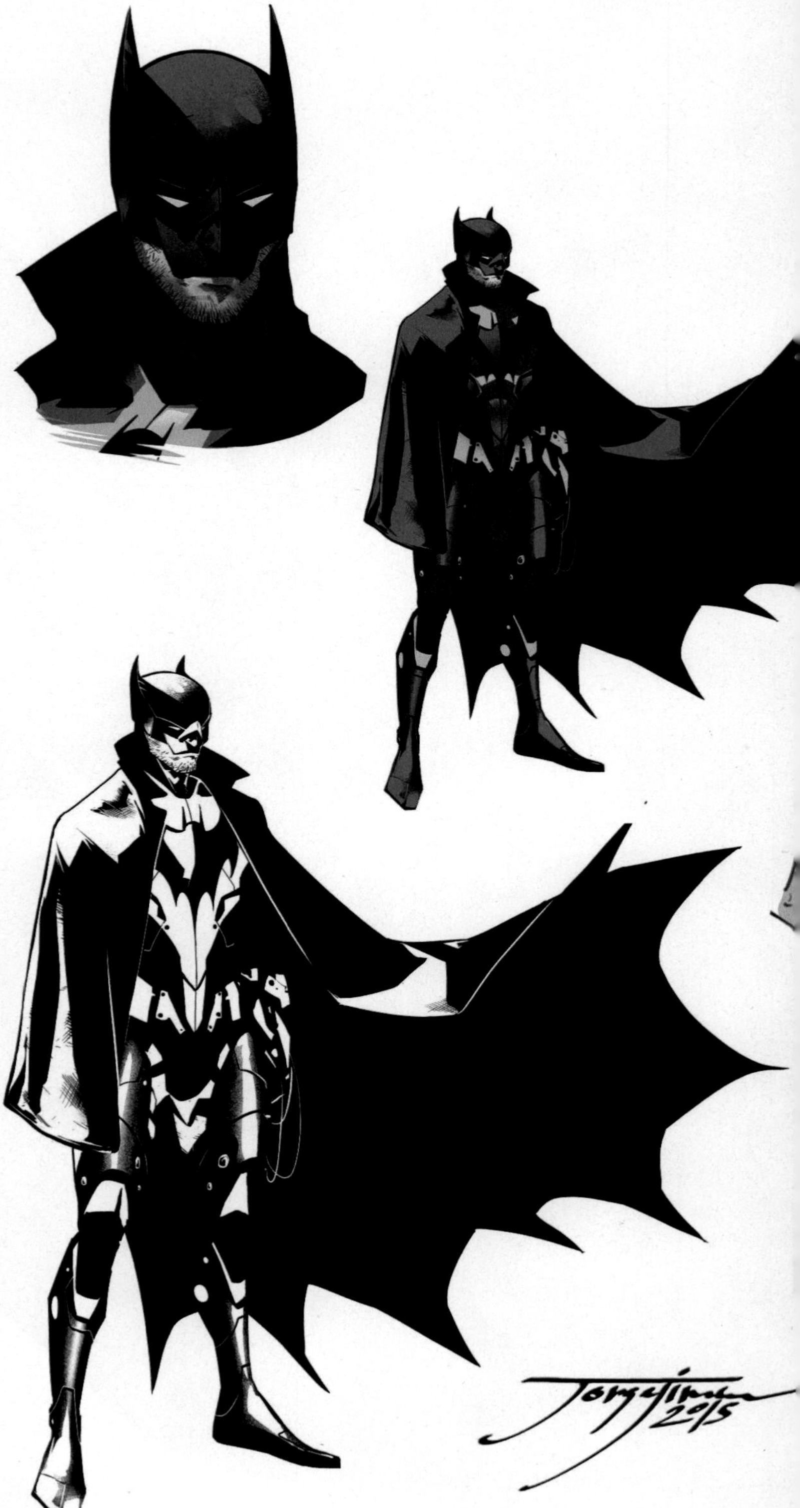
2015

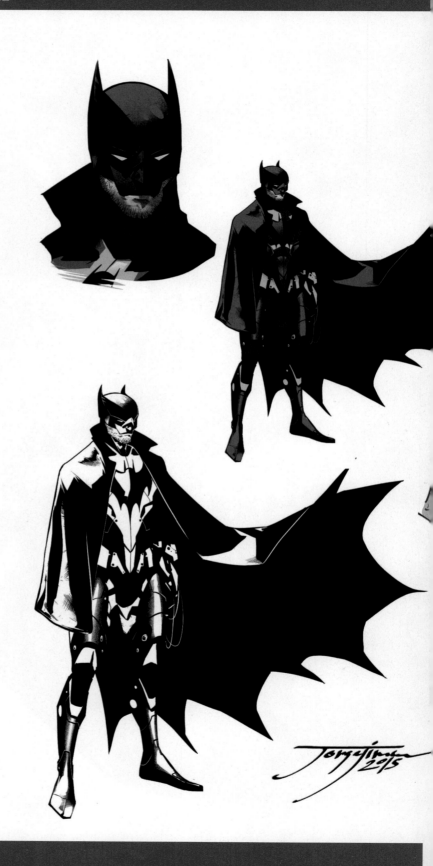

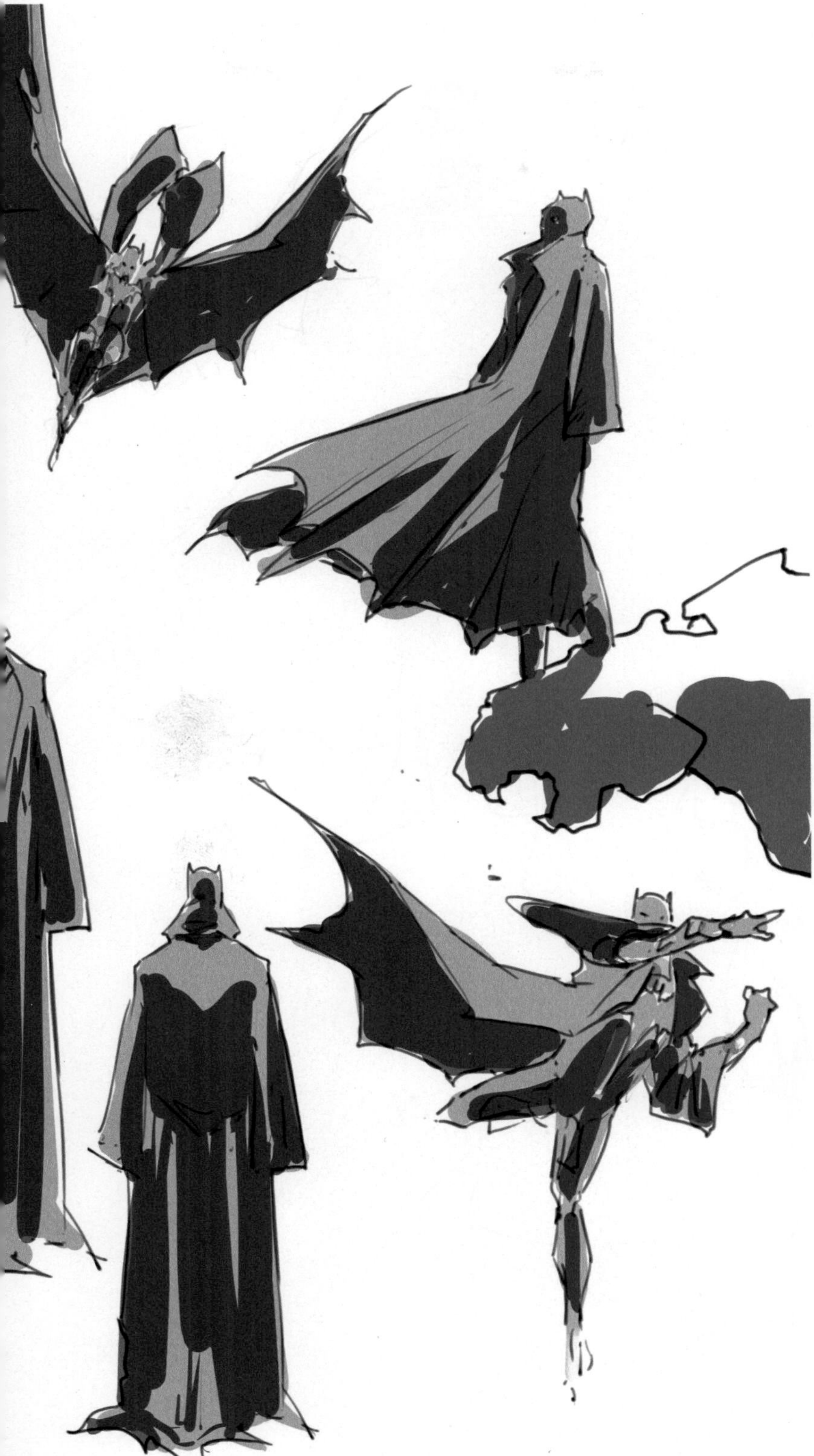

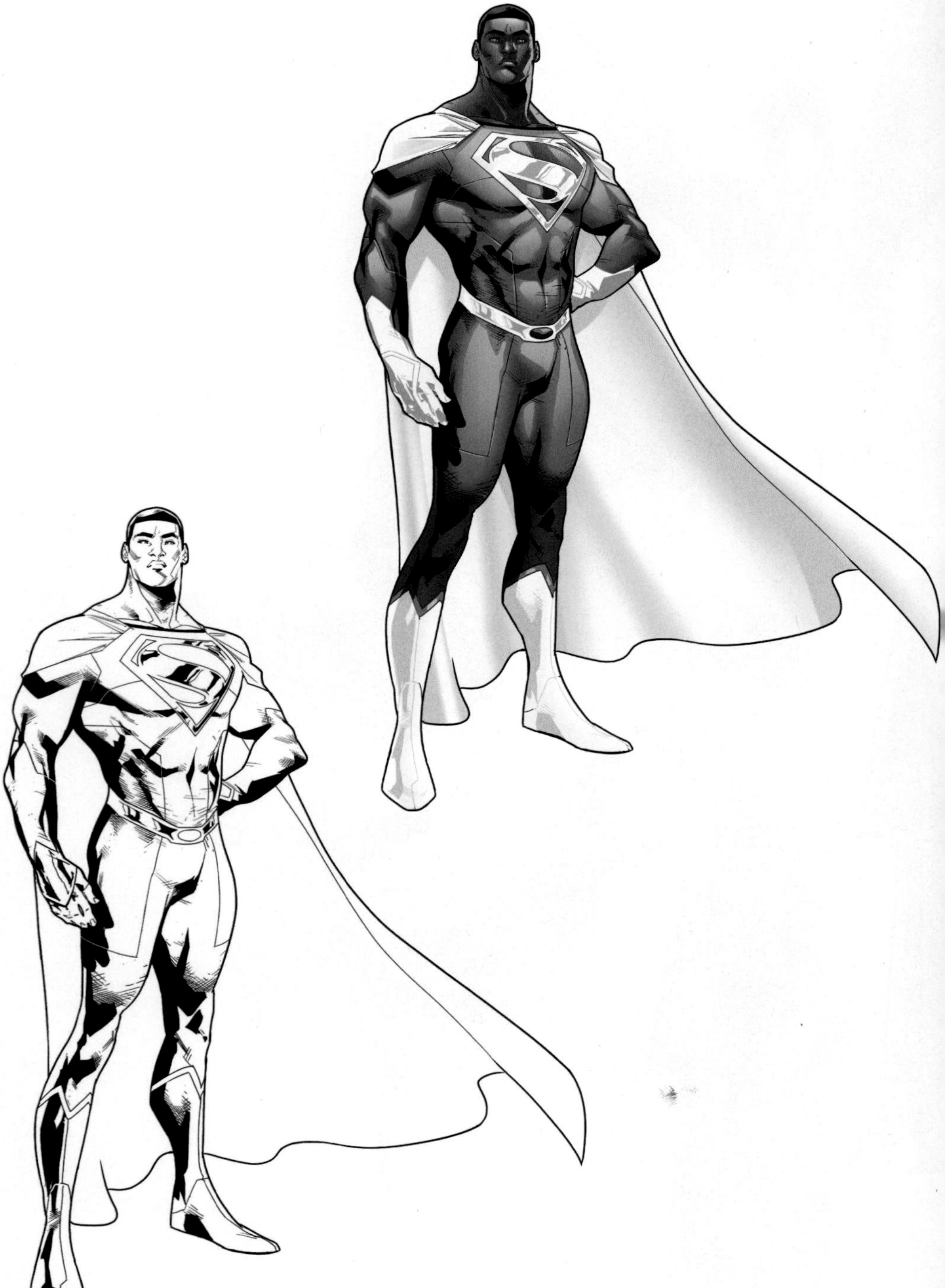

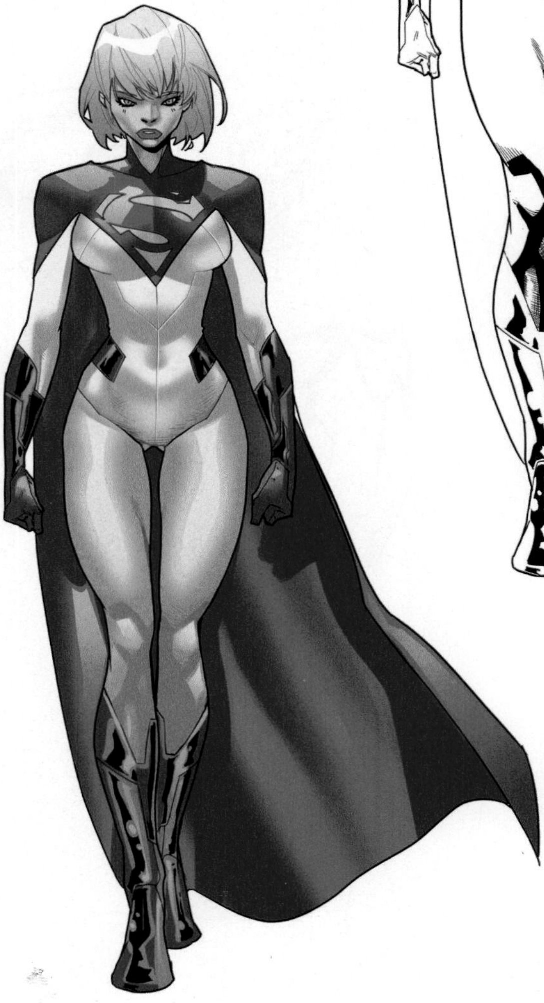
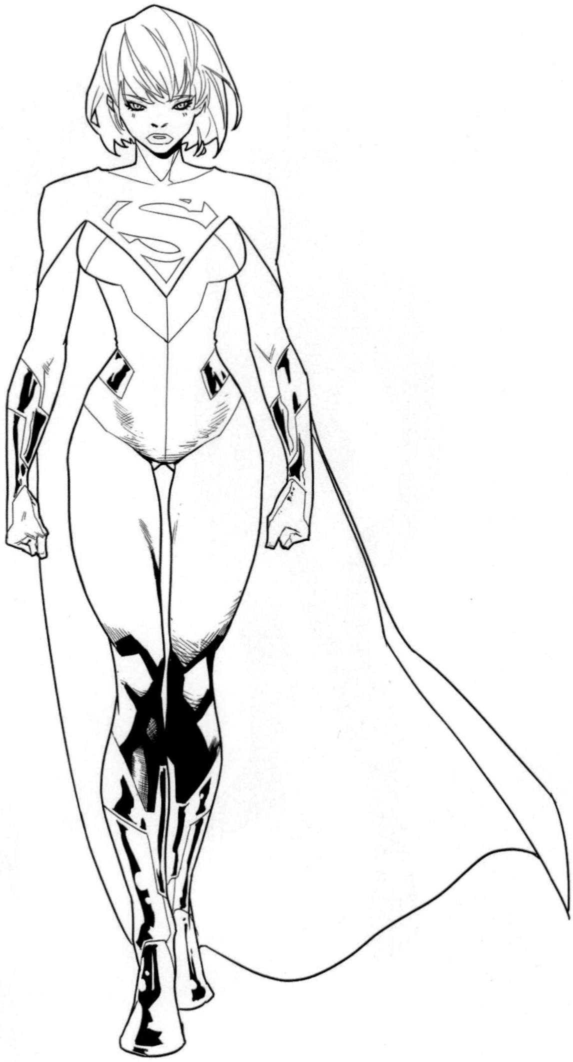

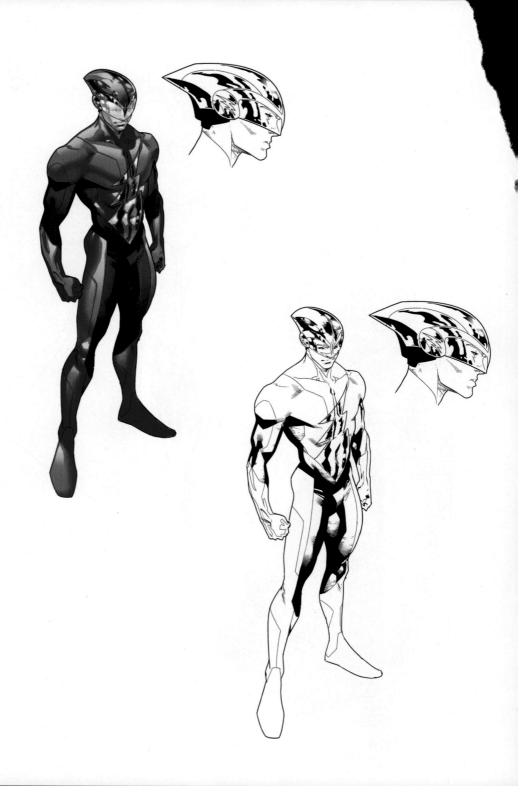

LOIS LANE

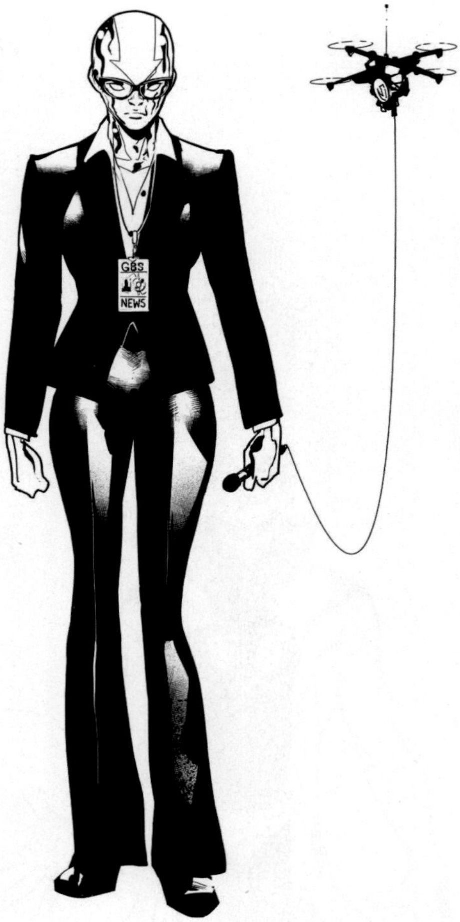
GBS
NEWS

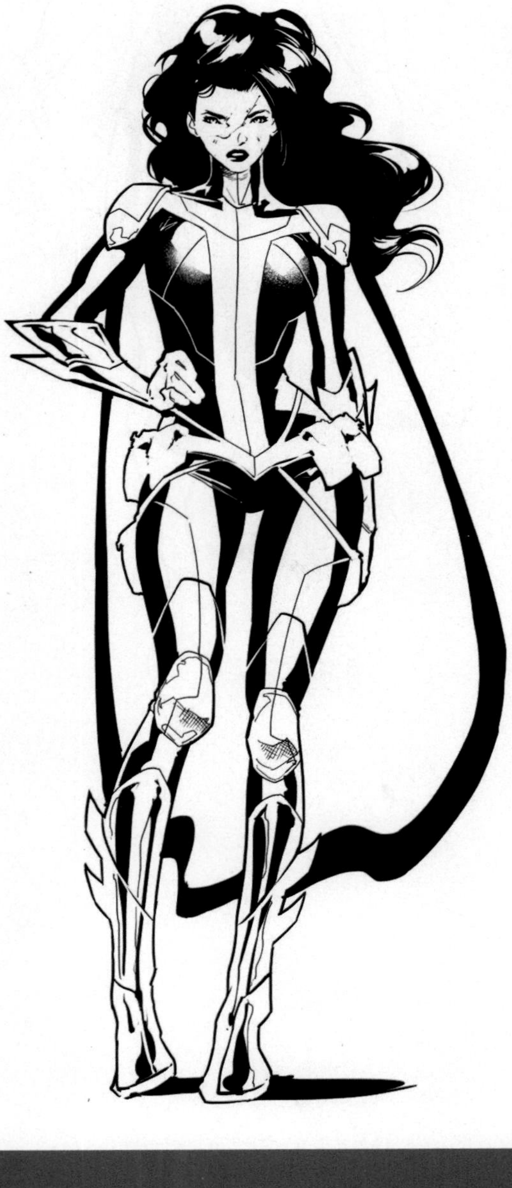

HUNTRESS

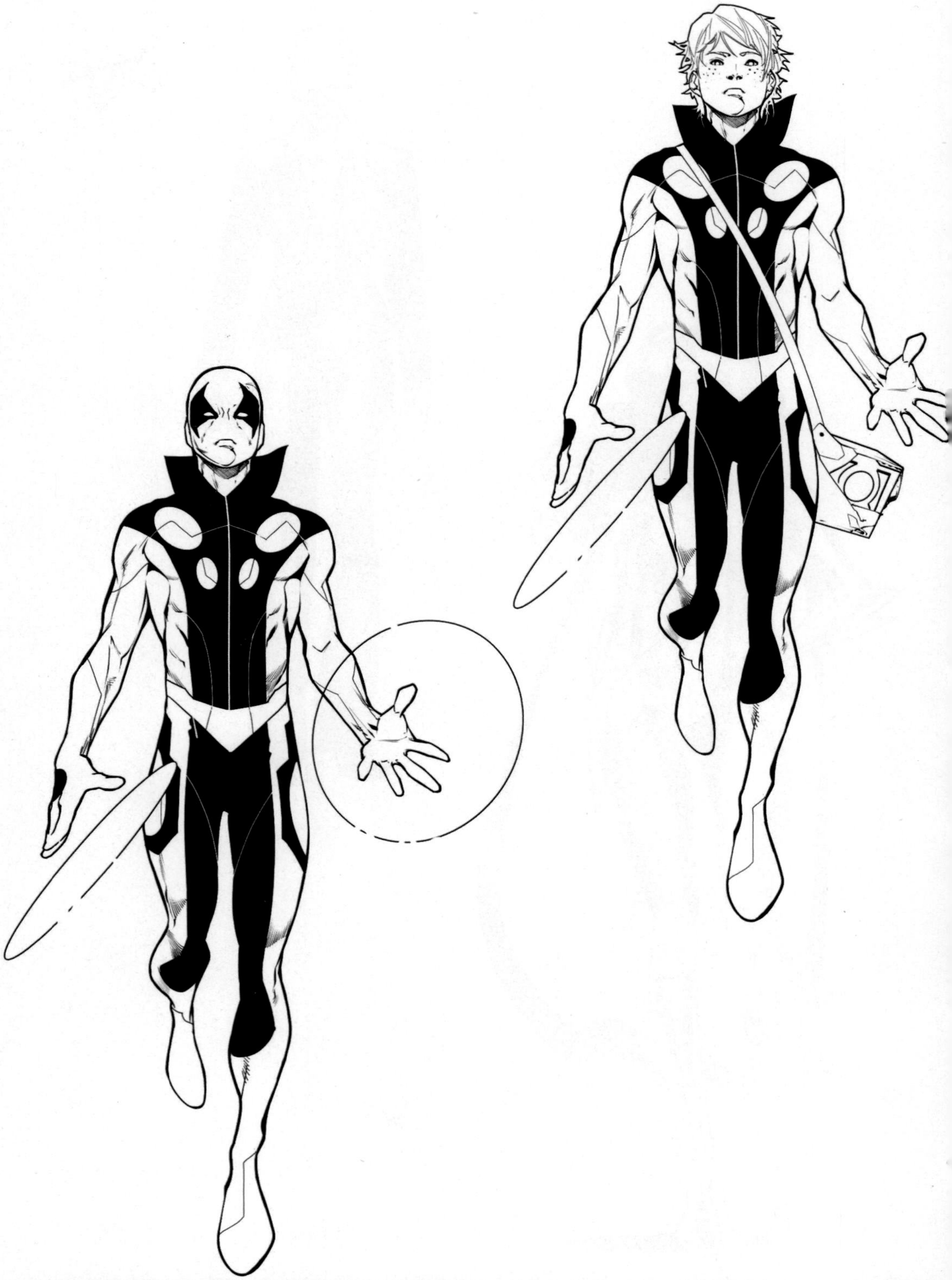